BEST
MUSIC
WRITING

2 0 0 8

BEST
MUSIC
WRITING

2008

Nelson George
GUEST EDITOR

Daphne Carr
SERIES EDITOR

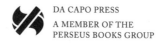

DA CAPO PRESS
A MEMBER OF THE
PERSEUS BOOKS GROUP

Designed by Timm Bryson
Set in 10.5 point Caslon by Cynthia Young, Sagecraft

Cataloging-in-Publication data for this book is available from the Library
of Congress.

First Da Capo Press edition 2008
ISBN 978-0-306-81734-2

Published by Da Capo Press
A Member of the Perseus Books Group
http://www.dacapopress.com

Da Capo Press books are available at special discounts for bulk purchases
in the U.S. by corporations, institutions, and other organizations. For more
information, please contact the Special Markets Department at the Perseus Books
Group, 2300 Chestnut Street, Suite 200, Philadelphia, PA, 19103,
or call (800) 810-4145, ext. 5000, or e-mail special.markets@perseusbooks.com.

1 2 3 4 5 6 7 8 9

CONTENTS

INTRODUCTION

GOD IN THE VINYL

When I was four years old, just tall enough to look into my mother's Motorola Hi-Fi on my tiptoes, I became fascinated with how music emanated from the fragile, round, black vinyl circles with colorful labels that my family purchased from record stores around Brooklyn. Now, the *obvious* path for a black kid with this interest was to draw on my God-given natural rhythm and become yet another celebrated Afro-American musician.

Problem was I had no rhythm, couldn't stay in tune, and didn't like practicing if a Curious George book was within reach. So I failed miserably at piano, trumpet, the glee club, and violin, though I did attain a fleeting mastery of the baritone horn in junior high.

These artistic setbacks didn't deter my love of music and, in fact, may have intensified it. In adolescence I got into the weird habit of listening to my favorite records three, four, five, sometimes as often as ten times in a row (a habit that worked best when I was home alone since it drove my mother and sister crazy).

If I listened often and deeply enough, I felt I could "see" the record. Not the musicians or singers, like in a music video, but in a more impressionistic way, as if sounds were colors and shapes. Some records inspired still images, but never literal recreations of the lyrics; rather, I imagined scenarios suggested by the chords, the choruses, and harmonies. A pop song could drop me in Alaska, a funk jam might take me to a Russian space ship, or a jazz classic would lift me to an apartment overlooking Central Park on a rainy day.

For me, these songs weren't movies, but experiences in which I could lose myself. There was a definite spiritual dimension to these repeat listens. When I fell into the records—like Alice fell down that rabbit hole—I'd land in spaces more elevated, inspiring, and, yes, divine than my mother's living room. John Coltrane's "Naima" did this for me. So did Bob Dylan's "Shelter From the Storm," and Otis Redding's "Cigarettes and Coffee." Even fragments of records transported: the backing vocals on Paul Simon's "Mother & Child Reunion," Al Jackson's licks on the obscure Al Green album track "One Night Stand," or the jingling bells in the intro to the Average White Band's "School Boy Crush." More than attending the Baptist church on our Brooklyn block or praying before bed, or anything officially "religious" in my life, these repeat listens felt spiritual, even transcendental. I was looking for God in the vinyl.

As musicianship continued to elude me, I searched for a way to get closer to the amazing spiritual force of music. Being a bookish sort, I began reading about music, seeking out a context for the albums, 45s, and cassette tapes I so loved collecting, and for voices that were as passionate about the feeling music could generate. In Leroi Jones's *Blues People*, a polemic about jazz, race, and politics, and Greil Marcus's *Mystery Train*, an imaginative journey through American history, class, and rock, I found two very different, very brilliant kindred spirits, and I found a calling.

I read both books at a crucial point during my teenage years—some time after my mother threw out my collection of Marvel comics and before the successful wooing of my first serious girlfriend. I'm pretty sure *Rolling Stone* magazine was my first regular introduction to music criticism, with the *Village Voice* soon to follow. Somewhere in my archives are mid-'70s rejection letters for my precocious unsolicited reviews sent to *Rolling Stone* and my future *Village Voice* mentor Robert Christgau. A few years later I started selling pieces to the music trade magazine *Billboard*, the black weekly *The Amsterdam News*, and teen appeal pulp magazine *Rock & Soul*. By 1981 I had finally cracked the *Voice* with a short piece on Luv Bug Star-ski, and my fate was sealed.

I give all this personal history because that search for God in the vinyl and the experiences of my early career significantly influenced which pieces I selected for this year's collection of best music writing. By accident of geography (living in New York) and by upbringing (having a soul music–loving mother), I ended up as a music journalist writing extensively about two musical/cultural movements rooted in African-American history. One was the evolution of rappin', street dance, graffiti, and fashion into something called hip hop. The other was documenting how technology, class, and opportunity remade R&B/soul into a record-selling juggernaut and altered its musical nature. One movement was a revolution that changed the sound of pop music, while the other was a reinvention of a beloved genre, a change fans still wrestle with today.

Throughout my career as an active music critic, roughly 1978 to the mid-'90s, the often competing, ultimately intertwined agendas of hip hop and contemporary R&B dominated my work and shaped my thinking about many things, including the role of the critic. For me there are three essential roles for a critic/journalist to play in chronicling music. First, and crucial to daily journalism (and the sale of music mags), is the ongoing assessment of established artists, musical genres, and changes in the making, selling, and distribution of music. In today's post–record label landscape, these threads interact with each other, creating both new opportunities and often considerable confusion. The core duty of the diligent music critic involves an evaluation of the performer's career, locating them in the history of their particular musical genre (or their ability to balance several genres), placing them in their current cultural context, and weighing their latest work against the standards of their previous recordings. The best music critics have a knack for looking deeply at a current work, holding it up as a mirror to the present music scene and as a window into the mind of its maker. This must be done without being too glib—glibness being the cardinal sin of folks who write too fast, too often, and about too many records.

Articles in the first category take on the challenge of defining major artists and trends in an increasingly confusing, diffuse musical landscape. Since indie rock is the defining musical movement for this generation's white critics, and since most of its most ardent supporters work online, it was fun to read *Slate*'s Carl Wilson's response to *The New Yorker*'s Sasha Frere-Jones's now notorious complaint that indie rock hadn't embraced the groove. I thought Frere-Jones made some strong points in his original piece. However, Wilson's very sharp analysis of how hip hop differs from earlier forms of black music, why economics and class divide white America's aesthetics, and what records Frere-Jones ignored in his argument, is a pimp slap sure to leave a mark. The dynamics of life within the "urban archipelago" that supports indie rock are the real concern of Bill Wasik, though he skillfully uses the journey of the North Carolina band the Annuals as his entry point. The interconnectedness of Pitchfork Media, MySpace, the South By Southwest music festival, and other related twenty-first-century social phenomena was made unusually lucid in Wasik's account. Clive Thompson mines similar territory in a piece from the point of view of a coffee-shop blogging Brooklyn singer-songwriter who feels trapped by his Internet success.

In a more frivolous, yet still effective manner, Jeff Weiss celebrates the one hit wonderfulness of Soulja Boy's winning web strategy. Outside of cyberspace, and very much in Oakland, Danyel Smith's profile of ascendant soul diva Keyshia Cole skillfully weaves together the journeys both women have taken from their mutual hometown. Poor Noah Berlatsky takes on the thankless job of defending contemporary mainstream R&B. I used to have that gig, so I know the frustration. What's sad is that much of what Berlatsky bemoans about how music critics treat young black singers could have been written in 1985 or 1995. Solvej Schou's account of auditioning for *American Idol* is first person journalism that takes us through an impersonal process while keeping her humanity intact. Ben Sisario's profile of Stargate—two prolific pop producer/writers named Erik Hermansen and Mikkel S. Eriksen—takes us into the contemporary world of manufacturing hits twenty-first-century style that captures the metallic dispassion of those faceless on the pop assembly line.

Having grown up around members of the Five Percent Nation and heard them preach endlessly about their "360 degrees of knowledge" on hot summer days, I was pleased to see how deftly Brandon Perkins used the Wu-Tang Clan's numerological bent to examine a once great collective who's artistic number is up. I know Grandmaster Dee very well and, aside from his role as a fine show DJ for Whodini, had never thought him an essential figure in hip hop history. What Jonathan Cunningham manages with Dee is to use a weekend in Jacksonville, Florida, as a window into the melancholy world of old school rappers on the growing hip hop nostalgia circuit. Sad without the nostalgic glow is Nadia Pflaum's "Pay 2 Play," which is equally insightful about hip hop away from the bright lights. Pflaum details how naïve and ambitious Kansas City MCs are ripped off by various bottom-feeding hustlers. It reads like the unwritten sequel to *Eight Mile*.

My favorite essay in this grouping takes on the hardest of critical jobs—to write intelligently about an artist with whom the culture is simultaneously obsessed and bored. Yet, despite *TMZ*, the E! channel and countless celeb gossip rags, Ann Powers does yeoman work in actually taking Britney Spears's new album seriously, even as she trashes it as an unholy mess. This is not work our culture is very invested in, not when Perez Hilton is just a click away. I'm not sure if feminism is dead or not, but Powers's deconstruction of Spears is in the best of that political/literary tradition.

The most exciting, vital role of the critic is to identify and advocate new movements, particularly those that serve minority taste and grow organically out of a community of like-minded individuals, be they a collective of DJs, music loving druggies addicted to the same substance and sounds, or bold dancers looking for their particular perfect beat. In many cases it is from some combustible combination of these elements that a true movement is born. I think that the ability to give voice and definition to such communities can be what makes or breaks a music journalist.

Not that the scene being documented is necessarily destined for world domination. One of the reasons I enjoyed Niki D'Andrea's "Bad Habits"—a piece about an odd group of Phoenix punks who call themselves NunZilla and who perform around their town in nun's habits and priest's collars—is the modesty of the entire inbred enterprise. Both D'Andrea and the band members know this isn't the next big thing, but take joy in what it *is*—a welcome break from their jobs and kids. My favorite piece in this section is J. Bennett's look at death metal stalwarts Dimmu Borgir for *Decibel* magazine. Bennett takes us to Norway and drops in on a band and subculture going through an identity crisis. You gotta love any article with quotes like, "Satan is limitless, so you must never limit yourself to the rules of a genre." Eric Pape goes into the Congo and finds not a heart of darkness, but a music industry of ruthless capitalism that's neither for the fainthearted nor thin-voiced. Though the Mark Ronson/Amy Winehouse collaboration made the sound of retro-flavored soul a hot international commodity, Andy Tennille points out that Sharon Jones has the same band, the Dap-Kings, and is a product of an underground soul scene in a tight-knit Brooklyn underground environs worth respecting.

The third, quite essential duty of this gig is to be a guide to the past for your readers. This means digging through the crates, both metaphorically and physically, to give play to the forgotten, hidden, or undervalued musicians and music. This tends to be the province of the true believer, a listener touched by the magic of a person, a record, or scene, and who is marked by that experience forever. These writers can be so touched that they run the danger of devoting unhealthy amounts of their adult life to trying to evoke a place, a time, a sound. This almost evangelical fervor can produce flurries of well-intentioned hyperbole or, on the upside, intense, passionate prose.

For these folks, mulling over the mod, the rocker, the b-boy, or the punk can drive them into an almost adolescent frenzy of attachment. It brings them back to a time that, in their mind, was unique above all others. Deeper still are those wonderful souls who had no direct geographical/racial/ethnic connection to the music but who, for a myriad of psychological/aesthetic reasons, get sucked in by the Delta blues, hard bop, or grunge, and have to know as much about it as the folks who were there at the creation. What's fascinating to watch is that the critic's second role, that of proselytizer for a emerging sound can, decades later, transform that writer into an archivist par excellence. What was once the energy of the youthful enthusiast becomes the passion of the wizened old collector.

I could have included a score of fine archival articles from *Wax Poetics*, which is my favorite revivalist magazine of the new millennium. Matt Rogers's take on Mandrill is a stellar representation of how *Wax*

Poetics unearths great funk, soul, and Latin acts from the past with panache and care. A nice companion to the Mandrill piece comes from, of all places, *The Nation*, in the form of Oliver Wang's breezy dissection of Joe Bataan and the brief, vivid craze for boogaloo music in the '60s.

I remember seeing *Saturday Night Fever* in the Paramount screening room a few weeks before its release in December 1977 and being caught off guard by its impact. Sam Kashner's loving recreation of its making brought me back to that odd moment when the Bee Gees were the best dance band in the world, and disco, which had peaked in New York by '76, was re-launched as a white ethnic movement by John Travolta's white suit.

Most of what's published in *Mojo* or *Oxford American* is gonna fit category three like a glove, which made Phil Sutcliffe on Pete Seeger and Jeff Sharlet on Lee Hays rich counterpoints. Though fellow travelers in the history of folk music, the ultimate paths of Seeger and Hayes were quite different, revealing much about the men and the America that shaped them. Like anyone who gives a damn about America's musical legacy, Larry Blumenfeld loves New Orleans. His ongoing reporting on the impact of the levee breaks is invaluable social history in the making, and here he looks at the tensions between the city's police and those upholding its long tradition of elaborate, second-line funeral parades.

Two giant musical figures of the 1990s get the assessment of origins they deserve. The blue eyes, flannel shirts, and primal screams of Kurt Cobain are decoded, along with the visual strategies of a documentary about Nirvana's late leader, in Sean Nelson's movie review, while ten years after the death of the Notorious B.I.G., Alan Light deftly uses oral history to recall the days before Biggie became big. Meanwhile Jody Rosen projects just the right mix of awe and amusement at the fact of Jimmy Buffett's ongoing, mystifying, and lucrative career in "A Pirate Looks at 60."

Is Alex Ross the best music critic, regardless of genre, working right now? If not, he's pretty damn close. His *The Rest Is Noise* book chapter turned *The New Yorker* profile on Finnish composer Jean Sibelius continues the impressive work that's made his reputation. Another longtime contender for the crown, Gary Giddins, is represented here with a brief, gracefully rendered look at the career of bossa nova inheritor Rosa

Passos, and that music's history. David Kamp's excavation of Sly Stone's lost years is, quite simply, the article scores of other journalists (like me) have wanted to write for twenty years, and Kamp made me even more jealous by doing such a fine job. And I know next to nothing about gay dance anthems or homo positive radio, yet Marke B's "Gayest. Music. Ever." is such a detailed and knowing overview of this scene's last ten years that I downloaded a couple of the compilations he writes about. Overall I disliked the music, but that didn't dampen my enthusiasm for Marke B's work since what mattered is that he cared so much he made me wanna listen.

Outside of my three admittedly rigid categories are all manner of odd, obsessive, fun works that slide up next to these traditional roles but exist outside them. I imagine many of these writers are seeking God in the vinyl, seeking transcendence through the forgotten history and left-field personal remembrances that music facilitates.

First is the story of Louis Armstrong, who I know many black folks viewed as an Uncle Tom because of all his jivey smiling. His standing up for civil rights back in 1957 was a tale I'd never heard before, and I thank David Margolick for telling it. 'Zines like *Eaves of Ass* exist to give folks like Craven Rock a forum for impressionistic navel gazing. I found his first person entries a wildly entertaining ride that bounced all over the place, musically, starting with Lynyrd Skynyrd and somehow ending satisfyingly with Rancid.

I suppose Tom Ewing's piece should have originally been categorized with the other archivist pieces, but there's an obsessive quality to his definitions of ABBA songs as "adult" and "dark" that leads me to believe Ewing spent a great many (too many?) hours listening closely to these records over and over in a closed room. That kind of focus, which could be viewed as committed or demented, depending on your view of ABBA's canon, is what makes this essay flow. To me it reads like the testament for some strange Scandinavian religion. When Ewing argues, "You may find that your life ends up more like an ABBA song than you imagine," he speaks for many of the writers in this collection, who would likely substitute their subject for ABBA in that same sentence.

—*Nelson George*

CARL WILSON

THE TROUBLE
WITH INDIE ROCK

IT'S NOT JUST RACE. IT'S CLASS.

The New Yorker pop critic Sasha Frere-Jones has often indicated bore-
dom and annoyance with a lot of the critically acclaimed, music-blog,
and/or NPR-approved "indie rock" of this decade. This week, in an article, a couple of blog entries, and a podcast, he tries to articulate why. His
answer? It's not black enough; it lacks "swing, some empty space and
palpable bass frequencies"; it doesn't participate lustily in the grand (and
problematic) tradition of musical "miscegenation" that's given American
music, especially rock 'n' roll, its kick.

To give bite to the accusation, Frere-Jones names a few names, beginning with the Arcade Fire and adding Wilco, the Fiery Furnaces, the
Decemberists, the Shins, Sufjan Stevens, Grizzly Bear, Panda Bear, and
Devendra Banhart, plus indie-heroes past, Pavement. He contrasts them
with the likes of the Clash, Elvis, the Beatles, the Rolling Stones, Led
Zeppelin, Cream, Public Image Ltd., Bob Dylan, the Minutemen, Nirvana, and even Grand Funk Railroad as examples of willful, gleeful,
racial-sound-barrier-breaching white rockers of yore.

As indicated in his pre-emptive blog post, the piece is a provocation,
as is Frere-Jones's M.O., and that is welcome at a time when musical
discussion revolves numblingly around which digital-distribution

1

method can be most effectively "monetized." (Current champ: Radiohead.) But many commentators have pointed out his article's basic problems of consistency and accuracy: Frere-Jones's story is that the rise of Pavement as role models and Dr. Dre and Snoop Dogg as rivals in the 1990s marked a quick indie retreat from bluesiness and danceability. Yet the conscious and iconoclastic excision of blues-rock from "underground" rock goes back to the '70s and '80s origins of American punk and especially hardcore, from which indie complicatedly evolved.

While it's possible to cherry-pick exceptions ever since, Frere-Jones does so selectively, overlooking the likes of Royal Trux or the Afghan Whigs in the 1990s, or more recently, the Yeah Yeah Yeahs, Spoon, Battles and the dance-punks LCD Soundsystem, Hot Chip, and Junior Senior, almost all of whom appear on his own best-of-the-year list in progress. Last March, in direct contradiction to what he says in this week's *The New Yorker* essay, Frere-Jones wrote in an LCD Soundsystem review: "About five years ago, indie rockers began to rediscover the pleasures of rhythm." Where are *those* indie rockers now? Vanished, because they would mess with his thesis. He isn't really talking about all of indie rock, but a folkier subset that's hardly trying to be rock at all. But to say so would be less dramatic.

The article also tends troublingly to reduce "black music" to rhythm and sexuality, and to elide the differences between, say, funk, soul, disco, folk-blues, Caribbean, and African influences in white rock. While he justifiably frames the issue as an American one, at least half of Frere-Jones's lauded precedents are British, a context in which appropriating black American music has vastly different connotations. His lead example, the Arcade Fire, is likewise un-American, hailing from Montreal (one of its leaders, Régine Chassagne, has family roots in Haiti). The piece also switches at its convenience between mainstream rock history and the "underground" genealogy of indie, while never balancing the scales by addressing current hit-making rockers like Fall Out Boy or the White Stripes, who remain heavier on groove.

One could go on playing "gotcha" at the expense of Frere-Jones's intended thrust, which mainly indicates that this piece needed another draft or two. This is odd, because "indie whiteness" is a subject he's been banging on about in many forums for several years. (Frere-Jones is also a sometime white-indie-rocker himself.) His consistent mistake seems to be to talk about musical issues as if they were nearly autonomous from larger social dynamics. It's the blind spot of a genuine music lover, but it grants music culture too much power and assigns it too much blame.

For instance, the separation of racial influences in American music arguably begins with the 1970s demise of Top 40 radio, which coincided with the Black Power movement and the withering of the integrationist ideals of the civil rights era. Frere-Jones nods in this direction when he talks about "political correctness," but he reduces the issue to an "academic" critique rather than a vast shift in racial relations and, more importantly, expectations. The brands of "authenticity" that both punk and hip-hop came to demand, which tended to discourage the cross-pollination and "miscegenation" of musical forms, are in keeping with the identity politics that became dominant in the 1980s as well as the de facto resegregation of black and white communities that began in the Reagan era. This is the counternarrative to the cultural-level "social progress" that Frere-Jones rightly points out, in which explicit racism has retreated, and black entertainers have come to dominate the mainstream.

It's not just because Snoop Dogg and Dr. Dre were such great artists that white people were afraid to imitate them—they're no better than John Coltrane, Jimi Hendrix, James Brown, Muddy Waters, and dozens of others whom white artists have happily mimicked in the past. Rather it's that this kind of "theft" became a capital cultural crime, and not just in the academy (how many '90s indie rockers knew by heart the verses in "Fight the Power," where Public Enemy calls Elvis a "Straight-up racist, simple and plain"?). If gangsta rap marked a break, it was because hip-hop became coded to reflect the retrenchment of the "Two Americas" and the resultant combative, near-separatist mood among African-Americans. It was deliberately made less assimilable, a development reinforced by the marketplace when white suburban kids turned out to love its more extremist voice.

You could argue that it's always incumbent on the artists to come back swinging by presenting an alternative vision. Some have tried—unfortunately, often in the form of jam bands and rock-rap groups—but the diminished street-level faith in an integrationist future means there's not as much optimism about integrationist music. What's more, racial lines in the United States no longer divide primarily into black and white. When "miscegenation" does happen in music now, it's likely to be more multicultural than in Frere-Jones's formula, as in rainbow-coalition bands such as Antibalas and Ozomatli.

Ultimately, though, the "trouble with indie rock" may have far more to do with another post-Reagan social shift, one with even less upside than the black-white story, and that's the widening gap between rich and poor. There is no question on which side most indie rock falls. It's a cliché to picture indie musicians and fans as well-off "hipsters" busily gentrifying neighborhoods, but compared to previous post-punk generations, the particular kind of indie rock Frere-Jones complains about is more blatantly upper-middle class and liberal-arts-college-based, and less self-aware or politicized about it.

With its true spiritual center in Richard Florida–lauded "creative" college towns such as Portland, Oregon, this is the music of young "knowledge workers" in training, and that has sonic consequences: Rather than body-centered, it is bookish and nerdy; rather than being instrumentally or vocally virtuosic, it shows off its cops via its range of allusions and high concepts with the kind of fluency both postmodern pop culture and higher education teach its listeners to admire. (Many rap MCs juggle symbologies just as deftly, but it's seldom their main point.) This doesn't make coffeehouse-indie shallow, but it can result in something more akin to the 1960s folk revival, with fretful collegiate intellectuals in a Cuban Missile Crisis mood, seeking purity and depth in antiquarian music and escapist spirituality. Not exactly a recipe for a booty-shaking party. While this scene can embrace some fascinating hermetic weirdos such as Joanna Newsom or Panda Bear, it's also prone to producing fine-arts-grad poseurs such as the Decemberists and poor-little-rich-boy-or-girl singer songwriters who might as well be James Taylor. This year even saw several indie bands playing in "Pops" concerts at summer symphony programs; that's no sin (and good for the symphonies), but it's about as class-demarcated as it gets.

Among at least a subset of (the younger) musicians and fans, this class separation has made indie more openly snobbish and narrow-minded. In the darkest interpretation, one could look at the split be-tween a harmony-and-lyrics-oriented indie field and a rhythm-and-dance-specialized rap/R&B scene as mirroring the developing global split between an internationalist, educated comprador class (in which musically, one week Berlin is hot, the next Sweden, the next Canada, the next Brazil) and a far less mobile, menial-labor market (consider the more confining, though often musically exciting, region-alism that Frere-Jones outlines in hip-hop). The elite status and media sway that indie rock enjoys, disproportionate to its popularity, is one reason the cultural politics of indie musicians and fans require discus-sion in the first place, a point I wish Frere-Jones had clarified in *The New Yorker*; perhaps in that context it goes without saying.

The profile of this university demographic often includes a sojourn in extended adolescence, comprising graduate degrees, internships, for-eign jaunts, and so on, which easily can last until their early 30s. Unlike in the early 1990s, when this was perceived as a form of generational exclusion and protested in "slacker"/grunge music, it's now been nor-malized as a passage to later-life career success. Its musical conse-quences might include an open but less urgent expression of sexuality, or else a leaning to the twee, sexless, childhood nostalgia that many older critics (including both Frere-Jones and me) find puzzling and irri-tating. Female and queer artists still have pressing sexual issues and identities to explore and celebrate, but the straight boys often seem to fall back on performing their haplessness and hyper-sensitivity. (Pity the indie-rock girlfriend.)

Yet this is a problem having to do with the muddled state of white masculinity today, and it's not soluble by imitating some image of black male sexuality (which, as hip-hop and R&B amply demonstrate, is dealing with its own crises). Are we supposed to long for the days when Zeppelin and the Stones fetishized fantasies of black manhood, in part as a cover for misogyny? If forced to choose between tolerating some boringly undersexed rock music and reviving the, er, "vigorous" sexual politics of cock rock, I'll take the boring rock, thanks—for now.

If class, at least as much as race, is the elephant in this room, one of the more encouraging signals lately might be the recent mania for Bruce Springsteen—as if a dim memory suddenly has surfaced that white working-class culture once had a kind of significant berth in rock 'n' roll, too. (It's now moved to Nashville.) I was unexpectedly moved by the video of Win and Régine from the Arcade Fire playing "Keep the Car Running" (Frere-Jones's No. 15 song of the year so far) live with the Boss onstage Sunday in Ottawa. The performance itself aside, their presence in front of an arena audience that mostly had no idea who the hell they were shows the chutzpah it takes to resist niche-market fragmentation. (And sure, I'd be at least as happy if they'd been doing it with Stevie Wonder, and even more if they were sharing the stage with Dr. Dre.)

My armchair sociology may be as reductive as Frere-Jones's potted rock history, but the point is that the problem of style segregation can't be solved by calling upon Sufjan Stevens to funk up his rhythm section. I'm as much a devotee of genre-mixing as Frere-Jones, when it works (I've even used the loaded term "miscegenation" in articles for years), but I've noticed that when indie musicians do grapple with hip-hop rhythms, using their own voices and perspectives (my friends in Ninja High School in Toronto, for instance), they're usually lambasted by critics who fancy themselves arbiters of realness for being an insulting joke. The culture-crossing inhibitions exist for reasons beyond mere timidity, and snorting "get over it" is not enough.

The impetus may have to come from the currently dominant side of the pop market—and increasingly that is what we're seeing. Kanye West doesn't much care about the race of the people he samples, while Justin Timberlake cares very much what race his producer is (African-American, please), and OutKast and Gnarls Barkley play teasing, Prince-like crossover games. If it's going to be re-established that such moves are legit, it will happen on the charts for a while before the more cautious and self-conscious rock-in-decline types feel free to do it too. Which, as a turnabout, seems rather like fair play.

BILL WASIK

ANNUALS

A North Carolina Band Navigates
the Ephemeral Blogosphere

On July 17, 2006, a blogger named Mike on a music site called Post-core.com made what can only be called a preemptive strike. "[W]ord on the street," Mike wrote, "is that Pitchfork"—the Internet's most influential music site, and arguably the independent music scene's chief tastemaker, online or off—"is getting the jump on this band tomorrow, which means we're going to throw it out there today." He went on:

> [T]his band's got it all: young songwriter who begs for the "wun-derkind" title . . . inventive and semi-electronic production, full sup-port from the most influential music blog out there (not this one), songs that explode halfway through, and about a hundred music blogs who feel the pressure to write about a different band every day. I'm just saying, get ready to get sick of hearing about this band.

"Get ready to get sick of hearing about this band"—it would be diffi-cult to think of a more apt motto for indie rock in the age of the Inter-net. A loose genre defined not by any sound but rather by its opposition to (or exclusion from) corporate radio and labels, indie rock evolved out of the hardcore scene of the 1980s, at a time when finding out about important new bands depended much on whom you knew or where you were: News spread almost exclusively through word of mouth, through photocopied 'zines (often with circulations in three or even two digits), or through low-watt college radio stations.

Today, indie-rock culture remains an underground culture, basically by definition, in that its fans shun mainstream music in favor of lesser-known acts. But now, MySpace, iTunes, and Internet radio make location and friends irrelevant for discovering music. Blogs and aggregators enable fans to determine in just a few minutes what everyone else is listening to that day. What you know, where you are—these matter not at all. To be an insider today one must merely be fast. Once Mike found out that Pitchfork would be posting about the new band, one cannot blame him for his haste, because après Pitchfork, le déluge: Unknown bands become all-too-familiar bands in a month, and abandoned bands the next month. Get ready, that is, to get sick.

As promised, half past ten on the morning of July 18 saw Ryan Schreiber, the founder and editor-in-chief of Pitchfork, place his imprimatur upon the new band, which he likened to "some fantasy hybrid of Animal Collective, Arcade Fire, and Broken Social Scene." His readers would know these names, bands that ranked among the most successful indie-rock acts of the previous four years, and all (not coincidentally) owed a debt to Pitchfork in getting there. Schreiber had essentially launched Broken Social Scene's career when he described their American debut album—which he had found just by "dig[ging] through the boxes upon boxes of promos that arrive at the Pitchfork mailbox each month"—as "endlessly replayable, perfect pop." More recently, a Schreiber review had conferred indie-rock superstardom on Brooklyn's Clap Your Hands Say Yeah; the group did not even have a record deal (the band had self-produced its album). What makes Pitchfork so powerful is not the size of its readership, which by web-magazine standards is small—one and a half million visitors each month, only a fraction of whom read the site regularly—but its stature in the firmament of indie-rock blogs as a kind of North Star, a point of reference to be measured against. A glowing Pitchfork review need not be agreed with, but it must at the very least be reckoned with.

In his post about the new band, Schreiber concluded with a wink to his site's clout. "Get familiar now," he wrote, "we could be writing about these dudes all year long." Predictably, by the end of August, more than thirty blogs had posted about the new band, and the album's leaked tracks became fixtures on the Top-20 list at Elbo.ws, a site that monitors plays of downloaded music.

Once Pitchfork blesses an act, any mention of that act on other blogs needs to be accompanied by an acknowledgment that one has lagged terribly behind the times. On September 7, Stereogum.com not only quoted Pitchfork's review but wrote, "The hype machine"—by which they presumably meant blogs like themselves, because not a single dollar had yet gone into promoting the new band—"has been in motion for this band, so we feel sorta silly calling them a Band to Watch (we know, we know . . . you blogged about them first.)" Even so, the first comment, just fifteen minutes after the post, began with one word in all caps: "DUH." By September 18, Idolator, the music blog of Gawker Media's online empire, could pull back for a world-weary dissection of the new band as phenomenon, complete with "Odds of Backlash," which it placed at five-to-one. On October 5, when *Rolling Stone* magazine's "Rock & Roll Daily" blog finally weighed in, with an unctuous pronouncement of phony hipness—"Trust us on this one: you guys are gonna seriously sweat us for introducing you" to this band—commenter "nick" unloaded with justifiably righteous scorn:

> yeah . . . everyone is really gonna "sweat you" for being (LITERALLY) the last blog on the Internet to write baout (sic) these guys.

The band is called Annuals, and they hail from Raleigh, North Carolina. I first heard the tracks on October 14, three days before the official release of *Be He Me*, Annuals' first album, but three months too late. Their sound is difficult to describe, especially to those who have not heard Animal Collective, Arcade Fire, or Broken Social Scene, bands that plumb the sonic *expansiveness* afforded by our high-tech, DIY musical age, when one can emerge from one's basement with meticulously untidy, offhandedly epic music. And if these other bands are epic, Annuals are more so. Within a single song, the vocal might rise from tender contemplation to a wail or even a hoarse, toneless scream; drums, hitherto absent, suddenly charge in, mammoth, driving, relentless, with two or even three kits going at once; arpeggios from various synths and strings wander in and out, while electronica decorates the margins, a layered sheet of rigorous noise. Whether you buy or steal I do not care; just find the tracks and listen. What they will sound like to you today I cannot say, but that autumn, Annuals sounded like the future.

Last Fall I met Annuals in New York at a vegan grocery/café on the Lower East Side. They had come to the city for the CMJ Music Marathon, a sort of indie-rock hajj for hundreds of bands, some of whom play to capacity crowds while others, bleeding flagellants, must play to almost no one—as I learned firsthand earlier in the week when, at the 7 p.m. set of a band I had liked online (a wistful countrified act called the Western States Motel), I found myself in an audience of perhaps a half-dozen, a situation in which one finds rock bands starting to make discomforting levels of eye contact. But already it had been guaranteed that Annuals would draw a crowd. Although the band's time slot was poor—number two on a six-band bill—their success at the festival had been essentially preordained, as everyone had seen the online blowup and modified their expectations accordingly. Even the New York Times, the day I met the band, had fingered Annuals, with their "grand, disheveled songs," as the festival act most likely to make good.

The orchestrator of Annuals is Adam Baker, a scruffy-but-strikingly-purposive twenty year old. A meld of hipster and hippie, he wore a green hoodie, rolled up cords, and junked-out white Asics, but also kept a little ponytail, a thin, messy beard, and a satiny blue choker. He spoke with a businesslike patter, his eyes darting around, a young man residing very much inside his own capacious head. With his mouth full of some sort of health food, he talked to me about creative control and how he aimed to maintain it. "That's been, like, our only rider throughout this whole thing," he said. "You can't force us to do it any other way than how we know how. We had tried recording with producers from the start, doing all the tracking with someone else and having them at the board? But it really makes us uncomfortable, and the sound doesn't come out exactly how we want it."

Instead, Adam recorded (often playing all the parts) and produced all the songs essentially by himself. If he owed the Internet for his band's sudden popularity, he owed his creative control to an equally revolutionary technology: PC-based sound-engineering software, particularly the cheap (a stripped-down version is free), remarkably powerful, and now basically ubiquitous ProTools; Adam is of a generation of musicians accustomed to producing CD-quality music in their teenage bedrooms. He has wrecked one of his eardrums, but unlike rockers of yore he incurred his injury not with amps but with headphones.

Lead guitar in Annuals is handled by Kenny Florence, a gregarious, almost antic nineteen year old with a baby face and thick black hair closely cropped. The six members of Annuals also play together as a band called Sedona, a sort of indie-bluegrass affair led by Kenny; Adam plays drums. In fact, it was while on tour as Sedona, in the van, that they got the call from a record label that had discovered Adam's Annuals songs on MySpace. Now Sedona lingered in the background while Annuals got its turn. "Annuals is our main project right now," Kenny said, "but we plan on putting out lots of different albums with lots of different styles and lots of different ideas. . . . We're planning on pretty much just, like—I don't know what the word is—exploding people's brains with all of the projects that we're doing, you know?"

"The intention is to get a dynasty together, I guess," added Adam. They spoke in the half-ironic tone affected today when expressing great dreams. In the meantime, Kenny still lived with his parents, while Adam roomed with the bassist Mike Robinson. "In my mom's basement," interjected Mike. "Can't lie."

"Can't afford a fucking apartment, man," said Adam.

"We're still climbing the hill," Mike said, philosophically.

Kenny, Adam, and Mike have been playing together since their early teens, when they started a punk band called Timothy's Weekend. They said that was in 2000—2000!—and suddenly their youth struck me. They played with the sophisticated sound of bands five or ten years older.

"We've been probably playing music together for the same amount of time they've been playing," Kenny pointed out.

"We just got a head start, that's all," offered Adam. He added that they hadn't even listened to Arcade Fire, Animal Collective, or Broken Social Scene until the comparisons started. His own influences, he said, tended toward Paul Simon and Brian Wilson. "They're just trying to compare us to bands that are current, you know?" he said. "There's not really anyone else they *can* compare us to." He paused. "*I think.*"

Everyone I know listens to indie rock. At the older end, some still hang onto bands from their day, while others are "graduating" towards classical or jazz; at the younger end, some fold mainstream hip-hop into their mix, while others dabble in metal or trance. But everyone I know listens to indie rock. They all vote Democrat, too, and in this regard we reside in the "urban archipelago," as a very smart essay in Seattle alt-weekly *The Stranger* called the urban-liberal consensus just after the heartbreaking (for us) 2004 election. But more remarkable than this nationwide political consensus is the nationwide cultural consensus that has sprung up within or alongside it, among hundreds of thousands of young adults, and not only in big cities, but in college towns and even rural retreats. Journalists rarely write about this consensus, perhaps because most of them reside squarely inside it. One might call it the hipster consensus, to use the somewhat unfortunate term that (for better or for worse) has come to denote these educated young Americans; and no cultural genre defines this consensus more than does indie rock.

If this hipster archipelago is a virtual community, it is building up its own virtual institutions, which use the Internet to harmonize the far-flung members, to allow these thousands of disparate agents to maintain a near-instantaneous and deceptively easy unanimity. Pitchfork serves as one of these institutions, as does the Gawker Media network of blogs (which includes the aforementioned Idolator, as well as Gawker in New York, Defamer in L.A., and a handful of other, nongeographically aligned offerings). But perhaps more intriguing than either of these is KEXP, a real-world public-radio station in Seattle that attracts a significant portion of its listenership online. Its three prime-time DJs play almost entirely indie-rock, with selections that (broadly) mirror the lineups, themselves converging, of the nation's indie-rock clubs. And indeed, a list of KEXP's top-twelve cities for online listenership reads like a hipster-archipelago roll call (albeit weighted understandably westward): 1. Seattle, 2. New York, 3. Minneapolis, 4. Portland, Ore., 5. Chicago, 6. San Francisco, 7. Los Angeles, 8. Washington, DC, 9. Vancouver, 10. Denver, 11. Atlanta, 12. Austin (Numbers 13 and 15, curiously enough, are Beijing and Guangzhou, in China).

Although it should be stressed that the actual online tribe of KEXP, like that of Pitchfork, is relatively small—62,000 unique visitors per week—it nevertheless functions as a crucial pollinator of sounds, injecting the same new bands at the exact same time into similar social groups around the world.

The week I met Annals, during the CMJ festival in New York, KEXP played host to a series of studio appearances by what one could only call, without any cynicism, some of the new bands of the season— Bound Stems, Hot Chip, White Whale, Forward Russia, Tokyo Police Club, What Made Milwaukee Famous—as well as appearances from such admired older bands as the Shins and the Apples in Stereo. (Annals had already recorded at the station in Seattle, a few weeks beforehand.) The day I visited, the show featured a Norwegian electronic band called 120 Days. In a blond-wood-paneled anteroom, the audience sat on folding chairs while behind the studio window the band gamely tried, as synth acts must, to give off the appearance of "rocking" while they attended to their machines. All of them strained to lurch about kinetically as they tweaked the knobs on their Korgs.

Midway through this rather arid demonstration, I sat down with John Richards, KEXP's morning-show host and probably the most listened-to indie-rock DJ in the nation. Richards has a slight build, an elfin face, and dirty-blond hair parted down the middle. Thirty-three years old, Richards started as an intern at the station (under its previous name, KCMU) and worked his way all the way up to drivetime. His taste is bulletproof; I find myself constantly checking the real-time playlist during his online broadcasts to catch the band names. When I asked him about the "virtual community" of indie rock, he knew just what I was talking about. He brought up the band Tapes 'n Tapes, a breakout act of spring 2006 (Pitchfork review: 8.3 out of 10) that, perversely, had not even attracted much of an audience in its own hometown of Minneapolis until it was picked up by the various blogs and by KEXP.

"A listener in Austin told me about it," Richards recalled. "I sent somebody off to find the music—find this right away, I said. . . . We got the demo from the band within a week, and started playing it." The trick in breaking bands, Richards said, is repetition. "Cowbell"—Tapes 'n Tapes' first hit, a driving raw thing—"was the song I was hitting constantly. And just kept hitting it, and hitting it, and hitting it, and then all of a sudden you saw their hometown suddenly react to a station playing their band. And then it just grew from there."

But why did so many of these bands disappear? What about the second album, or the third? Why did indie rock seem to have become wave after wave of disposable new bands? "You have these bands working really, really hard, they're writing great songs, they've had five years maybe; and their best material is going to make it on their first album," Richards said. But then, he went on, "you have a label involved at this point, you have deadlines now—another album in six months, nine months."

Richards said he now assumed that he would not even see second albums, no matter how good their sound. "Even an Annuals," he said. "I'm not even thinking about a second album from them. I just assume that this is the document that I have. . . . You think: 'This is a great movie—I hope there's not a sequel.'"

But Richards acknowledged that he and the other indie-rock tastemakers bore some share of the blame. "A big deal with us is discovery," he said. "And you're discovering not just a song; you're discovering a *band*. When you're just discovering a second album, there's not as much hype involved." He began to recount his own discovery of the Pixies, in 1988, and as he spoke his speech became subtly emotional, his hands began to clench. "I heard *Surfer Rosa*, and it changed my life. And you know, all the other albums I heard after that were great, but man, it never equaled that. . . . It was like a drug, I guess. You take the drug, you never get that high again, you know?"

He laughed at this, but he was coming to the crux of something: "It gets harder and harder to achieve that. You keep thinking—I want to be the one to discover that band. When you hear someone talk about Clap Your Hands Say Yeah, and you're hearing that David Byrne loves them, or David Bowie. And—wow, I saw them! And it was packed!

"But the second time," he went on, "well, now it sold out early, and it's at a bigger club. And *I'm not that guy anymore. I'm not the guy discovering them.* I'm just a guy who is with everybody else who also knows who they are."

One unlikely outpost of the hipster archipelago can be found in a strip mall in Carrboro, North Carolina. At the rightmost end of a startlingly hideous facade, the top half of which consists of some strange, brown, corrugated metal that harkens back to 1980s slapdash futurism, the Cat's Cradle sits nonchalantly, as if a rock club somehow naturally belonged there alongside the video store and the Amanta Gourmet Pizza. Despite its prosaic setting, the club is a longstanding and vital node in the national indie-rock network. To scan the list of bands playing at Cat's Cradle in any given year is to get a decent sense for the "big" indie bands that are touring the United States that year; one would find general overlap with any list of bands playing at, for example, the Bowery Ballroom or the Knitting Factory, in New York; at the 9:30 Club or the Black Cat, in Washington, D.C.; at First Avenue or the 400 Bar, in Minneapolis; at the Middle East, in Boston; at Hailey's, in Denton, Texas; at the Casbah, in San Diego; at the Earl, in Atlanta; at the Metro or the Abbey, in Chicago; at Bimbo's or the Independent, in San Francisco; at Chop Suey or the Showbox, in Seattle; at the shows put on in Philadelphia by Sean Agnew's R5 Productions, many of which take place in the basement of a Unitarian church—an even odder spot, perhaps, for indie-rock shows than a strip mall. In January, three months after I first met Annuals in New York, I came to see them in their hometown, or roughly so: All of them got their start playing music at the Cat's Cradle and the other clubs in Carrboro, and Chapel Hill, home to UNC, which Carrboro abuts. While the band waited to do their soundcheck, we sat around in the green room, which looked much like green rooms in seedy rock clubs anywhere: a dorm-room fridge, haphazardly arrayed scraps of torn carpet, fourth-hand upholstered furniture with the springs distended out the undersides.

"Whose Pop-Tarts are these?" asked Anna Spence, the slender redhead who plays keyboards in the band.

"Mine," said Kenny.

"Ours," said Adam, whose show preparations consisted of pacing around while using a lighter to burn decorative holes in his white collared shirt. "That's our rider, baby! Pop-Tarts."

By indie-rock standards, the past three months had been extraordinarily good to Annuals: an appearance on *Late Night with Conan O'Brien*, a full-page article in *Rolling Stone*. But they were still, as Mike had put it, "climbing the hill," and the band's patience with touring seemed to be fraying somewhat. "There's a plan to take a big break," Adam said, "because we've got all these other projects." He was speaking chiefly of Sedona, in which he drums—"I'm *dying* to get back behind the set," he said. He rattled off two other side projects: The bassist Mike had a "folk-pop" act called First Person Plural, plus Adam was planning an electronica act called Tundra.

Annuals was coming through their hometown with almost no fanfare, opening for the Dears—an unfortunately maudlin rock act from Montreal, whose songs, as a friend put it later during the show, resembled nothing so much as "a musical about an indie-rock band." I couldn't help but think about how the whole notion of a homegrown scene, here as elsewhere, had disappeared. Fifteen years ago, to be sure, national bands came through the Chapel Hill–area clubs, but the idea of a Chapel Hill band, or a Chapel Hill sound, was very much alive; the lo-fi pop sensibility of Superchunk, Archers of Loaf, and Polvo defined a local identity. Today in Chapel Hill, former members of Superchunk run Merge Records, arguably the nation's most influential indie label—but its bands hail from around the U.S., Canada, and even Europe. Annuals, whose label was based until recently in a cramped one-bedroom apartment on Fourteenth Street in Manhattan, summoned no more excitement in their own hometown than they did anywhere else.

The members are too young to have experienced this erosion of the local, but they grasp its import; Zack, Annuals' other guitarist, noted that thanks to KEXP, they had sold more records in Seattle than in their hometown. As music fans, they all recognized how the Internet shaped their own listening habits: the roaming for the new band that always lurks just around the corner. "There's two sides to that shit," Adam said, when I asked him about the Internet. "One side is it's a really wonderful way to discover all kinds of music. But then it also completely taints you. It makes you not enjoy music as long."

"It shortens your attention span," added Zack. "Because you can always access new stuff."

"Just like everything else, every day," said Adam, with resignation.

I asked about the name Annuals, a question I had been turning over in my mind ever since I first heard of the band.

"Actually, I remember the moment that I thought of the word," Adam said. "I was coming home from school, and I was looking at one of my mom's flowers. And I had just, like, started recording my little side project shit. And I thought: Annuals."

I felt relieved to know that the name did not mean for him what it had come to mean for me, a melancholy vision of a beautiful band built, constitutionally, to die. I had begun to imagine all of my wanderings through rock clubs and festivals, through blogs and social networks and download sites, as the meandering of a floraphile through resplendent gardens that will flourish only for a season; to imagine all the remarkable new bands, seemingly inexhaustible in supply, as dazzling marigolds, begonias, fuchsias, their palettes brilliant but their roots fragile, incapable of abiding a frost.

The South by Southwest festival, held each March in Austin, Texas, serves as indie rock's national convention, a four-day caucus at which all the ambitious indie acts clamor to mount the dais. The number of acts at the festival has swelled to more than fifteen hundred, performing on some sixty separate official stages, and this does not include the countless unofficial bands, on unofficial stages, hoping to be seen by the thousands of indie-industry functionaries who roam the streets with their all-access badges. Every alleyway or back patio of every club or store seemed to have a tent with a band blaring away underneath.

KEXP had set up shop on the UT-Austin campus, broadcasting its in-studio appearances from the set of *Austin City Limits*, the legendary music show. I caught up with John Richards the following afternoon, a Thursday, shortly after he signed off his shift, and we sat down in a spare, lofty office just off the set. Only half a year since Richards and I first met, I found him obsessed with an entirely new slate of bands. "It almost worries me that the burnout is going to happen in a week instead of six months," he said, only half joking. There was a wave of new British acts: pop-punk bands the Holloways and the Fratellis (the latter of which had just had their song "Flathead" turned into an iPod ad); the retro-soul songstress Amy Winehouse; and Fujiya and Miyagi, a hypnotic and danceable electronic outfit. (The station had been playing so much of these and other U.K. acts, Richards said, that fans were wondering if it had changed to an all-British format.) There were the other domestic bands of the moment, including Deerhunter, the Ponys, and Menomena, all smart, admirably difficult acts that had each released a couple of albums before but for some reason were just blowing up now. Annuals did not come up.

The very first band Richards mentioned in his list, the band "at the top of their game," as Richards put it, was Peter Bjorn and John, a Swedish act best known for their song "Young Folks," a laidback and likable dance number built on a dispiritingly addictive whistled riff.

Peter Bjorn and John had built this simple figure into a cacophony of attention, by way of the typical channels. Pitchfork bestowed an 8.5 on the full album, *Writer's Block*, and then chose them to headline the website's own South by Southwest party—a spot that one could imagine almost any of the 1,500 bands would have accepted. KEXP put them on their live bill, too; Peter Bjorn and John was the band I had come to see. They were to go on at quarter till two in the afternoon, and I sat in the near-empty bleachers and watched them set up.

The stage set of *Austin City Limits* seemed, at first glance, like an incongruous backdrop for indie rock. A kitschily stylized Austin skyline in the evening, it managed to render a too-sleepy city even sleepier-seeming in miniature. For that matter, Peter Bjorn and John (their actual names) seemed an incongruous indie-rock trio, at least visually speaking: The first two, who have played together for a decade, were mop-topped, fashionably unkempt fellows in tight black jeans, whereas the third, the drummer, wore a suit jacket over a crisp-white dress shirt, his black hair impeccably styled to one side, his overall look resembling that of a villainous investment-banker in an '80s movie (I later discovered he was not John, but a pinch-hit percussionist named Nino). But stage and band seemed to come together fine when they started up; the stands, which for the other bands that day had been half-empty, if that, were full.

Before I arrived in Austin, I realized that Annuals' season in a fickle sun had ended, and I found that my marvel at the ever-flowering garden of *good-enough bands*, had given way, I must confess, to a species of anger. Peter Bjorn and John, too, awed, and so did these other bands, but what about the bands from six months prior—Annuals, but also White Whale, Bound Stems, Tokyo Police Club, bands whose names even you, unfaithful reader, perhaps have already forgotten from just a few pages prior? I had begun to forget them, too. We falter like the others, enjoying the stories put in front of us today and forgetting the rest. How can we resist the new story, the one that everyone else is listening to, linking to, cueing up at parties? "Young Folks" was exactly that track, and as Peter Bjorn and John started, I couldn't help but get a thrill, despite myself, and the rest of the crowd clearly did, too. Some teenagers, who earlier on had improbably bounded out from the wings to sit Indian-style before the stage, now rose to their feet and began to dance, as unself-consciously as teenagers are able to, and in that heartbreakingly loose-limbed style they seem to prefer. Peter, it must be said, whistled with astonishing skill, performing the difficult riff over and over again without falter, *but wait*—halfway through, there is a malfunction; his lips unpurse and yet the whistle goes on—*he has been lip-synching the whistle*. And now, acknowledging his mistake, Peter begins to laugh as he sings, and Bjorn begins to laugh, too, and now John, as well, all cracking up at their mighty hit, cut off at the knees.

Annuals also performed at South by Southwest. As all the bands with any reputation did, they played multiple shows, of which I saw the first and the last. At the first, in a tented patio abutting a bar, they shared the bill with a band called Illinois, a dreamily ramshackle, banjo-driven rock act that was just then in the throes of blowup: Idolator that very week dissected Illinois' buzz in almost identical fashion to their post about Annuals six months prior, down to the same cynical "Odds of Backlash": five-to-one. The tent filled for Illinois, but most of the crowd stayed for Annuals.

The last Annuals show of the festival I happened onto by chance, as I walked with my wife up Trinity Street. The band was loading equipment from their big white van into the Austin Convention Center, where they were to tape a few songs for a radio station. While the band waited to go on, we all lay around on the floor in the main corridor, a sunny, echoing plate-glassed atrium some sixty feet high and three football fields long.

After the show, they had a two-week break, and they were finally going to use it to record as Sedona—Kenny's band, the band they'd been before Annuals got signed. Adam wanted to finish a few songs for Tundra. "And we might start on BandAnd," he added, then noticed my quizzical look and explained: BandAnd was the hard-rock band to be run by Zack.

"I think that'll have to be on our next break," Zack averred.

"It's like avant-garde metal fusion, pretty much," Kenny said.

"It's all of us trying to be as technical and heavy as possible," Zack said.

"We've got, like, little riffs that we've written for it," Kenny said. "We haven't put anything together fully, but we've got a *lot* of ideas."

Annuals might be the perfect name, I realized, in a different way than I thought. Maybe their destiny is to be a march of bands in themselves, not one fuchsia in the frost, but a thousand blooming in succession. Maybe they, and maybe we all, will learn to make art, to find narrative, in this churning, viral culture by embodying the churn, embracing it, by envisioning a life not as some decades-long epic, but as a succession of discretely plotted six-month shorts. Maybe, moreover, we are becoming so fragmented, so besotted on the specificities of our cultural subdivisions, that the future historians of the twenty-first century, maintaining their collaborative wiki-textbooks while they lounge about in silvery bodysuits, will identify our era to be when the story ended, as it were, the end not of history but of history as *narrative*—of the fiction that a culture, or even a subculture, is an arrow.

The last song Annuals played in the taping was one I'd never heard them do live: a sublimely meditative track called "Ease My Mind." Kenny had written it; he sang lead vocals and played a blistering acoustic. Where Annuals, lyrically, was achingly broken, this song was elliptically spiritual. "I like everyone to be this holy," Kenny sang,

> *Tell us, tell us, are you real?*
> *What do you feel?*
> *Spread the diamond dust because I need it*
> *More than peace of mind, this is—*
> *This is divine*

It was a gorgeous song, lilting and lovely. It was not an Annuals song, even though it was becoming that. It was a Sedona song. The same thing but another thing entirely.

CLIVE THOMPSON

SEX, DRUGS AND
UPDATING YOUR BLOG

Jonathan Coulton sat in Gorilla Coffee in Brooklyn, his Apple Power-Book open before him, and began slogging through the day's email. Coulton is 36 and shaggily handsome. In September 2005, he quit his job as a computer programmer and, with his wife's guarded blessing, became a full-time singer and songwriter. He set a quixotic goal for himself: for the next year, he would write and record a song each week, posting each one to his blog. "It was a sort of forced-march approach to creativity," he admitted to me over the sound of the café's cappuccino frothers. He'd always wanted to be a full-time musician, and he figured the only way to prove to himself he could do it was with a drastic challenge. "I learned that it is possible to squeeze a song out of just about anything," he said. "But it's not always an easy or pleasant process." Given the self-imposed time constraints, the "Thing a Week" songs are remarkably good. Coulton tends toward geeky, witty pop tunes: one song, "Tom Cruise Crazy," is a sympathetic ode to the fame-addled star, while "Code Monkey" is a rocking anthem about dead-end programming jobs. By the middle of last year, his project had attracted a sizable audience. More than 3,000 people, on average, were visiting his site every day, and his most popular songs were being downloaded as many as 500,000 times; he was making what he described as "a reasonable middle-class living"—between $3,000 and $5,000 a month—by selling CDs and digital downloads of his work on iTunes and on his own site.

Along the way, he discovered a fact that many small-scale recording artists are coming to terms with these days: his fans do not want merely to buy his music. They want to be his friend. And that means they want to interact with him all day long online. They pore over his blog entries, commenting with sympathy and support every time he recounts the difficulty of writing a song. They send email messages, dozens a day, ranging from simple mash notes of the "you rock!" variety to starkly emotional letters, including one by a man who described singing one of Coulton's love songs to his 6-month-old infant during her heart surgery. Coulton responds to every letter, though as the email volume has grown to as many as 100 messages a day, his replies have grown more and more terse, to the point where he's now feeling guilty about being rude.

Coulton welcomes his fans' avid attention; indeed, he relies on his fans in an almost symbiotic way. When he couldn't perform a guitar solo for "Shop Vac," a glittery pop tune he had written about suburban angst—on his blog, he cursed his "useless sausage fingers"—Coulton asked listeners to record their own attempts, then held an online vote and pasted the winning riff into his tune. Other followers have volunteered hours of their time to help further his career: a professional graphic artist in Cleveland has drawn an illustration for each of the weekly songs, free. Another fan recently reformatted Coulton's tunes so they'd be usable on karaoke machines. On his online discussion board last June, when Coulton asked for advice on how to make more money with his music, dozens of people chimed in with tips on touring and managing the media and even opinions about what kind of songs he ought to write.

Coulton's fans are also his promotion department, an army of thousands who proselytize for his work worldwide. More than 50 fans have created music videos using his music and posted them on YouTube; at a recent gig, half of the audience members I spoke to had originally come across his music via one of these fan-made videos.

When he performs, he upends the traditional logic of touring. Normally, a new Brooklyn-based artist like him would trek around the Northeast in grim circles, visiting and revisiting cities like Boston and New York and Chicago in order to slowly build an audience—playing for 3 people the first time, then 10, then (if he got lucky) 50. But Coulton realized he could simply poll his existing online audience members, find out where they lived, and stage a tactical strike on any town with more than 100 fans, the point at which he'd be likely to make $1,000 for a concert. It is a flash-mob approach to touring: he parachutes into out-of-the-way towns like Ardmore, Pennsylvania, where he recently played to a sold-out club of 140.

His fans need him; he needs them. Which is why, every day, Coulton wakes up, gets coffee, cracks open his PowerBook and hunkers down for up to six hours of nonstop and frequently exhausting communion with his virtual crowd. The day I met him, he was examining a music video that a woman who identified herself as a "blithering fan" had made for his song "Someone Is Crazy." It was a collection of scenes from anime cartoons, expertly spliced together and offered on YouTube.

"She spent hours working on this, "Coulton marveled. "And now her friends are watching that video, and fans of that anime cartoon are watching this video. And that's how people are finding me. It's a crucial part of the picture. And so I have to watch this video; I have to respond to her." He bashed out a hasty thank-you note and then forwarded the link to another supporter—this one in Britain—who runs "The Jonathan Coulton Project," a Web site that exists specifically to archive his fan-made music videos.

He sipped his coffee. "People always think that when you're a musician you're sitting around strumming your guitar, and that's your job," he said. "But this"—he clicked his keyboard theatrically—"this is my job."

In the past—way back in the mid-'90s, say—artists had only occasional contact with their fans. If a musician was feeling friendly, he might greet a few audience members at the bar after a show. Then the Internet swept in. Now fans think nothing of sending an email message to their favorite singer—and they actually expect a personal reply. This is not merely an illusion of intimacy. Performing artists these days, particularly new or struggling musicians, are increasingly eager, even desperate, to master the new social rules of Internet fame. They know many young fans aren't hearing about bands from MTV or magazines anymore; fame can come instead through viral word-of-mouth, when a friend forwards a Web-site address, swaps an MP3, emails a link to a fan blog or posts a cell phone concert video on YouTube.

So musicians dive into the fray—posting confessional notes on their blogs, reading their fans' comments, and carefully replying. They check their personal pages on MySpace, that virtual metropolis where unknown bands and comedians and writers can achieve global renown in a matter of days, if not hours, carried along by rolling cascades of popularity. Band members often post a daily MySpace "bulletin"—a memo to their audience explaining what they're doing right at that moment—and then spend hours more approving "friend requests" from teenagers who want to be put on the artist's sprawling list of online colleagues. (Indeed, the arms race for "friends" is so intense that some artists illicitly employ software robots that generate hundreds of fake online comrades, artificially boosting their numbers.) The pop group Barenaked Ladies held a video contest, asking fans to play air guitar along to the song "Wind It Up"; the best ones were spliced together as the song's official music video. Even artists who haven't got a clue about the Internet are swept along: Arctic Monkey, a British band, didn't know what MySpace was, but when fans created a page for them in 2005—which currently boasts over 65,000 "friends"—it propelled their first single, "I Bet You Look Good on the Dancefloor," to No. 1 on the British charts.

This trend isn't limited to musicians; virtually every genre of artistic endeavor is slowly becoming affected, too. Filmmakers like Kevin Smith ("Clerks") and Rian Johnson ("Brick") post dispatches about the movies they're shooting and politely listen to fans' suggestions; the comedian Dane Cook cultivated such a huge fan base through his Web site that his 2005 CD "Retaliation" became the first comedy album to reach the Billboard Top 5 since 1978. But musicians are at the vanguard of the change. Their product, the three-minute song, was the first piece of pop culture to be fully revolutionized by the Internet. And their second revenue source—touring—makes them highly motivated to connect with far-flung fans.

This confluence of forces has produced a curious inflection point: for rock musicians, being a bit of a nerd now helps you become successful. When I spoke with Damian Kulash, the lead singer for the band OK Go, he discoursed like a professor on the six-degrees-of-separation theory, talking at one point about "rhizomatic networks." (You can Google it.) Kulash has put his networking expertise to good use: last year, OK Go displayed a canny understanding of online dynamics when it posted on YouTube a low-budget homemade video that showed the band members dancing on treadmills to their song "Here It Goes Again." The video quickly became one of the site's all-time biggest hits. It led to the band's live treadmill performance at the MTV Video Music Awards, which in turn led to a Grammy Award for best video.

This is not a trend that affects A-list stars. The most famous corporate acts—Justin Timberlake, Fergie, Beyoncé—are still creatures of mass marketing, carpet-bombed into popularity by expensive ad campaigns and radio airplay. They do not need the online world to find listeners, and indeed, their audiences are too vast for any artist to even pretend intimacy with. No, this is a trend that is catalyzing the B-list, the new, under-the-radar acts that have always built their success fan by fan. Across the country, the CD business is in a spectacular free fall; sales are down 20 percent this year alone. People are increasingly getting their music online (whether or not they're paying for it), and it seems likely that the artists who forge direct access to their fans have the best chance of figuring out what the new economics of the music business will be.

The universe of musicians making their way online includes many bands that function in a traditional way—signing up with a label—while using the Internet primarily as a means of promotion, the way OK Go has done. Two-thirds of OK Go's album sales are still in the physical world: actual CDs sold through traditional CD stores. But the B-list increasingly includes a newer and more curious life form: performers like Coulton, who construct their entire business model online.

Without the Internet, their musical careers might not exist at all. Coulton has forgone a record-label contract; instead, he uses a growing array of online tools to sell music directly to fans. He contracts with a virtual fulfillment house called CD Baby, which warehouses his CDs, processes the credit-card payment for each sale and ships it out, while pocketing only $4 of the album's price, a much smaller cut than a traditional label would take. CD Baby also places his music on the major digital-music stores like iTunes, Rhapsody, and Napster. Most lucratively, Coulton sells MP3s from his own personal Web sites, where there's no middleman at all.

In total, 41 percent of Coulton's income is from digital-music sales, three-quarters of which are sold directly off his own Web site. Another 29 percent of his income is from CD sales; 18 percent is from ticket sales for his live shows. The final 11 percent comes from T-shirts, often bought online.

Indeed, running a Web store has allowed Coulton and other artists to experiment with intriguing innovations in flexible pricing. Remarkably, Coulton offers most of his music free on his site; when fans buy his songs, it is because they want to give him money. The Canadian folk-pop singer Jane Siberry has an even more clever system: she has a "pay what you can" policy with her downloadable songs, so fans can download them free—but her site also shows the average price her customers have paid for each track. This subtly creates a community standard, a generalized awareness of how much people think each track is really worth. The result? The average price is as much as $1.30 a track, more than her fans would pay at iTunes.

Yet this phenomenon isn't merely about money and business models. In many ways, the Internet's biggest impact on artists is emotional. When you have thousands of fans interacting with you electronically, it can feel as if you're on stage 24 hours a day.

"I vacillate so much on this," Tad Kubler told me one evening in March. "I'm like, I want to keep some privacy, some sense of mystery. But I also want to have this intimacy with our fans. And I'm not sure you can have both." Kubler is the guitarist of the Brooklyn-based rock band the Hold Steady, and I met up with him at a Japanese bar in Pittsburgh, where the band was performing on its latest national tour. An exuberant but thoughtful blond-surfer type, Kubler drank a Sapporo beer and explained how radically the Internet had changed his life on the road. His previous band existed before the Web became ubiquitous, and each town it visited was a mystery: Would 20 people come out? Would two? When the Hold Steady formed four years ago, Kubler immediately signed up for MySpace page, later adding a discussion board, and curious fans were drawn in like iron filings to a magnet. Now the band's board teems with fans asking technical questions about Kubler's guitars, swapping bootlegged MP3 recordings of live gigs with each other, organizing carpool drives to see the band. Some send email messages to Kubler from cities where the band will be performing in a couple of weeks, offering to design, print, and distribute concert posters free. As the band's appointed geek, Kubler handles the majority of its online audience relations; fans at gigs chant his online screen-name, "Koob."

"It's like night and day, man," Kubler said, comparing his current situation with his pre-Internet musical career. "It's awesome now."

Kubler regards fan interaction as an obligation that is cultural, almost ethical. He remembers what it was like to be a young fan himself, enraptured by the members of Led Zeppelin. "That's all I wanted when I was a fan, right?" he said. "To have some small contact with these guys you really dug. I think I'm still that way. I'll be, like, devastated if I never meet Jimmy Page before I die." Indeed, for a guitarist whose arms are bedecked in tattoos and who maintains an aggressive schedule of drinking, Kubler seems genuinely touched by the shy queries he gets from teenagers.

"If some kid is going to take 10 minutes out of his day to figure out what he wants to say in an email, and then write it and send it, for me to not take the 5 minutes to say, dude, thanks so much—for me to ignore that?" He shrugged. "I can't."

Yet Kubler sometimes has second thoughts about the intimacy. Part of the allure of rock, when he was a kid, was the shadowy glamour that surrounded his favorite stars. He'd parse their lyrics to try to figure out what they were like in person. Now he wonders: Are today's online artists ruining their own aura by blogging? Can you still idolize someone when you know what they had for breakfast this morning? "It takes a little bit of the mystery out of rock 'n' roll," he said.

So Kubler has cultivated a skill that is unique to the age of Internet fandom, and perhaps increasingly necessary to it, as well: a nuanced ability to seem authentic and confessional without spilling over into a Britney Spears level of information overload. He doesn't post about his home life, doesn't mention anything about his daughter or girlfriend— and he certainly doesn't describe any of the ill-fated come-ons he deflects from addled female fans who don't realize he's in a long-term relationship. (Another useful rule he imparts to me: Post in the morning, when you're no longer drunk.)

There's something particularly weird, the band members have also found, about living with fans who can now trade information—and misinformation—about them. All celebrities are accustomed to dealing with reporters; but fans represent a new, wild-card form of journalism. Franz Nicolay, the Hold Steady's nattily dressed keyboardist, told me that he now becomes slightly paranoid while drinking with fans after a show because he's never sure if what he says will wind up on someone's blog. After a recent gig in Britain, Nicolay idly mentioned to a fan that he had heard that Bruce Springsteen liked the Hold Steady. Whoops: the next day, that factoid was published on a fan blog, "and it had, like, 25 comments!" Nicolay said. So now he carefully polices what he says in casual conversation, which he thinks is a weird thing for a rock star to do. "You can't be the drunken guy who just got offstage anymore," he said with a sigh. "You start acting like a pro athlete, saying all these banal things after you get off the field." For Nicolay, the intimacy of the Internet has made post-show interactions less intimate and more guarded.

The Hold Steady's online audience has grown so huge that Kubler, Like Jonathan Coulton, is struggling to bear the load. It is the central paradox of online networking: if you're really good at it, your audience quickly grows so big that you can no longer network with them. The Internet makes fame more quickly achievable—and more quickly unmanageable. In the early days of the Hold Steady, Kubler fielded only a few email messages a day, and a couple of "friend" requests on

MySpace. But by this spring, he was receiving more than 100 communications from fans each day, and he was losing as much as two or three
hours a day dealing with them. "People will say to me, 'Hey, dude, how
come you haven't posted a bulletin lately?'" Kubler told me. "And I'm
like 'I haven't done one because every time I do we get 300 messages
and I spend a day going through them!'"

To cope with the flood, the Hold Steady has programmed a software
robot to automatically approve the 100-plus "friend" requests it receives
on MySpace every day. Other artists I spoke to were testing out similar
tricks, including automatic email macros that generate instant "thank
you very much" replies to fan messages. Virtually everyone bemoaned
the relentless and often boring slog of keyboarding. It is, of course, precisely the sort of administrative toil that people join rock bands to
avoid.

Even the most upbeat artist eventually crashes and burns. Indeed,
fan interactions seem to surf along a sine curve, as an artist's energy for
managing the emotional demands waxes and wanes. As I roamed
through online discussion boards and blogs, the tone was nearly always
pleasant, even exuberant—fans politely chatting with their favorite
artists or gushing praise. But inevitably, out of the blue, the artist
would be overburdened, or a fan would feel slighted, and some minor
grievance would flare up. At the end of March, a few weeks after I
talked with Kubler in Pittsburgh, I logged on to the Hold Steady's discussion board to discover that he had posted an angry notice about
fans who sent him nasty email messages, complaining that the band
wasn't visiting their cities. "I honestly cannot believe some of the
emails, hate mail and otherwise total [expletive] I've been hearing, " he
wrote. "We're coming to rock. Please be ready."

Another evening I visited the message board for the New York post-
punk band Nada Surf, where a fan posted a diatribe attacking the bass
player for refusing to sign an autograph at a recent show, prompting an
extended fan discussion of whether the bass player was a jerk or not. A
friend of mine pointed me to the remarkable plight of Poppy Z. Brite, a
novelist who in 2005 accused fans on a discussion board of being small-
minded about children—at which point her fans banned her from the
board.

When Jonathan Coulton first began writing his weekly songs, he carefully tracked how many people listened to each one on his Web site. His listenership rose steadily, from around 1,000 a week at first to 50,000 by the end of his yearlong song-a-week experiment. But there were exceptions to his gradual rise: five songs that became breakout "hits," receiving almost 10 times as many listeners as the songs that preceded and followed them. The first hit was an improbably cover song: Coulton's deadpan version of the 1992 Sir Mix-a-Lot rap song "Baby Got Back," performed like a hippie folk ballad. Another was "Code Monkey," his pop song about a disaffected cubicle worker.

Obviously, Coulton was thrilled when his numbers popped, not least because the surge of traffic produced thousands more dollars in sales. But the successes also tortured him: he would rack his brain, trying to figure out why people loved those particular songs so much. What had he done right? Could he repeat the same trick?

"Every time I had a hit, it would sort of ruin me for a few weeks," he told me. "I would feel myself being a little bit repressed in my creativity, and ideas would not come to me as easily. Or else I would censor myself a little bit more." His fans, he realized, were most smitten by his geekier songs, the ones that referenced science fiction, mathematics, or video games. Whenever he branches out and records more traditional pop fare, he worries it will alienate his audience.

For many of these ultraconnected artists, it seems the nature of creativity itself is changing. It is no longer a solitary act: their audiences are peering over their shoulder as they work, offering pointed comments and suggestions. When OK Go released its treadmill-dancing video on YouTube, it quickly amassed 15 million views, a number so big that it is, as Kulash, the singer, told me, slightly surreal. "Fifteen million people is more than you can see," he said. "It's like this big mass of ants, and you're sitting at home in your underpants to see how many times you've been downloaded, and you can sort of feel the ebb and flow of mass attention." Fans pestered him to know what the band's next video would be; some even suggested the band try dancing on escalators. Kulash was conflicted. He didn't want to be known just for making goofy videos; he also wanted people to pay attention to OK Go's music. In the end, the band decided not to do another dance video because, as

Kulash concluded, "How do you follow up 15 million hits?" All the artists I spoke to made a point of saying they would never simply pander to their fans' desires. But many of them also said that staying artistically "pure" now requires the mental discipline of a ninja.

These days, Coulton is wondering whether an Internet-built fan base inevitably hits a plateau. Many potential Coulton fans are fanatical users of MySpace and YouTube, of course; but many more aren't, and the only way for him to reach them is via traditional advertising, which he can't afford, or courting media attention, a wearying and decidedly old-school task. Coulton's single biggest spike in traffic to his Web site took place last December, when he appeared on NPR's "Weekend Edition Sunday," a fact that, he notes, proves how powerful old-fashioned media still are. (And "Weekend Edition" is orders of magnitude smaller than major entertainment shows like MTV's "Total Request Life," which can make a new artist in an afternoon.) Perhaps there's no way to use the Internet to vault from the B-list to the A-list and the only bands that sell millions of copies will always do it via a well-financed major-label promotion campaign. "Maybe this is what my career will be," Coulton said: slowly building new fans online, playing live occasionally, making a solid living but never a crazy-rich one. He's considered signing on with a label or a cable network to try to chase a higher circle of fame, but that would mean giving up control. And, he says, "I think I'm addicted to running my own show now."

Will the Internet change the type of person who becomes a musician or writer? It's possible to see these online trends as Darwinian pressures that will inevitably produce a new breed—call it an Artist 2.0—and mark the end of the artist as a sensitive, bohemian soul who shuns the spotlight. In *The Catcher in the Rye*, J. D. Salinger wrote about how reading a good book makes you want to call up the author and chat with him, which neatly predicted the modern online urge; but Salinger, a committed recluse, wouldn't last a minute in this confessional new world. Neither would, say, Margo Timmins of the Cowboy Junkies, a singer who was initially so intimidated by a crowd that she would sit facing the back of the stage. What happens to art when people like that are chased away?

It is also possible, though, that this is simply a natural transition point and that the next generation of musicians and artists—even the avowedly "sensitive" ones—will find the constant presence of their fans unremarkable. The psychological landscape has arguably already tilted that way for anyone under 20. There are plenty of teenagers today who regard themselves as "private" individuals, yet who post openly about their everyday activities on Facebook or LiveJournal, complete with camera-phone pictures. For that generation, the line between public and private is so blurry as to become almost nonexistent. Any teenager with a MySpace page is already fluent in managing a constant stream of dozens of semi-anonymous people clamoring to befriend them; if those numbers rise to hundreds or even thousands, maybe, for them, it won't be a big deal. It's also true that many recluses in real life flower on the Internet, which can famously be a place of self-expression and self-reinvention.

While researching this article, I occasionally scanned the list of top-rated bands on MySpace—the ones with the most "friends." One of the biggest was a duo called the Scene Aesthetic, whose MySpace presence had sat atop several charts (folk, pop, rock) for a few months. I called Andrew de Torres, a 21-year-old Seattle resident and a co-founder of the group, to find out his story. De Torres, who played in a few emo bands as a teenager, had the idea for the Scene Aesthetic in January 2005, when he wrote a song that required two dueling male voices. He called his friend Eric Bowley, and they recorded the song—an aching ballad called "Beauty in the Breakdown"—in a single afternoon in Bowley's basement. They posted it to MySpace, figuring it might get a couple of listens. But the song clearly struck a chord with the teen-heavy MySpace audience, and within days it had racked up thousands of plays. Requests to be the duo's "friend" came surging in, along with messages demanding more songs. De Torres and Bowley quickly banged out three more; when those went online, their growing fan base urged them to produce a full album and to go on tour.

"It just sort of accidentally turned into this huge thing," de Torres told me when I called him up. "We thought this was a little side project.

We thought we wouldn't do much with it. We just threw it up online."
Now their album is due out this summer, and they have roughly 22,000
people a day listening to their songs on MySpace, plus more than
180,000 "friends." A cross-country tour that ended last December net-
ted them "a pretty good amount of money," de Torres added.

This sort of career arc was never previously possible. If you were a
singer with only one good song, there was no way to release it independently on a global scale—and thus no way of knowing if there was a
market for your talent. But the online fan world has different gravitational physics: on the basis of a single tune, the Scene Aesthetic kick-
started an entire musical career.

Which is perhaps the end result of the new online fan world: it allows a fresh route to creative success, assuming the artist has the correct
emotional tools. De Torres, a decade or more younger than Coulton and
the Hold Steady, is a natural Artist 2.0: he happily spends two hours a
day or more parsing notes from teenagers who tell him "your work totally got me through some rough times." He knows that to lure in listeners, he needs to post some of his work on MySpace, but since he
wants people to eventually buy his album, he doesn't want to give away
all his goods. He has thus developed an ear for what he calls "the perfect
MySpace song"—a tune that is immediately catchy, yet not necessarily
the strongest from his forthcoming album. For him, being a musician is
rather like being a business manager, memoirist, and group therapist
rolled into one, with a politician's thick hide to boot.

JEFF WEISS

SOULJA BOY

CRANKING THE CHAIN
No One Understands the Murky,
Download-Rampaged World of
Major-Label Rap Better

Carl Carlson: I don't get all this eyeball stuff. Uh, what are they
supposed to represent? Uh, eyeballs?
Moe Syslak: It's pomo!
[Blank stares from all.]
Moe: Postmodern!
[More staring.]
Moe: Yeah, all right—weird for the sake of being weird.
Guys: Oooh!

Soulja Boy is not weird for the sake of being weird. He's weird for the sake of being lucrative. Which actually might make him post-postmodern, or maybe just post-post-Diddy. Either way, he's harnessed the power of the post-MySpace, post–Lonely Girl, Web 3.0 world better than anyone else in music. Of course, some may say, "But Radiohead just sold 1.2 million downloads in the first week," but one year ago, Thom Yorke was still the pinup boy of seemingly every sensitive and bespectacled indie-skewing individual on the planet, while Soulja Boy was just another one of the 300,000-plus unknown musicians on MySpace, YouTube and Sound-Click.

Yet at one point this month, the Yahoo! home page featured blaring headlines trumpeting the 17-year-old Atlanta rapper's fifth nonconsecutive week at the top of the *Billboard* Hot 100 singles chart, an astonishing feat for any musician, let alone a senior in high school. And like most great successes, the reason behind Soulja Boy's rise to fame is both astonishingly simple and unsurprisingly complex. The short answer behind Soulja Boy's ability to move more units than recent efforts from Redman, Pharoahe Monch and Public Enemy combined lay just one click away, in the video for his smash hit, "Crank That."

Commencing with a shot of a perplexed label executive trying to figure out who this Soulja Boy character is and why his children are obsessed with his dance, the video for "Crank That" essentially summarizes Soulja Boy's mythology and rapid ascent from anonymity to the most popular artist in America (at least this month). Accordingly, there are numerous shots of Soulja Boy uploading videos to his YouTube page (now the 43rd most subscribed in the site's history, with nearly 1.5 million channel views) and inking a deal with Mr. Collipark, of Collipark Records, the former label of fellow Atlanta crunk-rappers the Ying Yang Twins.

In and of itself, the song is good in a mindless sort of way, with the inanity of its lyrics buoyed by a standard snap beat colored with an infectious and hypnotic steel-drum loop. Its true brilliance, however, lies in Soulja's instinctive marketing genius—and, of course, the deep-moneyed Interscope pockets behind him. Both "Crank That" and its accompanying instructional dance video, "How to Do the Soulja Boy Dance," serve as flawless exercises in brand building, featuring a ticker tape of come-ons to visit Soulja Boy's Web site (Souljaboytellem.com, which also serves as the actual name of his debut LP), his online merchandise store (now available—Soulja Girl booty shorts), the number to text to buy his ring tone, and—of course—the linchpin in any 2007 rapper's strategy: the MySpace page.

In a genre where every MySpace page seems more pimped-out than the Bishop Magic Don Juan drinking out of a bejeweled cup rolling through the seedy part of Santa Monica Boulevard in a lime-green Caddy, Soulja Boy's page is the Holy Grail. Enter and visitors are immediately treated to the sight of Soulja Boy, arms outstretched—triumphant—dipped head to toe in his Soulja Boy clothing line (complete with white sunglasses with the words *Soulja Boy* written on the frames). Scrolling past the perfunctory streaming songs and profile pic (pasted across Soulja Boy wallpaper) reveals a 3-D cartoon character of Soulja Boy shilling his album; "Crank That" Soulja Boy signs made by his legion of female admirers; and YouTube videos of "Soulja Boy's Hottest Videos and Performances." Not to mention homemade videos involving the Soulja Boy dance (including a Winnie-the-Pooh dance and members of the Texas Longhorns football team) and a separate reserved area for celebrities doing the Soulja Boy dance (good to see that the possibility of jail time hasn't gotten Lil Wayne too down).

No one understands the murky, download-rampaged world of major-label rap better than Soulja Boy. After all, the kid was born in 1990. To his generation, old-school means a world pre-MySpace/YouTube. Unabashedly expressing his admiration for 50 Cent, Soulja Boy has taken his idol's mogul aspirations and draped them in the familiar aesthetics of the cash- and status-crazed world of the post–Cash Money/Bling era of hip-hop, while using the Net to create a grassroots fan base from scratch. Think of him as one part Lonely Girl, one part Bruce Barton and one part Dem Franchise Boyz, a product of the sort of blurry meld of art and commerce that has inexorably marched on since the day Andy Warhol made his first silk-screen, or at the very least the moment Run-DMC sewed up their first Adidas.

With his facility in the flattened Web 3.0 world, Soulja Boy essentially created an open-source template that catapulted into a global phenomenon within a matter of months. Cynics who point out that he's just another product of the Interscope machine underestimate the hustle of the 100-plus videos Soulja Boy uploaded before Jimmy Iovine ever heard his name. And if you don't think the other labels haven't noticed and aren't already trying to find the "next Soulja Boy," then welcome back to Earth; hope that nine-year space flight went well. It remains to be seen whether Soulja Boy will turn out to be anything more than a one-hit wonder, but what's clear is that you should expect to see a lot more of this in the world of mass-market hip-hop, with more and more '90s-born, technology-weaned rappers attempting to follow Soulja Boy's blueprint. Weird.

KEYSHIA COLE
HELL'S ANGEL

It's 1998. Keyshia Cole is 16 and on her own. She should be in the 10th grade.

Brandy and Monica are big with "The Boy Is Mine." Janet Jackson has "I Get So Lonely." It's been more than a decade since the start of the crack tsunami, and the Oakland Unified School District has experienced triple-digit increases of assaults, sex offenses, and drug and alcohol offenses. Clinton cops to Lewinsky. The hot new show is HBO's *Sex and the City*. Keyshia walks in to a West Oakland recording studio at about two in the morning. Alicia Keys is at work in one of the rooms, as is D'wayne Wiggins of the recently disbanded East Oakland R&B group Tony! Toni! Toné! There is a hazy, after-hours vibe in the place. Somebody says Keyshia wants to get on the mic. The "young lady sound good," they say. Keyshia sings a song now lost to legend, then she leaves. Wiggins wakes up at dawn and listens to the track. He asks the room, "Who was that chick who was here last night?"

Now it's 2007, and here's what we know about "that chick" Keyshia Cole. She's an American Music Award–nominated singer-songwriter whose second album, the much-anticipated Just Like You (Imani/Geffen), has just been released. Keyshia's a platinum-recording artist—and it's no easy feat in this era of digital downloading to sell more than one-and-a-half million copies of any album, even one as deeply felt as Keyshia's 2005 *The Way It Is*. Her "Love" song was painful to listen to, but it was also huge—rising to No. 3 on Billboard's R&B/Hip Hop chart. Then, in 2006, with Sean "Diddy" Combs, Keyshia had the biggest pop hit of her career (to that point) with "Last Night" (Bad Boy). She also stars in a highly rated BET reality show ("Keyshia Cole: The Way It Is") in which the "reality" is her life. Keyshia has a reputation for being a magically emotive live performer and often plays to sold-out crowds. Keyshia Cole, everyone says, is Mary J. Blige's heir apparent. So, okay: But who is Keyshia Cole? Keyshia Cole is an Oakland type of chick. And I'm one who might know a little something about that.

Keyshia came up in East Oakland off of 84th Avenue and East 14th Street. I claim 83rd and East 14th, and so can my mother, my grandmother, and my great-grandmother. For the first 27 years of my life, I never left Oakland except for Los Angeles, so I didn't know to say that I "loved" Oakland, or that I'd ever "miss" Oakland, or that I was an Oakland type of chick. All I knew was that Oaktown (called that corruptively and affectionately) was wide-open, dangerous, sometimes pretty, and ferocious with crack and the seemingly cool, vicious, sweet guys who sold it in small and sometimes big ways.

Sixteen years separate Keyshia and me, as well as the circumstances of our upbringings (though, of course, we all have our crosses to bear) but she—with her grimy sweetness, underdog mentality, and what can only be called a reflexive stank attitude—reminds me of the girls I ran around with when I was young and living in Oakland, trying to figure out how to get out of—but still be of—the 'Town.

East Oakland, when I was a kid in the '70s, was borderline—the worst was winos hollering; some rode the white horse. It was a big deal to hear a gunshot. Crack was a whisper in the wind. But by the mid-'80s, when I was 20, and Keyshia's mother had given her up to the California foster care system (charged as recently as 2004 with being a "kids-for-cash" program, Cali has what some consider one of the worst child welfare services in the country), crack had trounced wine, heroin, and the 'Town.

Me and mine watched the biggest crack dealers like they were movie stars. And by the early '90s, when Keyshia was about 12, people in

Oakland clocked the murder rate like it was an A's game. Fools were, as we used to say, straight gettin' shot up—it was hella crazy.

But while I took the hell East Oakland had become for granted, as a normal evolution of a small city, at least I had old memories to romanticize and rely on. Keyshia has only known Oakland as Cokeland (like a criminal, my hometown has mad aliases). An angel with a dirty face, she grew up essentially unsupervised in hellish personal situations. She'd seen ugliness up close and beauty in her surroundings (have you been to the Bay Area?) as well as in the mirror. And she knew she was talented.

So with the logic of a kid for whom public education is either raggedy, or not an option, or plain old intimidating, Keyshia decided that the road to being "the biggest entertainer I could ever become" was more realistic than the road to becoming her childhood dream—a veterinarian. She became her own guardian—and guided herself from harm and toward the light. She reminded herself: *I am talented.*

"Coming from Oakland," Keyshia says via phone from Miami, "I shouldn't have seen a lot of things I've seen. Now I've overcome everything, and I'm looking in the mirror, trying to figure out who I am. I'm realizing I'm a real strong woman."

She had to be strong to come up through the Bay Area's black music scene—by the late '90s, a frustrated, pre-hyphy wilderness—a scene that had roots in groups like The Whispers, the Pointer Sisters, and Sly & the Family Stone, a scene that flowered in the early '90s with MC Hammer, Too $hort, En Vogue, Tony! Toni! Toné!, Digital Underground, and Club Nouveau. Keyshia caught the ragged tail of it all. She auditioned for Hammer before she was 13, met Tupac ("You a lil' comedian," he told her) around the same time. From everything I've heard about Keyshia in her Oakland days, she was broke, unruly, thorough, and immaculately manicured. She loved hard. She talked shit. She valued loyalty. And in the vital, dicey, alterna-Oakland universe, Keyshia, with her poverty-fueled ambition, was one of the best the 'Town had to offer. But she knew that if she didn't leave and become a part of the world, she'd never do the big things she barely knew, back then, how to articulate. She'd remain a smart-ass chick in the wrong dress with the right shoes, with a man who loved her but was bitter because he'd barely gotten

100 miles (spiritually or physically) beyond the city limits himself. There are a lot of girls like that in Oakland. It's a complicated town.

"Think about the championships brought home by the A's and the Raiders," says East Oakland native Todd "Too $hort" Shaw, who appears on both of Keyshia's CDs. "Blue collar teams, and Oakland is a blue collar town. People work *hard* in Oakland, work for survival—purchase homes, raise kids. The Black Panthers. And the Hells Angels— tough-ass white boys who kicked ass. The East Bay Dragons, a black bike gang—they personify the image of the 'Town as real no-nonsense. From Oakland? We go *anywhere*."

"I love Oakland," Keyshia says, "but I'm not *just* a girl from Oakland. I'm not."

"When I first saw the house," she says, "I was like, *This is it right here. I didn't know if I could afford it, but I was like, *I'm buying this house*."

Keyshia lives right outside of Atlanta now.

"It looks like a castle," she says matter-of-factly of the six-bedroom mini-mansion with a finished rehearsal studio. She likes describing it, but is as pleased with herself for having purchased it. "I'm being responsible," she says. "Investing, buying things I'm supposed to buy."

She's a bit overwhelmed about what furniture to put where. The country air bothers her urban sinuses and sensibilities. She's unsettled about just how pitch black it gets in the foresty suburbs. Police lazily patrol her very low-crime environs, and it freaks Keyshia out. "I don't trust people," she says. "Don't trust police. We don't need help, we got guns in the house and they're registered. We got guns because it's all women in the house. Who knows what men are going to do?" Men have been a source of pain throughout Keyshia's life, from the father she never met, to the men who broke in and raped her sister, to an old producer boyfriend who never made good on his promises. She brought some of that baggage along when she moved to ATL (Alpharetta, Georgia). Keyshia wanted to put bars on her windows, but, "The police said, Huh?"

It's not just that Keyshia makes no bones about being one of seven children born to a drug-addicted mother—her sister Neffy, with a drinking problem, and her oft-arrested, oft-jailed mom are both posted up on this season of *The Way It Is*. They've even moved into Keyshia's Atlanta dream home. Also in residence is Gizmo, a three-pound teacup Yorkie, and Lyric, a Maltese Keyshia got for herself when her first single, the 2004 Kanye West–produced "I Changed My Mind" was released. Lyric's been to "dog jail" for biting, twice. Keyshia says that one of the hardest things she's ever had to do is "help my family adapt to who I'm becoming at this point in my life. They always say, 'You're not Keyshia Cole to me.'" She tells the story of whom she's becoming in fits and starts. "I say this with all respect, but I've never been a [true] Bay Area artist," she says. "There was one song I did with Messy Marv [2001's "Nubian Queen Remix"]. He's the only person in Oakland who ever paid me—$300," she says. And then, with pride: "I felt like somebody that day."

She notes without bitterness that she never sang at Oakland hotspots like Yoshi's or even clubs in nearby San Francisco. "Manny [her manager] was like, 'Yo, we about to go to these [other] places because people are paying for you.'" Part of Keyshia's fable includes the idea that, back in 2003, she caught a boyfriend in the act of cheating, and that within "minutes" she was in her car, driving to Los Angeles to make herself happen.

"I had like $7,000 in my account when I left Oakland," she says, "and when I got down to about three Gs . . . it was like, I can't go back to Oakland. Not broke, anyway. I prayed. He heard my call."

She snagged an interview with then–A&M Records President Ron Fair, who has been instrumental in the careers of Christina Aguilera, the Pussycat Dolls, and Mya. "I was 21," she says, cool as can be. "He signed me after he heard half a song. Ron [now chairman of Geffen Records] took me to [Interscope Geffen A&M Records Chairman] Jimmy Iovine that next week, and then 'I Changed My Mind' came out." From the gruff urgency of her soprano, to the strut she worked in the video, to her strident declaration of the words in the title, the song rocked worlds. She seemed like every girl who had ever loved the wrong guy—but this time, Every Girl had the kind of sassafras that only grows in Northern California. "When she came out with that first video?" says Too $hort. "With that burgundy hair? That was the Oakland in her."

Hers was the rash, reaching voice of a have-not on the verge of be-coming a have—and that sound is recognized far beyond Oakland. Even the *New York Times* called Keyshia's debut one of the best albums of 2005. On her new *Just Like You*, Keyshia's voice remains raw with the after-burn of a difficult romance and thick with old scars in tender places. And there are undercurrents of revenge, too, as well as soft wicked notes glowing with I-told-you-so.

Keyshia wrote all 13 songs on *Just Like You*. The song that most re-flects where she's at now is "Got to Get My Heart Back." It's a strong song. "Everybody who has ever loved or lost love can understand where I'm coming from," she says. "Once you feel that pain, you're like, *Damn man, I ain't going through that no more.*"

Everyone wants to hear someone sing out like the world will change, like the lover will return if the song is played enough times in a row from car speakers with the windows down. It's why Keyshia's fans have the kind of zealous affection for her usually reserved for Mary J., for Jill Scott, for singer/songwriters who yell the kind of truths women are of-ten afraid to whisper. Her specialty is the ability to leap between rous-ing, rah-rah individualism—note the first single, "Let It Go," featuring Missy Elliott and Lil' Kim—and wallowing, unrequited love—note the Internet-only cut "Trust."

Sean "Diddy" Combs says he'd wanted to work with Keyshia for a long time when they decided to do "Last Night." Having worked with Mary J. at the beginning of her career, he has thoughts on the ways Cole and Blige are alike—and different. "Vocally," he says via phone from Miami, "it's two different styles. Maybe because I worked with both of them so closely, I can see it, hear it. They have different ap-proaches, and the textures of their voices are different. Mary's voice is definitely deeper than Keyshia's. But there's a similarity between them as far as . . . the pain. Most vocalists can't really translate pain through their voices. And they both come from the hip hop generation. They both know how to ride beats like a rap artist."

When Keyshia claims that she's in the music business for the money, it's clear she really means she's in it for the security and steadiness. Even the music biz in its troubled state is stable compared to how Keyshia came up. She's very conscious of her professional worth, and like a lot of people raised with next to nothing, ultra-conscious of what she has and where it is. "I get $6,000 for a track, period," she says without hesitation or smugness, like it makes her feel good just to say it out loud. "I get more than 50 grand for a show, so at this point in my life, I'm not hurting for no money. It's like . . . what you gonna do? With your artistry? Are you going to grow? As an entertainer? What you gonna *do*?" A short pause, like she's counting. "I own my house," she says. "And we're going to stay doing this reality show—I own that. I own my car. And that's just from the first time around."

Reginald Hudlin, President of Entertainment at Black Entertainment Television, says one of the biggest compliments he's received about BET's reality shows is that they are "more real" than other networks'. "I loved going online and seeing kids debate about the finale of the *Keyshia Cole* series," he says from his New York office. "Some thought she was disrespectful to her imprisoned mother. Others said . . . when you have an addict in your family, you have to come at them with tough love—that's real talk about real issues."

There are reality *shows* we watch for entertainment and participate in for money and notoriety—and then there's the actual truth of one's bonafide reality. "I'm in this [business] because I care," Keyshia says finally. "I'm open with my life because people learn from that. And because I've been through a lot—it feels like . . . overcoming." I wonder what exactly she means by "a lot"?

"A lot is, your mother has been a drug addict all your life. A lot is, getting adopted, your sister getting raped, and everything with men and the trials and tribulations with that. Being in a foster care family, knowing that this is not your biological family. *Where's your family? Where's your dad?* Getting in a situation and thinking you're in love, and a guy is messing around, playing tricks on you, thinking this is the only thing you have and realizing that's really not anything to hold onto. Realizing that you're alone, by yourself, and now it's your time—that you're grown. You have to *do* stuff. Even though you didn't ask to be in this world, you gotta do something about it." She pauses. Sounds like she's trying to be patient. "Once I figured out that," she says, "I was like, *Look, ain't nobody gonna do this for me. I gotta do this by myself.*"

In New York City, it's a warm evening in Midtown at a restaurant named Mr. Chow. All-white linen tablecloths and no menu to speak of—the waiter just brings you what he thinks you'll like. Keyshia, clearly not on her first visit, requests the crispy seaweed with the candied walnuts. She's drinking water, and working the hell out of some jeans, a white ribbed tank top, and a sweater that covers her back only to her shoulder blades. Her hair is short, blonde, asymmetrical, and sleek. Her makeup is lustrous in the right places, almost invisible every place else. Her manicure is fresh: delicate ivory paste bows atop a flawless French. Keyshia might not be 5 feet tall in heels and is more beautiful than she looks in any photo or video. She's not cynical. She's wary.

Is she comfortable with the pomp and circumstance of the restaurant? Almost. Does she want to talk about Young Jeezy, to whom she was rumored to be engaged? No. Enter waiter with gleaming, steaming plates. There's steak that comes rare and Keyshia picks only at the slices cooked to medium-well. She doesn't, though, send it back.

Although she talks a lot about her future, it's the thing about her that seems most murky. The idea of having kids, for example, doesn't necessarily appeal. "I got kids I'm taking care of right now," Keyshia says, alluding to her siblings and mother. "And I got so many things I'm trying to do, so many things I *want* to do. I don't want right now to do the baby thing." As Keyshia makes agonizingly clear in her music, she's trying, like many of her fans, to figure out how a talented woman with ambition and issues figures into a lasting relationship.

"*What* is the problem?" she'd asked a few days before via phone. "Shit! They should want somebody who wants to be something, somebody who knows what they want out of life, a woman with the intelligence to take herself where she wants to be. Motherfuckers want somebody who's going to sit around and be all 'Alright, Daddy, wassup? What we doing?'"

Like, where the party at? And there's jumpy laughter from us both. "And always *beneath* a nigga," she says without bitterness, like it's as clear a fact of life as death. "We can do all that, and I'm cool, but what about this side?" She gestures toward herself. "What about the woman?" There's silence. "What about me?"

She wants to say the right thing, the real thing, but opts instead for the safe, vague thing. Is she getting the tiniest bit refined? That way raw talents tend to when they become well known? The manner to which Mary J. Blige, former ultra-undisciplined girl, aspired and finally achieved?

"I'm trying to get it together," Keyshia says. "I'll be cool in three or four years, I know that because I know where I want to be." Then, wistfully: "A lil' girl," she says, and though she's back to the idea of kids, the idea of possibly having a daughter, Keyshia as easily could be speaking about herself. "Maybe one day. It'll be okay one day." Well, it's a long way home.

Back in 1998, that morning after she sang in the West Oakland studio, D'wayne Wiggins asked around for the girl who folks said was "Keyshia." Then he drove around and ended up leaving a message with a person at a random house. "I never thought she'd get it," he says now from his home in Oakland. "Keyshia came back through, though." He found out later that she was living someplace else, in a shelter.

It would be the same old 'hood description, if it wasn't a description of the flatlands of East Oakland, Keyshia's blocks: the check cashing centers, the beauty supply stores crammed with Palmer's Cocoa Butter Formula and deep-cleaning no-lye relaxers. The housing projects, the crack corners, the storefront churches, the closet-sized donut shops with rows of Bubblicious and Pixy Stix. The public schools struggling. The fights about gentrificaiton. The dope. Oakland can be a bizarre place, even if you're from there.

But the 'Town can be an amazing place sometimes, especially if you're from there. Front and center is Lake Merritt—crowned with a Necklace of Lights, it's a tidal lagoon that sits just east of downtown. The swanky hills of Oakland, the place where Keyshia wants to buy a home some day, are fragrant with eucalyptus trees. From the top of those hills you can see the Bay, San Francisco, and the Pacific beyond.

The sight of it all can take the sting from Oakland's bites—and make you want what's out there as much as the fickle comforts of the block.

"She's carrying the torch for Oakland," says $hort. "The legacy. She's our shining star right now."

Yep. $hort claims her. Wiggins claims her, too. Everyone in the 'Town claims her. Foster child or not, Keyshia is a daughter of the City of Oakland, population 400,000, but when she's up on that stage, she is a sister to us all, the one who grew up from the concrete like a rose, the one who looked at Hell, and said, *I got to go—Heaven's missing an angel.*

"I don't know how to be fake," Keyshia says in a way that's both captivating and confrontational, a combination of moods that those of us from there believe to be quintessentially Oakland. "What I feel like is what I feel like. How you gonna take that away from me? I don't talk this way for nothing. I am who I am for a reason. My mother was a drug addict and I've been in a crackhouse, but all that created who's before you. Who am I to hide my facts? People *know* now." It was a phone conversation, and Keyshia's voice came through like a song she might have written, playing on faraway radio. "Who I've become," she says, "is who I want to be."

Noah Berlatsky

UNDERRATED OVERGROUND
Give Contemporary R&B a Chance

To say LeToya's self-titled debut is perfect pop does the album a disservice. It's packed with distorted beats, oceanic harmonies, and miraculous songwriting—and the production makes it feel like the music is being broadcast from the precise center of your skull. "Tear da Club Up" combines an OutKast sample, a propulsive stuttered opening, and skittering beats worthy of Aphex Twin. "All Eyes on Me" features a titanic pseudo-Bollywood loop that pretty much defines "fat." Even the tossed-off bits—like a gorgeous, easygoing duet with a recording of Yolanda Adams on the outro—are spectacular. In other words, this album struts. It's one of the most accomplished and creative recordings I've ever heard, in any genre.

Alas, this is a minority opinion. LeToya's album, which came out this summer, generated huge popular excitement—in part because it was her first release since her split from Destiny's Child six years ago—and last month it was certified platinum. But critical response has been, um, reserved. Most outlets didn't even bother to review it. Those that did had little to say, and even less that was laudatory—RollingStone.com called the arrangements "tepid" and pronounced "Torn," the disc's first single, "passable."

Not that this was a big surprise. Few genres are as despised by critics as contemporary R&B. Pick a review of an urban diva at random and you'll likely be informed that her street posturing is laughable, her lyrics are monotonous, and her voice is an embarrassment. Even positive assessments often feel backhanded. A write-up of *Kelis Was Here* on Pop-Matters provides the singer's fans with talking points so they can counter their friends' inevitable skepticism. And last week in this paper, Jessica Hopper praised Ciara's latest . . . because it wasn't quite as bad as Gwen Stefani's.

Different strokes for different folks, of course. But only to a point. Many of the criticisms leveled against contemporary R&B are confused enough to be misleading. Take one of the most common contentions—that the performers' voices are lousy. I've heard this said of Ashanti, Ciara, Kelis, Teairra Mari—even, bizarrely, Mariah Carey. It's true that few current R&B performers can belt out a tune like Aretha. But the thing is, they don't need to and probably shouldn't try. Contemporary R&B has very little to do with classic 60s southern soul. Rather it's rooted in the high-gloss production and intensive harmonies of Motown and Gamble & Huff. There are a few exceptions: on her recent debut, *Point of No Return*, Shareefa deftly combines an old-school soul singer's grit with new-school studio sheen, and Faith Evans's unbelievable "Mesmerized" sounds like Stax on steroids. But in general, adding a big voice to giant production makes for a faux-Broadway disaster (hello, Christina Aguilera). Contemporary R&B just works better with less dramatic singers.

Tweet and Monica, for example, both have smooth, creamy voices that swirl languidly into the backing tracks. And Cassie's vocals might be kindly described as wispy. That doesn't hinder her a bit, though. On her self-titled debut she's so processed and multitracked she becomes just one more electronic element among many—part of a robotically flawless glucose-delivery system that makes Pizzicato Five sound clumsily robust.

Even if every singer in the genre could holler like Marion Williams, though, I doubt it would convert the music press. Critics want scrappy, they want subversive—or at the very least they don't want ingratiating. As Jim DeRogatis puts it in his chronicle of 90s music, *Milk It!*, "Rock 'n' roll is a spontaneous explosion of personality and it is an attitude." That just doesn't describe R&B at all. Misogyny is still the easiest way for rock, hip-hop, and country artists to demonstrate their edginess, but contemporary R&B is a female-dominated world—as such it doesn't really do that kind of "attitude." And it's impossible to pretend that a prepackaged product of reality TV like Danity Kane is in any way scrappy.

Though divas do occasionally talk about "keeping it real," the ambivalence about selling out that's used to signal authenticity in hip-hop and alternative barely exists in R&B. On the contrary, performers tend to cultivate a girly, XXXOOO relationship with their fans. This is why Beyoncé can cheerfully shill for her latest Hollywood movie, *Dreamgirls*, on *B'day* and present it as an extraspecial bonus moment for her listeners. And it's why she and so many of her rivals use only their first names: it's both more intimate and more suggestive of a corporate brand.

Personally, I find this straightforward embrace of commercialism refreshing. Even if you insist on the dubious proposition that mass entertainment ought to be subversive, though, contemporary R&B does have something to offer. It's largely performed by lower-class women of color, many of them still teenagers—in fact it's one of the only ways any lower-class teenager can reach such a large audience. Sure, sometimes what they have to say isn't any more thoughtful than "this junk in the trunk'll put a bump in your pants," as Brooke Valentine quips in "Taste of Dis." But you don't have to listen to too many tracks to find more substantial material.

The common thread running through contemporary R&B isn't drippy sentiment or party-girl mindlessness. Instead the performers emphasize self-worth, independence, and strength, even as they acknowledge the importance of close relationships. Like classic country (or classic R&B for that matter) the music is about love, joy, loss, and—most of all—dignity. In "No Daddy," Teairra Mari expresses sympathy for and solidarity with sex workers without lapsing into moralism or pity—no mean feat. ("No I don't strip in the club / Nor trick in the club / But I got friends that do / So my girls that's getting the dough / The best way they know / No hate girl, I got you.") Mya's "Late" is a smart and funny account of an accidental pregnancy—with some tips on proper condom care thrown in. Cherish's "Oooh" is about teen abstinence. Kelis's "Ghetto Children" has a heartbreaking refrain—"No matter what teacher say to you / Ghetto children are beautiful" —that's just about the best two-line condemnation of our educational system you're likely to hear.

The best thing about contemporary R&B isn't the lyrics, though. It's the music. Sometime in the late 90s, R&B moved from the groove-based vibe of TLC and early Timbaland toward extremely complex song structures. Production capabilities, already phenomenal, climbed into the stratosphere. The result is music of painstaking craft: layers of sound morph and twist through multiple bridges and intricate arrangements while a multitracked vocalist sings rings around herself. Often it's impossible to tell which real instruments are involved, if any, just as it's difficult to know who's ultimately responsible for the final product—most songs seem to have three to five writers, not to mention the producers and executive producers.

Contemporary R&B is a bit like the shoegazer pop of the 90s and a bit like the most polished Philly soul, though in many ways it's more intense than either. Certainly it can sink into bombast or undifferentiated mush. At its best, though, it's unearthly. LeToya and her peers are stretching the boundaries of how music can be made and what it can sound like even as they remain firmly in a popular idiom. In this, they're not unlike the first great swing or rap performers—and just as in those cases, it may take a decade or two before critics start to appreciate them. In the meantime, everybody else has the opportunity to listen to some of the best American music ever made. And it's right on the Top 40 station of your choice.

SOLVEJ SCHOU

FIRST PERSON

Auditioning for this Season's *American Idol*

I've been singing since I was 4 and performing in bands since 15. Nothing, however, could prepare me for auditioning for TV's hit competition *American Idol*.

It was a chilly morning in August.

I slept through my alarm, set to 3:30 a.m. A friend's call half an hour later woke me out of my nervous sleep. After quickly shimmying into a bright red vintage dress, I rushed over to the Rose Bowl stadium in Pasadena for the Los Angeles area audition (airing on Fox on Jan. 31 at 9 p.m.).

Bleary-eyed and shivering in the pre-dawn darkness, I took a place in line along with 10,000 other aspiring contestants—from teenagers to those like me in their late 20s.

People brought their mothers, fathers, best friends and aunts. One read "Idol" judge Simon Cowell's "I Don't Mean to Be Rude, But . . ." Some piled on makeup. Others rehearsed their songs—loudly or whispering. Most everyone yelped and screamed at the Fox cameras twirling past.

I came alone (it was too early for everyone I knew) and murmured lyrics under my breath. Friends called to keep me company. My feet started to hurt.

I'm a blues-singing garage rocker at heart, not someone prone to trying out for a commercial endeavor such as "Idol." Yet prodding from friends and family prompted me to give it a chance. Even my bandmates said, "Hey, why not? Go for it."

The song I chose to audition, "Rock Steady" by Aretha Franklin, was a favorite—soulful, sassy. Not as ubiquitous as "Respect," but still bold. I felt committed. I had already been wearing my "Idol" audition wristband for two days.

Once inside the stadium, after hours of waiting for the gates to open and then that mad dash inside, I found my seat, surrounded by a mix of saucy trash-talkers and shy couples.

Mostly, the tension was palpable—somewhere between wide-eyed hope and crushing anonymity. But there was also something else in the air: a joyful love of music. It felt easy to get caught up in that rush, regardless of the odds.

Questions looped through the crowd.

"Are Simon Cowell, Randy Jackson, and Paula Abdul here?"

"No they're not."

"I heard they are!"

It turns out they weren't—by a long shot.

The cool morning air had already turned wickedly hot. Across from where we sat, way on the other side of the stadium, were a dozen tented booths, side by side. Behind that . . . exits.

Once we settled in, a jubilant emcee roared us to our feet to sing the L.A. audition's retro theme song—"Daydream Believer" by the Monkees. Well, the chorus of it, at least, over and over.

We waved to the swooping camera, we yelled "I'm the next 'American Idol'!" and we waited.

Row by row, we lined up to audition in front of one of those 12 booths, four participants to a booth.

Sure enough—no Simon, no Randy, no Paula.

By the time I got to that line, I was jittery yet pumped, repeating the feisty intro to "Rock Steady": "Rock steady baby! That's what I feel now. Let's call this song exactly what it is."

An "Idol" staffer ushered me over to a booth along with three others in line. I had noticed earlier that a woman dressed as a homecoming queen (a nod to the chorus of "Daydream Believer") got the coveted golden ticket allowing her to move to the next round. Could she sing? Who knows. Few others followed in her footsteps.

At the judging table in front of us sat two 20-something producers. One was a young woman with sunglasses so large, she could have been napping behind them. The other was a young man with his head propped up in his hands. He said nothing and looked bored.

Suddenly Simon seemed not so rude after all.

Each of us would be given roughly 15 seconds of our chosen song to perform. No questions, no names.

Two of the singers next to me were great, even passionate. Another one, not so much.

Then I stepped forward and sang, belting out the tune with all I had. It's Aretha, after all.

I was louder than the rest, working my vibrato, stretching my arms out. The bored guy perked up a little, but still said nothing. This was the moment I had waited six hours for.

After less than 20 seconds, it was over.

Afterward, the young woman with the sunglasses turned to all of us, thanked us for auditioning, and said we would not be needed for the show. There was no banter between judges. No comments to us about our performances—snarky or otherwise. Not even a little canned applause.

Instead, we were instructed to go, our wristbands were cut, and we walked out of the stadium.

As I turned to leave the booth, the girl who cut my wristband exclaimed, "Rock steady, baby!"

I smiled at her, containing my exhaustion as I went to my car.

Days later, my band Naughty Bird performed at a local club and I felt a deep sense of relief—to sing our own songs in that cramped, dark place, on our own terms, to loud applause.

Ben Sisario

WIZARDS IN THE STUDIO, ANONYMOUS ON THE STREET

The songwriting session was so fresh that the aroma of the evening's chicken wings still lingered. Behind the vast mixing board of a dimly lighted Manhattan recording studio, two producers and their co-writer greeted a record executive who had come to hear their work. With the press of a button, the room filled with sound: somber guitar arpeggios over a slow, sleek hip-hop beat, with layers of falsetto harmonies leading to a big, glittery, instantly memorable chorus. It was pure candy—sweetly melodic, but just funky enough to have a dance groove.

"I'm thinking Jennifer," the executive said. "It's perfect for Jennifer Hudson."

As three more songs that had been written in the last 24 hours blared from enormous speakers, the producers sat calmly, waiting to hear which superstars their songs would be pitched to. But they weren't the Neptunes or Timbaland or Dr. Dre or anyone else ardent followers of the Top 40 would be likely to recognize. They were Tor Erik Hermansen and Mikkel S. Eriksen, wholesome-looking, milk-complexioned Norwegians who, despite having no public persona, have quickly become two of the most in-demand figures in pop music.

Better known as Stargate, Mr. Hermansen and Mr. Eriksen have had an enviable string of hits since arriving in the United States two years ago, including Beyoncé's "Irreplaceable," Rihanna's "Unfaithful," and "So Sick" by Ne-Yo, a rising 24-year-old singer from Las Vegas who is a frequent co-writer. (Ne-Yo's new album, "Because of You," released Tuesday on Def Jam, includes two Stargate songs.) Add to those Lionel Richie's comeback single, "I Call It Love," and "Beautiful Liar," the steamy track by Beyoncé and Shakira, which shot to the top of the iTunes best-seller list when released in March. At a time when the music industry is starved for hits, Stargate has had repeated success with a relatively simple approach: sugary, lilting R&B in the Michael Jackson vein leavened with the kind of melody-rich European pop that paints everything in bright primary colors.

More potential hits are in the works. The executive visiting them, Larry Jackson, senior vice president of A&R (artists and repertory) at J Records, confirmed that Ms. Hudson would be recording their song "Can't Stop the Rain." And the Stargate name is attached to many other "priority releases"—projects that record labels, managers and radio programmers are expecting to be the most popular and profitable.

"In the industry, their name recognition is as powerful as Timbaland's," said Jeff Rabhan, who manages Elliott Yamin, the "American Idol" alumnus whose self-titled new album has two Stargate tracks.

But in this age of the superstar producer, Mr. Hermansen and Mr. Eriksen are an exception, and not just for their perky Scandinavian accents and the plain T-shirts and sweats that make them look like refugees from a college soccer team. Like the Brill Building songwriters of the 1950s and '60s, they are behind-the-scenes workaholics, preferring to spend their time in a cramped studio.

"We have the No. 1 record in the country for 10 weeks, but when we walk down the street no one knows who we are," said Mr. Hermansen, who like his partner is 34, shiny of scalp and beanstalk thin. "It's great."

With no videos to shoot, no tour dates and no solo albums to record, they are able to devote themselves to writing and recording, and they churn out new songs with astonishing speed and regularity. While labels and artists frequently wait weeks or even months for a new song from a top producer, a typical Stargate workday yields two, three, four or more.

"A lot of American producers have a great difficulty with pop," said Barry Weiss, president of Jive Records, who recently hired Mr. Hermansen and Mr. Eriksen to work with Usher, Chris Brown and Joe. "But these guys were raised on pop. They grew up on Abba. They grew up on Boney M. Those influences lend themselves to them making very melodic pop records, with great hooks and choruses. You plug in the right top-line writer and you got one plus one equals three."

Arriving at noon at their studio on West 25th Street six days a week—"We get Sundays off," Mr. Eriksen said—the men of Stargate keep the music industry's equivalent of banker's hours. Working in a modest room so crowded with recording gear that they spend much of their time toiling inches apart, Mr. Hermansen and Mr. Eriksen say they usually finish up by midnight or 1 a.m.—around the time many of their competitors might be beginning their own sessions.

Life in a recording studio can be slow and numbingly repetitive, but on a recent afternoon Stargate was a blur of musical multitasking. After tweaking some instrumental tracks, the producers convened with a co-writer over lyrics to a new song, and recorded it a couple of hours later. On and off throughout the day, as one restaurant delivery after another came through the door—eggs and bacon, Chinese, burgers—they sketched out yet another tune and discussed their favorite topic: the pride and constant stimulation of working in the United States.

"We can be in the studio till 1 o'clock in the morning," Mr. Hermansen said, "and then we walk out on the street and right outside we meet the president of Atlantic Records and the head of A&R over at Def Jam. And we'll talk about projects—'O.K., we'll come by your office tomorrow.' Then we'll be up there at 11 o'clock playing songs."

Their work carries on a tradition of Scandinavian bubble-gum artistry that stretches from Abba to Max Martin, the Swedish mastermind behind the late-'90s heyday of Britney Spears, 'N Sync et al. But while Mr. Martin has lately been developing a more rock-influenced sound in songs like Kelly Clarkson's "Since U Been Gone," Stargate has followed a lifelong love of the Michael Jackson-Prince school of R&B.

"In Europe we've only been hearing the biggest American hits," said Mr. Eriksen, the quieter of the two, who has a thin, blond goatee and moves in quick, precise jolts at the console, like a video-game virtuoso. "That's what we've been listening to and trying to measure up to."

Formed a decade ago in Norway as a trio—the third member, Hallgeir Rustan, left two years ago because he did not want to come to America, and remains a producer in Norway—Stargate had its first successes in Britain, with dozens of singles by teen-pop acts like Blue, Atomic Kitten and Hear'Say reaching the Top 10. The three men remixed American hip-hop and R&B songs, sweetening them for European radio with layers of added melody. Soon they began to set their eyes on a studio in New York.

"We knew that to make the records we really wanted to make, we had to go to America," said Mr. Eriksen.

After some exploratory missions, they settled in New York in the spring of 2005. Work was slow at first until a chance meeting with Ne-Yo (whose real name is Shaffer Smith) in a hallway at Sony Music Studios on West 54th Street. "They told me they did R&B, and honestly I didn't believe them," Ne-Yo said.

But he was impressed by their work, and on their first joint songwriting date they knocked out six songs, among them "So Sick," which was No. 1 for two weeks. Then came Ne-Yo's next hit, "Sexy Love," then Rihanna, then Beyoncé. . . .

In the usual Stargate M.O.—common in pop and hip-hop production—Mr. Hermansen and Mr. Eriksen create an instrumental backing track and then let a collaborator write the lyrics and vocal melody.

For Ne-Yo, Stargate's strength has as much to do with the music it makes as the music it doesn't.

"You hear some tracks where the producer is absolutely trying to be the star," he said, "the way they do so much with the track that it's almost difficult to write—you can't find any space to put a song in there. But I never had a problem with these guys. They are the epitome of simple and to the point."

For their recent writing session with Ne-Yo, in Studio D at Sony Music, Mr. Hermansen and Mr. Eriksen brought a CD with sketches of 11 songs. Scanning through it, Ne-Yo picked one midtempo track with sharp, resonant acoustic guitar—"That's nasty!" he said—and sat down with a notepad, playing the track on a loop while Mr. Hermansen and Mr. Eriksen sat for an interview a few feet away.

After about 40 minutes, the singer leaped out of his seat. "I got it," he announced, and sang his brand-new verse and a chorus. Everyone agreed that the song was hot, and once Ne-Yo removed his heavy gold chains—to keep them from clanging while at the microphone—assumed their recording positions.

In about two hours, they had finished a textbook Stargate song. Over a spare beat that would not be out of place in a vintage Run-D.M.C. track, the guitar laid out a palette of bright, bold chords and the weaving melody that remains a focal point throughout the song. Ne-Yo's vocal—recorded in a couple of takes, with layer upon layer of harmonies added in quick succession—was soft and soulful, climaxing in a chorus that, with a swell of synthesizers behind it, seemed to glow with neon. "No matter what I do," Ne-Yo sang, "I can't stop the rain."

Stargate's speed is a big attraction to clients. The duo's unobtrusive production style is another, and cannily plays to the ego dynamics of pop stars: everybody wants a hit, but nobody wants to be upstaged by the producer.

"Most pop, hip-hop and R&B producers," said Mr. Rabhan, the manager, "are so distinctive that their music becomes instantly recognizable and overshadows the artist. Stargate has really been able to make a footprint without making it all about them."

But that footprint is often faint. While a song produced by Timbaland or the Neptunes is recognizable no matter who the artist is, the Stargate signature is more difficult to detect, because to some degree the duo's style is an adaptable method, not a specific sound.

"They're chameleons," said Steve Lunt, an A&R executive at Atlantic Records who last worked with Stargate on songs by the teenage singer Gia Farrell. "But if you put a bunch of Stargate songs together you will see the thread running through them."

Mr. Hermansen and Mr. Eriksen dismiss the idea that their remarkable productivity might be helped by songwriting formulaics.

"There's a craft to any art form," Mr. Hermansen responded. "You have to master the craft, but at the same time you have to be creative within the format you're working in. We have a certain . . ."

". . . musical language, so to speak," said Mr. Eriksen, finishing his colleague's sentence as if picking up a verse. "You shouldn't be afraid of that either. Even though it might remind you of something else you shouldn't shy away from it. Because it's our expression."

In the largely black milieu of R&B, Mr. Hermansen and Mr. Eriksen have gotten their share of double takes. More than once, they said, visitors to their studio have misdirected their obeisances to the people they meet at the door: the two black British men who are Stargate's managers.

But there are a growing number of well-known white R&B producers, including Scott Storch, Mark Ronson and Jonathan Rotem, as well as performers like Justin Timberlake, Amy Winehouse and Robin Thicke (who is also a successful producer).

What sets Stargate apart from producers black or white is its image. Or, rather, the lack of one. The two do not stake their reputations on hip-hop authenticity; Mr. Hermansen and Mr. Eriksen, who are both married and have young children, remain deliberately invisible and clean-cut. When a photographer was about to snap their picture, Mr. Eriksen carefully moved an empty beer bottle so it wouldn't appear in the shot. A laptop computer in their studio is set to Norwegian time, and they make it clear that the biggest draw of living in New York is the work.

"We're like players who just got off the bench and started scoring," Mr. Hermansen said.

Beginning their recent studio date with Ne-Yo, they took their places behind the console, unloading discs and various devices from a backpack. A young member of Ne-Yo's entourage who was surfing the Internet on a studio computer caught Mr. Eriksen's eye and asked him if they have a MySpace page.

Mr. Eriksen shook his head no.

"Why not?" the young man asked.

"Don't have time," Mr. Eriksen said, and began punching buttons at the mixing board.

WU-TANG

WIDDLING DOWN INFINITY
*CAN A BUNCH OF OLD, DIRTY BASTARDS SAVE
HIP-HOP FOR A THIRD TIME OR WILL THE MATH
JUST COLLAPSE UPON ITSELF?*

The mathematics should've worked out. 819 days after the death of Ol' Dirty Bastard {8 + 1 + 9 = 18; 1 + 8 = 9}, The RZA announced the forthcoming arrival of Wu-Tang Clan's fifth release and first in nearly six years. Breaking down the digits, it all added up to 9, and there couldn't be a number more abiding of the single greatest hip-hop group of all time. Not only does the seductively top-heavy numeral enumerate the group's original members and their own genesis but also the origin of us all; there are 9 months in the gestation period of a human embryo. The number is so definitive to the New York crew that it now stands out as an era lost to the cruelly neutral cosmos of mathematics. You can't mention 9 and Wu-Tang in the same breath without having to remind yourself of the need to subtract 1.

According to Supreme Mathematics—a Five Percent philosophy and belief of the Wu, used to describe the Earth's mechanics—the number 9 means "to bring into existence," and this meant everything to the group's first record. It took 9 MCs, each with 4 chambers of the heart {2 atria, 2 ventricles}, to give rise to *Enter the Wu-Tang:*

36 Chambers {9 x 4 = 36}, and hip-hop was never the same. Referencing the Kung Fu films that Wu-Tang so revered, the Clan arrived onto the rap scene with the 36 chambers of hip-hop mastery when everyone else was striving to attain the knowledge of 35 lessons. With 108 pressure points on the human body {1 + 0 + 8 = 9}, only the Wu-Tang seemed to grasp that 36 of those are deadly {9 + 36 = 45; 4 + 5 = 9}. *Enter the Wu-Tang* was so definitive that when they released a self-aggrandizing, double-disc sophomore album four years later called *Wu-Tang Forever*, no one even fucking blinked. No artist or group— hip-hop or not, before or since—has defined itself by such a brilliantly conjured and successfully united mythology. And though 9, and thus 36, was the key, it certainly wasn't the entirety.

From the announcement of death to that of birth, it all seemed so simple then. Wu-Tang Clan's fifth record would be called *8 Diagrams*, finishing off the trio of classic martial arts flicks that helped define the group's mythology, and the math continued to add up. 8 members to record *8 Diagrams* {8 x 8 = 64}—it's as if 9 members couldn't balance the equation. God bless Ol' Dirty Bastard's soul, but maybe he had to die so *8 Diagrams* could be born. One door closes and another door opens, like the black and white of a chessboard's 64 squares. Chess is a paramount part of the Wu—from constantly spinning lyrical metaphors to the cover of GZA's *Liquid Swords*, perhaps the greatest Clan solo project—and the 64 squares extend beyond the board. It is an equally life-defining integer and an organic evolution not only of the crew's numerology but also of its history.

"64 is a very important mathematical number," says The RZA, sitting near the back staircase of Hollywood's Roosevelt Hotel. "You add 6 and 4, of course, you get 10. You add 1 and 0, you come back around to get 1—knowledge, the foundation for all things in existence."

But existence might not happen. The math might be all wrong. Unlike 1993, when hip-hop was redefined by the gritty streets of Shaolin, and unlike 1997, when Wu-Tang helped save hip-hop from shiny-suited R&B hooks in the wake of The Notorious B.I.G.'s and Tupac's tragic deaths, 2007 might not mean the resurrection of Wu-Tang and, in turn, hip-hop. 2 + 0 + 0 + 7 = 9. But that's not Wu-Tang's number anymore.

SMALLEST INTEGER WITH EXACTLY 7 DIVISORS

"If Wu-Tang is foolish enough, and it's possible to be foolish," RZA says with a wide-eyed look of devastating reality, "if however many members of Wu-Tang are foolish enough to fall for the bureaucracy of the industry in 2007, then they are fooling themselves and taking themselves out of the realm of heaven."

9 members meant 9 personalities meant 9 individual egos, and sometimes that worked {9 x 9 x 9 = 729; 7 + 2 + 9 = 18; 1 + 8 = 9}. The dynamics inspired some of the greatest art of the past 20 years, as well as some of art's biggest frustrations. 64 can be divided by 64, 32, 16, 8, 4, 2 and 1, but Wu-Tang has faced uncounted divisors on all fronts. After reinventing the industry in 1993 by forcing a contract with Loud Records that allowed the members solo deals by other labels, those same industry forces have turned on Wu-Tang over and over again.

From Method Man telling *Blender* that RZA's brother, and Wu-Tang Corporation's co-CEO, Divine is "number one on my shit-list" to U-God blaming RZA for his lack of solo success to nobody reportedly visiting Dirty in jail, it's never been a rap utopia. And though members have always returned for the good of the W, things are proving most difficult in 2007.

"If the business is not taken care of [then] there will be no album or tour," says Raekwon's manager, Mel Carter, via e-mail. Raekwon canceled his appearance at the Wu's scheduled photo shoot for *URB*, and Bodog, *8 Diagrams*'s European label, two days before the shoot was set to go down in mid May. Rock the Bells, the multimillion-dollar hip-hop bonanza, which Wu is scheduled to headline in August with Rage Against the Machine, has already sold out its run. It ain't Wu-Tang without Raekwon's inventive slang or infinitely quotable rhymes on "C.R.E.A.M."

"When it comes to photos and press and all that shit, I agree with anybody in the crew that say, 'Yo, I want my business straight before I start talking to people,'" RZA says. "I understand that. I told them that's their prerogative."

Carter has since told *URB* that the business is "all good," but the outside influence weighs heavy in RZA's voice. Sometimes anger carries the brunt while other times it is an audible sadness, but it's entirely un-avoidable when more numbers are added into the mix.

"That's a problem," says RZA. "You talk to someone like Mel Carter, who's my buddy or whatever. He's not a Wu-Tang member. He could never understand the importance of what Wu-Tang is. He can only see it from a business point of view. Everybody be talking about the deals. Fuck the deals. We aren't special because of no deals; we special because when we come together, we make music that changes the world."

Even without the dotted I's and crossed T's of a contract, Raekwon still came through and recorded new verses for *8 Diagrams*. In fact, as of the beginning of June, everyone has come through and recorded new verses, at least three apiece, according to RZA, except Ghostface Killah.

Can Wu-Tang exist without Ghostface? In today's world, Ghost is the Wu's most relevant solo member. His *Supreme Clientele* is widely credited as keeping the group afloat, and his recent string of prolificacy has built up the greatest body of solo work. He was also RZA's room-mate when Wu-Tang Clan was created and perhaps, most significantly, the first Clansman to unsheathe his sword on the first song of their first album.

"I told Ghost, 'Yo, I'll do this album without you, Ghost,'" says RZA. "'I'll do it without you, man, because it ain't about you; it ain't about me; it's about Wu-Tang. It's about what it means to the people. It ain't about what it means to us no more.'"

With the loss of Ol' Dirty Bastard, the Clan's number shrunk from 9 to 8 . . . 4 x 9 = 36 . . . 8 x 8 = 64. 7 may be the God number, but 7 is only prime because it has no divisor other than itself and one. There is no Wu-Tang with 7, regardless of what RZA says.

64 CELLS

What begins as conception, when sperm and egg meet, turns to meiosis when a cell splits into 2 cells, then into 4, then 8, then 16, then 32 and eventually arrives at 64 {2 + 4 + 8 + 16 + 32 + 64 = 126; 1 + 2 + 6 = 9}. Before life exists, it spreads. There wouldn't even be concern about Wu-Tang's fifth album if it weren't for the influence of *36 Chambers* and the 14 years of Wu that have passed since.

The only place to begin is the beginning, and the only things found there are words like "blueprint," "renaissance" and "revolutionary." It was a time when hip-hop was dominated by the two extremes of Dr. Dre and the Native Tongues crew: lush, G-funk bass complemented by gangsta mantras and, respectively, jazzy samples accompanied by textbook cleverisms. Dre defined the West Coast while Tribe, De La and the rest were too ethereal to claim earthly locations, so for the first time in hip-hop history, New York was without a definitive sound. Then, a sample from the Gordon Liu–helmed film *Shaolin vs. Wu-Tang* came from the gutter before turning into the grimiest drums anyone had ever heard, and the streets of New York were defined on record so thoroughly that listeners could practically smell the piss.

The sophistication of Wu-Tang's street persona rarely moved dance floors—even RZA leaves the Roosevelt Hotel's club when the DJ strings together too many Wu cuts—but it was something *worth* listening to, especially when weed was in the air. Fuck, there are 88 castanet claps on the idiophonic-heavy "Wu-Tang Clan Ain't Nuthin' Ta F' With," just like the 88 keys on a piano—but the only piano within hearing distance is leering in the corner with a butcher knife. The lyrics of these 9 MCs with 9 immediately differential voices used comic books, Five Percent knowledge, chess and Kung Fu films to narrate complicated tales of New York life at the tail-end of its crack era.

That revolutionary renaissance left a blueprint for The Notorious B.I.G., Jay-Z, Nas, Mobb Deep and countless others throughout the '90s . . . and that's only '70s babies. Even in today's hip-hop world, the slang and Mafioso aspirations laid by Raekwon and Ghostface Killah—especially on *Only Built 4 Cuban Linx*—are unavoidable in the lyrics of Clipse, Young Jeezy, Lil' Wayne, and more. It's an artistic expression that, regardless of its high-minded origins and perhaps unavoidable progressions, has become the politically correct cop-out for criticizing the black community in America.

"Everyone in my crew is either a dropout or a felon. And to have that side of America express art was different," RZA says before quieting down, "but at the same time, it was detrimental. Because now you have guys who have more of a wild-style mentality, the ghetto-hood type of life, and it followed us and caught up to us in one way or another by making us a target."

RZA may mean "Wu-Tang" when he says "us," but it's easy to connect the dots and hear "black America." Wu practically invented the strong codes and street ethics that, in the wake of Imus Gate, are being "investigated" on *60 Minutes*, but there was always a moral—even if it was just "survival of the fittest"—in the group's cinematic take on poverty's trials and tribulations. But with Wu-Tang's gangsta-rap profile being lower than it's ever been, the Clan wasn't dragged into the "Stop Snitchin'" argument.

"How has the South dominated hip-hop for the last four, five years without lyrics, without hip-hop culture really in their blood?" RZA asks. "Those brothers came out representing more of a stereotype of how black people are, and I think the media [would] rather see us as ignorant, crazy motherfuckers than seeing us as intelligent young men trying to rise and take care of ourselves."

WHEN I'M SIXTY-FOUR

Even in the face of Wu-Tang's glaring lyrical maturity on *36 Chambers*, there is no escaping their youthful indifference. From the carefree chorus on "Shame On a Nigga" to Method Man and Raekwon's battle of torture threats ("*I'll sew your asshole closed and keep feeding you and feeding you . . .*"), Wu-Tang's exuberance at even the most gutter of scenarios is that of men who haven't pondered life's finite quality—not because death was unfamiliar, but because there was no time to think about it.

"In our generation, twenty-year-old niggas got lost 'cause we were supposed to be in jail or dead at twenty-five," RZA says. "So we remained kids. How many niggas play video games at thirty now?"

The Beatles' Paul McCartney romanticized old age on the *Sgt. Pepper's Lonely Hearts Club Band* ditty, "When I'm Sixty-Four," to a level that would've been incomprehensible to the young members of Wu-Tang who spent their teens ditching school to drink 40s and watch martial epics from the Far East in Time Square pornography houses with the homeless. "When I'm Sixty-Four" is pure schmaltz—the bubblegum antithesis of Wu-Tang's sound—that swoons for a time when a couple grows old together, but growing old has never been something hip-hop has ever glorified. The closest thing to a 30-year-old rapper in the 100 best-selling albums of all time is Will Smith's *Big Willie Style*, and there's no equation needed for the significance of those numerals.

"I don't think we're going to achieve some of the same things that some so-called hip-hop artists do," RZA says. "Let's say Chris Brown—he's considered a hip-hop artist, but he doesn't rap, and he sells millions of records and has a real young audience. How do we compete with that? We don't. Wu-Tang needs to aim at what's us, what's ours."

What's theirs is an increasingly Web-savvy and dollar-stingy group of hip-hop purists who are more discriminating when purchasing music, if not downright indignant at the very idea of paying for it, than any other demographic with expendable cash. This group has a number in mind far from 9, 64, or even $9.99. It's 0. Certainly, the decade-old *Wu Forever* went multi-platinum on the strength of committed fans and not its chorus-less, 338-second, 1,031 word single, "Triumph," but those pre-Napster days were, quite literally, in a previous millennium. {1,031 + 338 = 1,369; 1 + 3 + 6 + 9 = 19; 1 + 8 = 9; remember that?} Even if The RZA isn't targeting the young'uns, he's not discounting their possible participation in a Wu resurgence.

"Just look at the media heroes of the sixties and seventies," he says. "Shaft was a grown-ass man. Super Fly was a grown-ass man. Everybody wanted to be Shaft and Super Fly; these were grown-ass men that kids wanted to be! I think that we have the potential to be those grown-ass men that kids want to be."

THE CRAYOLA 64 BOX

There has never been a more colorful character in the history of hip-hop than Dirt McGirt, aka Big Baby Jesus, aka Osirus, aka Dirt Dog, aka ODB, christened Russell Tyrone Jones, but born Ol' Dirty Bastard. Method Man depicts his flow on 36 Chambers's intermission better than anyone ever has, saying he's the Ol' Dirty Bastard "*'cause there ain't no father to his style.*"

"Real" hip-hop may have been birthed out of James Brown samples, but no rapper had, or has, ever captured the power of grunts, off-melody emotion or spontaneous combustion like Dirty.

"George Clinton said to me, 'ODB brought to music a cadence that no other performer ever did,'" RZA relays. "A cadence means where your words hit, how they hit and the rhythm of those words. The cadence that ODB brought was unheard of. He was so unpredictable as a performer that it couldn't be duplicated or imitated—he left a blueprint of originality."

> "*Here comes Rover, sniffin' at your ass*
> *But pardon me bitch as I shit on your grass*
> *That means ho, you been shitted on*
> *I'm not the first dog that's shitted on your lawn*"

There is absolutely no reason those four bars should even be recited, never mind be one of the most enjoyably memorable moments of hip-hop in the '90s, except for Ol' Dirty Bastard and his cadence that George Clinton was talking about. Few artists in the universe of music could make the nasty nursery rhymes of "Dog Shit" as *pure* as the Dirty did, but like the intro to "Shimmy Shimmy Ya" suggests, he truly did create a new chamber. And yet, Dirty is better known for his rap sheet than his raps.

"That's America for you, in the way that there are a lot of American heroes and idols that we know their name and what they stand for, but we don't know their music," RZA says. "Take James Brown, the Godfather of Soul. His name is probably famous around the world, but can somebody name 10 of his songs? Maybe not."

ODB died nearly 4 years ago, but it's been 10 years since he impacted a Wu-Tang release. From being the first person arrested under a then-new California law barring bulletproof vests to multiple other offenses, rehab stints and eventual jail time—a bizarre world that still isn't trumped by his bizarre flow—he wasn't much of a presence on *The W* and *Iron Flag*, his only appearance on the two albums being the first verse and chorus of *The W*'s "Conditioner," recorded while on the lam. (As well as an unforgettable jailbreak performance at the Hammerstein

Ballroom.) It might not be a coincidence that his absence of color caused the drop-off in both sales and respect for those albums, but he's as much Wu-Tang as the rest of the nonagon.

"He has a sixteen-year-old son that acts just like this mother-fucker—dance like him, talk like him, potbelly like him," RZA says. "I'm potentially gonna have [him] come in and do a hook on the album—to give us his blood on the album. I'm looking for ways to make that happen, and I'm looking for ways to put money in his family's pockets."

I-CHING'S 64 HEXAGRAMS

Today's hip-hop appears to be eons removed from the time when a Raekwon purple tape set the culture on fire and even ages from the day when a Wu-Tang CD brought hope to the horizon. It's not just album sales that are down, but it's the belief that hip-hop still has the ability to inspire that has plummeted to an all-time low. People are dissatisfied with the state of rap, and much like the Great Fire of Rome in 64 AD when Nero mythically danced nude in the mountains playing his lyre while the city burned, rap's elite seems happy to exist in penthouses and boardrooms while the whole thing is in flames. On *8 Diagrams* Wu-Tang is faced with the challenge of change, certainly from the culture at large, but definitely from within.

For the first time, Cappadonna will sign as an official member of the Wu-Tang Clan. An affiliate for life, he was never far from any track involving Ghostface or Raekwon and, in fact, helped tutor many members of the Wu in the art-form of rhyme. Although his capacity as an official member is exciting based on the man's track record on songs such as "Winter Warz" and "Daytona 500," it does fuck up the numbers a bit. 9 living members can't create *8 Diagrams*—despite the issues, RZA is certain that Ghostface will come around—it just doesn't equate.

"I'm not a part of the 8 diagrams, I'm just the 7 in the center," RZA says, in reference to the Five Percenter Universal Flag. "They're the 8-pointed star; they're the ones that shine out. I'm the one that maybe fed it to them, the source of it."

The star needs to shine at full force for Wu-Tang to overcome all that is upon them. Every member, no matter how they fit within the diagram, needs to remind the world why hip-hop was the voice of those muted by poverty and a muse for the world's creativity. Whether it's Cappadonna or ODB's son, an unavoidable hunger needs to be expressed . . . otherwise the American public just won't eat it up.

"Right now, as far as the freshest voice on the mic, it's the person you least expect," RZA says. "U-God is on fire. Now how could U-God be on fire after all these years? After all the shit that he done been through, after U-God came on the radio publicly blaming me for his life. He's the most in-tune motherfucker right now. . . . This is a nigga that hates me."

Part of RZA's enthusiasm for the most often overlooked MC of the Clan's newfound fire is U-God's excitement over RZA's evolution in production. After scoring 8 or 9 feature films, RZA has expanded his sound palette to include what Raekwon calls that "orchestral shit." He's still The RZA, but he promises that in addition to the gritty sound people expect, there'll be more than just that on *8 Diagrams*.

"I'm making songs, nigga, songs that you can have Carnegie Hall play one day," RZA says, also announcing that for the first time Wu-Tang will bring in big name outside producers (Marly Marl, Q-Tip, Easy Mo Bee, and perhaps Dr. Dre) to add to RZA's newly unearthed vibe. "I'm making songs that you can write out on a piece of paper and give it to another band, and they'll do it."

The ancient Chinese philosophy of I-Ching uses 64 hexagrams to plot the inevitability of change in the universe. There is no questioning that Wu-Tang's universe has changed—from the members to the state of hip-hop that surrounds them—but they've been in similar positions before. Each of I-Ching's hexagrams represents a specific statement about the world at large, and the 64th is simply translated as "not yet completed," something very familiar to the probability of *8 Diagrams*.

If you look hard enough, any number is everywhere. Squinting at the world through a filter of digits there are infinite equations that provide answers that we're all seeking. Numerals can block reality as much as they pierce the truth, but their infinity can never be contained by paragraphs. 9 drags on a cigarette turns into 36 into 64 into $9 + 36 + 64 = 109$ into $1 + 0 + 9 = 10$ into $1 + 0 = 1$, Supreme Mathematics' number of knowledge, and yet it also turns into 9 + 3 + 6 + 6 + 4 = 28 into 2 + 8 = 10 into 1 + 0 = 1, knowledge. And the knowledge that one, final, great Wu-Tang Clan album exists may be just enough to save hip-hop a third time.

"It's gonna happen. It's gonna happen because it's inevitable—it has to happen," RZA says. "[But] if it's not coming this year, it ain't coming at all. That's my opinion. If it doesn't come this year, it don't mean nothing no more."

Jonathan Cunningham

FREAKS COME OUT AT NIGHT
Grandmaster Dee Cuts a Wide Swath
on the Comeback Trail

It's almost midnight in the lobby of the Jacksonville Sheraton Hotel, and Grandmaster Dee, legendary DJ and key member of Whodini, is acting the fool. With his low-cropped fade, blue Jumpman tracksuit, and white sneakers, he does not stand out as a celebrity at all. That's the problem—or make that, *part* of the problem. His speech is slurred, his eyes are glazed, and he's clutching a Heineken bottle like a microphone, hollering at every passing female about how he's a member of Whodini—the seminal hip-hop group from the 1980s. You remember Whodini, don't you?

Some of the women clutch their purses closer. Others cling to their husbands tightly and walk rapidly by, eyes downcast. Dee's friends try to corral him back to his senses, but the scene drags on for 20 minutes. This is Grandmaster Dee at his worst, a guy who reeks of washed-up hip-hopper.

Dee, born William Drew Carter, is in Jacksonville on this chilly Friday to perform at the Funk Fest alongside other throwback artists such as Lakeside, MC Lyte, Bobby Brown, Cherelle, and Frankie Beverly and Maze. The daylong extravaganza of popular rap, R&B, and soul acts from the 1980s is a big deal to Jacksonville's African-American population. A weekend of heavy partying is already in full swing, and the mood in the Sheraton, where all of these groups are staying, is laid-back, except for Dee, the one knucklehead causing a ruckus.

Not 30 minutes later, *that* Grandmaster Dee is gone. The other one, the one who still commands respect, is making a beeline for the DJ area in the packed Deep Blue nightclub. The club's resident DJ sees him approaching and announces on the mic that "Grandmaster Dee from Whodini is officially in the building!" and the patrons on the dance floor start going crazy. In a flash, Dee is on the turntables, scratching records with his elbows, forearms, and hands and doing behind-the-back tricks.

This is a DJ master class. It's hard to believe this is the same guy who could barely stumble up a flight of stairs a half-hour ago, the same guy who was almost turned away at the door for being drunk and not meeting the club's dress code. But there he is, on point and rocking the turntables with pinpoint precision. His "set" lasts barely five minutes, but he's flawlessly controlling the crowd. It all looks so effortless, and a knot of patrons presses forward toward the DJ area to see a legend at work.

Now people are walking up to *him* and extending their hands in introduction. Women are trying to flirt, and their boyfriends are getting jealous. This is Grandmaster Dee in his element.

It's been 25 years since Whodini first burst out of Brooklyn. Back in 1982, the group's three cocky kids—Jalil Hutchins (one of the few rappers to go by his real name), Ecstasy (with his trademark Zorro hat), and DJ Grandmaster Dee—quickly made a name for themselves as one of the most versatile hip-hop crews in New York City. No thorough anthology of old-school rap is complete without Whodini classics like "Freaks Come Out at Night," "Friends," and "Five Minutes of Funk," key tracks that helped hip-hop break out of R&B and into the pop charts and the national mainstream.

For a time, their prominence was paralleled only by Run D.M.C.—another New York-based group that Whodini regarded more or less as friendly rivals. The two groups played many shows together, but according to other hip-hop acts on those tours, Whodini was the more popular act.

"There's no question that Whodini was killing it every night," Public Enemy's Chuck D says from Long Island. "You gotta understand, between '84 and '87, you've got a group that nobody wants to play behind. Run D.M.C. didn't want to play behind them. And it caused tension. It was like the Four Tops and the Temptations. Hell, they got along, but they were out to smash each other every night."

Doug E. Fresh is another hard-core fan. "I think because there were people who had something against Whodini, people haven't told the whole truth within the history of hip-hop," he says. "You can't leave them out. They did hip-hop *and* R&B, and the combination is different than most. A lot of rap fans almost hold it against them that they were able to bring those two worlds together."

Whodini penned songs that appealed to women as well as men—a trick Run D.M.C. never figured out. "You know, Whodini were the first true sex symbols of hip-hop," old-school rapper Dana Dane says. "You had Grandmaster Dee with the green eyes, X and Jalil had their own style, plus they always dressed fly. They were getting NBA-type groupies before ballplayers were getting 'em. They were rock stars, basically."

By the time *Escape*, their 1984 record, hit the streets, they were regularly playing shows in Germany, England, and Japan. Aside from Kurtis Blow and the Sugar Hill Gang, rap groups touring internationally were still virtually unheard of.

Whodini ruled hip-hop when the culture was still fighting for recognition. At the time, hip-hop was still pretty much confined to the five boroughs of New York City, and the so-called smart money said the music was just a fad, that it would die out by the end of the summer. You could barely hear it on the radio, and television shows like *Yo! MTV Raps* were still years away. As for hip-hop-based ad campaigns, forget it.

Whodini was the first rap group to use official dancers in its live performances, the first to shoot a music video (for the single "Magic Wand"), and the first hip-hop group to go platinum.

But rap in the 1980s morphed at rapid speed. Each hit song, each new artist, spawned whole new fads and styles. Groups that were hot in January were played out by August. Sure, that happens in all forms of music, but early rap's turnover was especially brutal.

"We were a party group, and we made party songs," Carter recalls. "We liked champagne, liked the Hennessy. The other groups drank domestic beer, but we always had Heineken. We had a lot of fun back then, sometimes too much."

The band didn't shy away from substances that were harder than Henny. Cocaine was the group's illegal drug of choice. They may not have been rockers, but they lived the Mötley Crüe lifestyle of sex, drugs, and rock 'n' roll to the hilt. Worse, so did their bosses.

"Back in that era, the whole management company was doing drugs," Hutchins says of Whodini. "All of 'em. And half of the artists. We all had bad habits. But it's hard to keep a career going and have all of your business handled properly when even your management's on drugs."

Bill Adler, a hip-hop historian who also served as Whodini's publicist, recalls that the trio's addled behavior was a frequent source of frustration for him. "They would blow off professional commitments," Adler says. "They would disappear into a hotel room, get stupid high, and you couldn't reach them. When someone blows off big interviews, it hurts. And it hurt my reputation as well."

The bottom started falling out in 1987, a pivotal year in hip-hop history. *Open Sesame*, the group's fourth album, failed to produce a hit. Meanwhile, gold chains and the first stirrings of the gangster vibe were creeping into the music. Even a "conscious rapper" like KRS-One was taking rap in a more hardcore direction with the release that year of *Criminal Minded*. Whodini's Harry Houdini schtick seemed played out—the group was suddenly about as fresh and relevant as 'NSync is today. They'd gone from being superstars to near non-entities in the genre they had played such a huge role in legitimizing.

"My man [Ecstasy] used to come out on stage wearing leather shorts and cowboy boots and a hat," Adler says. "He was beautiful and built, and he was going to let you admire how cut he was. But when you look at those pictures, it looks dated at best. And at worst, it looks fruit . . . unmanly. Hip-hop is hypermasculine. And here you got songs like 'The Freaks Come Out at Night' that expressed sexuality in too overt a way to be taken serious for any length of time. The lines of hetero- and homosexuality were blurred. I think by the end, people just didn't get it."

For Carter's part, he's moved past the gripes and shortfalls of Whodini's time on top. "My mind goes way past the past and to the future," he says. "I'm focusing on us coming out with new material soon."

They may not make it back to the pinnacles they climbed in their early, groundbreaking days. But now they're pioneers of another sort— explorers on the old-school hip-hop revival circuit.

"My objective is to turn things back around. I don't want to jinx it, but I have ideas that I want to do," Carter says. "Me, I feel like Carlos Santana. He took a break, and now he came out again, like a rebirth. I say we got stock in the game called hip-hop."

His plan is to rise to the top from right here in the bottom of America. Two-thirds of Whodini's members now live in Atlanta, and Carter lives in Plantation. The group is touring again. Carter is working out an endorsement deal with DJ equipment giant Stanton, and he just landed a weekly residence at the Marlin Hotel in South Beach. There are tentative plans for the group to star in a reality-TV series about the lives of old-school rappers, and Melle Mel, MC Lyte, and Big Daddy Kane have all made commitments. Carter also hopes to get back to making music, and he thinks now is a perfect time for some of the old-school rappers to come back and show the youngsters in the game a thing or two.

Then and now, you could make a case for Grandmaster Dee as the star of the group. Carter was born in the Bedford-Stuyvesant section of Brooklyn in the summer of 1962. On old Whodini album covers, it's his hazel-eyed, bronze-skinned mug that stands out the most, and his magnetic personality comes through with mesmeric intensity when the group is on stage.

But this is the Saturday morning after a long Friday night in Jacksonville, and as the clock strikes noon, Carter is already at the hotel bar enjoying a liquid brunch of Heineken and Hennessy. Ecstasy and Hutchins are upstairs sleeping after driving in from Atlanta, where they share a house, and Carter is too busy double-fisting to take care of business. Whodini hasn't actually rehearsed for a gig in years, but Carter typically handles the soundcheck before their shows. Right now, he's supposed to be 15 minutes away at the Jacksonville Metropolitan Park, making sure the system is tight. Instead, he's holding court at the bar and talking shit about the wackness of last night's groupies. His attire is almost identical to what he had on the previous night. He's rocking in the same Jumpman tracksuit—worn partly because Michael Jordan is his second cousin—and a similar white T-shirt, not to mention the same slurred speech that followed him to bed around the break of day. Forget about a soundcheck; as time passes and more alcohol slides down his throat, you start to wonder if he'll be in any shape to perform at Whodini's show later that day.

For the duration of this weekend stint, Carter is sharing a conjoined suite with another legendary partier—longtime friend Bobby Brown. Brown spent much of Friday evening out of sight—save for a 3 a.m. appearance at Carter's hotel room, where, soaking wet and dressed in nothing but a towel, he looked to borrow something. For his part, Dee spent the wee hours with three middle-aged groupies who planted themselves in his hotel room until it was time for this reporter to get lost.

It's hard to tell if Carter's buzz is freshly acquired or lingering from the earlier one, but either way, he's especially talkative about hip-hop and what's kept him going for the past 25 years.

"There's just something about going out there and having 20,000 people in the palm of your hand every night that's addictive," he says. "I had to make sure my game was tight, because it was about showmanship back then. You really had to stand out and be different for anyone to notice you, because all the DJs were so good."

"Drew had beautiful timing," Adler remembers. "He was the drummer basically, and he did it with flair. He could cut a record with his nose. I mean [Grandmaster] Flash was incredible, and he could spin around and cut with his elbows, but Drew could do it with his face."

"All the DJs wanted to be like Grandmaster Dee 'cause he was the best," Dane adds. "Even Jam Master Jay, who was one of the greatest ever, wasn't as incredible as Grandmaster Dee. Dee had control of every cut, every motion. He could read the crowd, the MCs; he knew when to drop the record, when not to, and could let the fellas do what they had to do."

"Drew was always ahead of the game, even back when we first got together," says Dr. Ice, who has now joined the entourage at the bar. While some may remember Dr. Ice from his time in the group U.T.F.O. and their breakout 1985 hit "Roxanne Roxanne," he was also a part of the Keystone Dancers alongside his partner Kangol Kid; the pair were brought on to enhance Whodini's live performances. Although Kangol has retired from hip-hop, Whodini still includes Dr. Ice in all of its current shows so that rapping, scratching, and dancing—three of the four vital elements of hip-hop—are represented each time they take the stage. "We came up in the days when DJs were party rockers," Dr. Ice says, "and a part of what makes Drew so good is that he still has that quality about him today."

By now, Ecstasy and a few longtime Whodini affiliates are flanking Carter at the bar. Everyone is laughing, cracking jokes, and reminiscing. Turn back the aging process and you could be looking at one of today's rap posses.

Carter says his first encounters with DJ'ing were through Masta Don from the Def Committee and DJ Whiz Kid, who took him under their wings his freshman year at Julia Richman High School in Manhattan. "Every day after school, we'd work out on the turntables," he says.

The first time he heard the music, as a freshman on his high school's basketball taxi squad, he was electrified. "I went to the lunch room one day, and they had the boom box set up, and I remember hearing with the echo effect, '*Yes yes y'all, and you don't stop, you are listening listening, to the sounds sounds of DJ Afrika Afrika, Bambataa Bataa, and the mighty mighty Zulu Zulu Nation Nation.*' And I was like, 'What was *that?*' like, ooh, I want to be down with that."

Soon enough, he was. Everything about hip-hop was growing at an exponential pace, and Carter's DJ'ing skills were no exception. By 19, he already had his own group, Grandmaster Dee and the Devastating Two, with Carter on the turntables and two female MCs called Dimple D and Giggle G.

Around 1980, he also fell in love with the late-night broadcast of New York's preeminent radio host, Mr. Magic, on radio station WHBI. It was the only radio show in town where you could hear hip-hop, and Carter tuned in religiously. Though he didn't know it at the time, this would eventually lead to the formation of Whodini.

"Me and Jalil didn't even know Drew back then," Ecstasy says. "We had our own group, the Quadra Brothers. This would have been like

'80 or '81. But we were fans of the Mr. Magic show. We recorded a little radio jingle, like a commercial bigging up his show, and Magic used to play it on the air. After that, we started working at the station—just answering phones to help out, and the first person to call in every [Saturday] night was Grandmaster Dee. He used to call in *every* night to check in."

Magic rented the Saturday-night graveyard slot between 2 and 4 a.m. for $75 an hour. Anybody who cared about hip-hop was glued to the radio. Carter laughs as he recalls his standard catch phrase, which was echoed through boom boxes across New York City each Saturday night. "I used to call up and say, 'Yo, what's up, Mr. Magic? This is Grandmaster Dee, and, yo, I'm checking out Mr. Magic on WHBI, 105.9.'" Although it was pure shameless self-promotion, both Jalil and Ecstasy were intrigued by his resolve. The three met and practiced together, but they didn't become a trio for a few more years.

Jive Records, which was based in England, flew to the United States and wanted to record an album with Mr. Magic, but Magic decided against it. Instead, he pushed the deal into the hands of Ecstasy and Jalil, who quickly signed with Jive in early 1982. Ecstasy remembers how Jive named the group. "Back then, everyone was the Funky Four +1 or the Furious Five, so here we come as Whodini, and everybody's like, 'What the fuck?' But it worked."

The duo recorded their first song, "Magic's Wand," produced by London-based synth-pop pioneer Thomas Dolby, and it became a worldwide underground hit, getting heavy radio play throughout Europe and Australia as well as in the United States. It ended up selling close to 100,000 units. That was one of the perks of signing with a British label—while Whodini worked it stateside, their material was also getting a sizable push overseas, an advantage Whodini's New York–based competition didn't have.

But without a DJ or an extensive catalog, some of their initial shows overseas were rough. "We'd tour in Europe and do hour-and-a-half sets, but we only had two singles," Ecstasy recalls. "We used to borrow material from *everybody*—Grandmaster Flash, Kurtis Blow—whoever had material out, we'd borrow it just to stretch out our sets."

By 1983, the duo realized they needed Carter to legitimize them as a group. He was brought on officially as a tour DJ that year and made his debut on wax on 1984's breakout album, *Escape*. Carter laid all the scratches and DJ blends on the record, and his musical knowledge gave the album a distinctive sound. Russell Simmons, who handled most of the major acts in hip-hop at the time whether they were signed to Def Jam or not, became Whodini's manager.

"We would have followed Russell anywhere back then," Ecstasy laments. "He was our manager, and we loved him, but it couldn't last forever."

There's a notable sigh of disappointment whenever Simmons' name comes up. As the posse parts ways to prepare for the show, Carter is noticeably sullen. Alcohol and nostalgia have worked Dee into a funk. He disappears for a couple of hours, opting not to answer his phone.

Carter the man and Grandmaster Dee the legend are two different people. The former is an all-too-human everyday citizen, a divorced parent and grandparent who struggles with his vices. Grandmaster Dee, on the other hand, is flawless. After 20 years of catering to audiences, his music selection and scratching prowess are superb.

Still, knowing that Carter has spent the better part of a morning and afternoon "getting nice" at the bar and in his hotel room, it's astounding to encounter him hours later, the transformation into Grandmaster Dee complete. He's dressed in an all-white linen outfit with tan-and-white leather shoes, and he has put the boyish hip-hop antics to rest for the moment. On stage a little after sundown, he exhibits no noticeable effects of his afternoon bender. His audience—most ranging in age from 30 to 60—is at his feet, dancing to Dee's warm-up set of tracks by Donna Summer, Chic, and the Gap Band. It's an assortment of old-school hits he spins before Hutchins and Ecstasy join him to officially start the set.

Looking out from the stage, his gaze meets a sea of clapping hands and swaying bodies. On this evening, there's a singular surprise. Old friend Doug E. Fresh has flown in as a guest, walking on stage with the members of Whodini, exciting the crowd. The impromptu 45-minute set zips along perfectly—though a few sound-quality issues come back to bite Carter in the ass.

The foursome belts out classics like "One Love," "Big Mouth," "Friends," and "Freaks Come Out at Night." Carter seems to absorb the

MCs' nearly invisible cues. Like Dwyane Wade on a fast break, he's in the zone, pulling records off the turntables—yep, he's still using vinyl—and softly tossing them behind him like Frisbees. His pace is frenetic, and he barely breaks a sweat while seamlessly switching between two different catalogs. As the show winds down, just after Doug E. Fresh beatboxes the intro to "The Show" and the crowd sings along on a raucous rendition of "La Di Da Di," the ground behind Carter is littered with records.

After the show, the scene backstage is incipient debauchery. Whodini's dressing room quickly fills with groupies, girlfriends, and industry types. Bottles of Moët are popped, the cognac flows, and the backstage antics typical of hip-hop today—minus a cloud of weed smoke—are in full effect. Brown makes a grand entrance—the decibel level picks up as he strides in the door, loud and proud. He's the king of the scene tonight, and his presence swells the heads of the rank-and-file groupies.

Meanwhile, a groupie who has worked her way backstage has her eye on Carter, lifting her shirt and flashing her breasts in his direction. Hutchins takes a shot of Hennessy, and despite a torn ligament under the brace on his knee, he playfully falls to the ground, rattles off a couple of dozen good pushups, and limps back to his chair. Save for the brace, you'd think he was 20 again.

When Carter steps out of the room, Fresh gushes about his longtime friend. Neither Carter nor Whodini have gotten their due, he says. When the topic of VH1's *Hip-Hop Honors* (one of the closest things in existence to a hip-hop Hall of Fame) comes up, Fresh can't hold his tongue. "They should have already got it," he says. "They might have to change it to *Hip-Hop* Dis*honors* in a minute."

Ecstasy chimes in that he'd like to be honored, if only so that his kids will know that their father isn't just talking shit about being an unheralded legend. But he doesn't want to come across as bitter. "I don't want to be the angry rapper that says, 'What about us, what about Whodini?' We made our music, and the crowd still loves it. I don't care if they honor us or not."

"Truth is truth," Fresh insists. "And a lot of this has to do with your time on Rush Productions."

It's the second time the *R*-word (referring to Simmons) has been mentioned. The mood in the dressing room remains jovial, but the Hennessy and champagne are loosening tongues.

"When we started working with Russell, he booked us on the Fresh Fest, the Def Jam tour," Hutchins says. "He made sure we were on all the major tours. So I ain't go no beef with Russell, and I ain't got no beef with [Russell's business partner] Lyor Cohen. They got a beef with us. As far as they were concerned, there could only be one of us on top. And we were running on Run and 'nem [Run D.M.C.]. They live and they do their thing, but come on. We were kicking their ass too. Whodini ain't no joke!"

Minor controversy mars the tail end of Funk Fest 2007. Carter is supposed to DJ Bobby Brown's set, but the promoters pulled the turntables off stage, and their co-performance never happened. Brown and Carter believe that the organizers didn't want them to upstage the headliner, Frankie Beverly and Maze. And Brown and Frankie Beverly can't stand each other. They've traded words in public before, and Brown is seething. Brown and Carter may have shared bills for nearly 20 years, but tonight would have been the first time they would have performed together. When Beverly's entourage—led by Beverly himself, clad in a black suit topped with a bright-red hat—brushes past Brown's, it's the last straw.

"Oh, you're wearing the red hat tonight, huh, Frankie?" Brown says as Beverly slides past, pretending not to hear. "You lucky I don't knock that hat off your head, you faggot motherfucker."

The Whodini and Brown crews head out to a club across town. Brown arrives with his new girlfriend, several cousins, and his father, Herbert "Pop" Brown, in tow. They've eschewed the VIP room and are hanging out on the dance floor—bewildering curious onlookers who marvel at Bobby Brown in their midst.

Carter arrives a little later in a stretch Hummer, lugging a heavy crate of records to the DJ booth. Soon he's playing a mix of reggae, funk, and hip-hop while Dr. Ice works the crowd, basking in Carter's grooves. Suddenly, Brown decides to join in. He heads to the DJ booth—he's had a bit to drink—takes the microphone out of Ice's hand, and starts freestyling. The crowd goes apeshit. It's not the duo performance the two had in mind, but as organically and spontaneously as possible, Carter and Brown are working the club in unison. Carter drops the beat to Notorious B.I.G.'s "Warning," and Brown raps it word for word. It's more like karaoke than a real performance. Brown is too drunk to be coherent, and Carter is mostly playing songs with words instead of spinning instrumentals. From a purely musical standpoint, it's a shambles, but the two old friends are cracking up and having a blast.

Much later in the evening, everybody still on the premises is herded over to the VIP area in a separate building. There, Carter takes over a different set of turntables and spins an exclusive set that lasts until the wee hours. Brown alternately tends to his girlfriend and 77-year-old Pop (who is partying at least as hard as everyone else in the building) and occasionally busts out with what looks like a few choreographed New Edition dance moves. Despite it all, nothing about the night reeks of celebrity.

The night finally concludes after 5 a.m. A second posse of groupies has gathered in Carter's hotel room, and they get a bit out of hand. They're loud, and they start hitting on Pop Brown, who's more than game. He maintains that he's "got his Viagra ready and needs a woman like a fish needs a raincoat," but his son boots the girls out.

Most A-list rappers today are a lackluster album away from seeing their careers vanish, though it's hard to detect the undertow while it's happening. Whodini is lucky; there's an old-school circuit that can help keep a rap group afloat. But before a group can bounce into that market, things have to get ugly.

It's not necessarily the conversation that Carter wants to have, but he's stuck, driving in a car for six hours from Jacksonville to Plantation with a reporter who won't let him off the hook. During the drive, which includes stops at the home of a childhood friend, an extended nap, and a lot of hip-hop trivia, Carter is candid and hungover. He misses touring, and he's glad the phone is ringing again.

"Back in '85, '86, I was making more than $100,000—easily," Carter says. "I was taking in around $150,000 just off touring and hip-hop. And that's 1986 money. We'd be hanging with Mike Tyson, partying at the Roxy with Madonna. And I'll be honest, I shared a lot of that money with other people from around the way or whatever. It wasn't like I wanted to have fun by myself."

By the time Whodini released its *Greatest Hits* album in 1990, it was a foregone conclusion that the time in the spotlight was finished. By 1994, all three members of Whodini were in Atlanta, where they signed with Jermaine Dupri's So So Def label. A decade earlier, Whodini had given an adolescent Dupri his start in the music business when they let him be one of their dancers. The group had high hopes for their So So Def debut *Six*, but it was a commercial failure.

Carter stayed in Atlanta for two more years after the So So Def deal wound down, leaving only after a run-in with the police outside of Club 112 that left him with a broken arm. After a subsequent stay in Memphis, he moved to Miami briefly before settling in Plantation a year and a half ago.

Carter doesn't remember when tricks became part of his repertoire, but he delighted fans with antics such as scratching records with his sneakers, Chapstick, and anything else he could get his hands on. "The first time I went to Japan, I started doing tricks with the chopsticks," Carter remembers. "I went and got a dozen of them, took four, put them together, and just started scratching—the crowds would go crazy when I pulled that one off. I remember we started doing something in the middle of the second tour where, at the end of the show, the group would pick me up with my feet in the air, trying to pull me off stage like, 'Yo, we gotta go,' and they're pulling me away from the turntables but I'm still scratching the records. We were always giving them something different. That's what made our live shows so fun."

Speaking of tricks, one of the original Houdini's most astounding illusions was making a 10,000-pound elephant disappear. Audiences never figured out exactly how a five-ton elephant vanished into thin air, but it bears a special relevance to this juncture in Carter's career. An obvious topic that most people around Whodini these days choose *not* to discuss is whether there's still room for the group to reemerge in the rap industry with new material. Their stage shows are tight, but the genre as a whole is hurting. The question is: Would audiences even care? That's the five-ton elephant in the room.

"There's a fantastic market for their music right now," Chuck D insists. "Now is a good time for them to make some music, some videos, and use them as advertisement for their live shows. With today's market—MP3s, digital downloading—all they need is to play their shows, no different than the Dells play shows, and they'll be fine."

Carter can't argue with that, and, in fact, he's hoping his old friend is right.

"Like I always say, if you could last 25 years and still do what you do and love what you do and still eat without a record out, then you've done something right," he says. "Nobody is making music catering to the older crowd. That's where we're going to step in. Not just for us but to save hip-hop as a whole."

Nadia Pflaum

PAY 2 PLAY

Hip-Hop Hustlers Are Making Off with Kansas City Rappers' Hard-Earned Cash

Twenty-six-year-old Robert Hardiman, otherwise known as Realla Re-zob, stands outside the Walgreens at 39th Street and Broadway in a plain white T-shirt, the straps of a backpack looped loosely over his slim shoulders. Inside the bag are dozens of CDs tucked into yellow envelopes with slips of white paper detailing the contents.

Hardiman sells these mixes for $5 each and packs them with songs by the same artists whom 16-year-old girls breathlessly request on urban radio: Akon, Cupid, T-Pain and Hurricane Chris. For this mix, Hardiman has also sneaked on his own song. Called "J's," it's an anthem dedicated to Nike Jordan shoes.

When an employee in a Walgreens vest comes outside, she doesn't run off Hardiman for soliciting on store property. Instead, she smiles in recognition and goes back inside to get her purse.

Even though he hasn't recorded an album, Hardiman is well-known on the local hip-hop circuit—mostly because of his tireless efforts to sell homemade mixes on street corners.

Hardiman wins over customers with his easy smile, his come-hither eyes and the tale of his latest success. His song "Smashin'"—a hyperactive, danceable beat with a hook that goes *Big wheels on our ride, lookin' fly/ We smashin' state to state makin' tycoon moves/In our customized whips when we dips on through*—was recently included on a collection of songs at SnoopDoggDemo.com, a Web site that offers music for free download.

Hardiman entered "Smashin'" in a Snoop Dogg mix contest after seeing an ad on the Internet.

"I had to send them $250," he says. "But they still chose it over, like, 250 million other songs."

Though Snoop Dogg's photo was on the Web site, the contest didn't appear to be sanctioned by Snoop Dogg or Geffen Records, Snoop's label. (Several of the site's pages simply read "Coming Soon!")

Still, Hardiman figured the $250 was money well spent. Even if the site didn't stick his song in the middle of a downloadable mix of music, he believed that the site's operators might remember the track and use it for a future mix.

But he didn't receive any hard copies of the CD, something that similar companies promise and deliver. Hardiman might have been better served by simply uploading his song to a MySpace page for free—which he eventually did.

Meanwhile, last month, SnoopDoggDemo.com went dark.

Dewayne Holmes, who works for Geffen's Midwest urban-promotions department, says he is unfamiliar with the Snoop Dogg demo site. "There's a lot of frauds out there, so people have to do their research before they commit to something," he says.

Rappers bump fists and advise one another to stay on their hustle—keep writing rhymes and making beats, keep logging hours in the recording studio, keep selling mixes out of car trunks.

But a swarm of other hustlers waits to skim money from the naïve and the uninitiated. They'll talk novice rappers into paying for slots on tours that fall through or charge a premium to let them open for national acts visiting Kansas City or fleece them for airtime on local radio.

Some of these hustles are illegal, others simply unethical. But all are hurting local artists.

In Anti-Crew's short career, the lucky breaks have outweighed the unlucky ones. The two MCs, Matt Peters and Jeffery Shafer, formed their hip-hop duo in 2000. They rocked mics at the Peanut at Ninth

Street and Broadway before they could legally drink at the bar, and they had recorded an album, *The Progressive Movement* (which earned positive reviews in *The Pitch* and *The Kansas City Star*), before they graduated from Lincoln Prep Academy.

To get so far so young, Peters and Shafer had to have some business savvy. They knew enough to put together a professional-looking press kit to send to newspapers and to set up their own Web site and MySpace pages to attract people to their music.

They figured the effort was paying off when they got an e-mail from a New York company called 721 Productions.

By then, Shafer was in his freshman year at Columbia College in Chicago, where he studies marketing and communications while taking courses in music business. Peters had left Columbia College and returned to Kansas City after his father, Kansas City Symphony bassist Steven Peters, was murdered in a botched robbery. (Steven Peters' killer received a 25-year prison sentence last year.)

721 Productions asked Peters and Shafer to send their press kit and some music samples, plus a registration fee of $20, to be considered for future 721 projects. Shafer and Peters did so, and on December 15, 2005, they received a letter in the mail.

According to the letter, Anti-Crew had been chosen to join 721 Productions' "Tour 2005/2006" lineup; nationally famous rap acts Styles P, Mobb Deep, Fat Joe and Redman would also be on the tour. For $1,000, the letter promised, Anti-Crew could join the performers on a five-city leg. The money would pay for transportation, hotel rooms, plugs on urban radio stations, and promotion on fliers and posters.

Shafer researched the company the best way he knew how: He Googled it. His Web search found several small newspaper stories about 721-sponsored shows in the New York area. The invitation letter included the company's address and phone number as well as information on refunds.

Peters and Shafer sent their money.

About a month later, they got a packet and chose a list of dates when they'd be available. Then they started talking on the phone with people at 721. They learned that Ludacris had been added to the tour.

"I was in steady contact with them, and they had answers to everything," Shafer recalls. "They would even call me on occasion."

But on February 15, 2006, Shafer and Peters received an e-mail.

"Our staff at 721 Productions have made a unanimous decision to cancel this year's Tour 2006 Season due to a sudden death in our staff in early January 2006," it read. "We lost our Financial Coordinator and Sponsor Correspondent and as a result we will begin reorganizing and changing the structure of our endeavors beginning April 1st 2006."

The letter explained how refunds could be obtained for a period of 180 days and included an e-mail address and a phone number to contact with questions. Shafer and Peters followed the instructions but have yet to receive their money.

"What's kind of embarrassing, too, is that it was money we made from our album sales," Shafer says of their $1,000. He says he can't get anyone from 721 Productions to return his calls.

No one from 721 returned *The Pitch*'s call, either.

Shafer says he and Peters have consulted an entertainment lawyer to decide what to do next. But the company is in New York, Shafer and Peters are in Illinois, and their music keeps them busy.

"This really humbled me," Shafer says. "Nobody should ever pay to play. We don't charge plumbers to fix our water pipes, so why charge artists to play music?"

Until September, Club Kandi was located in a low-profile building between abandoned-looking storefronts advertising Black Cat fireworks in the industrial West Bottoms.

Not every night was poppin' there, but when touring acts came through—Club Kandi booked the Youngbloodz, Slim Thug, E-40 and Trina in 2006—the place was packed with smoke, bass and people out to see and be seen. Cars with spinning rims and custom paint jobs lined North James Street.

In June 2006, Dem Franchize Boyz, a group from Atlanta that had been signed to Jermaine Dupri's So So Def record label, was scheduled to perform there.

The show would be huge—everyone knew the words to the group's song "Lean Wit It, Rock Wit It" and had its snap-dance moves down as soon as the video hit YouTube.

Vell Williams, a 26-year-old member of AllInOne, was looking for a way to get his group heard. So far, they'd printed water-bottle labels with their logo and rapped for a Mr. Goodcents ad (which still hasn't made it to the airwaves). Getting out in front of 2,000 people at Club Kandi seemed like the promotional break his crew was looking for.

"People have heard us perform before, so we have a reputation of doing good shows—remembering our lyrics and not having our hands on our crotches the whole time," Williams says.

He approached Club Kandi owner Chad Waldrop about opening for Dem Franchize Boyz. Williams says the two of them drew up the standard Club Kandi contract: $500 would pay for AllInOne to perform a few songs before the headliners took the stage. Williams says Waldrop never asked to hear his music.

The show was unforgettable for Williams and his trio—people in the crowd tried to slap their hands and nearly drowned out the music with their approving shouts.

"I was getting pulled off the stage. That was exciting like hell," Williams says. "The amount of respect we got from that—it was real."

Williams vacillates between thinking it was worth $500 and thinking that paying to play is wrong. He acknowledges that club owners who spend thousands of dollars to bring in a national touring act want to recoup their investment. And Williams admits that nobody twisted his arm to pay for the chance to play. But he wishes that club owners would give artists a break. "Charging us to perform—that's not even an even trade," he says. After all, it costs money to record with top-of-the-line equipment, buy beats from producers, print T-shirts and press CDs. "It's hard out here for a rapper. Easy for a pimp."

Waldrop now runs the Hurricane in Westport and has changed Club Kandi to a nonhip-hop format. He says he never kept the $500 fees he charged artists to open at Club Kandi.

"A lot of the promoters are from out of town, so we collect money for the promoters, and when they get in town to do their event, we give them the money when they get here. That's how it goes. The club doesn't get that money. Wish we did."

But Waldrop acknowledges that the Hurricane doesn't charge rock and punk bands to play. "Not at all," he says. "Rock bands ain't got no money. They're barely alive, living day to day, where most of these rappers are funded by drugs."

"He ain't talking about me and AllInOne," Williams counters. "That didn't ever fund my music, and it don't fund my music now. I know my people in my crew. Anything we get, we earned, and we work hard."

Akbar Akram—DJ Ak—gazes out at a gyrating cauldron of arms and legs and shaking booties. He's making a November guest appearance in the basement of Skybox, a smoky den where the walls are painted with half-finished graffiti murals.

Akram has played with an impressive list of performers—he has connected with Shadyville, a group of DJs who have access to artists on Interscope Records, and has toured with Bubba Sparxxx, Fonzworth Bentley, and the Ying Yang Twins. Recently, Akram has been DJ-ing behind the Shop Boyz, promoting their hit "Party Like a Rock Star." His voice-mail recording features a personalized greeting from 50 Cent.

In KC, most DJs don't touch a microphone, but Akram is talking to the crowd all the time, introducing new remixes and shouting out the tracks by local rappers. To do so is second nature, considering his last radio gig in town.

In 2005 and 2006, Akram hosted *The Takeover*, an hourlong show featuring local hip-hop that aired every Saturday at midnight on KPRS 103.3, a locally owned station with the highest ratings in Kansas City.

According to Akram, KPRS first approached him about hosting a weekly local mix show. Akram would own the show, station reps told him, because he would pay for his airtime: $250 a week for a total of $1,000 a month.

Akram named his show *The Takeover* to let local artists know that he was putting the power in their hands. Before his show started, he says, local hip-hop got airplay maybe twice a year. But he played area artists every week.

"This was funded right here," Akram tells *The Pitch*, patting the pockets of his jeans three times for emphasis. "Nobody else gave me money to try and launch this. It's not like I'm a millionaire or I'm rich."

To meet his monthly fee, Akram solicited advertising. Dayton Wheel and Tire, a shop in Belton, paid to sponsor Akram's show, as did the owners of urban clothing stores in places such as the Blue Ridge

Shopping Center and the now-closed Bannister Mall, Akram says. "My sponsors were only paying $500 or $1,000, whatever it may be, but they were getting endorsements they could reuse."

He also held a launch party at the Red Vine restaurant (which has since gone out of business) at 18th Street and Vine. DeShai Hampton, aka Mz Shai, who hosts *The Show-Me Mix Show* on community radio station KKFI 90.1, remembers a line of local hip-hop heads trailing out the door. The cover charge was $10, and it cost more money for rappers to audition for Akram—Hampton says figures varied from $50 to $150.

"So, OK, they're going to charge you to get in, charge you to perform, and at the end there's no guarantee he'll ever play their music," Hampton says. "There's no need to do all that to people."

Akram says it was a matter of simple economics. "They [KPRS] didn't want me to charge people to be on my show or charge sponsors or anything, but they expected me to pay them," he says. "It doesn't make sense."

Artists had plenty of opportunities to recoup the money they paid him, Akram says. He'd set up autograph sessions for them at the clothing stores that sponsored him, he says, which gave them the chance to sell their CDs and T-shirts.

But Akram clashed with KPRS Program Director Myron Fears. Akram says Fears reserved the right to edit *The Takeover*, which offended Akram because he'd paid to own the show. Akram says Fears once declared a song too profane because Fears thought he heard the artist Cam'Ron say "dipshit" when he was really shouting out the name of his hip-hop crew and its record label, the Diplomats, by saying "Dipset."

KPRS discontinued *The Takeover* in the spring of 2006. "Basically, the guy was hard to work with, he did not follow directions, and he thought he knew everything," Fears says of Akram. "In terms of pay-for-play, that is not what we're all about here at [KPRS owner] Carter Broadcast Group."

Akram now works for Shadyville's Sirius satellite-radio station, Shady 45, where he occasionally hosts programs such as the uncensored, two-hour mix show Rep Yo Set, which airs on Sundays.

Kenny Roberts, known on the air as Kenny Diamonds, replaced Akram as the host of KPRS's local radio show in the summer of 2006.

The show moved to Fridays at midnight and is called *Underground Heat*. Roberts dishes out street slang on the air, but he holds a master's degree in communications from Central Missouri State University. (He pledged the Kappa Alpha Psi fraternity, symbolized by a diamond, hence the nickname "Diamonds.")

"For the first year of my show, I was my sponsor—$200 a week out of my pocket," Roberts says from behind a desk at the KPRS studios. He has just finished recording an interview with two young rappers called Flash (Steven Brundidge) and Jae Casino (Justin Ewing, who is Roberts' brother).

Roberts worked in the promotional department at KPRS before he landed his show, so he was often on location for remote broadcasts at cell-phone depots and clubs. Roberts says people would come up and ask why it was so expensive to get their music played on KPRS.

"For me it was like, 'Well, it's not supposed to cost. That's illegal,'" Roberts says. "You can't play music [in return] for money."

Answering those questions was embarrassing for Roberts, so he decided to handle fundraising differently.

"You can definitely sell commercials, just like any syndicated show," Roberts says. To avoid conflicts of interest, he says, he lets the station's sales department sell ads rather than doing it himself.

But Roberts has found a way to turn his job at KPRS into additional business.

"Basically, I turned *Underground Heat* into a marketing company," Roberts says. He'll sponsor a mix or put on a concert and charge unknown artists to open for bigger acts, which helps him defray the cost of booking a big name. "If I can put your name on a flier and get 800 people to go to the show, I'll pay you," Roberts explains. "But if I keep your name off the flier and I can still get 800 people to go to the show, you pay me. It's a cold game. But it's what you think it's worth."

Roberts also charges fees for his knowledge of the music industry. For a price, he can put together a promotional package for an artist and help the artist shop it to labels around the country.

He used to share his knowledge for free, but after a while, he started to see people he'd mentored paying others for access to their connections. "At least my connections are real," he says.

Keejuan Carter, 28, opens the door to his east-side apartment wearing a white sleeveless shirt and sweatpants. Then he settles back down on his couch. A game show is blaring on TV.

Carter is the manager of Van Brunt Entertainment, a collective of rappers who grew up together near Van Brunt and 27th Street. The artists have each put out solo albums, but they promote one another together. They won't speak to journalists individually, preferring that all media contact go through Carter.

Carter explains that the group began with a rapper called D-Loc da Chop, who recorded a song with Tech N9ne (one of Kansas City's few successful hip-hop exports) when D-Loc was only 17. D-Loc's friend, a rapper who now goes by Cash Image, told him to get serious about the music.

"He [Cash Image] was like, 'We gonna call [producer] Don Juan. We gonna get you about 10 beats, gonna get a suite, bring up a boom box. We gonna write, and we gonna buy some studio time,'" Carter explains. "D-Loc da Chop started Van Brunt Entertainment there."

Another rapper, Slopp da Gambla, played a song for D-Loc, and D-Loc declared Slopp his rapping partner on the spot, Carter says. D-Loc, Slopp and Cash Image got busy recording. They also got their promotional materials together, splashing the Van Brunt Entertainment logo across T-shirts that they wore in clubs and on the street.

Carter made sure that the Van Brunt artists took care of licensing and registering their music with organizations such as ASCAP (the American Society of Composers, Authors and Publishers) and BMI (Broadcast Music Inc.), which protect artists' music while making sure they get royalties for each spin.

This year, Cash Image came out with a hit song, "In My Chevy," which was heavily requested on *Underground Heat*. Carter and his crew found a way to get "In My Chevy" on a ring tone that their fans could download.

Van Brunt Entertainment has been able to make pay-for-play work for them.

"We paid our dues, and it eventually works—if you got talent. I've seen with my own eyes: You pay $200, $300 for a 15-minute set, that's four songs. If you got a table set up in the back with merch, it's a given.

Eight hundred people are falling in love with you after four songs, and you can make that $200 back in CD sales."

But even they fell for a recent contest that wasn't what it seemed.

On Wednesday, September 5, one of the regular contributors to a forum at hiphopkc.com posted this message: "I was in Westport tonight and some guys were handing out fliers outside the Hurricane. They gave me a flier and said they were promoters for the Source and that the Source is having a contest at the Emerald House on Main on Friday night where they'll pick one singer/rapper from KC (who wants to pay $75 to enter the contest) to advance to another contest in New York where the winner will be the Source's next Unsigned Hype. Regular admission is a whopping twenty bucks!!!"

During the days of Tupac and Biggie, hip-hoppers pored over the glossy pages of *The Source* each month. But in recent years, the magazine's influence has waned. When that Friday night rolled around, the crowd at the Emerald House was lackluster, but local musicians stepped up to compete. Cash Image paid the $75 to enter, and his infectious hooks won over the judges.

As Carter understands it, the prize for winning was that Cash Image would be flown to New York City to compete in the next round of the contest. But when the November date grew near, Cash Image passed on the opportunity.

"We were thinking that they were going to pay for the tickets and things of that sort, but they didn't," Carter says. "We would have had to pay for them ourselves, at the last minute."

Carter and Cash Image weren't the only ones who misunderstood the rules of the contest.

The phone number on the contest flier rings Willie Williams, a promoter from Illinois. Williams tells *The Pitch* that he signed on to *The Source*'s tour under the impression that he was working for employees of the magazine. Under his contract, he says, he was to pay for *Source* representatives to fly to a handful of cities on the 30-city contest tour, where they would judge the contest. Williams says he paid for the judges' hotel rooms, meals, and airfare, along with $5,000 a night to handle the advertising that would lure contestants and audiences to each tour stop.

If that sounds backward, it is.

But for his end of the deal, Williams kept the $75 that each contestant paid to enter the contest and collected all the cash from the door. If he did his job well, he had the potential to rake in more than he spent. But at the Emerald House, it didn't work out that way. "I think I lost $7,000 in Kansas City. Probably more than that," Williams says.

A bigger surprise came at his next tour stop.

In Houston, Williams says, he ran into some people he knows who actually do work for *The Source*. They told him that the people he was working for weren't affiliated with the magazine. Rather, they were with a St. Louis company called Fyreboy Records.

Williams says it was embarrassing for him because he was the one who would be blamed for any miscommunication, given that his number was on the flier. He felt misled.

Fyreboy Records owner Willie Spratt tells *The Pitch* that his company ran *The Source*'s contest for the magazine as a marketing strategy. "I have a contract with them. It states there would be no money exchanged between my company and *The Source* but that this was to be a straight marketing venture between us and *The Source* for us to find artists for them to feature in their magazine."

Spratt acknowledges that Fyreboy collected money from small promoters like Williams, who in turn paid for the privilege of promoting the shows and collecting money from audiences and contestants.

"I think I paid them a total of $16,000 alone," Williams says. "And they did about 30 cities."

It seems that everyone involved with the Unsigned Hype contest, from the contestants to the judges, paid money to make money.

Ché Johnson is the executive vice president of brand development at *The Source*. In an e-mail, he told *The Pitch*, "I am able to let you know that technically FryeBoy [*sic*] was allowed to execute events in conjunction with *The Source*. They operated completely independently however and I have heard of countless issues and problems with the execution. Of course I am the last person that they would let know what transpired as I opted not to get involved with their promotion because I foresaw problems in execution that would potentially damage *The Source*'s already tarnished name and reputation."

Williams says he ended his involvement with the tour that night in Houston. "I lost $3,000 because I couldn't get my money back. But I didn't want to take advantage of people."

Spratt says his company tried to be upfront about the terms of the contest.

Meanwhile, Fyreboy Records' CDs were on sale at every stop on *The Source* contest circuit, and the label's artists performed live each night. "They got their record label's name out there," Williams says. "It was a good hustle."

On the upside, the KC leg of the contest tour made Williams a fan of Cash Image. Now, Williams says, "I listen to his CD all the time."

Ann Powers

IT'S TIME TO KICK THIS ADDICTION

Blackout, the new album from Britney Spears, is as intoxicating as a snort of high-grade white powder. Like that nightclub indulgence, it's an expensive ride, crafted by a team of top producers exploring the outer reaches of cybernetic pop. Its dazzling studio effects, rhythmic reconstructions and vocal shape-shifting drag the listener in, as each song elaborates on the power of desire and desirability. It's hard to resist.

But maybe it's time to start just saying no.

Since it leaked online a few weeks ago, *Blackout* has been receiving buzzy attention. A few reviewers have trashed it, but most have called it a comeback. Spears's musical presence on the album may be minimal (dance-pop notables, including Keri Hilson, Europop darling Robyn and L.A.'s own Nicole Morier shore up her vocals throughout, and Spears has just two deeply buried writing credits), and her public behavior remains cause for concern, but apparently that doesn't matter. The music's fun, the beats are fresh, and the Spears that *Blackout* promotes isn't a person anyway but a publicly traded fantasy. Cynicism clearly outweighs compassion when it comes to poor, sad Brit.

The public agrees that Spears is a product worth purchasing. *Blackout*, which was released Tuesday, is expected to chart at No. 1 next week, moving about two-thirds of the 527,000 units Carrie Underwood did the week before. This even though, beyond a sleepy and rather sad phone-in appearance on Ryan Seacrest's KIIS-FM radio show Wednesday, Spears isn't promoting the release. Maybe she's too caught up in the loss of her kids in a custody battle; maybe (even this seems possible with her) she really doesn't like *Blackout* all that much.

After all, it's not really her album, is it? It's one thing to recognize the fluid collaborative process that has made for great music since the days of disco, and jazz before that. It's another to blithely dismiss the importance of the figure who carries that music forth into the world. Spears is listed as executive producer of *Blackout*, and the *Wall Street Journal* reported that it earned her a nearly $4 million advance. So the idea of Britney it presents must have some relation to her own idea of herself.

At any rate, there are three Britneys now. There's the tragic celebrity going through a public breakdown, who seems to have little command over her own actions and less over how others treat her, including the public that's circling and scorning her. Then there's the Britney created by Spears and many others over the course of a decade, an embodiment of the feminine libido in an age when empowerment and exploitation are often confused. Finally, there's the Britney the public imagines, a repository for our fears about what today's tough little girls might become and our disgust and fascination with the fame machine.

Blackout is an attempt by Spears and her latest crew of in-studio plastic surgeons to reconcile those three Britneys. But as seductive as the music is, it fails. Instead of reconciling the fantasy Britney with the one who breathes, these songs push aside her pain and defeat and substitute an almost militant wantonness. In the process, they abandon what made the invented Britney so appealing: her stance on the knife's edge between virtue and corruption, the innocence of a girl brash enough to declare "I'm not that innocent."

As the living, breathing Spears continues to crash downward in plain view, few seem troubled by the disconnect between the success of this album and the sorry state of its nominal maker. Even more disturbing, no one seems to care that the songs on *Blackout* uphold the very attitudes about femininity, sexual power, and the blur between reality and television-tabloid "reality" that have dragged Spears into misery—and those of us enthralled by her into a state of callousness and cynicism.

Let's assume that Spears still wants to connect to the spirit of sexual liberation that took shape in the 1970s and went pop mostly through Madonna's efforts in the 1980s. *Blackout* contains some direct Madonna references. The CD booklet photo showing Spears sitting on a priest's lap, which has outraged the Catholic League, is an obvious nod. More generally, the album's mix of avant-garde dance music and libertine lyrics echoes controversial landmarks such as "Justify My Love" and "Erotica," which blended explorations of explicit subject matter with cutting-edge dance beats.

But Madonna's libertinism was always tied to a community—an underground of self-identified queers and other sexual outlaws who saw erotic freedom as part of a larger movement toward gay and women's liberation. In comparison, the mood of *Blackout* is oppressively retrograde.

Enlisting her signature panting coo, Spears presents herself (or is presented by the songwriters representing her) as a girl gone wild, driven incoherent by desire. "What I gotta do to get you to want my body?" this mother of two implores on "Get Naked." The song is subtitled "I Got a Plan"—but the voice that claims that plan belongs to a man, background singer Corte Ellis, not Spears. Spears plans nothing. She occupies the centuries-old stereotype of the woman in heat, unable to control her sexuality, finding relief only when a man takes her in hand.

The other message *Blackout* strongly conveys is that notoriety is its own reward. In "Piece of Me," the song most often cited as proof that Spears possesses some level of self-awareness (though she didn't write it), Spears responds to being surveilled by the tabloids by listing the violations for which they cited her: She's too fat, too thin, a grocery-store flasher and working mama who trots her kids around to her photo shoots. Most of all, she's "shameless," a word that has sounded truly defiant in the mouths of Garth Brooks and Ani DiFranco but that, dully voiced by Spears, becomes a condemnation she's willing to embrace.

This list of sins is made musical within a choppy, mechanical setting that reinforces the aggressive petulance of the vocals. The title phrase suggests a threat without following through. A few songs later, "Freakshow," which Spears did co-write, presents Team Britney's solution to the quandary of constant surveillance: "Make them clap when we perform."

In this scenario, a woman who's been branded as overly sexual can respond only by becoming truly pornographic. It's the culmination of the self-objectifying process that reality television and the fever for celebrity promotes, in which any kind of interior life, including both sexuality and artistic creativity, gets flattened out and transformed into an empty commodity.

If these songs represent Britney talking back, her response is disturbingly adolescent and predictable, with none of the redeeming emotion and individuality of other celebrity answer songs, like "Get in the Ring" by Guns N' Roses or "Leave Me Along" by Michael Jackson. W. Axl Rose wanted his enemies bloody; Jackson wanted to escape to Neverland. Britney doesn't want to fight or retreat. Her solution to being exploited is only to exploit herself further.

But lyrics don't matter in dance music, right? Real meaning resides in the way its rhythms move the body and its inventive sonic twists expand the mind. If words are present, though, they communicate. Think about the dance songs you love most: They're built around ritual incantations that express freedom, sorrow, pride, or communal connection: "I Feel Love," "I Will Survive," "I've Got the Power," "Groove Is in the Heart." Even chilly Madonna built a utopian vision of the dance floor as a free space in songs such as "Vogue," in which striking a pose becomes a means to self-realization.

There's no self-realization on *Blackout*, nor is there celebration. There's only addiction—to sex, to powerful men, to exhibitionism. If this is how Spears wants to be perceived, she's even more troubled than the tabloids tell. If it's what those entrusted with her best interests think is most enticing—and if the marketplace proves them right—then we're all hooked on some pretty nasty stuff. I wonder, will we ever be able to kick it?

Niki D'Andrea

BAD HABITS

NunZilla's Punk-Rock Catechism
Will Leave You Praying for More

On a cool, clear Friday night in early February, about a hundred people
are packed into the Casa Blanca Lounge on Van Buren Street in downtown Phoenix. Many of them have come for "communion" with local
punk/thrash quartet NunZilla. But the "nuns" here aren't anything like
the ones who rapped your knuckles with rulers in Catholic school, and
this communion is more like an anarchistic tent revival.

Onstage, the female members of NunZilla wear nun's habits, while
the drummer (the group's only male) rocks out in a priest's frock. A
video projector displays a collage of cartoonish nun art on the wall behind them, complete with images of nuns leveling cities with laser
beams that shoot from their eyes and sexy nuns in red miniskirts holding machine guns.

The band's "mascots"—three large, blow-up Godzilla dolls—are being
molested by the crowd. People hump them, dance with them, kick them,
punch them, put clothes on them, ride them, beat each other over the
heads with them, put them together in lewd positions, throw them on the
stage. It's like some warped version of Disneyland for drunken adults.

While the nuns are screaming red-faced through one of their many
two-minute tunes, like "Eat Shit and Die," the smoke machine onstage

103

goes out of control, blasting out a thick, white cloud that quickly consumes the band until all the audience can see are green and blue stage lights glowing somewhere in the fog and the occasional blow-up dinosaur flying back out into the fray.

The show is interactive, with drunken audience members jumping up onstage, knocking over band members' beers and mic stands, and falling over the amplifiers. There's a "pit" in front of the stage, but the mood is more goofy than violent—everybody's just dancing around, and nobody pushes, punches, or elbows anybody else. The "slams" are more like gentle nudges, and when somebody slips on some spilled beer, two guys help him up. Before bopping him over the head with a giant blow-up Godzilla doll.

NunZilla is loud, fast, and probably too obnoxious for the mainstream. It's highly unlikely that it'll be Phoenix's next "breakthrough" band, but that's not its goal. This is all about *fun*, about blowing up the theater of the absurd into a lowbrow three-ring circus, whether the nuns are wearing creepy clear-plastic bank robber masks or standing on 10-foot-tall boxes in extra-long robes to appear as though they're levitating near the ceiling.

The congregation flocks to NunZilla for the crazy experience and to have a good time. The band's built a following on the strength of its smoke-and-mirrors live shows (and its MySpace page), leaving many fans wondering when the first NunZilla record—completed in February—will be released. The band says that'll happen in the next month or so. In the meantime, they're tending to their surprisingly regular lives and ordinary day jobs, and gearing up for their performance at the "Zombie Ball" in Tempe, a music and fetish event slated to take place the day before Easter in honor of "Zombie Jesus" rising from the dead.

The members of NunZilla swear they aren't out to be blatantly blasphemous. But two of the four members do have backgrounds in Catholicism, something that seeps into their stories—and their attitudes—about being in a band that makes the Catholic clergy look like a bunch of cartoon characters.

"We can have a gimmick, and that's what we have, but it's only intentional in the sense that we thought it was funny," says NunZilla's Sister Kenyattasaurus Rex. "But it's one thing to have a gimmick and totally suck. And me, personally, I don't think we suck. I thought we could back up our gimmick."

"It was the idea of the theatrics and the stage show, shit that you don't see around that makes *us* laugh," she continues. "And if everybody else is laughing, great, but it doesn't matter. It doesn't matter."

"We're just having fun," adds bandmate Sister T-Raptor. "What else are we going to do? Sit home and watch TV?"

The members of NunZilla—Sister Kenyattasaurus Rex (vocals, bass), Sister T-Raptor (guitar, bass), Sister Taryndactyl (lead guitar), and Father Stone (vocals, drums)—are characters, and they have a lot of fun being in character, too.

"There comes a time in every person's life when god calls upon them to ritualistically remove their own liver," Sister T-Raptor wrote on Nun-Zilla's MySpace blog (www.myspace.com/nunzillacomes). "Let it be known that while my body lies here in Applebee's bathroom full of riblettes and those little cheese thingies, but empty of a liver; the rest of me is in a better place and surrounded by the spirit of the lord . . . P.S. You fucking cremate me and I'm going poltergeist on your ass."

Nunzilla's MySpace profile boasts more than 1,300 friends and 11,000 profile views, thanks largely to a calculated bum rush of comments the band left on other people's MySpace pages, saying things like "Say your prayers! NunZilla comes!"

But you can't always be in character, right? Well, when the members of NunZilla show up at Monroe's downtown on a Thursday night to just drink, eat, and gab (they're not playing or anything), they're all in their costumes. Three nuns and a priest, drinking beer and whiskey in a basement bar, singing impromptu backup baritone vocals for Brian Blush (formerly of The Refreshments), who's performing "Folsom Prison Blues" by the bar. How on Earth does something like this start, anyway?

Oh, with some ducks. Before they were Father Stone, Kenyattasaurus Rex, and Taryndactyl, they were Jason Stone, Kenyatta Turner (formerly Shircliff), and Taryn Moore, and they were neighbors, living across the street from Encanto Park in the spring of 2005. And one day, they lugged bongos and a banjo across the street and just started jamming down by the water.

"And while we were playing, out of the corner of my eye, I saw these ducks," Jason says. "And I turned to look, and there were all these ducks around us, just looking at us really intently. And we stopped playing, and they all waddled off. So we thought, 'That was weird,' and we started playing again, and they came back. And every time we stopped, they'd leave, and they'd come back when we started playing again and just sit there and listen to us. And I thought, 'Hey, if we can entertain these *ducks*...'"

"And then the sprinklers came on and drenched us and we had to run away," Kenyatta says.

But the seed had been planted. They had to play in a band together. It wasn't that the thought had never occurred to them before—Kenyatta and Taryn had both met Jason at shows around Phoenix in the mid-'90s, and Kenyatta's known Sister T-Raptor (nee Tana Youmans) since 1990. But like many other musicians in Phoenix's incestuous punk rock scene, they were busy with multiple band projects. Jason's drummed for Beelze Bullies and The Mongoloids for years, Tana's the bass player for Asses of Evil, and Kenyatta and Taryn are both in The Dropouts.

Their extemporaneous sprinkler symphony for the ducks at Encanto helped them realize the musical chemistry they had, and there were more practice sessions in the park. "It would always be too late, and we weren't supposed to be there," Kenyatta says. "So we'd be looking out for the cops, and we had beer, ready to run back across the street."

"Our Encanto Park sessions were fantastic," Tana says.

"Finally, we were like, 'We could move [practices] into our house if we wanted,'" Taryn says with a laugh. "Like, 'Okay, let's plug in!'"

There were some jokes about becoming a Heart tribute band (Tana really is a ringer for Ann Wilson), but a plastic toy put them on the right trajectory.

The "Nunzilla" toy, a 3-inch-tall wind-up doll manufactured by Archie McPhee Toys, has light-up, Kryptonite-green eyes and spits sparks when she waddles. She is to thank for Phoenix's NunZilla. When the band was still in its infancy, the members found themselves at Hidden House off Osborn Road, playing with this wind-up nun to everyone's amusement. Somebody suggested they call themselves

NunZilla, they found nun's habits at Easley's Costume Shop, launched the NunZilla MySpace page in August '05, and that was it.

Well, okay, that wasn't really it—blow-up Godzillas, nun collage films, "levitating nun" stunts, and fog machines followed.

"Everything we do, we do for our own amusement," Kenyatta says. "If other people are amused, great."

And if some people are offended?

"We do not expect anybody to take us seriously," Kenyatta says. "If somebody's offended, then please, listen to something else. Watch something else."

Besides, as Tana points out, how much reverence should you offer the Catholic Church when "We live in a city where a bishop [Bishop O'Brien] ran over a man, killed him, and tried to get away with it?" (O'Brien was convicted in 2004 and resigned from his position but never served jail time, being sentenced to probation and community service instead.)

And it's not as if NunZilla is inventing a new, irreverent "pop culture nun" trend anyway. Just last year, UC Davis professor Frances Dolan toured universities delivering a lecture titled "Why Are Nuns Funny?" which focused on the image of nuns as humorous, absurd figures as far back as the 16th and 17th centuries. And ever since Sister Luc Gabriel (a real nun) cut a record as The Singing Nun in 1963, pseudo-sisters have been everywhere, from TV (*The Flying Nun*, *Brides of Christ*) to the stage (*Nunsense*, *Late Night Catechism*) to the big screen (everything from European "nunsploitation" films of the '70s like *Killer Nun* to modern musicals like *Sister Act*) to a 2005 Kabbalah party to celebrate the Jewish holiday of Purim, where the ever-controversial Madonna dressed as a nun.

The whole NunZilla thing started as a joke, and it still is. Of course, not everyone finds it funny. "You wouldn't believe what I had to go through to get this shirt," Jason says, pulling on his priest's frock. "I went to an actual Catholic church supply store, and the guy working there was real quiet and speaking in that hushed Catholic voice, asking me all these questions, like 'What church are you with?' And I told him I wasn't with any church, I just wanted a shirt. And so I got the shirt, and I swear to God, when I went to pay for it, he wouldn't take the money from me. So I set the money down on the counter, and he picked up each bill slowly, and he'd punch a button on the register, and take this really long pause before punching the next button, like he was wrestling with his conscience.

"But you know what's really weird? I went into the convenience store that's in the *same building* as the church supply place right afterwards, and I was feeling all creepy about the shirt-thing, and there [were] all these display cases with stuff like crack pipes and bongs and cock rings."

Then there was that photo shoot with the Arizona Derby Dames' Schoolyard Scrappers team in late February, when NunZilla showed up to pose with the team at photog Andy Hartmark's suggestion and almost caused a brawl. According to the band, one of the roller girls refused to pose with Jason dressed as a priest, saying she felt it was sacrilegious. The team captain insisted, and a heated argument ensued. "I thought we were gonna see a fight," Kenyatta says.

In the end, everyone calmed down and agreed that posing with Nun-Zilla should be optional. A few of the derby dames opted out.

"I felt kind of bad," Tana says. "We don't think anything of it. We're just having fun, and it kind of came to fruition there that somebody might have a problem with it."

"I didn't feel bad about shit," Kenyatta says. "I don't know why she was so upset when she was dressed up like a Catholic school girl with her boobs hanging out."

"I told her, 'It's only a shirt,'" Jason says. "I'm drinking a 40 [ounce] the whole time we're taking the fucking pictures."

Tana has another theory for Jason. "It could have been that cucumber wrapped in tin foil that you had in your pants, sweetie."

The members look at it this way: If the Virgin Mary can appear on a tortilla and Jesus can appear in a tree in New Mexico, then why can't four Phoenix punks wear clergy costumes and scream out silly songs about eating souls?

NunZilla's first show, on December 31, 2005, at the Cypress Lounge, should have been an omen.

"I've got a scar on my head from the first show we ever played," Jason says. "I hit myself in the eyeball just about as hard as you could fuckin' hit yourself in the eyeball. The drumstick came back and I closed my eyeball, and it was like, Wham! Just super-hard, like where you hear noise in your head. I thought I'd yolked my eye."

So Jason ran to the bathroom after the song, determined that his eye was okay (even though it was all watery and red and "hazy and out of focus") and got back onstage to finish NunZilla's set. The real carnage was about to begin.

Jason had cracked a cymbal before the show, but he'd talked Nick (a.k.a. "Sludgegutts"), drummer for local band Dephinger, into letting him borrow his brand new, expensive cymbal. During NunZilla's last song, two of Jason's old friends in the crowd took a rolling chair and did a high-speed launch into his drum set, knocking over Sludgegutts' cymbal and cracking it.

Kenyatta recalls the moment it all came crashing down. "[Jason] leapt over his drum set and caught his friend in midair and took him down."

"I freaked the fuck out," Jason says. "I dove head-first at my friend I've known since I was 12, and I had to kick his fucking ass. But I couldn't hit him in the face, so I was jumping up as hard as I could and landing with my ass and elbow on his head. It was pretty violent. So I'm kicking his ass, and there's broken glass everywhere, and I put my hand in this broken bottle. And when we finally stopped, there was blood spurting out of my hand."

Jason was the first person admitted into the emergency room at Thunderbird Hospital on New Year's Day 2006.

"That was a great show," Kenyatta says. "Fabulous first show."

Then there was the time NunZilla played during a hockey game intermission at Castle Megasports, right out on the ice, and kept sliding all over the place in front of a bunch of baffled kids. And the show in Las Vegas, when Jason wore his priest's shirt through a casino, carrying three beers and two shrimp cocktails, much to the chagrin of casino security, who followed him and tried (unsuccessfully) to grab him for questioning. "I totally dodged them and ducked behind some slot machines," Jason recalls.

And of course, there are always the blow-up Godzillas.

"The best is when you can kick the dinosaur and hit the guy right up front in the crotch," Tana says. "Like the power kick! After one show, this one guy came up and was like, 'I couldn't believe it, I was just standing there and then I got kicked in the crotch with this dinosaur! I love you guys!' He was so happy it happened to him."

"You can get a lot of momentum with those things, if you're standing close enough," Kenyatta adds.

And that's what NunZilla thrives on—the insane aesthetic of the live show. "Visuals, it's all about the visuals," Kenyatta says. "Give 'em something to watch."

It's about flexibility, too, or maybe just the willingness to be bizarre. "We're like a spaghetti Western," Jason says. "We could do anything in this band. Somebody could play a banjo. I might just tap a cymbal for our next big hit."

"We are weird," Tana says. "We are so weird. We're just a weird bunch of people."

So who are these weird people, anyway? And what are their ties to the Catholic church besides being a punk-rock parody of its clergy?

Well, as deviant and demented as some might deem the band members' music and image, the members of NunZilla lead surprisingly normal lives.

Kenyatta is 32, divorced with no children, has a college degree in computer information systems, and has worked for DeVry University for 13 years, doing everything from career services and counseling to teaching and marketing. She recently bought her first house.

Taryn is 30, single with no kids (but she has a boyfriend), and works for a nonprofit agency that provides supportive services for homeless youth. She also works as a tattoo artist at a friend's private studio.

Tana is 37, married with two children (an 18-year-old son and a 13-year-old daughter), and works in the human resources department of a local staffing firm, handling payroll, benefits, and administration.

Jason is 32, married with a 4-year-old son, and works as operations manager at AM political talk radio station KFNX 1100 (ironically, a conservative station that airs programs like *The O'Reilly Factor* and *The Dr. Laura Show*). He was also recently a coach at the YMCA for a soccer team of 6-year-olds.

Those are the pedestrian stats. The most interesting aspect of the band members' "real" lives, as they pertain to NunZilla, is their religious backgrounds and current beliefs. Jason's background with Catholicism is particularly interesting, as he seems to have crossed paths with every corrupt clergyman in Phoenix.

Jason was raised Catholic, and he says when he was a boy, he was baptized in Mesa by Father Dale Fushek, former Vicar General for the Roman Catholic Diocese of Phoenix, who resigned in 2004 amidst a slew of sexual abuse charges. "Yeah, the main molester guy," Jason recalls. "The blond guy. Honest goddamn truth."

Later, Jason started training to be an altar boy, and spent a couple of hours a day in a creepy monastery. "The monastery is like this dark fucking dungeon, with circular seats and dark wooden walls, and you'd hear shit behind them and we'd be freaking the fuck out," he says. "We were there a couple hours a day and we'd have the whole suit on and stuff, and then we'd put back on our Catholic gear and go out to the playground and shit. It was really fucking weird."

One day, Jason's priest suddenly disappeared without explanation. –Jason found out later that he'd been sent to the Vatican, but by that time, his mom had pulled him out of altar-boy training, uneasy about the priest's mysterious disappearance.

Although he was born into and raised with the Catholic religion, Jason says he's spiritually "searching" right now. But his Catholic past does play a role in his attitude toward NunZilla. "There's a small part of me, with my background and stuff, that likes throwing up my middle finger, sticking the tongue out, and wearing the shirt, just thinking, 'Loosen the fuck up,'" Jason says. "When you get into some deep Roman Catholic shit, it's like this unbelievable, weird-ass shit, cult-fucking-crazy crap.

"I've met Bishop O'Brien—the hit-and-run-cat—several times," Jason continues. "All those priests that I knew, they just need to loosen up. You could look at my life, and any priest's along the way, and I'll probably win. Instead of touching boys, I teach soccer."

Tana was also exposed to the Catholic religion (her mother is still devout), along with other faiths. "My great-grandmother, whom I call Mammy, was deep-rooted in the South, and was staunch Pentecostal— the whole strychnine-drinkin', snake-charmin', speaking-in-tongues-type stuff," Tana says. "And when you're a child and you see stuff like that, it's fascinating and it's scary. Right now, I consider myself a spiritual person. I live by the golden rule. But religion, in general, for me, I don't buy into it. I think it's such a joke."

Initially, Tana's Catholic mother didn't approve of NunZilla, but after seeing the band play live, she presented Tana with her favorite rosary and told her she was proud of her. "It felt really good. For her to do that was a big deal," Tana says.

Taryn wasn't raised in a religious environment and doesn't attend church. "I don't follow organized religion. I believe many truths exist in all religions," she says. "There are many gods, and many great stories, but I've chosen to celebrate life and believe in that."

Kenyatta grew up Baptist, and her mother is now Muslim, but she says she hasn't found a faith that floors her yet. "My mom went to several different churches when we were growing up, and she eventually settled on Muslim, but before that, it was all about Jesus and reading the Bible. And one day, she was like, 'Nope, that's not it. It's this,'" Kenyatta says. "So watching her search for that thing that she needed really opened my eyes to the fact that some people just have something that they need, and they're trying to find the thing they're most comfortable with.

"I have not been looking for that thing," Kenyatta continues. "If it truly, really exists, when it hits me, I feel I won't be able to deny it. Because if it's really there and it's really the way some people describe it, I won't have a choice. For me, that hasn't happened yet. I don't think I'm fighting anything; it just hasn't *gripped* me the way some people seem to be gripped. So I'm not gonna make something grip me because somebody says I should, or because my family is or my friends are."

At this point in the conversation, Tana has a suggestion: "Let's just start our own church."

On a Saturday night in late February, NunZilla is sneaking into a certain studio/rehearsal space on the west side for what they call "guerrilla practice." They're really not supposed to be there, but they're cool with some people who actually pay to rent a rehearsal room in the building, which sits inconspicuously at the dark end of a street, amid construction workers' lights and industrial buildings.

NunZilla "borrows" the space to practice whenever they can. The deal is that they can use the renters' access codes, space, and PA system, provided they don't break anything, and they leave some beer in the minifridge.

The band brings plenty of beer. Most of the rehearsal is spent drinking, laughing, talking, and teasing each other. The vibe is more like a spontaneous jam among old friends than a serious, studious, buckledown vibe. There's tons of giggling and no bickering. "We're all great friends," Kenyatta says. "It's awesome. We don't get together because we have to, we get together because we want to."

"There's no fights or drama," Tana adds. "It's just like, whatever. Very easygoing."

The band's easygoing attitude is reflected in their "songwriting process" as well, which is not really a process at all, but again, more of a jam. "Someone will come up with a riff, we lay the riff down, and layers progress from there," Tana says, before pointing at Taryn. "*You* whip shit out of your ass all the time."

Speaking of which . . .

"Hey, I've got a new riff," Taryn announces, strumming it out on her guitar.

Kenyatta stands in front of Taryn with her bass and listens, then begins figuring out and mimicking the chords. Then Jason starts thumping out a bass drum rhythm behind her. This is how all NunZilla songs were born, right down to improvised lyrics that nobody bothered to write down until it was time to record their debut album, which the band recently completed.

"We recorded at one of the most awesomest studios in Phoenix, Full Well," Tana says.

NunZilla cut the record with local producer Mike Bollenbach (The New Romantics, The Impossible Ones), who was so taken with the band that he wanted to have a dinosaur stage name, too. So now he's "Bollbasaur."

"This [recording experience] was just glorious," Jason says. "Mike was all energetic and crazy and just rockin' out."

The band plans to self-release its 11-song CD, titled *Killing Faith*, in April or May, as soon as the mastering's finished. "We're very proud of our work," Tana says of the album. "We did [it in] six days. Six long days, but we did it. We're happy with it."

As for the band's plans after they release the album, they have no grand delusions about being a Top 40 act or playing arenas. "I'd just like to point out, first of all, that we're dressed as three nuns and a priest, and we write ridiculous songs that are really loud and fast," Jason says.

"Plans?" Tana asks. "Well, we're gonna keep living life. And, uh, if someone would like to donate a van to help us haul our stuff, we'd love that."

They've been talking about shooting their first video with Andy Hartmark (probably for their theme song, "NunZilla") and plan to play more shows in Phoenix, Flagstaff, and "maybe L.A."

But their greatest desire is their simplest. "We want the CD to help spread the gospel," Kenyatta says.

And as NunZilla fans know, there's nothing like the gospel of a Godzilla to the groin.

J. Bennett

DIMMU BORGIR

Thanks to bands like Dimmu Borgir, black metal has bridged the once-frozen divide between underground obscurity and mainstream acceptance. But has it crossed to the other side intact? *Decibel* travels to Norway and investigates.

Norway is surely many things to many people, but to black metal enthusiasts it is nothing less than the one true Unholy Land. The anti-Bethlehem, if you will [or even if you won't]: a latter-day Bikini Atoll. Standing in the hills of Holmenkollen in February, overlooking Oslo, one sees snow in almost every direction. The Oslofjord, former home and painting subject of Edvard Munch, spreads its frozen tendrils to the south. The towering Holmenkollen ski jump, which dates back to 1892, looms in the distance. Further on, another, more pertinent landmark appears: Holmenkollen Chapel, which was famously burned to the ground in 1992 by three of the most notorious figures in black metal: Burzum mastermind Varg Vikernes, Mayhem guitarist Øystein "Euronymous" Aarseth—who was later murdered by Vikernes—and Emperor drummer Bård "Faust" Eithun, who had himself killed a man just two nights before the arson. Restored in 1996 through the pecuniary goodwill of Norway's Princess Astrid and a handful of other well-to-do philanthropists, the chapel stands as a reminder, for some, of not so much the fire that blackened its hide and razed its rafters, but of a different blaze—the one In The Northern Sky, as it were—that ignited a small but decidedly global musical revolution.

Having cut a swath across Scandinavia, England, mainland Europe and eventually North America, the results of that conflagration are now hosting a banquet at the Holmenkollen Park Hotel. Thirty journalists from all over the world have converged upon this site to hear *In Sorte Diaboli*, the seventh and latest album from symphonic black metal sorcerers Dimmu Borgir. All six of the band's members are in attendance, *sans* corpsepaint: vocalist Stian Thoresen (a.k.a. Shagrath, also of Chrome Division), guitarist Sven Atle Kopperud (a.k.a. Silenoz), bassist Simen Hestnæs (a.k.a. ICS Vortex, also of Arcturus), guitarist Thomas Rune Andersen (a.k.a. Galder, also of Old Man's Child), keyboardist Øyvind Mustaparta (a.k.a. Mustis) and drummer Jan Axel Blomberg (a.k.a. Hellhammer, also of Mayhem), as are various representatives from the band's label and management, Ulver mastermind Kristoffer "Garm" Rygg and famous Norwegian cartoonist Lise Myhre. After a three-course meal accompanied by the merciless consumption of untold quantities of Norwegian *øll*, the party moves upstairs, where the bar remains open until the last glass is emptied. If the prevailing image of black metal is a couple of dudes dressed up in spikes and corpsepaint posing for a black-and-white picture by torchlight in two feet of snow, this is about as black metal as a dinner party at an Aspen ski lodge.

And therein lies black metal's dichotomy: While Varg Vikernes scrawls pornographic images of big-dicked hobbits on the walls of his Tromsø jail cell, penning screeds denouncing *Lords of Chaos* authors Michael Moynihan and Didrik Søderlind and biding his time until the next installment of the *Lord of the Rings* trilogy is screened in the prison day room, the genre he helped create has, like many genres before it, split into at least two distinct factions: the mainstream and the underground. On the mainstream side, bands like Dimmu Borgir, Cradle of Filth and (to a slightly lesser extent) Satyricon sit like corpsepainted kings, lording over a modest musical empire complete with major label record deals (Cradle and Satyricon), slots on Ozzfest

(Dimmu and Cradle; Satyricon actually turned Sharon down last year) and hundreds of thousands of records sold. On the other side: just about everyone else. There are those with higher profiles than others, of course—Enslaved, Emperor, Mayhem, Darkthrone, Immortal—but even these world-class sons of northern darkness haven't achieved the kind of semi-ubiquitous Hot Topic status that Dimmu Borgir and (especially) Cradle seem to enjoy amongst the great unwashed. More to the point, perhaps, is the widespread perception amongst black metal enthusiasts that Dimmu and Cradle are somehow manipulating black metal for commercial purposes—or are even no longer "true" black metal musicians at all.

Which is pretty much where tonight's feature presentation begins.

ENTER THE DEATH CULT

To date, Dimmu Borgir's 2003 album, *Death Cult Armageddon*, has sold over 111,000 copies in the US. Its successor, *Stormblåst MMV*, a re-recorded version of their 1996 album of the same name (minus the MMV), has sold 31,000 units. Which is why the release of *In Sorte Diaboli* is such a big fucking deal; with the ridiculous tab Nuclear Blast is presumably footing—wining, dining, flying in and putting up 30 journalists from all corners of the earth—expectations are clearly high. And the marketing dominoes have already begun to fall: The band recently shot a *Braveheart*-style video for the album's first single, "The Serpentine Offering"; a three-track iTunes single (including two non-album tracks) was made available three weeks prior to the album's official release, and a five-week North American tour (with Unearth, DevilDriver and Kataklysm) will be underway by the time this article hits the stands.

This kind of full-bore, tits-out marketing scheme is a far cry from the decidedly underground dissemination of Dimmu Borgir's mud 'n' treble 1994 debut, *For All Tid*, which was released like an errant fart via No Colours Records, the German home to some of Nazi black metal's heaviest hitters—Graveland, Nokturnal Mortem, etc. Silenoz and Shagrath are the only members of Dimmu Borgir who remain from that era. "If you listen to the first album and the new one, it sounds like two different bands today, and that's a good thing," says Shagrath, sitting in one of the Holmenkollen's many dark-wood dining halls. "We have black metal ingredients and concepts, and what we stand for is kind of black metal-oriented, but I think we have gone beyond that term. It's still extreme music and can be related to as black metal in many ways, but it's much more than just black metal."

Of course, public perception of Dimmu Borgir has changed just as much as the band itself, and their transformation from vaguely grim underground notables to slick symphonic superpower has been a slow but steady process. "We're not a pure black metal band," Shagrath admits. "We never have been. There have always been a lot of people saying bad things about us: We're sellouts, *blah blah blah*. It was never our intention to be a pure black metal band anyway. That's probably also the reason why a lot of people can actually find something they like in our music: It's varied. It's extreme, but you can find a lot of elements that you cannot find in other extreme music. That's probably why we have more followers than many other bands. So maybe there's jealousy from small bands that say Dimmu are sellouts, but we never paid attention to those people. We've always done our own thing and gone our own way."

Shagrath's statements ring true with Nachtmystium vocalist/guitarist and Battle Kommand Records founder Blake Judd, a.k.a. Azentrius, a keen observer of and active participant in underground black metal culture. When *Decibel* calls him, Nachtmystium are in a van somewhere in the Midwest on tour with Norway's 1349. "Ironically enough, before you called me we just finished listening to [Dimmu Borgir's 1997 album] *Enthrone Darkness Triumphant*, so I obviously don't hate them," he says with a laugh. "I'm not really into their newer stuff, but I wouldn't call them sellouts—it's just that their shit happens to be trendy right now."

Still, Judd points out that neither Dimmu Borgir nor their mainstream black metal counterparts from the British Isles are regarded as black metal in underground circles. "I think both Dimmu and Cradle are great metal bands, but I don't even really consider them black metal anymore because there's nothing really intimidating or provocative about their music to anyone over the age of 16 to 18 years old," he says. "I think that's the main reason why you see the separation of the underground people: Things have to get more extreme. People are always looking for the next extreme mindset or next extreme approach to music. So it doesn't really surprise me that you could probably talk to 10 dudes in corpsepaint and probably not one of them would own a Dimmu Borgir record."

Erik Danielsson, a.k.a. E., vocalist/bassist for cult Swedish black metal horde Watain, sees the dichotomy between underground and mainstream black metal as a matter of bastardization: "I think black metal is to be defined by whomever, unfortunately," he says over the phone from Madrid, the latest stop on Watain's tour with Celtic Frost and Kreator. "Black metal, no matter what we would like it to be, is a rebellious subculture based upon music. It started out good, and it went very wrong. There is a stem that I can still relate to with a lot of branches that I cannot relate to."

THE PRINCIPLE OF EVIL MADE CASH

Back in the States, Dimmu Borgir guitarists Galder and Silenoz are being chauffeured around Los Angeles by their manager in a rented PT Cruiser ("At least it's black," Galder laughs). Upon their arrival at Nuclear Blast headquarters in Hawthorne, they seem well aware of the fact that Dimmu Borgir has little-to-no "true black metal" status amongst the self-nominated underground elite. "People say Dimmu is not real black metal, but once the topic of black metal comes up, they always mention us," Silenoz points out. "We're born-again anti-Christians— I guess you could say it that way. We still have a traditional black metal riffing style, but we have evolved it around our own expression. We're on a totally different level musically and in mentality than what's considered old school black metal. I mean, that's the type of black metal I prefer to listen to, but it would be boring to play."

"There will be some people who won't like the new album," Galder adds, "but if you turned it around and *For All Tid* was our new album, you'd get a totally different reaction. You can't please everybody—there are some magazines that *hate* this band. But it's always the same people [who] give us the bad reviews . . ."

"I don't mind that," Silenoz cuts in. "I think it just gives us more pro-motion. And once we've recorded the new album, we're satisfied, you know? Otherwise, we wouldn't give it to the label. Once the label has it, it's out of our hands and out of our control, and people are entitled to think whatever they want. Of course it's great to be liked—don't misun-derstand me—but it's great to be hated, too."

If Dimmu Borgir are hated in underground circles, Cradle of Filth are loathed. According to England's *Metal Hammer*, Cradle are the most successful British metal band since Iron Maiden (2004's *Nymphet-amine* has sold over 147,000 copies, while last year's *Thornography* has already moved 50,000 units). They've been the perennial subjects of self-induced "controversy" (in particular the infamous masturbating-nun/"Jesus Is a Cunt" shirts of the mid '90s and the band's decision to wear "I Love Satan" shirts to the Vatican) and near-constant derision.

"I look at a kid in a Cradle of Filth shirt the same way as I look at a kid in an Insane Clown Posse shirt," says Judd, "And I worked in a Hot Topic when I was 16, so I know what I'm talking about to a certain ex-tent. Cradle of Filth have taken marketing to a whole different level. They've always been on an offensive-imagery merch[andising] cam-paign—they know how to market shock value. I think of them the same way I think of Marilyn Manson, who to a certain degree I have a ton of respect for. He captured the minds of 14- to 17-year-old kids through-out the late '90s and made a fucking mint off it."

Danielsson of Watain also has some choice words about the differ-ences between his own band and Cradle of Filth. "While I see us all as musicians, the main difference between Watain and the members of Cradle of Filth—even though I do not know them personally—is that they make their art out of taking pieces of what other people have done before because they know it has been successful. They know that people are a bit fascinated by darkness—they know what the kids want, so to speak. They know that horror sells, and that's how far their ideology goes. We, on the other hand, are the artists that make the art that they are inspired by. What they do as businessmen, we do because our lives are based upon horror and darkness. What we do is take a knife, open a square around our hearts, take the heart out, put the microphone to the heart and let it speak."

Calling England, anyone?

Unsurprisingly, Cradle of Filth ringleader Dani Filth has heard all this before, if not in person from disgruntled "fans" or quoted from the pages of magazines, than certainly on every Cradle of Filth–related message board discussion that hasn't taken place on the band's own forum. And even then . . . well, who knows? "I think we're really too busy now to worry about what other people think," Filth says dismissively. "But it doesn't bother us, because when we were 'true underground black metal'—our first demo and the first Darkthrone album came out at the same time—these people weren't even a glint in the eye of the milkman. Why would you have a 16-year-old rant at you, 'Oh, you're not true black metal.' Well, you were a fetus when we were making our demo, mate."

While neither Danielsson nor Judd were fetuses in 1990, Filth's point is taken: The concept of "true black metal" is limiting and exclusionary at best; ridiculous at worst. "I think there's only one true black metal fan, and he lives on the edge of a cold lake on a cold mountain in the middle of Norway just moaning to himself," Filth offers. "He's gone insane, because he's been living on the streets of Oslo for so long whilst Dimmu Borgir and Satyricon drive around in flash cars drinking loads of beer."

And what about Satyricon? The Norwegian tag team of Frost (drums) and Satyr (everything else) *did* put out *Volcano* on a major label in 2002, winning a Norwegian Grammy in the process. Satyr declined to be interviewed for this article, but did send us a brief, if predictable, statement. "Despite of our achievements and commercial success, Satyricon have never compromised our music, image or lyrics. We have always firmly stood up for what we believe in and are passionate about. Regardless if people like us or not, most people recognize and respect that kind of attitude in a band. The only obligation we have is to follow the direction our hearts point out. We know no other way and our fans are aware of that."

But let's not confuse motivational assumptions or disdain for shock-tactic marketing with the shunning of fame and fortune. In fact, Danielsson, Judd and Filth are in agreement when it comes to the subject of maximizing one's potential. "In Watain, we have no limits as to how big we want to become," Danielsson admits. "Slayer said it already in '83: Evil has no boundaries. If you have boundaries, you cannot pretend to play Satanic music. We know what we do is strong enough to burn the world. And if we sit with the key to something that can actually change the course of history, why hide in the cellar and release a demo? In the end, frankly speaking, we are not here to play black metal—we are here to fuck the world."

"It's easy to shun success when you're not successful," Judd points out. "If you're true to your heart and you know when you track your shit that you're making something that means something to you, if other people like it that should only make you happy. And if it doesn't, don't make it available. But don't put records out and get upset when people like it. That 'cult' black metal shit—I don't get it, man. Those people don't realize that they're just as much of a herd as people who shop at Hot Topic for Cradle of Filth shirts."

Like Judd, Filth views the elitist attitude of the underground as the antithesis of the Satanic ethos in which black metal is steeped. "People don't have a god-given right to give rules to bands," he seethes. "Music is supposed to be about freedom. 'Do what thou wilt shall be the whole of the law; every man is a star,' *blah blah blah*. The whole thing is about freedom. Satan equals adversity, not being told what to do by a select committee of people saying, 'Ooh, that's not evil enough!' It's like, fuck off. We're supposed to be a *black metal* band."

WHAT WOULD SATAN DO?

When Filth quotes Old Man Crowley, he makes a cogent point about Cradle of Filth's—or any truly or even pseudo-Satanic band's—rise to success. One of the prevailing themes of Crowley's *The Book of the Law*, Church of Satan founder Anton LaVey's *The Satanic Bible*, or even "Ragnar Redbeard's" *Might Is Right* (the 1896 book that inspired LaVey and, possibly, Hitler) is the unfettered facilitation of the will to power and/or success. Whether it's by dispensing with the moral standards of the day, good old-fashioned Social Darwinism, or simply crushing one's enemies, driving them before you and hearing the lamentations of their women, all imply a flagrant and often calculated disregard for The Rules, whatever they might be. Clearly, Satan would approve.

"Satan is limitless, so you must never limit to yourself to the rules of a genre, of a subculture, of a scene or of an underground," says Danielsson. "As soon as you do that, you become just as much of a sheep as Cradle of Filth are to the music industry. You must always be there with a torch in one hand and a knife in the other, ready to strike down everything that is in your way. And that goes for the underground mentality as well. You need to be able to sacrifice everything—even your underground credibility—in order to reach certain goals. We are prepared to sacrifice a lot more than underground credibility to do what we have to do."

Judd echoes Danielsson's sentiments about limits when talking about his own band, Nachtmystium. "We're gonna make music that we like whether one person or a million people buy it," he says. "But if more people get into it, yeah, we're gonna take those steps to ascend to a higher level. I mean, that's what a Satanist would do—fully excel and sit above those around him. Be a king amongst your peers. That's not where I'm coming from, but if you put it together with something that a band like us is doing, that's the real shit, if you ask me."

Ravn, vocalist for acclaimed Norwegian corpsepaint commandos 1349, totally agrees—even if, like Judd, he doesn't necessarily consider himself a Satanist. "If you put rules on black metal, it's not black metal," he says. "Rules are for religious people to follow. Guidelines are one thing—if you have a vision, you can use the guidelines to achieve what you want. But if I'm going to do something, I have to do it for myself. I have to do what I feel I need to do. That might be seen as a Satanic way to think by the Church of Satan's definitions, but I'm not a religious person."

Although he wouldn't call either Dimmu Borgir or Cradle of Filth "true" black metal bands, Ravn recognizes their ability to function as gateway drugs that may eventually lead fans to his own band. "I don't count them as black metal at all, but they do their thing and make a living, and I totally respect that," he says. "But they can have a way of opening up the doors to black metal because people see the corpsepaint and everything, and they might dig into it more. So these bands might also have positive effects as well."

Ravn says 1349 aren't necessarily gunning for the commercial successes of Dimmu or Cradle, but they're not rejecting it, either. "Whatever happens, happens," he offers. "We're not working toward a goal like we want to be as big as any of these bands. That's not the reason we do it. We do it because we have a vision and a feeling that we need to create this art. If people want to listen to it, then good—whether it's one person or 10,000 or 100,000."

Of course, then the question becomes: What makes certain black metal bands commercially successful, and what keeps others underground? The prevailing wisdom points to obvious contributing success factors like melody, clean vocals, slick production and highly financed marketing campaigns, but none of those things account for "true" one-man American black metal units like Xasthur, Leviathan and Draugar, who are happy to stay underground: They don't play live, rarely give interviews and often limit how many copies of their albums are pressed. And that's before you even address the issue of What the Music Sounds Like.

One of the oldest and most respected of the fiercely "true" black metal outfits is undoubtedly Darkthrone. Formed in Norway in 1986, the band hasn't played live in over a decade (despite having released half a dozen studio albums in the same period), gives few interviews and even turned down a Norwegian Alarm Award nomination in 2004. "There is no guidebook for Satanism or black metal 'success,'" Darkthrone drummer/lyricist Gylve Nagell (a.k.a. Fenriz) tells *Decibel*. "We never made any plans. Darkthrone is led by coincidences. Trying to control nature is definitely Christian. But of course, we know our trade." For Fenriz, the elements of black metal success are purely arbitrary, and one only has to peruse heavy metal history for proof. "Motörhead and Venom had underground production [and] sound but became huge," he points out. "Many soft black metal bands with plastic sounds remain unknown. Those in the know are constantly supporting what matters."

When it's suggested that the Cradle/Dimmu axis enjoys little to none of the underground credibility that Darkthrone has maintained for two decades, Fenriz lives up to his reputation as a dude who does not give a flying fuck: "That's their problem," he says. And with that, our interview is over.

THE HELLHAMMER FACTOR

Perhaps no single person straddles the frozen divide between black metal's mainstream and underground factions more prominently or successfully than Jan Axel Blomberg, a.k.a. Hellhammer, who has not only been playing drums in Mayhem for nearly 20 years but who has been Dimmu Borgir's official session drummer since 2005, playing on both the re-recording of *Stormblåst* and *In Sorte Diaboli*. Having spoken only informally in Oslo, we have our first on-the-record talk via telephone. "Of course, Mayhem will never sell 300,000 copies of a record like Dimmu Borgir has," he laughs. "We're lucky if we sell 40,000, but we have a solid fan base. But Dimmu Borgir's success is due to hard work—they've been working harder than most other black metal bands, and they've taken a lot of shit from the so-called 'true' people. They may not sound like Mayhem, but who are these people to decide what is 'true' or not? Dimmu Borgir have been true to their style of music and their lifestyle. That's different than jumping on a bandwagon and claiming to be evil."

Thoughts from our man in England? "People always groan when anything gets too popular," Filth points out. "Now people are moaning at Darkthrone, and I love it. When people accuse Darkthrone of selling out, it's like, where are they gonna go next?"

Incidentally, Filth has this to say about Dimmu Borgir: "I think they're great—always have. Beneath us, they're the next thing along. They always get blamed for copying us, but sometimes that's a bit untrue . . . *sometimes*. But they're a great band in their own right."

Beyond his own aspersions, Filth cites as a source of contention what he feels is a fan-generated beef between Cradle and Dimmu based on the fact that the two bands both previously included blastmaster Nick Barker amongst their ranks: "I think what fueled the fire was the fact that Nicholas was a member of their band, so everybody thought, 'Oh, there must be a bone of contention there,' but that never was the case. I'm sure it's exactly like Guns N' Roses and Mötley Crüe—or Maiden and Ozzy. It's like, 'Go on, you fuckers! Have a fight!' I think people want to see that happen. Maybe it's just because we're the two most popular bands."

Hellhammer's subsequent assumption of Dimmu Borgir's drum throne comes with its own public perception issues. "I'm sure I've ruined Mayhem for some people by joining Dimmu," he jokes. "But then again, I don't care. Of course, Mayhem has always been underground—there is no point denying that. But, honestly, I don't think the commercial success of Dimmu is doing any harm at all for me personally. And I know for sure it doesn't harm Mayhem in any way. I'm sure there are people who think I should only play in Mayhem, but they don't get to decide that."

Besides, those who bemoan Hellhammer's involvement with Dimmu Borgir could find far more questionable material in his lengthy session résumé: This is the man, after all, who played drums on the Kovenant's disco-tastic *S.E.T.I.* album. "That was the worst piece of shit I ever played on," he laughs. "They tried to be commercial and they thought they were going to sell a hell of a lot of records, but it really flopped. *That* was really selling out. We're all friends and that kind of stuff, but when I heard the finished record I just said, 'I'm sorry—I'm out of this shit.'"

In a perfect world, somewhere over the rainbow, as it were—or at least over the phone from Norway—it is the creator who decides what to call his art. "The word 'true' has been destroyed by idiots," Hellhammer says. "The people who claim this are actually putting restrictions on themselves. It's funny for me to read someone claiming, 'this is true black metal' or 'this is *not* true black metal.' I mean, who the hell invented this black metal stuff? It was *we*, you know?"

ERIC PAPE

"WE SING EVERYTHING. WE HAVE NOTHING ELSE"

A polished yellow Hummer with tinted windows coasts over potholes and debris toward an intersection lined with metal-roofed shacks and street-side vendors hawking watches, sunglasses, and sodas. Young men loiter and bicker near ragged beggars and open sewer trenches. Then someone reads the Hummer's license plate and yells out "MM!" a local abbreviation for "Rich Man." As the rest of the crowd looks closer, they realize that a pop star is lounging in the cush backseat. They call out his name, Koffi Olomide, until a window opens. Air conditioning spills out into the blazing heat. "What do you want?" Rich Man says, in a studied, soft baritone.

"*Pognon!*" one kid shouts in French. "Dough."

"Papa!" young men plead from all directions.

"Give us some money," one demands.

Rich Man hands a stack of bills to the guy standing nearest to the window and orders him to share. But when the crowd swells—some wild-eyed with hunger and dehydration, some on crutches, still others scooting along the ground with their useless legs trailing behind—the cash dump seems more like cynical self-defense than guilt-induced compassion. Boys and men push, shove, and even wrestle in the dusty street, as the Hummer emerges from the scrum unscathed.

This is Kinshasa, capital of the Democratic Republic of Congo in the heart of central Africa, where the decadent flaunt their wealth in one of the most devastated nations on earth. As the Congo River runs from the country's heartland to the capital near its western edge, the nation's music also seems to pump from countless diverse regions through the city known as "Kin." The country's artistic wealth may rival its rich diamond and gold deposits, but Kinshasa's culture of corruption, moral decay, and negligible resources have created a music scene that can be best described as Darwinian. It's a place where the average musician survives by writing songs that shout-out rich, powerful patrons—politicians, criminals, or foreign "investors"—who pay a nominal fee for the privilege. An absurd world where even the biggest pop stars feel compelled to offer tributes to regional warlords.

Once the country's anchor, Kinshasa today is the center of international efforts to resuscitate a nation (formerly known as Zaïre) scarred by what has been called Africa's World War, which lasted from 1996 until 2003. The conflict started as a sideshow to the Rwandan genocide of 1994, but it soon became the region's even more deadly main attraction. Starvation, disease, pillaging, and gang rape were common. Precious resources like diamonds, gold, cobalt, oil, and timber helped to draw eight neighboring countries into the fighting; in all, more than 20 armies or rogue fighting forces clashed. Nearly 4 million were killed—with more than a million others displaced—the highest single-war total since World War II.

The hardship drove hundreds of thousands of country dwellers—including thousands of former child soldiers—into the capital. It left Kinshasa's dynamic music scene, which has long been one of the few gateways to a better life, on more perilous ground than ever. But Congolese music, rather than reflect the horror in society, has always danced on the tumult, its dominant sound being soukous, from the French word *secouer*, meaning "to shake."

Soukous is rooted in 1930s Caribbean music, which evolved into African big-band versions of the Cuban rumba—dubbed "lingala" or "congo"—and enjoyed great popularity across the continent in the 1950s and '60s. By the early '70s, the group Zaïko Langa Langa (known as "the Congolese Beatles") pioneered modern soukous, dumping the horn sections and wind instruments and rocking out by emphasizing the snare drum and slick electric guitars. The result was high-energy music that spawned dozens of hits and dance crazes, stretching from big-city Africa to major European capitals. It also launched the careers of many of the 20-strong band's members, most notably world-music legend Papa Wemba.

But by the '90s, artists like Koffi Olomide (a Wemba protégé) and the group Wenge Musica were turning soukous into the raunchy dance music ndombolo, which inspired convulsive booty-shaking across the region and into the Congolese diaspora of Europe and the United States. But while the country's political and economic structure crumbled, the songs still celebrated outrageous wealth (Olomide was seen wearing fur coats in the tropics). And choreographers almost seemed to mock the grim landscape—one dance mimicked walking and hopping through a minefield.

Now, after years of war, and with masses of nobodies desperately clinging to meager hopes of pop star success, you end up with today's surreal, rigidly hierarchical music scene. At the top, stars like Olomide and Wemba, as well as J.B. Mpiana and Werrason, still display expensive cars, scantily clad women, and conspicuous bling in videos and onstage. Papa Wemba and Olomide have international followings and can charge up to $80 per seat for a local concert. (Kinshasa has a large upper class of international aide workers, military officials, politicians, and businessmen, such as diamond traders and their entourages). Popular artists make little money in the Congo from CDs and cassettes, both of which are quickly copied and hawked for a couple of bucks on the streets.

Another class of musicians aspires to such stardom by projecting a second-hand image of wealth and glamour. Fally Ipupa, whose soaring vocals highlight strummed guitar ballads, is a flashy Olomide protégé. Less brazen artists perform in a relatively new style called "other music," which incorporates elements of rap, folk, jazz, and Caribbean music. In one song, "other" musician Jean Goubald sings plaintively and powerfully from the point of view of an adolescent soldier searching for his lost childhood. The rap group Kinshasa Mafia Style (KMS) decry a bribery-driven society. But mostly, it is a scene of disenfranchised musicians who try to mobilize followings in their neighborhoods while hustling for handouts.

Finally, there is the music of the street itself—from the homeless kids singing as they bang sticks on rusty car rims to the local mechanic blasting songs into the wee hours, to the policemen who sing as they run up and down stairs for exercise, to the laborers packed into truck beds who vocalize as they're transported through town. Music is everywhere in Kinshasa. For all but the wealthy, going out at night usually means singing and dancing in a vacant lot, a dirt-floor "bar," or any outdoor space.

"We can't go to the movies or shopping," says Tshala Muana, the hip-shaking "Siren of Soukous," who has largely given up music to work in politics. "Here, it is all music. It is soccer once in a while, but music is every day. We sing village songs or memories or Celine Dion or Michael Jackson. We sing everything. We have nothing else."

Out of all this, miracles do happen. As music fans from Brooklyn to Berlin to the Bay Area recently learned, Kinshasa's scene is still on the cutting edge. In a country that has endured so much, it's not surprising that the songs often deal with death—just not in the way that one might expect. Referred to as "Konono music" (after the group most identified with the style) this sound migrated to Kinshasa about 30 years ago via minstrels from near the Angolan border who believed that their spiritual role was to link the living to the dead. When the soft percussive thumping of their small metallic thumb piano (known as a *likembés*) was overwhelmed by the raucous noise on the outskirts of Kinshasa, they created motley Rube Goldberg-like amplification systems. Old car alternators became microphones that pumped music through colonial-era megaphones. Unable to eliminate feedback and distortion, the musicians integrated it into their sound, adding grooves pounded out on frying pan lids and car parts, under call-and-response chants. The harsh-yet-hypnotic polyrhythmic music, released in the west via two collections called *Congotronics 1* and *2*, caught on in dance clubs and have sold tens of thousands of copies in Europe and the

United States, inspiring Konono No. 1's international tour last fall. It's such a success story that it inspires a million dreams—and delusions—back in Kinshasa.

I meet Jean-Rene Mbungo in October 2006 when he asks me for bus fare home. He is clad in a black Marithé Francois Girbaud long-sleeve T-shirt, cuffed blue jeans, a designer watch, and a white hat that looks like it was made for a flamboyant fisherman. In one ear, JR, as he is known, wears a diamond ring and his right wrist is bound by a black leather Dolce & Gabbana bracelet with silver studs.

"It is real," he says firmly. This 23-year-old is so casually chic and utterly metrosexual he looks as if he could have been leaving Joe's Pub in Manhattan after a soul gig. Instead, he's attending a political rally for interim president and candidate Joseph Kabila (who was installed in power after his father, President Laurent Kabila, was murdered by a bodyguard in 2003). "You never know what they'll give out," JR says. It could be T-shirts, food, or even money, as JR well knows from his visits to several rallies for Kabila's opponent, Jean-Pierre Bemba.

"When you have $10, that's a lot," Papa Wemba, who opened up for Peter Gabriel on his massive Secret World tour in the early '90s, tells me last fall. "If money blows in the wind, people will chase it. It describes the misery of our people. In Europe, this would be a scandal."

JR proudly says that he is a member of the band Quartier Bel-Air, which is on indefinite sabbatical because their leader went to France to record a CD. JR's own recording efforts fell apart after he spent his entire savings of $200—several months' salary—in a studio last year before even laying down vocal tracks. With his wife pressuring him to find work so they can care for their sick infant, JR joined this rally to ask Kabila for assistance. To JR, this was job prospecting. If he could sing for Kabila, he might get a paying gig for the day or the chance to perform at other political rallies. Unfortunately, his audience was limited to other hopefuls, hungry women, and Kabila's military police.

Despite the problems he faces as one of the multitude of singers and musicians on the streets, JR exudes self-confidence. "I was born with the music in me," he says. "At ten, I started singing in an orchestra of 18 people." He pauses. "If I went to your country, I'd become a big star."

Down the street, dehydrated Kabila "supporters" stand around in the baking midday sun. As I pass, a crowd of men gathers behind me.

"We want me some money," one demands.

"Water," says another.

"Shouldn't you guys be talking to Kabila?" I reply, quickening my pace. "You did walk across town to see him."

"I'm hungry," one very muscular man calls out.

The only food I have is some peanuts in a plastic bag. I pass them around, and that's when I get a good look at the group—a dozen stunningly hip young men, mostly in their 20s. Some wear do-rags, earrings, and big stone necklaces. Others have stylish hair braids, (fake) brand-name sportswear, and Congolese knockoffs of black Converse sneakers.

"Aren't you guys sort of well-dressed to be here?" I ask.

"We're musicians," one says. The others nod. I briefly wonder whether all musicians in Kinshasa look like cherubic Harlem rappers. I ask who sings.

"Me," a man with a do-rag says. "And him," he adds, pointing at another guy whose short dreads stick out from a multicolored baseball cap. "He's the president."

He isn't talking about Kabila. He's referring to the "president" of their band, Talon Lumire (Heel of Light). The person who throughout most of the world would be considered the lead singer gets an honored title here. Another young man, who wears wrap-around sunglasses and goes by the name X-Or, declares: "And I am the Secretary General."

The importance of titles in Kinshasa can be traced back to the reign of the dictator Mobutu Sese Seko. In 1960, Belgium pulled out of the Congo after brutally exploiting the colony for decades, and the country enjoyed its first democratic election. But with Belgian influence still strong, mining interests of great importance to the west, and Mobutu stirring up fears of communism in the region, the CIA backed his successful 1965 military coup. Mobutu went on to set a template for garish authoritarian power that is firmly imprinted on Congolese society nearly a decade after his death in exile. A man who demanded glorification while inspiring terror, Mobutu defined the way that most Kinshasans interact with authority even today. His ferociousness toward real or perceived enemies resulted in grotesque torture and high-profile executions, sometimes before crowded stadium audiences. One resistance figure who returned from exile after a promise of amnesty was publicly mutilated—his limbs amputated one by one—while he was still alive.

Later, Mobutu moved from the stick to the carrot by instituting a system of graft that funneled billions of dollars to Swiss bank accounts, even as Zaire's infrastructure collapsed and the nation defaulted on international loans. Still, his cult of personality surged to absurd proportions. He took on the name Mobutu Sese Seko Kuku Ngbendu wa za Banga (translation: "The all-powerful warrior who, thanks to his endurance and unbending victorious will, shall advance from conquest to conquest, leaving fire in his wake"). The nightly news opened on the image of Mobutu descending from clouds.

But as such fanfare lost its impact, and corruption worsened in the '70s, Mobutu sought other ways to win over the people and began co-opting the nation's thriving music scene. He ordered traditional songs and dances performed at political rallies, but insisted the lyrics be changed to celebrate Zairian identity and Mobutu himself. Political praise songs flourished, primarily because the musicians were paid, directly or indirectly, by the state. It created a perverse situation: an oppressive, authoritarian leader who strongly supported his country's musicians—as long as they lauded him.

It is no surprise, then, that Congolese music has almost no history of artistic rebellion or direct criticism. Lyrics rarely go beyond highlighting the challenges of daily life; they almost never remark upon the venal misdeeds that make those challenges insurmountable. "There are, traditionally, no activist artists in the Congo," says Papa Wemba. "Today, [most] people sing about carnal love. We don't denounce politics for fear of being jailed or killed, even if there is a crisis. It is permanent, this fear. Historically, a musician's job was to glorify the chief, like in a village."

It is difficult to attend any major concert in the Congo, or even listen to the radio, without hearing lyrical shout-outs that salute politicians, businessmen, military officials, or other high-profile figures. This is *libanga*, the Congolese language of musical flattery. In one stirring live performance, Koffi Olomide dished up libanga for Kinshasa's imposing chief of police: "Commander Raus et la ville est tranquille" ("[With] Commander Raus, the city is calm"). The more prominent the mention, the higher the fee—generally from $200 to $2,000.

When Werrason boasts that he is a superstar who can fill the biggest stadiums, sell more CDs and cassettes than anyone, and influence elections, he is basically negotiating for an increase in his rates. For Werrason, libanga is simply advertising. Others in the Kinshasa scene say that for Werrason, it makes no difference if he is shouting out a humanitarian organization, a corporation, or even a diamond smuggler, as long as he's paid. "Western Union got in contact," he says. "Usually, (a company or an individual will) write me by e-mail and say they want a 'mention.' I say, 'Transfer money to my account.'" The fruit of that transfer is clear. A few minutes into his song "King of the Forest," whose flashy video is filled with pricey sports cars and a bevy of women in bikinis, he suddenly declares: "Western Union, the fastest way to send money abroad." Unlike rappers who name-check Hennessy and Cristal as essential to a bling lifestyle, this is a straight-up commercial endorsement.

The target audience for many such plugs are the more prosperous Congolese immigrants in places like Paris, Brussels, and Oakland, who send money back home, which helps explain Western Union's interest. (A Western Union representative said that the company "supports African artists when we can.") When a diamond dealer pays top dollar to have his name injected in a chorus, it is to spread his fame as far as possible, and the artist who can do that best will get the most money. As libanga has become the norm, those who do cash in tend to wave it in everybody's face.

"When I arrive in a neighborhood, people start to call out my name," says guitarist and singer Jean Goubald. "They want me to drop money out the window. I don't. They think I'm rich. I'm not. But other musicians do it. They want to give the impression that they are rich, even though the songwriters' rights association is going out of business. If we earned royalties on our songs, we might get rid of libanga."

That is unlikely, but Werrason, for one, learned a grave lesson about selling his services during the presidential campaign. Soon after accepting what he described as a "symbolic amount" of money to sing on behalf of Joseph Kabila, a bus pulled up in front of his rehearsal studio. Thugs filed out, broke in, stole musical instruments and computer equipment, then set the place on fire.

"It was [presidential candidate] Jean-Pierre Bemba's supporters," alleges Werrason. "Bemba's people said it wasn't them, but it was." Werrason made typically outrageous claims, saying he lost $250,000 in materials, for which he is seeking compensation—from Kabila.

They live on the edge of urban darkness. You might hear them scraping in the dirt as you sip a beer on an outdoor patio. Or lurking between parked cars, behind palm trees. Some even climb out of uncovered sewer holes or rise out of filth-laden drainage ditches. Everyone in Kinshasa knows that the night belongs to the unwanted children of the slums of Kinshasa. Many came to the big city in search of opportunities but ended up becoming untouchables.

Up close, their eyes often have the yellowy glaze of an old street lamp. Their breath stinks of toxicity—the residue of huffed glue or shoe polish. When they have a little money, they reek of cheap alcohol or marijuana. In the areas where they skulk, there is little sympathy. Nightclubs, pizzerias, and gas stations hire security personnel armed with sticks. Ask a guard why and he will invariably use the name with which Papa Wemba tagged them long ago: "shege," for rough and radical Che Guevara–like kids. Shege is an ugly word, a dehumanizing epithet that encapsulates the fears of the privileged and the tiny middle class.

But on election day, no one on Kinshasa's main drag was denigrating the shege. Walking down the Boulevard du 30 juin on the morning of October 30, 2006, was like surveying a ghost town. Amid fear that fighting would break out between those loyal to the opposing candidates, many of the wealthy simply left the country. There was no urban activity. No traffic. Shops and restaurants were shuttered. Street vendors had taken the day off. People voted in their neighborhoods and returned home to pray that the United Nations, which was overseeing the election with the largest peacekeeping mission in its history, could prevent violence from breaking out. Just about the only people on the boulevard were the shege and the walking—or crawling—wounded.

When the votes were finally counted, Kabila won a decisive victory, making him the country's first elected president in more than 40 years. And after protests of election irregularities and some shootouts—minor, by national standards—the fiery rebel leader Bemba accepted defeat. Ultimately, the election amounted to a small step forward, as the scarred nation tried to put itself back together like a jigsaw puzzle that's missing several key pieces.

But on that day last October, nobody knew that the Democratic Republic of Congo would enjoy a rare electoral success story. Rumors flew that Kabila had stationed foreign mercenaries along the nearby Congo River, just in case, and that Bemba loyalists were gathering at another border. As I walk down the boulevard, I realize that it's the first time no one is harassing me for money.

It's because I'm walking with Patrick Manzenze Mangala, a man in a ragged JE VOTE JOSEPH KABILA T-shirt with two crooked buckteeth jutting out from his mouth. Patrick looks much younger than his 23 years. Born the eighth of nine children to civil servants who strained to make ends meet and then divorced, Patrick spent virtually all of his teen years sleeping on cardboard on the verandas of closed restaurants. Now he easily chronicles the shege's suffering, like a tour guide of misery. He might not aspire to be a professional singer, and his music may amount to little more than the street noise that surrounds him, but he has the socially conscious street rap of Kinshasa down pat.

"We, the shege, are like cliff climbers; we can stick to walls," he says, as though speaking of comic book heroes. "We are courageous. We have to know many things just to survive."

When I'd first met Patrick, outside the Ministry of Social Affairs on Election Day, his curled-in body language projected fragility and anguish, as he slowly dragged his sandals in the dirt. But now, among the desolation around us, he proudly struts, almost projecting the confidence of a rebel leader.

"I have an organization," he says of the homeless youth. "These are some of my members. They report to me."

Before you traverse the streets of Kinshasa—an activity discouraged by foreign aid workers as well as locals—you will be warned not to believe what you hear. It is generally good advice. Nearly everyone who approaches you on the street has a story of woe, leading up to the pitch: "Could you spare a dime—or 20 bucks." Some tales are surely true; many are complex lies. So I'm skeptical of Patrick's claim that he is the prince of the shege. His cocky tone seems to echo that of Werrason or of a politician arranging deals. From Mobutu to the pop stars to the most neglected souls on the streets, this dynamic is the same: If you appear powerful enough to promise some crumbs of recompense, people will follow you. And if you're a follower, maybe you can begin to negotiate your way to greater power and wealth.

Then Patrick delivers his spiel. After a wrenching litany of reasons why I should give him money—to share it with the squalid humanity around us, for one—he offers insight into enduring Congolese power relations. "You must have pity on us," he says. "Have pity and it will help you." It will help my network of patronage, my conscience, my sense of solidarity, and even my relationship to God, he says.

On the boulevard, Patrick has already positioned himself as the strongest, healthiest, and most able. With his members focused completely on him, his swagger almost seems intimidating. And with his taut biceps, he is an imposing presence. In the eyes of his fellow shege, there are hints of deference, awe. They really do respect him. The question is the same for Patrick or Kabila or the countless Kinshasa singers who might eventually get before a microphone. Will they use their moment in the spotlight to help bring about change? Or will they just empower themselves and return to throw a few bills into the breeze?

Andy Tennille

THE RETURN OF REAL FUNK & SOUL MUSIC

Sharon Jones and the Dap-Kings

Fifty years ago this year, an aspiring, young country fiddler from Memphis, Tennessee, borrowed some basic audio equipment from his barber and began recording music in his wife's uncle's garage, thus laying the roots for the one of the world's preeminent soul and funk labels.

Borrowing $15,000 from his sister Estelle Axton, Jim Stewart founded what would ultimately become Stax Records in a renovated old movie theater at the corner of McLemore Avenue and College Street in south Memphis. From 1957 until its close in January 1976, Stax artists such as Otis Redding, Booker T. & The MGs, Sam & Dave, Rufus & Carla Thomas, Isaac Hayes, Albert King and the Staple Singers produced more than 800 45s and 300 LPs, scoring over 160 hits on the Top 100 pop charts and 240 Top 100 R&B classics during its nearly 20-year run.

Unfortunately, the label's meteoric rise to fame would not last. In 1972, Stax minority owner Al Bell struck a distribution deal with Columbia Records, using a six-million-dollar loan from that label to buy out Stewart. The handshake arrangement between Bell and Columbia Records President Clive Davis disintegrated when Davis was fired, sending Stax into bankruptcy and forcing its closure in January 1976.

In March 2007, Concord Music Group relaunched the label with the release of *Stax 50th Anniversary Celebration*, a two-disc compilation of more than 50 classic tracks. Media trumpeted the news of Stax's return as the revival of American soul and funk music, but they had it all wrong. For the past six years, a tiny record label run out of a dilapidated brownstone in Brooklyn's rough Bushwick neighborhood has been quietly producing authentic soul and funk music the likes of which has not been seen in America since Stax shut its doors more than 30 years ago.

Gabe Roth looks exhausted.

Slumped on a brown couch in the control room of the studio at Brooklyn-based Daptone Records, the label chief, producer and bass player hides behind a pair of dark sunglasses, fresh off a redeye flight from Los Angeles, where, the night before, he played in the house band at the 2007 ESPY Awards.

For the better part of the past year, Roth has been a busy man: engineering and arranging new albums for R&B starlets Amy Winehouse and Lily Allen; collaborating with famed DJ/producer Mark Ronson; producing new albums by Staten Island–based rising Afrobeat stars the Budos Band and late-'60s soul duo Bob & Gene; overseeing reissues by Deep Funk pioneers the Poets of Rhythm, organ boogaloo trio Sugarman Three and Fela Kuti devotees the Daktaris; and playing in the backing band on Winehouse's recent world tour.

Today, Roth is wrapping work on *100 Days, 100 Nights*, the upcoming studio album from Gotham funkmasters Sharon Jones & the Dap-Kings, slated for release October 2 on Daptone.

Tomorrow, the 33-year-old bassist and bandleader who plays under the stage alias Bosco "Bass" Mann will reunite with the Dap-Kings for a show at Brooklyn's Kingsborough Community College, the group's first gig in almost three months and the beginning of the supporting tour for *100 Days, 100 Nights*.

Life hasn't always been so busy for the founder of Daptone Records. Growing up in Riverside, California, Roth got his start in music playing drums in high school garage bands covering "My Sharona," "Wild Thing" and "Wipe Out" at parties for pot and beer money.

"My parents were kind of hippies, so they always had lots of Motown records, Beatles, Stones and James Brown," he recalls. "The Stax music, James Brown and the Motown stuff were things that were in my ears early on. When I came to New York to visit my sister while I was in high school, a friend of hers turned me on to the Meters. That stuff really opened up my mind. It was really powerful, rhythmic music that as a teenager I could sink my teeth into."

After high school graduation, Roth followed his older sister to the Big Apple and enrolled in New York University. Arriving in Greenwich Village, he quickly found fellow funk fans and formed bands with names like Dine-O-Mite and the East Side Soul Congregation.

"Around that time, I was really getting into buying records," Roth remembers. "I couldn't really afford the 45s, but I was getting a lot of compilations and reissues and beginning to dig a little deeper. When I went back to California to visit my parents, I'd go around to these places that sold jukeboxes. Anybody that dealt jukeboxes usually had a trailer someplace where they stashed all the 45s if they didn't throw them away. So I'd go to these places and just dig and get dusty. That was the period when I really started falling in love with soul music."

One of the labels that piqued Roth's interest early on was Pure Records, a Paris-based reissue imprint owned by avid French collector Phillipe Lehman.

"Pure was putting out some of the nastiest funk compilations that were coming out at that time, and I used to buy all of them," Roth says with a nostalgic laugh. "Phillipe was a rich, eccentric guy and a huge collector. A mutual friend introduced us when he was in New York because Phillipe wanted to try to produce new funk records. We hit it off immediately. He had all these records that he played me the night we met, like the Poets of Rhythm's *Practice What You Preach*, and eventually we decided to start our own label."

Founded in 1996, Desco Records' first releases were 45s featuring soul singers Lee Fields and Joseph Henry backed by Roth, Lehman and a variety of like-minded musicians keen to continue the tradition laid down by Stax, Muscle Shoals Sound and Motown Records.

"The first one we did was 'Steam Train' with Lee Fields in 1996," Roth says. "I must have gone to every record store in the city trying to sell them for two dollars a piece. I couldn't get rid of that thing, so I went home, got some newspaper and rubbed them with it to try and make them look like some old record. . . ."

While Roth's faux-antiquating method might not have succeeded, it spawned an idea. Obsessed vinylphiles were always looking for old, limited-edition pressings of rare funk and soul 45s, the more obscure the better. A few months later, Desco issued *The Revenge of Mister Mopoji* by an unknown group named Mike Jackson & the Soul Providers, heralding it as the long-awaited reissue of a soundtrack to an obscure '70s kung fu movie.

"It was a fake reissue of a soundtrack to a kung fu movie that never actually existed," Roth confesses with a sly grin. "We would go to record shops in New York to sell the album and store clerks would tell me, 'I don't want that. I got the original.' There was no original soundtrack; there was no fucking movie to begin with. It was unbelievable. That's when I realized how full of shit most of these people were."

Despite its fictitious origins, *Mister Mopoji* was a cult hit for Desco, selling a few thousand copies. For the follow-up, Lehman and Roth assembled the same musicians at a heavy metal studio in Long Island, stuck with the Soul Providers moniker and issued *Soul Tequila*.

"That record went nowhere," Roth says. "We tried different covers, we tried pitching it differently. Nothing worked. Nobody wanted that record. We couldn't understand how people had loved a fake soundtrack record but didn't want to buy a real record by the same band."

Unfortunately, the trend stuck. From 1997 until its dissolution three years later, Desco released straightforward, honest funk and soul 45s and albums such as the Other Side's *Don't Look Back Behind the Shack* and Lee Fields' *Let's Get A Groove On* that were largely commercially ignored, interspersed with records with fabricated back stories including Nino Nardini & the Pop Riviera Group, the Daktaris' *Soul Explosion* and Ravi Harris and the Prophets' *Funk Sitar Man* that ultimately would be among the label's best sellers.

"I definitely struggled with that because we weren't really trying to fool anybody," Roth says. "We just wanted to make records we liked. But whenever we made a record that we were being honest about, we couldn't throw it down the garbage disposal. Nobody wanted it. Only when we spun some story around it about being a soundtrack or something goofy did people buy it. The one great thing that came out of that was, once they saw it as an old record, they would compare it with other old records. It was great for us because that's really where we wanted our records to be sitting anyway. Even if they lost—and they always lost and still do to this day in my mind—those are the records they should be up against."

While Desco never achieved commercial success, Roth did not leave the label empty-handed. In 1996, a wedding singer and former Riker's Island prison guard named Sharon Jones was called in to sing backup vocals on a few tracks for *Soul Tequila*. The session served as Roth's introduction to the singer who would eventually become the face of the Dap-Kings.

"Sharon showed up, knocked out the harmonies on 'Let a Man Do What He Wanna Do' in a second and that was the first time I listened back to the tape in the booth and it sounded like a real record to me," Roth gushes. "She came in on the background vocal and all of the sudden it was official—the shit was legit. We had done a lot of cool stuff up to that point, but she helped us finally make a real record."

Sharon Jones was born Sheron Lafaye Jones on May 4, 1956, in Augusta, Georgia. The youngest of six children, she grew up in a house equally influenced by gospel hymns and the music of Augusta's most famous native, the Godfather of Soul, James Brown.

"I remember singing a lot in church and I remember my brother Henry used to sing and dance at home like James Brown," Jones says. "He'd imitate James Brown so I tried to do it too. We'd dance around and sing. I was born in 1956, so in '66, I was 10 years old. I was at the right age."

As a teenager in the '70s, Jones began singing outside the church in talent shows and local funk groups in Brooklyn, where her mother had relocated. Throughout the '80s, Jones made a living performing in wedding bands and doing sporadic recording sessions while also working as an armed guard for Wells Fargo Bank. While Roth's memories of her first Desco session are fond, Jones was a bit skeptical about the 21-year-old producer at the mixing console.

"I remember thinking, 'What the hell does this little white boy know about funk?'" Jones says, laughing. "But Gabe knew what he was doing. We finished the session that day and I remember walking out of the studio thinking that that boy was reincarnated—he was a 55-year-old black man in a little Jewish boy's body."

Jones began singing as part of the Desco Super Soul Revue alongside Lee Fields, Joseph Henry and gospel singer Naomi Davis, but the label would not last. Conflicts between Roth and Phillipe Lehman dissolved Desco Records in early 2001. Lehman went on to start Soul Fire Records, which released numerous reissues as well as original 45s and LPs before closing in 2003.

With original Soul Providers guitarist Binky Griptite, organist Earl Maxton, percussionist Fernando "Boogaloo" Velez, trumpeter Anda "Goodfoot" Szilagyi and baritone saxophonist Jack Zapata in tow, Roth recruited tenor saxophonist Leon Michels and drummer Homer "Funkyfoot" Steinweiss of teenage Desco recording artists the Mighty Imperials and Sharon Jones & the Dap-Kings was born. Based on Desco's growing reputation as a purveyor of modern funk and soul music, the Dap-Kings landed a club residency in the summer of 2001 in Barcelona but needed a recording to sell at the shows. With a handful of old Soul Providers songs, Roth penned some new tunes and recorded *Dap Dippin' with Sharon Jones & the Dap-Kings* on an eight-track in the basement of a Brooklyn kung fu dojo that doubled as an Afrobeat nightclub.

While *Dap Dippin'* may not have been recorded in acoustically ideal environs, the album's raggedy feel aids the music's funky vibe. Opening with a classic intro mc'ed by Griptite, the 11 tracks written by Roth ooze pulsating rhythms punctuated by precisely placed horn blasts, slinky guitar riffs and Jones' sultry vocals.

"I realized from the very beginning that it wasn't any divine inspiration or genius on my part that was going to make this music work," Roth says. "It's not that I can smoke the right shit, look at the right colors and all of a sudden, beautiful things are going to pour out of my ass. It's never been that way. My approach to songwriting is more like a craftsman. I can figure out this chord will work with that chord because they have the same notes in them. I can write lyrics pretty fast because my mind rhymes things even if I don't want it to. So I was just trying to write things that sounded cool and then basically put them in the hands of some really talented and soulful people."

Needing a vehicle to issue the album, Roth borrowed money from his family and founded Daptone Records with saxophonist Neal Sugarman of Sugarman Three fame. *Dap Dippin'* was the label's first longplayer, followed quickly by the Sugarman Three's *Pure Cane Sugar* and the Mighty Imperials' *Thunder Chicken*.

"It's always been a real family affair with us," Roth explains. "After Desco ended, we had all these people playing in these different bands. We had the Dap-Kings, but Binky and I were also playing in Antibalas. Leon and Homer had the Mighty Imperials but were playing in the Dap-Kings. Neil joined the band when Leon left to start the El Michels Affair and Truth & Soul Records. Tommy Brenneck, who was playing in Dirt Rifle and the Fast Breakin' Classics out on Staten Island, joined too. It was when the Dap-Kings and Antibalas started doing better at the same time when it started becoming a conflict. Eventually, we all had to pick a horse. That was real hard for all of us."

Over the next three years, the Dap-Kings toured extensively in both the United States and Europe, where the burgeoning Deep Funk scene was growing with bands like Speedometer, the New Mastersounds and the Soul Destroyers and supported by DJs like Keb Darge and Snowboy.

"It was real interesting because our music was some raw, take-your-pants-off shit and over in England, they're coming off Northern soul and methamphetamines," Roth says. "Their stuff sounds really hyper to my ears and our stuff that sounds great to me puts them to sleep. They're also into a lot of syncopation, staccato stuff like the Meters and Tower of Power. We kind of got further and further away from that stuff and got more into the dumpy, Lee Dorsey grooves."

By the time Jones and the Dap-Kings returned to the studio to record the follow-up to *Dap Dippin'*, Roth had rented a run-down building on Troutman Street in Brooklyn and built a recording space over the course of several months in the winter of 2002 with the help of the other Daptone musicians.

"I'd show up in my overall jeans and say, 'What do you want me to do?'" Jones remembers with a smile. "We had some professionals come in to do the main box, but Gabe and I did a lot of the electrical wiring and plumbing work by reading a book we got from Home Depot."

"That was the coldest winter of my life," Roth says. "There was a 24-hour plumbing store down the street, so I'd go over there and the guy behind the counter would sell me a torch and explain to me how to do sweat-soldering. I'd be down in the basement in the middle of the night trying to fix the pipes and gas lines with the torch and my hands were completely numb. It was fucking awful."

While Antibalas' *Who Is This America?* was the first album to come out of the new Troutman Street studio, *Naturally*, the Dap Kings' sophomore effort, followed soon after. Released in January 2005, the record was a huge musical jump for Roth and the Dap-Kings. In the three years since *Dap Dippin'*, the band had played hundreds of gigs all over the world and gelled as a group. Roth had improved as a producer and arranger and upgraded to 16-track recording.

"*Naturally* was a big step," Jones agrees. "Everything was more organized and everyone was contributing. Gabe would have some of the charts written out with what he wanted, but somewhere along the way the guys started adding their own stuff too because they were feeling it. We were all feeling it."

Not only did *Naturally* represent a vast improvement musically, but the album's release also meant larger crowds at the band's shows. The group played *Late Night with Conan O'Brien* and was invited to festivals in Europe and the States. In addition to the Dap-Kings, the label signed the Budos Band, a group of Staten Island Fela Kuti fanatics, and issued their debut recording in November 2005. As the popularity of *Naturally* grew, so did the reputation of Daptone Records as the home of modern funk, soul and Afrobeat music.

"It was around that time that I got a call from Mark Ronson," Roth says. "He was a DJ over in London that had a big album coming out called *Here Comes the Fuzz* and he'd sampled a Sharon Jones song on it. So he called and we worked it out and eventually he asked if we'd be interested in doing some projects with him. The first thing we did was the Amy Winehouse album."

With the Dap-Kings as her backing band and Ronson and Roth twisting the knobs, Winehouse's *Back to Black* was an immediate hit, selling millions of records and gaining widespread radio airplay.

"I don't think they gave Daptone and the Dap-Kings enough recognition," Jones says. "From the Desco days, we have been out here for 12 years now doing this. To hear other people say that they brought this music back out is not right. I want us to be recognized. Everyone needs to know about us. I ain't trying to say we want millions or anything like that but I think we deserve our just due. We are keeping it real. We make real music and I think everyone needs to hear it."

With the overnight success of Winehouse's *Back to Black*, Ronson enlisted the band for Lily Allen's *Alright, Still* as well on tracks off his own new record, *Version*.

"Working with Mark was really easy," Roth says. "He knows what he wants, he knows what we do and he wants us to do what we do. After we did that work with him and a couple of runs with Amy on her tour, it became a little distracting for me because I wanted to work on our stuff. That's around when we started working on *100 Days, 100 Nights*."

"With *100 Days, 100 Nights*, everything's just gotten better. Just like the difference between *Dap Dippin'* and *Naturally*, the musicianship on the new record is so much higher. The horns really resonate on this album, and the rhythm section is badder than they've ever been. Binky and Tommy's playing has never been tastier, Sharon sounds better than she ever has and everyone is just humming on this record."

As if on cue, Roth swings around in his chair in the control room at the studio on Troutman Street and hits a button on the mixing console. Jones' distinctive voice fills the room as she belts out "Answer Me," a cover of a Dorothy Norwood gospel song that the singer turns into a hallelujah-shoutin' rave-up. If *Dap Dippin'* was the Dap-Kings at their funkiest and *Naturally* was their most soulful hour, *100 Days, 100 Nights* is the band's turn at rhythm and blues. And like all great R&B albums, the songs on *100 Days, 100 Nights* are about love— lamentations over lovers lost, painful memories of broken relationships, appeals for affirmation and tales of unrequited love. Opening with a spooky, New Orleans jazz funeral–like horn intro, the album's title track is driven by Jones' woeful ponderings on the mysteries of men's indecisiveness. Jones demands her lover's attention on "Tell Me" and sings "Humble Me" with the passion and clarity of a woman who's experienced the perils of opening her heart. With its downright dirty bass line and rattling drums, "Nobody's Baby" sounds like a classic Tina Turner track from an era of music long gone. All in all, *100 Days, 100 Nights* may be the most Stax-like of all the Daptone releases to date.

"It is probably more like a Stax record than anything we've done before," Roth says. "I got a chance to meet Booker T & the MGs recently when Sharon did a gig with them. I had it all planned out. I wanted to ask them how they made certain records and tell them my favorite things about what they did. In my mind, we were all hanging out at Peter Luger's having steaks and throwing Frisbees in the park. So we get backstage and Sharon's like, 'Steve, Duck, Booker, come here. This is the guy I was telling you about, Gabe. He leads our band and really wants to meet you guys.' And the only thing I can say is, 'Thank you for what you have given to the world.' I was completely dumbstruck. I was standing there in a room with these guys who are my heroes and just fuckin' freaked."

"Out of all the music that I've been into over the years, Stax is the most inspiring. It's been a huge inspiration to me. Stax was something that hadn't been done before or since. Motown was a factory, but Stax was a family.

"That's what we've got going on here. Daptone is a family."

In memory of Soul Brother No. 1, William Grant Tennille (1944–2007).

Marke B.

GAYEST. MUSIC. EVER.

The death of circuit, Energy 92.7 fm,

and the new queer dance floor diaspora

Something *horrible* happened.

The promo package, marked *Special*, arrived on my desk in May from Ultra Records in New York City. Hastily, I tore the envelope open and yanked out the CD within, letting squiggles of packing confetti fall where they may. A bronze and glistening, near-naked, possibly underage Brazilian boy stared fiercely from the cover. His bulging genitalia were not quite stuffed into a Gummi-red Speedo. His hair dripped with viscous product. Posed stiffly against a seaside shack the color of processed cheddar, he looked like he was about to either blow me or feast on my liver. The text across his sculpted, slightly veiny torso read *DJ Ricardo! Presents Out Anthems 2*.

Oh, good lord.

If there's anything that turns me off more than DJs with exclamation points appended to their monikers—OMG! The '90s! Low carb! Wow!—it's some gay fool from Ultra Records in New York City trying to tell me what my "out anthems" are. Sorry, but tin-eared "Don't Want No Short Dick Man" remixes, spacey-diva "Deeper Love" covers, mindless melodramatic thumpers, and obnoxious washes of sizzle and screech don't quite sum up my raggedy, faggoty lifestyle or speak to my proud, if occasionally morally compromised, experience.

I adore dance music—it's my life. Any packed dance floor is a good thing in my book. But I also have some taste, and this was the apogee of cheesiness. The presumption that these bland corporate farts are the tunes of my loony-queer times crosses a clear homo-to-homo line in the shimmering sands. (For the record, Ultra Records, my current personal out anthems are the Cinematics' "Keep Forgetting," Shazzy's "Giggahoe," and Gladys Knight and the Pips' "Love Is Always on Your Mind." Go mix *that*.)

Listen, I can ride with the tsunami of cheap and sleazy DJ dance compilations that has flooded various music stores, in-boxes, and jittery Wal-Marts for the past decade or so, featuring tightly clenched glutes, toxic tans, and spandex-stretching silicone explosions. (And that's just the music. Someone should really publish a picture book of all of the blindingly awful, grinding-Barbie-in-headphones cover designs. Title suggestion: *Writhe the Ibiza Abysmal*. Or how about just *Champagne and Crap*?) There's definitely a market out there for pulsating pabulum, and I dug my own grave with two coke spoons and a mirror ball when I became a nightlife critic. I was even OK with the knowledge that because I had *Out Anthems 2* grasped shakily in my hot little palm, it meant that *somewhere out there an* Out Anthems 1 *must exist*. You go, DJ Ricardo!! Work it however you can. No, that wasn't the horrible part.

SPLICING THE MONOLITH

The horrible part was this: I actually kind of liked it.

Bursting with a weird glee that's unique to our media-saturated moment—"Holy shit, you've got to hear-see-watch this, it's the most horrifying thing ever!"—I had rushed the CD over to my boyfriend Hunky Beau's house before listening to it, eager for us to put it on and tear it a new one together. That's our modern gay love.

Yet once I'd slipped the disc into Hunky's Mac and readied myself a hot shot of *schadenfreude*, I realized I don't hear this sort of heinous stuff when I'm out and about as much as I used to. The once-omnipresent, thousand-nostriled behemoth of overbearing, poorly produced circuit and "progressive house" music has been somewhat tamed. Sure, much of the CD was atrocious, but now that this cookie-cutter hokum is no longer forced on me at every gay turn I take, pouring forth from restaurant patios and flashy video bars, after-hours megaclubs and fisting pornos, open gym windows and passing Miata convertibles, I could listen to it not as some soulless dominant paradigm that was threatening to rob gay culture of every last ounce of scruff and sparkle, but as mere tacky noodling: harmless fun in an ironic way, if you're into irony anymore. (Not poor Hunky Beau, though. A die-hard devotee of skinhead mosh and East Bay punk, he dived beneath the covers as soon as the first few high-hat sprays had rung in the air, moaning like he had aural hepatitis.)

What happened that night—a night that found me wriggling around in my Underoos and torturing my man with shouts of "Look at me! I'm a tweaked-out fan dancer!"—sparked the more masochistic aspects of my curiosity.

Ever since the supastar DJ scene of the late '90s and early '00s became economically impossible to sustain—the Sisyphean task of convincing thousands of people to spend $40 to hear a scrawny dude from Manchester, UK, or Miami spin *yet again* burned many promoters out—the dance floor playing field has blown wide open. Megaclubs, with their monolithic sounds, gave way to smaller venues where independent promoters could experiment with fresh ideas and vent their wacky stylistic impulses, minus hefty cover charges and pat-down security. Clubs became more like house parties: the kid with the most friends or the biggest iTunes collection could plug into the DJ booth and let 'er rip.

Gay clubs, especially, had followed the newfound freedom from big-time pressure and flight-booking budgets in myriad zany directions. Today's gay club scene is more diverse than it's ever been. Almost every night of the week there are *options*.

So maybe it was time for me to reappraise a style that I'd grown to hate, now that it was fading from mainstream gay scene ubiquity in favor of sleek hip-pop and '80s hair bands. Maybe I could stare into the numb, drooling jaws of circuit and progressive terror and dance, dance, dance. Could it really be as bad as I remembered? Was I ready to let go of my bitterness toward a music so insidious that even my grandmother thought my life was one big party scene from—gag—*Queer as Folk*?

Was it possible for me to tune into KNGY, 92.7 FM (Energy), the aggressively gay-friendly "pure dance" local radio station that had become synonymous with such music—and had recently hosted a party spotlighting, yes, DJ Ricardo!—without retching uncontrollably at the first few modulated wails?

Perhaps. I dug out the hand-crank radio from my earthquake emergency kit because, like, transmission radio—who still listens to that? I reacquainted myself with how to adjust a dial. Then I turned the volume up.

DOWNSIZE QUEENS

Mention Energy 92.7 to most gay men, and curious things happen to their bodies. The shoulders pop, the eyes roll, the hands begin to gesticulate wildly. Those are the gay men who love the station. The others absolutely loathe it. Their bodies convulse in a spasm of disgust. Their faces twist into ghoulish grimaces. Spittle flies from their lips. The hatred is *palpable*. There's no middle ground when it comes to Energy. I've been in cars where people have fought over it until blood spurted.

Such reactions may be the legacy of the circuit party scene. Fifteen years ago, if you asked the average straight person to close their eyes and think about "gay music," the image that would first leap to his or her mind would be a turtlenecked show-tune queen clipping pink rosebuds in her garden while whistling something from *Les Miz*. Or, if the hetero were more contemporary, the archetype called up would be a sweat-dripping, mustachioed disco nymph collapsing into a pile of Studio 54 fairy dust or a bleached and tragic Madonna fan in an oversize cable-knit sweater with a regrettable yen for cheap eyeliner. Many gay club kids today would gladly take those images over what replaced them in the mid-'90s: buffed-out 'roid heads in sailor caps and tighty whiteys frantically tooting whistles while some faceless diva yelped them into an aerobic frenzy.

The colossal circuit scene had its strengths: with its world-conquering voraciousness, it served as an accessible entry point for the vast numbers of gay men who came out at the time. Clattering circuit beats and ecstatic progressive swells and breaks—the natural evolution of corporate rave music in a mainstream gay environment—pushed many HIV-positive men through despair in the time before effective AIDS meds became available, and served as an all-purpose celebration template afterward. But circuit parties also marginalized queers with no taste for militaristic conformity, gratingly regurgitated tunes, or the alphabet soup of designer drugs then in vogue. The fact that the circuit had once been a credible, if snobbish and expensive, underground movement held no sway when it hatched into a gargantuan space tarantula from Planet GHB that swallowed all semblance of queer individuality. It was the *Will and Grace* of clubland, and most of us got jacked.

But that was then, this is *neu*. Dissing the circuit scene for gay club music's discouraging popular image is like nail-gunning a dead, glitter-freckled horse. "The scene has really downsized, along with the whole megaclub thing in general," a popular San Francisco circuit DJ confided to me recently. "The energy we're riding on is nostalgia."

Michael Williams, co-owner of Medium Rare Records in the Castro, the go-to store for dance mix compilations, told me, "We still sell a lot of that music, but people aren't asking for it as they once did. I think the market got oversaturated and quality became a real factor. People began asking, 'Where's the talent?' Our biggest sellers now are more complex artists like Shirley Bassey, Thelma Houston, and Pink Martini, or DJs who really work to have an interesting sound, like Dimitri from Paris." Even the odiously corporate *Out* magazine declared the circuit party over in its current issue, so you know it must be true.

Still, the sour taste of the circuit era in many alternaqueers' mouths has proved hard to wash out. And the stereotype of awful gay club music still reigns supreme in the straight world. Even though Energy 92.7's been around for less than three years and is in truth, as I found out after tuning in, more prone to playing *Billboard* Hot 100 pop remixes than actual circuit music, it's had to bear the backlash brunt. As the most visible mainstream gay dance music giant of the moment, it's become guilty by association.

CREEPIN' LIKE BOUGAINVILLEA

> Greg: "*Oh my god, he is such a freakin' moron.*"
> Fernando: "*Thirty-six percent approval ratings is far too high for this president.*"

> Greg: "*The only way my gay ass would be impressed by [George W.] Bush is if he put a VJ in the Oval Office. Bitch, please—how many more troops have to die?!*"
> Fernando: "*You're listening to Energy, 92.7 FM. Here's Rihanna with 'Don't Stop the Music.'*"
> —FERNANDO AND GREG IN THE MORNING

This is how gay Energy 92.7 is: when I first visited the station recently, the station's party promoter, Juan Garcia, recognized my hair product from 50 paces. "Little orange can, girl?" he called out to greet me.

This is how gay Energy 92.7 is: when I sat in on the morning show with hosts Fernando Ventura and Greg Sherrell, they agonized during songs over the fact that something called the "smart-fat diet" forbade them to eat nuts for a week. "You can write anything you want," Sherrell, a high-voiced, blond spitfire who frequently informs listeners that he's wearing his most expensive jeans, told me. "But if you don't say I'm thin, I finna kill you."

Fernando and Greg in the Morning, on air weekdays from 6 to 10 a.m., is one of the most popular shows on Energy, which has a potential reach of 3.2 million listeners. The show could be accused of a lot of things—gay minstrelsy, pandering to stereotypes, making me get up at 4 a.m. to sit in—but it could never be accused of being unexciting. It's the only openly gay morning show on commercial radio, and some of the live quips traded by DJ Fernando, Greg "the Gay Sportscaster," and their "straight man" producer Jason are dizzy scandal. Vaginal pubic hair "creeps up like bougainvillea," poppers are bad on first dates "because they'll make your throat sore," and Kylie Minogue gets the verbal knockdown but "Oh, we love her: she had breast cancer!" Interspersed with segments like "Homo vs. Hetero," during which one caller of each orientation is quizzed about the other's lifestyle, are Kelly Clarkson and the Killers remixes, "Vintage Beats" by Blondie and Michael Jackson, and current dance-chart toppers by Bananarama, David Guetta, and the Sunlovers.

It's a thing of wonder in a society still riddled with homophobia— I dare you to find a YouTube video with more than 5,000 views that doesn't have the word *fag* in the comments—to have such an unequivocally queeny experience, with a strong straight following, sail through the airwaves each morning. The tunes take a backseat to the dish. "At 9:30 in the morning you can only get so adventurous with your music selections," Ventura, an easygoing, bearish guy, told me. "I mostly stick with the hits."

The station, located in a murky green downtown office building, is a buzzing hive of fluid sexuality and good-natured candidness. The hyper-drive strains of DJ Tiesto and Deepface fill the air. As the only independently owned and operated commercial radio station in San Francisco, Energy's done well. As a suitor of the gay audience, it's done spectacularly. Even though its press materials emphasize its appeal to a broad variety of dance music fans, Energy's known as "the gay dance station" to most San Franciscans. (That's not so much the case across the bay, where Energy has gained a lot of traction in the Latino and Asian communities.)

Balancing a constant need for revenue with gay political intricacies can get tricky. A chill shot through me when I saw "Energy 92.7 owns the gay community" printed in bold and underlined in the station's media kit—apparently we're all slaves to remixed Cher. And even though the station is a major sponsor of most large gay charity events, there have been a few controversies. The gay media has fussed that Energy is co-owned and run by a straight man, Joe Bayliss, and the station has been blamed for dumbing down gay culture to grasp the pink dollar (although that's like saying Britney Spears's performance sucked because her heel broke). And last year Energy released a branded compilation mix CD—with an Army recruitment ad slipped into the packaging.

"We made a mistake. It was just stupid and insensitive on our part," Bayliss, a frank, handsome man with a ready smile, said when I asked him about the Army debacle. "This institution offered us a lot of money, and hey, we're a struggling, independent business. We answered every complaint personally to apologize. We learned our lesson." (A new, military-free compilation comes out next month, to be carried by Best Buy, with proceeds going to local AIDS charities.)

PROGRAMMED RAINBOWS

That's the politics, but what about the music? "I'm starting to build up a dance music collection," said Bayliss, who's been working in radio since he was a kid. "This particular format tested through the roof in this market when we were looking to buy the station. I had no idea who Paul Oakenfold or Kaskade was when we started. I used to run a country station, and I didn't know Merle Haggard from a hole in the ground either. But we're 100 percent committed to this music and its audience. We have to be—our listeners are very dedicated."

Rabid may be a better word. The phone lines were jammed while I was there, and according to programming manager John Peake, the in-boxes are full every morning with e-mails from gaga enthusiasts. Good portions of Energy listeners stream the station online, and employees interact continuously with members of Energy's E-Club virtual community. Even the afternoon DJs were leaping up and down in the booth while I was there, pumping their fists heavenward.

"Often we'll get these enormously long e-mails from people listing every song we played that night, going into intense detail about each one and exactly why it was so important to them," Peake told me. "We get a lot of e-mails at six in the morning."

Looking compact in a lavender oxford, faded jeans, and a kicky Italian snakeskin belt, Peake took me through the music selection process. Each week he and music programmer Trevor Simpson go through new releases, recently submitted remixes, and requests from the station's fans. They form a playlist based on what they think will most appeal to listeners and then program their picks into a hilariously retro MS-DOS program called Selector with, I shit you not, a rainbow-colored interface. "It's tacky, but it's bulletproof," Peake said, laughing. DJs either punch up the tracks automatically or refer to the playlist to make their own mixes using Serato software. Zero vinyl's involved.

Peake and I talked about the criteria for choosing songs. "It's a moving target. There's definitely a ton of music out there that falls within our brand, and our nighttime and weekend DJs get to play a huge variety of mix music from around the world, so there's a lot of latitude. I think our biggest challenge right now is figuring out the role of hip-hop. Our younger listeners demand it, but a lot of our demographic is still afraid of it. If we play something with rapping in it, we get flooded with angry callers screaming, 'How dare you play this! Don't you know it's homophobic?'"

Later I spoke with Energy's promotions director, Tim Kwong, about the backlash against the station. "We get it from both sides," Kwong, a young Bay Area native with impressively gelled hair, said. "Trance and progressive fans say, 'Why don't you play more harder, locally produced records?' Rock and hip-hop fans want us to play fewer remixes of their favorite songs. We try to strike a balance, but the truth is what we do works for our audience."

"I can totally understand the frustration people feel when a certain image is projected that doesn't fit them," he continued, addressing the gay question. "As an Asian American with a punk and indie background, I have a lot of experience with stereotypes, believe me. But we try to be as broad as possible in our appeal and acknowledge differences. And we're not bribing people to listen to us."

(OTHER)

To their credit, the folks at Energy also acknowledge that their programming may not be in sync with what's going on in the gay club scene now. "It's apparent when you listen to the morning show that I don't go out to clubs very much," DJ Fernando told me. "But when I do, I notice there is so much more choice these days. In the past there were a bunch of huge nights or clubs, and everybody went. Now there's a night or a bar for everybody."

"Ick! I think it's total crap. It's like the dance music equivalent of Weird Al," said Bill Picture, who, along with his partner, DJ Dirty Knees, is the city's biggest gay rock club promoter, when I asked him his opinion of Energy. "We're much more into visceral rock energy and seeing live, local queer punk. But a lot of gay people *do* like that kind of music. And I'm glad that there's a radio station that they can tune in to. How boring would it be if all gay people liked the same things? We're happy to be an alternative."

The alternatives have arrived aplenty. In addition to Picture's metal events, there's DJ Bus Station John's bathhouse disco revival scene, which fetishizes pre-AIDS vinyl like the smell of polished leather. There's DJ David Harness's Super Soul Sundayz, which focuses on atmospheric Chicago house sounds. There's Charlie Horse, drag queen

Anna Conda's carnivalesque trash-rock drag club that often—gasp!—includes live singing. Queer-oriented parties with old-school show tunes, square dancing, tango, hula, Asian Hi-NRG, hyphy, mashups, Mexican banda, country line dancing, and a bonanza of other styles have found popularity in the past few years. The night's a sissy smorgasbord of sound.

There's even a bit of a backlash to all of this wacky fracturation and, especially, the iTunes DJ mentality. A segment of gay club music makers is starting to look back to the early techno and house days for inspiration, yearning for a time when seamless mixing and meticulously produced four-on-the-floor tunes—not sheer musical novelty—propelled masses onto dance floors.

Honey Soundsystem, a gay DJ collective formed by DJs Ken Vulsion and Pee Play and including a rotating membership of local vinyl enthusiasts, attempts to distill Italo disco, Euro dance, acid house, neominimal techno, and other cosmic sounds of the past three decades into smooth, ahistorical sets spanning the musical spectrum from DAF's 1983 robohomo hit "Brothers" to Kevin Aviance's 1998 vogue-nostalgic "Din Da Da" to the Mahala Rai Banda's 2006 technoklezmer conflagration "Mahalageasca (Felix B Jaxxhouz Dub)."

"Girl, that shit must be pumped out by a computer with a beard somewhere," the 21-year-old Pee Play opined of Energy 92.7's music. I didn't tell him how close to the truth he was as he continued, "But I'm over most of the goofy alternashit too. I never lived though circuit, but the music is fucked-up. I'm just really into quality. I want to play records that every time you hear them, they just get better."

PLAY LIKE BROTHERS DO

I'm not sure if there's such a thing as gay music. If there were, its representative incarnation would probably be closer to experimental duo Matmos's homophilic soundscapes, like those on their 2006 album *The Rose Has Teeth in the Mouth of the Beast* (Matador)—each track named for a gay community hero and composed of poetically related sampled objects ("Sequins and Steam for Larry Levan," "Rag for William S. Burroughs")—than anything that ever soared from Donna Summers's throat. As far as gay dance goes, the epochal choreography of the un-compromisingly out Mark Morris, currently the hottest dance maker in the country, may prove more historically resilient than the image of semiclothed bears raving on a cruise ship.

Yet despite the Internet drain, clubs are still where homos meet to get sweaty, and the music they get sweaty to has a big impact on the culture at large. Dance music is ephemeral in the best sense: how good it sounds has everything to do with how and where you experience it and what and who you experience it with. Energy's playlist was per-fectly amusing in a broadcast booth full of campy, happy people or while twirling half naked in my BF's bedroom. But in a club setting, maybe not so much—it all depends on who my been-there, done-that ass is dancing next to, no?

I recently spoke with Steve Fabus, one of the original DJs at San Francisco's legendary Trocadero Transfer gay disco, launched in 1977. He's been spinning continuously for 30 years and has pretty much seen it all. "Dance music is magic—it's what gay people *are*," he explained. "It brought us together and kept us going through some incredibly hard times. Disco gathered everyone under one roof, and then house came along and did the same. Circuit was fun in the beginning, but it got too aggressive, and people of color or people into other things didn't feel welcome. It took over everything, and, of course, it burned out."

"I love that kids are expressing themselves in smaller clubs, with dif-ferent kinds of playing. It's encouraging," he continued. "But it's a shame that circuit took the big clubs down with it, where everyone could share in this experience together. Of course, there are other factors involved—crystal meth, the Internet, economics. You have to be very clever to be gay and live here now. It's just so damned expensive."

"But oh well," he said with a laugh. "Everything comes in cycles."

PETE SEEGER

You'd say it was the heart of America, if America had just the one heart. On a breezy summer morning, two thousand souls gather by a river— the beautiful Hudson river, two miles wide, framed by the tall spans of the Newburgh-Beacon bridge.

Pick-ups and well used cars, older guys with long hair and whiskers and wonderfully cheery wives, a few younger families too, are assembling at Beacon's small waterside park for the Strawberry Fair. It's an annual fund-raiser for the Clearwater sloop project, which, since the late '60s, has been campaigning to clean up the river.

There's plenty to interest and delight: a smithy, a bouncy galleon, the Hudson Bio-Diesel Co-op, Patricia's Presents, radical badges ("That's *Mr* Faggot to you"), and the eponymous strawberry shortcake stall— 1,200 pounds of fruit and whipped cream at your service.

A tinny tannoy pipes up, the DJ's opening selection Woody Guthrie's "This Land Is Your Land." Then "Deportee."

Over by the stage—a grassy mound—a long, lean man, plainly old, yet radiating vigor, unloads an array of paraphernalia from his estate car. A sledgehammer. A tyre with a lump of tree trunk affixed to it. A banjo.

Pete Seeger. At 87, the living library of American folk music. Woody Guthrie's friend and constant champion. Parent or foster-parent of "We Shall Overcome." "Where Have All The Flowers Gone?," "If I Had A Hammer." Pathfinder for Dylan, Baez, the whole '60s folk and protest song movement. Honoree of Bruce Springsteen's recent *Seeger Sessions* album. And chief instigator of both fair and sloop club.

He's lived just outside Beacon (pop. 14,000, 60 miles north of New York City) since 1949 when, with Toshi—his wife for 63 years (currently manning the cream whipper)—he bought a cheap patch of hillside, cleared it, and built a log cabin (augmented by more modern accommodations in the '80s). They brought up their three children there.

So the town's used to having him around, both the music legend and the activist who'll begin his address at the Clearwater tent with the line "When I was a Communist . . ." Even beyond liberal circles, he is appreciated. "Very down to earth," they say. A storekeeper adds that the riverside park was a dump with "rats this big" and all the trash bulldozed into the Hudson weekly until Seeger and the sloop club campaigned and city hall spent $800,000 on reclamation.

At midday, the appointed time, Seeger, a plate of waffles in hand, strides over to *Mojo* and suggests we talk over a picnic table. Before a question's asked, he's introducing a ruminative aside with one of his recurring phrases: "If we're still here in a hundred years . . ."

He talks like an American freight train, long, slow, meandering, unstoppable, weighty. That weight comes not just from what he's sung. It comes from what he's done.

This is the man he is. Back in 1955, at the height of America's Red Scare paranoia, an official drove up the track to Seeger's cabin and handed him a summons to testify before the notorious House Un-American Activities Committee (HUAC) about alleged Communist links.

As the McCarthy era's key instrument of political persecution, HUAC's objective was, via the tacit but potent threat of blacklisting, to coerce its victims into confessions of Communist/pinko/liberal fellow-travelling and then, piling disgrace on terror, to denunciations of their friends.

That August in New York, Seeger stood before the Committee's inquisitors and took the toughest course available, the one that could lead to imprisonment. When they asked whether he'd performed at Communist Party benefits, he refused to "plead the Fifth," the legal sidedoor favoured by most perfectly sound lefties. It meant you had the right to remain silent, but Seeger bridled at its implication of incriminating evidence withheld. Instead, he asserted his Constitutional First Amendment right of free speech.

He told the Committee, "I'm not going to answer any questions as to my associations, my philosophical or religious beliefs . . . I think they are very improper questions for any American to be asked, especially under such compulsion as this."

The following year, HUAC indicted him for contempt of Congress, but then delayed the trial until 1961, when he was sentenced to 12 months imprisonment. He appealed and, a further year on, was finally cleared—the judge declaring him constitutionally correct, although politically "unworthy of sympathy."

In his Seeger biography *How Can I Keep From Singing?*, David Dunaway writes that during this period and beyond he "became the most picketed, blacklisted entertainer in American history. . . . If Seeger had been made of soft wood instead of oak, he would have cracked."

Yet Seeger bluffly denies both fear and courage in holding the line: "I didn't have any job to be fired from. I could keep on singing for lefty groups and schools and colleges. So I was able to take a stronger stand." (Of course, in a sense, Toshi and the children took that stand with him, and he has often hailed their support as a crucial bulwark when he's out rampaging for a cause.)

Stronger stands have been Seeger's lifelong habit. He stood on picketlines in the early '40s under threat from police and strikebreakers. He kept on singing his radical songs when, in 1942, his first group, The Almanac Singers, were blacklisted out of record deals, radio shows, and gigs. He sang for 1948 Progressive Party Presidential candidate Henry Wallace and got pelted with rotten eggs and tomatoes when the campaign swung through the South. The following year, in Peekskill, near Beacon, he sang on a bill with black Communist movie and opera star Paul Robeson at an outdoor benefit for the Civil Rights Congress and drove home through a hail of rocks thrown by New York state Ku Klux Klansmen (his father-in-law shielding the Seeger infants in the back of the car). In the late '50s and '60s, with civil rights workers being murdered weekly, he sang in cottonfields and churches and marched to Montgomery with Martin Luther King.

Resonant macho phrases like "he never backed down" aren't relevant. Seeger has readily admitted to physical fears, occasionally running from baton-wielding cops for example. But he kept the faith.

Ask how he came by his inexhaustible commitment and he immediately harks back to childhood: the influence of novelist and American Boy Scouts founder Ernest Thompson Seton—"I tell people I became a Communist at age seven because of his stories of how the American Indians shared whatever they had; I decided that's the way people should live"—and of his father, Charles, a passionately socialist academic who was forever devising schemes to bring classical music to "the masses" (they proved singularly ill-suited to the desperate days of the '30s Depression).

Still, when Pete didn't take to the classics, Charles bought him a ukulele and later introduced him to 5-string banjo, the fundamental instrument of mountain folk music. Pete always remained close to his father and his radical precepts, such as "The question is not 'Is it good music?' but 'What is the music *for?*'"

While President Roosevelt's New Deal began hauling America out of the mire in the late '30s, Seeger went to Harvard, joined the Young Communist League, failed his exams, and so stumbled into his vocation. His father introduced him to Alan Lomax, already working for the Library of Congress in Washington. He put Seeger to work "listening to thousands of folk and blues records." In these songs, Seeger once noted, he discovered the "meat of life." Through Lomax too, he met folk and blues originals Leadbelly, Aunt Molly Jackson, Sara Ogan— and Woody Guthrie, the estate agent's son who'd reinvented himself as the ultimate Okie troubadour.

Lomax dated "the renaissance of American folk song" to the first Seeger-Guthrie encounter, at a "Grapes Of Wrath" benefit in New York on March 3, 1940. Soon after, Guthrie moved into the spartan Greenwich Village apartment Seeger shared with his fellow Almanac Singers. As a popular and prolific songwriter with apparent working-class credibility the others lacked, he was welcomed into the band.

Seeger often wondered why Guthrie liked him when he "didn't drink, didn't smoke, didn't chase girls." For his part, Seeger loved Guthrie's music and style and studied him devotedly. When they hitchhiked to Texas together in 1940, it was Seeger's boho-hobo finishing school.

On the road with Guthrie, he co-wrote his first song—"66 Highway Blues"—but the Woody life curriculum went much further. "He taught me to speak bad grammar," Seeger laughs. "And he told me, 'Pete, if you go in a bar, sling the banjo on your back, buy a nickel beer and sip it as slow as you can. Sooner or later somebody'll say, Kid, can you play that thing? Say "A little," and keep on sippin' your beer. Sooner or later somebody'll say, Kid, I've got a quarter for you if you'll pick us a tune. *Now* you swing that banjo around!'"

Guthrie showed him how to ride the freight trains too. "You don't jump on it inside the railroad yard," Seeger advises. "Wait till it's outside of town, you trot alongside, grab hold of the steel rungs and climb up to the roof."

Seeger soon felt so confident the left Guthrie with his family in Texas and set off on his own—up to copper-mining Butte, Montana, over to coal-mining Harlan County, Kentucky. "With Woody's advice I was able to learn about my country the way I never would have if I'd stayed at Harvard," he concludes.

Guthrie even gave Seeger an early lesson in coarse realpolitik. From 1940, the Almanacs had followed the American left line by writing peace songs—because, following the 1939 Hitler–Stalin non-aggression pact, war would mean fighting Communist Russia. Then in June, 1941, the radicals flew into a dither when news broke that Germany had invaded Russia. Guthrie got back from a cross-country jaunt that day. "I opened the door and there was Woody with a wry smile on his face," Seeger recalls. "He says, Well, I guess we won't be singin' any more peace songs. I say, What? You mean we're gonna have to support Churchill? He says, Yup, Churchill's callin' for 'All aid to the gallant Soviet allies!' Churchill's flip-flopped. We gotta flip-flop."

And so they did. War songs instead of peace songs. Seeger even joined the army (a few years later he drifted out of the Communist Party having realized Stalin was actually a monster rather than a "hard driver").

For the next ten years he dedicated himself to his mission: breathing life into traditional folk, developing new topical and political material, and always remembering to get the audience singing because if it wasn't *their* music it was no use at all. For a couple of years from 1950 he did give commercial folk a try with The Weavers. They sold millions, but he agonized over bowdlerizing songs like "Irene, Goodnight"—Leadbelly's original featured morphine and sex—and they got their topsy-turvy pay-off when, regardless of their anodyne music, they were blacklisted to death for their lefty connections.

Even in strait-laced late '50s America, the blacklist proved an ineffective censor among large swathes of the first rock 'n' roll generation. With Toshi finding a lot of customers who "didn't care for HUAC," Seeger reeled off 200 to 250 solo gigs a year. It was one of McCarthyism's more accidental spin-offs: Pete Seeger inventing the college circuit and becoming the cornerstone of the '60s folk revolution.

"I sang from college to college, summer camp to summer camp," he says. "Probably the most important job I ever did in my life was carry on the music of Woody Guthrie like that. A lot of talented new songwriters came along to pick up where he left off."

The gawky veteran became a lightning rod. Joan Baez saw him in California, Tom Paxton in Oklahoma, Bob Dylan in Madison, Wisconsin, January 1961. Seeger's potent connection to the past, to a sense of purpose, reached ever wider as his songs—the anti-McCarthyite "If I Had A Hammer," the anti-nukes "Where Have All The Flowers Gone?" —began to chart, albeit sung by other artists.

Dylan, imbibing New York by the barrel, and Seeger, ever alert to new talent, probably first met in February 1962 at a gathering of contributors to seminal new folk magazine *Broadside* (a handcranked effort running on $35 a week provided by the Seegers). "I remember sitting there with Bob and Phil Ochs thinking, I'm in the same room as two of the greatest songwriters in the world!" he says. By the end of the year Seeger was playing Dylan's "Masters of War" and "Hard Rain," promoting him as he had Guthrie.

Dylan appreciated the acceptance in a community where, as he wrote in *Chronicles Vol. 1*, "They didn't know what to make of me. Pete Seeger did, though."

Their rapport was cemented in July 1963, when Dylan, unusually, stepped up to the political frontline by playing with Seeger in Greenwood, Mississippi, at a black voter registration rally—300 fieldhands in a cotton patch.

Of course, their harmonious phase came to a notorious end at Newport Folk Festival in 1965 when Dylan went electric and Seeger, in one of his rare yet comprehensive outbursts of temper, rushed the sound desk hollering that he'd like to cut the cables with an axe—for the very Seeger reason that "I wanted to hear the words."

In Scorsese's documentary *No Direction Home*, Dylan recalled how pained he was to realize he'd upset Seeger: "Someone whose music I cherished and someone I highly respected *(he clutches his chest),* oh no, it was like a dagger. The thought of it made me go out and get drunk."

They sort of reconciled later; Dylan sang at Seeger's Guthrie memorial concert in 1968 and Seeger always remained an admirer of his music, even attending a Dylan concert at a minor league baseball stadium near Beacon in 2004.

By the end of the '60s, Seeger's moving and shaking days were over—although he strode on through middle and old age gigging and campaigning as ever, he says bluntly, "I could have kicked the bucket, my job was done." At least he'd been able to close the era with one of the greatest audience-participation routines ever: leading half a million singing "Give Peace a Chance" at the climax of the 1969 anti–Vietnam War demo in Washington.

But, in 1998, the reawakening of interest due a living legend began with a double CD tribute, "Where Have All The Flowers Gone?" Although Roger McGuinn, Ani DiFranco, Donovan, Billy Bragg, and more covered Seeger-related songs, Bruce Springsteen, who sang "We Shall Overcome," was to prove the most significant contributor.

He'd listened to every Seeger record he could find and, at the time, he said: "Pete had a real sense that songs were tools, and righteous implements when connected to historical consciousness. At the same time he always maintained a tremendous sense of fun and lightness. Everything I wanted. I found there. I wanted to continue doing things that Pete had passed down and put his hand on."

The seed sown, it took eight years to germinate into *The Seeger Sessions* album, an event that caught Seeger on the hop: "1 didn't know about it until Bruce called me when it was ready to be produced. He's a great singer and it was an honour. But I wish he hadn't used my name because now my cover's blown. The mail comes in by the bushel."

Does he actually like the album?

"Oh, some of it's really great. "Old Dan Tucker" was the hit song of 1844 and Dan Emmett, who wrote it, would be proud of Bruce's rendition. I'd prefer "Oh Mary Don't You Weep" in a major key so everybody can join in. He changed it to minor. . . ."

Seeger hears himself being a persnickety old folkie and laughs, takes a bite of waffle, and commences a discourse on the immutable perfection of "Danny Boy." "It was written 400 years ago, you know. . . ."

Seeger has always been wary of ego and personality, but he still loves to perform. He's up on that grassy mound all afternoon announcing acts, plugging the strawberry shortcake, talk-singing a few choruses—"Sorry, my voice is so gone now"—and picking his long-necked five-string Deering banjo. Around the skin it still says—after Woody—"This machine surrounds hate and forces it to surrender."

At the end of the day, he spends some time clearing up litter. Then, spying Mojo, with a gleam in his eye he picks up that six-pound sledgehammer, swings it way back over his head and smashes it down onto a railroad spike protruding from the top of that previously enigmatic log-and-tyre contraption. He falls into a rhythm, grunting phrases of a chaingang chant with each swing. John Henry lives . . .

Breaking off, he's not too puffed to proffer an "If we're still here in a hundred years . . . it will be because we've all become involved in local events like this." Before we're done he'll add a "The human race has a 50/50 chance of being around in a hundred years if we learn that the happiest people are those who are working together."

But it would be simplistic to take him for some kind of fool to optimism. In the private journals to which he gave the biographer, Dunaway, access, Seeger wrote: "I seem to stagger about through this agonized world as a clown dressed in happiness, hoping to reach the hearts and minds of the young. When newspaper reporters ask me what effect my songs have, I try and make a brave reply, but I am really not so certain."

Such doubts must be the bitter part of his inner truth. Yet they can never negate his heartfelt, life-force decency.

Closing our interview, he mentioned a song he'd learned recently: "It was written in Arabic by an engineer in Beirut. It starts, 'Sing to her, call to her, and though she is far away she will come closer, but you must call to her.' Well, who is she? 'Light of the sun, light of the moon, the countries in all four continents are but a drop in your ocean, oh Freedom.' Now you know. She's Freedom. You sing the opening again, and you sing that line, 'But you must call to her,' over and over. Isn't that wonderful?"

The Story of "We Shall Overcome"

A silver voice echoed round the Lincoln Memorial and soared high above Washington until the quarter of a million people assembled to demand that congress pass President Kennedy's Civil Rights Bill were all singing with Joan Baez, "We shall overcome, we shall overcome someday."

It was August 28, 1963. Rather better remembered, naturally, is that Martin Luther King was about to say, "I have a dream. . . ." Even so, it was the day the great freedom anthem met its destiny.

Pete Seeger traces the song to a hymn called "I'll Overcome Someday," composed in 1903 by Philadelphia preacher Charles Tindley, a slave's son. Its first recorded step beyond black communities came in 1946 when Zilphia Horton, music director at radical, desegregated Highlander Folk School in Monteagle, Tennessee, learned it from strikers, mainly black women, at a Charleston, South Carolina, tobacco plant. They'd secularized the hymn and switched the "I" to "We."

Horton knew Seeger and taught it to him. He published it in his *People's Songs* magazine and started singing it everywhere he went, adding verses and probably shifting the "Will" to "Shall" because it sang better. In 1952, touring California, he passed it on to white folkies Frank Hamilton and Guy Carawan.

Carawan then became the song's key promoter. After Horton's death in 1959, he took over as music director at Highlander, by then a civil rights movement hotbed. But Carawan found that black activists had largely forgotten "We Shall Overcome," so he started using it in song workshops.

Meanwhile, it kept changing. When police closed Highlander for breaking segregation laws—they arrested four teachers, including Carawan—student Mary Ethel Dosier responded with the "We are not afraid" verse. When the school reopened in Knoxville, Bernice Reagon, founder of The Freedom Singers and Sweet Honey In The Rock, shifted the rhythm from stolid hymnal to what Carawan called "the Motown beat."

But it really took off after 1960's founding convention of the mixed-race Student Non-Violent Co-Coordinating Committee in Raleigh, North Carolina. Carawan attended, introduced some campaign songs and "We Shall Overcome" took hold. Within weeks it soundtracked every sit-in, freedom ride and march news clip.

Seeger sang it with Dylan and The Freedom Singers at a voter registration rally in a Mississippi cotton field. He sang it again in a black church in Meridian, Mississippi, the night in 1964 when student campaigners Goodman, Schwerner, and Cheney were found dead (murdered by the Klan).

He notes that, at the time, not everyone thought it ideologically sound. Seeger's fellow HUAC inquisitee, playwright Lillian Hellman, railed at him "We shall overcome *someday, someday?*" But Bernice Reagon replied, "If we said, 'next week,' what would we sing the week after next?"

"We Shall Overcome" was copyrighted in 1960 by Carawan/Hamilton/Horton/Seeger—the late Zilphia Horton represented by her husband Myles, who founded Highlander—but they assigned all royalties in perpetuity to the We Shall Overcome Fund, which still gives annual grants for "art and activism against injustice in the South."

JEFF SHARLET

THE PEOPLE'S SINGER

THE EMBATTLED LEE HAYS

In 1950, Lee Hays sent his siblings the first proof of his existence they'd had in more than a decade: baby-brother Lee, all three hundred pounds of him, harmonizing his deep, dark bass voice on a recording of "Goodnight, Irene," the No. 1 hit in the nation. Lee was thirty-six, but his voice sounded old and smooth, and at the same time hard, exposed: an oak shivered open. "Stop rambling, stop your gambling," Lee sang, a verse ironic in more ways than one:

> Stop staying out late at night
> Go home to your wife and family
> Stay there by your fireside bright

Last any Hays had heard of Lee, he was on his way to getting lynched, a gentle fool of a giant running after dangerous dreams: lilywhite Lee planning a black Boy Scout troop in Mississippi, pinko Lee organizing a mixed-race union of sharecroppers in Arkansas, "Professor" Lee teaching Yankees how to put on Communist plays in Southern churches. And then he'd gone missing. In a ditch? In a river? To Moscow? Now he resurfaced on top of the charts, in *Time* magazine, singing on TV for Uncle Miltie. He was the foundation of a "folk sensation," a hillbilly quartet by way of Greenwich Village: the Weavers: Lee's bass, Freddy Hellerman's neat baritone, Ronnie Gilbert's fire-alarm alto, and the wry tenor of Lee's old pal Pete Seeger, all dipped in the syrup of an orchestra imposed by the record company and loved only by Lee. He appreciated a sound as big as his belly, his politics. He called himself a socialist, but he liked to say he didn't know what kind. That wasn't quite true; he was the singing kind. As far as he was concerned, collectivism meant four-part harmony. He hated to sing alone, took no solo bookings, insisted on sharing credit for his songs. "Sharing made him a little less vulnerable," remembered a guitarist who backed him. "Lee needed a group to be Lee Hays," says one of his protégés, the singer Don McLean. "That's why he invented the Weavers." They were all Lefties, but it was Lee's longings—one part Red, one part religion, one part the angry empathy of a closeted gay man raised holy-roller in rural Arkansas—that provided the tilt that made "Goodnight, Irene" lilt so lovely out of jukeboxes across the country.

Lee and Pete had borrowed the song from an idol of theirs named Leadbelly. A good many of the Weavers' songs were Leadbelly's. Lee and Pete probably first gleaned "Midnight Special," "Rock Island Line," "Goodnight, Irene," and the tune to which Lee wrote "Kisses Sweeter Than Wine"—all huge Weaver hits—gathered round Leadbelly's twelve-string guitar and a bottle of bourbon in his Lower East Side apartment. Both Lee and Pete worshipped the black ex-con *Life* magazine had called a "Bad Nigger"—an actual headline. The real Leadbelly was a sophisticated artist, a font of American songs. Not just the blues, but also ballads and folk and gospel and reels, country, jazz, and pop. He remembered everything he ever heard and mixed it together as the spirit led, as the hour demanded, as the liquor flowed. Leadbelly taught Pete what Lee already knew: "authenticity" was a trap, purity was a dead-end, no song belonged wholly to anyone. Lee didn't "appropriate" Leadbelly's songs, he made *sub*-versions, each one a variation of an old song both new and noisy with the ghosts who'd sung it before him. "Art is a weapon," went a radical slogan of the day; Leadbelly was an armory.

Pete memorized the notes; Lee felt them. He was loose with language. Not careless; agile. Before he went North, he specialized in what he called "zipper songs." He'd make them out of hymns and sing them at the secret meetings of the sharecroppers union back home in Arkansas—"zipping" radical words into a song like "The Old Ship of Zion" ("It's that *union train* a-coming-coming-coming"), prepared, he explained, "to break into the hymn words if gun thugs should appear."

But that was back in the '30s, when Lee led with a movie-star chin and followed with smiling blue-sky eyes, when he was still filled with enough Holy Ghost—Lee always had the Ghost—to believe that change was coming soon. "See the lynch rope a-swinging," he'd write, "see the torches burn/The people said, wake up, it's time to learn/Time to get together, drive the evil men out/And make a new land in our own South."

In the end, though, it was Lee, no fighter, who got driven out, running North by stages: to Cleveland, where he educated himself working in a library, reading all the books marked with a black stamp as indecent—D.H. Lawrence, Upton Sinclair, tales from a renaissance said to be taking place in Harlem; to Philadelphia, where he became "Uncle Lee" to the household of the avant-garde poet Walter Lowenfels; to New York City, where he shared a place on West 10th Street with a gangly green banjo picker named Pete Seeger, a living catalogue of five hundred songs, enthrallee of Lee's Southern storytelling bona-fides. "Lee and I found we got along very well," Pete would tell Lee's biographer, Doris Willens. "He liked the sound of my banjo accompanying him, and I really admired his way with an audience."

Lee's signature song was "State of Arkansas," a dirge about the miseries of his home state that shifts effortlessly to hillbilly humor. The song's narrator pays for a bottle of whiskey with a mink skin and gets "three 'possum hides and fourteen rabbit skins for change." Then the song turns again, ending, like most of Lee's thoughts, somewhere between mournful and funny:

> *If you ever see me back again*
> *I'll extend to you my paw*
> *But it'll be through a telescope*
> *From hell to Arkansas*

Pete, built like his long-necked banjo without the curves, empty-pocketed scion of the New England Seegers all got-up in sharecropper drag, became the straight man to Lee's shambling, smoky lush, big-eared and bag-eyed, a black suit draped over his giant frame. Joining them was a half-pint Okie already of some renown, Woody Guthrie, with whom Lee shared a bottle nightly, more frequently if it could be arranged. Woody was fond of ripping Pete's working-class affectations to tatters, pointing his nose in the air and dripping Harvard vowels. Pete—known as "The Saint"—couldn't or wouldn't come up with a response, so Lee would find himself defending the Yankee barely out of his teens. Together with a revolving cast that included Cisco Houston, Josh White, and Sis Cunningham, they called themselves the Almanac Singers. They were the group from which Bob Dylan would take his talking blues, and to which every folk, pop, rock, and hip-hop radical who followed owes a debt of rebellion. "If you want to know what's good for the itch, or unemployment, or Fascism, you have to look in your Almanac," Lee declared in a radical newletter he put out later in the decade, *People's Songs*. "That's what Almanac stood for." Soon there were more Almanacs than Lee could count, singers and songwriters and guitar pickers and accordion squeezers crowding into unheated urban communes Lee called Almanac Houses. They sang "Which Side Are You On?" in churches, "Get Thee Behind Me, Satan" in union halls. "Songs about peace, white collar workers, air raid wardens," Lee wrote, "the sinking of a destroyer, love, unemployment, coal miners, songs about the Almanacs themselves."

They also sang the party line, although often as not they fell out of tune. As "order-takers," Lee confessed, they were a failure. Lee sang for the Communist Party, campaigned for it, believed in its goals. But he never joined it. "If Communists liked what we did," Lee summed up, "that was their good luck."

But even up North, Lee couldn't escape the torches burning, the lynch-rope swinging. In 1949, after the Almanacs had dissolved because of the war and because Pete kicked Lee out (some would say it was politics; Lee would say it was because he'd been lazy), and after a union of radical folkies they'd organized folded (Lee, lazy, kicked-out again), a mob of lowercase people, actual workers and farmers, attacked a concert Lee and Pete helped organize in the Hudson river town of Peekskill, just north of New York City.

The headliner was Paul Robeson, the stage and screen star of *Show Boat*, *Othello*, and *The Emperor Jones*. The "Russia-loving Negro baritone," the local *Evening Star* called him, an advance man for Moscow. The paper urged the local citizenry to stop Robeson and his Red friends by any means necessary.

On the scheduled day, the Leftist novelist Howard Fast (later the author of *Spartacus*) arrived early on the scene. It was one of those afternoons when the sun seems too sleepy to set, a goldenrod evening. The concert ground was a meadow at the end of a dirt road, its entrance a bottleneck; gathered around it like a noose was a crowd jeering at each passerby. Fast found a group of teenagers. "Just keep cool," he told them. "Nothing will happen."

Then a boy came running around the bend. Fast and a few dozen others followed the boy back to the entrance: Down from the banks of the road poured a mob of three hundred attackers.

Fast, a veteran of the Jewish street gangs of New York, found himself in command. He formed a small group of concert-goers into a defensive line at the entrance to the concert grounds, flanked by a ditch on one side and wetlands on the other. Fast surveyed his troops—skinny boys from Harlem in church clothes, summer-camp counselors, bohemian hoboes whose fingers were more used to plucking six-strings than making fists—and told them that now they'd learn to fight. "We stood in line in the gathering dark, arms locked, singing, 'Freedom is our struggle, we shall not be moved.' Every few seconds, there was a sickening thud as a rock crashed against the skull of one of our boys," Fast would write for *Daily Worker*. "Some held their places with the blood pouring from their torn scalps; others went down."

Night fell, a lull followed. They saw that the policemen had vanished. The mob shifted shape. Veterans in American Legion caps remembered their wartime lessons. They charged through the dark in waves, men with billies and men with bottles, Red-scared men swinging posts ripped from white picket fences.

Lee and Pete later memorialized the fight in a song, "Hold the Line," which would become an anthem of the Civil Rights movement:

> *Hold the line! Hold the line!*
> *As we held the line at Peekskill*
> *We will hold it everywhere*

But the truth was that they held the line only by backing it up, foot by bloody foot, till they were forced into a ring around the stage. Someone smashed the lights. Women led crying children in "The Star Spangled Banner." The mob chanted "Kill a Commie for Christ!" The night turned brilliant with a bonfire of two thousand folding chairs. A wooden cross burned. Three government men in suits stood taking notes as the townsmen, now some seven hundred strong, gathered up songbooks and sing-along sheets and threw them into the flames.

The concert's organizers rescheduled for the following week. And up from the city, from Brooklyn and the Bronx and the Lower East Side, came an army of three thousand union men to defend the concert-goers. Instead of the originally planned audience of two thousand, twenty thousand showed. Pete brought his banjo and belted out Lee's lyrics to their new song, "If I Had a Hammer": "I'm hammering out danger!" And Robeson sang his famously radicalized version of "Ol' Man River":

> *I must keep fightin'*
> *Until I'm dyin'*
> *And Ol' Man River*
> *He'll just keep rollin' along*

After a few more numbers, the Lefty crowd was ready to declare victory and get the hell out of Peekskill.

The townspeople had made plans, too. With the help of some nine hundred local and state police officers, another mob funneled the concert-goers onto the aptly named Division Street—"a long gray tunnel" Lee called it in an account he wrote for the radical *Sunday Worker*. Thousands of protestors waited, pre-stacked rock piles at the ready. State troopers looked the other way; a police helicopter thumped overhead; local deputies cheered as each car had its windows smashed. "White niggers get back to Russia!" rioters screamed. Or, reduced by rage to one word, "Jews! Jews! Jews!" They began flipping vehicles, dragging out men first, and then women, for beatings with clubs and brass knuckles and, most of all, shoes—work boots and wingtips and women's pumps swinging into the bellies and teeth of schoolteachers and garment workers and railroad porters.

Lee and Woody made it out on a bus, Lee close to crying and Woody cracking wise. "Anybody got a rock?" Woody called. "There's a window back here that needs to be opened." Then Lee started to sing: "I'll sing out *danger!*" he began, in the middle of the lyric, his great barrel of a voice transcending his terror. "I'll sing out a warning!" Woody joined in: "I'll sing out love between my brothers, all over this land."

The next day started late in Peekskill. The sign at the outskirts that declared PEEKSKILL IS FRIENDLY TOWN was joined by another, replicated in store windows up and down Main Street: WAKE UP AMERICA! PEEKSKILL DID.

If this was America, Lee thought, it's not mine. "Sometimes I live in the country," went the number he now sang after Peekskill, "Goodnight, Irene," a subtler, sadder kind of zipper song.

> *Sometimes I live in town*
> *Sometimes I take a great notion*
> *To jump into the river and drown*

Pete's banjo plucks the rhythm, Ronnie Gilbert's alto slips into the water, Lee's big bass aches the lullaby. That's all it was to the hit parade, but to Lee, especially, "Goodnight, Irene" was a secret language, "a great notion"—all that could be said for a nation that responded to folk songs with burning crosses, the "drowning" as much of an allusion to Leadbelly's darker words (a junkie's lament, a love gone cold) as Decca Records would allow. For those who could hear, the song was thick with broken-hearted meanings, an elegy for wrong choices and a hope for the sweet, revolutionary bye and bye.

Irene, goodnight. Irene, goodnight
Goodnight, Irene, goodnight, Irene
I'll see you in my dreams

In 1950, when Lee sent out records of "Goodnight, Irene" to his siblings—one each to brother Reuben, a banker; to Bill, a salary man; and to Minnie Frank, a newspaper poetess—he attached a note relaying as much as he figured they'd be able to understand about where he'd been, what he'd seen, the revolution that didn't happen. His letter was just six words long: "This is what I've been doing."

That was as true as the three minutes and twenty-two seconds of "Goodnight, Irene," from the first swell of the strings glued on by a hit-conscious record company to the fade of four voices.

This is what Lee had been doing:

After he'd given up on Reuben, Bill, and Minnie Frank for hopelessly bourgeois, Lee found new brothers and sisters among the black and white labor organizers who became his heroes, his muse. One evening, late 1930s, riding with them in a rump-sprung car through the cold Arkansas night, Lee discovered that singing could save him from his constant fear. Not the words of a song, but simply the sound of his voice mixing with others, those who sang along with him and those who'd sung before him, most of all his father. He'd been a big man, an itinerant preacher who carted a vast, eccentric library around Arkansas. He died in a car crash when Lee was thirteen; Lee's mother went insane shortly thereafter. There was a sense in which Lee, too, never recovered.

Lee was not a brave man. Despite his size—his mastiff shoulders and a head as large and hard as a tree stump—he shrank from physical confrontation, from physical activity in general. He was tubercular, though he didn't know it then, and the diabetes that would, piece by piece, rob him of his legs in later years may have already set in. He had run away from home, but he believed his family had abandoned him. (In a sense they had: His siblings were scattered across the country.) Hunger and loneliness aged him. Beneath the deep bass and behind his hillbilly routines, Lee was *afraid*, as permanent a condition as the sexual desires he referred to, obliquely, in a pseudonymous review of now-forgotten novels by gay writers he deemed too "defensive" about their longings. "Have you ever been married?" acquaintances who didn't know better (which was most of them) would ask, and Lee would crack his broad thin lips in a grin, his little liquor-soaked teeth like a row of corn on the cob, and tell a tale about his first time, way back when, with a "golden-haired girl," in a Confederate cemetery; no more questions, please.

His old fears were strong that cold night in the rump-sprung car. It was marked for violence, as was its owner, a labor organizer who'd once been whipped by bosses with the belly band of a mule harness. "The organizer drove warily, hunched over the wheel," Lee wrote. "The young Negro boy beside him watched the road just as carefully, and his feet pressed the floorboards every time the organizer stepped on the brakes. The Negro man and the white woman who sat in the rear with me were tense, and I could feel their bodies tightening up every time we passed a car or went through a town.

"The organizer started singing."

Ordinarily, they'd sing union songs. "But in this cold night we sang hymns." They'd all been raised in the church and all had converted to the union; they believed in deliverance, here and now, not salvation in the hereafter. But they remembered the old words, harmonies swelling and breaking ("Floods of joy o'er my soul like the sea billows roll") bass voice giving way to sweet soprano, the organizer's raspy baritone coming in with a verse or a chorus, one hymn after another, and all the voices searching, working for harmonies unheard and unknown, perfect blends of tones and feelings and fears.

I wondered about this, why we found such comfort in the old hymns, we whose eyes were fixed on a new day and a new way of life. For awhile it was possible not to be scared, even.

But the answer was there, and it came to me that the words of the song didn't matter. They were there and we sang them, but what mattered was that we were singing.

Lee was a believer. Like his father who died pinned to the wheel of his overturned open-top Ford on a two-lane outside of Booneville, Arkansas, like his mentor, Claude Williams, a radical Presbyterian known as the Red Preacher, a white Arkansan beaten and jailed for the same Christian hope Martin Luther King, Jr., would die for decades later.

But Lee's god wasn't God, it was "The People," that great abstract many-faced mass. You could call Lee's religion communism, but he'd just as soon call it a song. "One dreams of a great people's song," he wrote in 1948, as close as he ever came to declaring a creed, "of our marching song which will come again, but hasn't yet; of the great song which is still unsung." He believed it would be a battle hymn, remembered for generations, a victory song, like John Brown's glory. He wanted in on it. He tried zipping labor and race into "We Shall Not Be Moved." He wrote the words to "If I Had a Hammer." He rang his aching vocal chords like two-ton church bells on "Hold the Line."

And yet Lee harbored few illusions about his faith: He knew that the People, like the Lord, could be fickle or mad or mysterious, vengeful or loving or silent—painfully silent—in the face of injustice. The People, Lee's divine, were only human. Maybe that's why Lee could almost never get through some solemn labor anthem without a goof, a twist, a joke, sometimes a fable.

"I never knew but one person in my life that didn't like singing or music in any form," went a story he liked to tell between songs. "He was a Southern preacher who belonged to a church that thought all music was sinful, etc., etc. I would argue with him about it by the hour and say, 'Preacher, I just can't understand your point of view. Music is divine, it's the language of the angels. It defines the indefinable, expresses the inexpressible.' But he would just say, 'I wouldn't care if it unscrewed the inscrutable, it's sinful and I don't like it.'"

In 1951, Lee alone among the Weavers realized that the battle was lost. When they hit the top of the charts with "So Long (It's Been Good to Know Yuh)" and Pete seethed over being booked in swanky fat-cat clubs in Hollywood and Vegas instead of union halls in Arkansas, Lee ordered room service and toasted every jukebox in America that made the Weavers the most popular group of the summer.

Besides, it was only a matter of time before some goon dug up their past and reported that the tuxedoed quartet was in truth a singing sleeper cell direct from Moscow. Some goon! An actual Judas, an F.B.I.

informer named Harvey Matusow, aka "Harvey Matt," the former head of the People's Songs Music Center.

Matusow would later describe his fatal kiss in a book called *False Witness*. He and the editors of a newsletter called *Counterattack*—three former F.B.I. agents who functioned as a faucet for J. Edgar's leaks—found themselves frustrated as they mulled over the Weavers' success. They loathed such hits as "On Top of Old Smoky," "Pay Me My Money Down," and "Midnight Special"—America-hating music, they believed, Commie-code. But they had nothing on the Weavers themselves. "They could not be placed in the Communist party," Matusow wrote. "Having known all four of them, not as Communists, but as friends, I triumphantly said, 'I know them, and they are Communists.'"

And that was it. Bookings disappeared. Records disappeared. Top of the charts in 1950, by the end of '52 their names weren't safe to whisper. Called before HUAC in 1955, Pete invoked the First Amendment, a move that earned him a prison sentence of a year. Lee wasn't so brave. Lacking Pete's puritan pride, he was too scared to admit he even knew his own words. "We have just heard one of your songs, entitled, 'Wasn't That a Time,'" said the committee's counsel. "Were you the author of it?"

Lee declined to answer.

"I don't think I have ever felt so damned alone as on that day," he'd remember in 1981, the year he died. "When I got home my heart hurt and I place the beginnings of my heart trouble to that day."

Lee would sing again, but in a sense the rest of his life was just a long, slow exhalation. Don McLean recalls Lee circa 1968. He lived on a half-acre up along the Hudson. His neighbors were fellow blacklist veterans. His visitors were young musicians who heard the love but not the danger in the song that paid for Lee's liquor, "If I Had a Hammer," made into a hit by Peter, Paul, and Mary. Some days were very fine. He still had his legs then, and he loved to garden. Some days he was afraid of what lay beyond, what he'd left behind. Some days he was just mean. He'd disappear into his cottage, waste the day filling an ashtray as big as an urn. "Lee still had his voice," remembers McLean, "but he was shrinking. Like the air was coming out of him."

At the end of 1955, the Weavers held a reunion. Their manager beat the blacklist by renting Carnegie Hall for a nameless quartet and then selling it out before anyone could complain. Their opening number was "Darling Corey." If you've ever wondered what the Left once was in America—the Old Left that organized American labor and did FDR's heavy lifting and fought fascists in Spain in 1936 and in Peekskill in 1949—listen to "Darling Corey" as the Weavers sang it in 1955. It's a ghost, a memory even then, but still it's more thrilling than anything that played on the radio that year—or last year, for that matter—a punk battle hymn for four voices. Pete tears it open with a single note, spitting bullets out of his long-necked banjo. He was mad and proud and bitter, playing for the fallen and the falling, for Leadbelly and Woody—who was two-thirds gone now, dying of Huntington's Disease in Brooklyn—and for the Weavers themselves. It was a new sound for Pete, Woody's sound. Not the jokes, but the anger. The difference between Pete and Woody could be seen on their instruments. In a neat circle bordering his banjo, Pete wrote, *this machine surrounds hate and forces it to surrender.* Across the hips of his guitar, Woody scrawled, *this machine kills fascists.* That night in 1955, Pete turned his banjo into Woody's old killing machine. The first spray of notes is followed by a plummeting spiral like a man stepping— leaping—off a cliff. Enter four voices: *Wake up, wake up, darling Corey!*

The song is about a moonshining mountain woman, but as Lee would say of his favorite hymns—he'd zip one of his hee-haw routines into "Amazing Grace" later that very evening—the words don't matter. The opening blast of harmony is Gabriel's horn, a mash-up of the Red Army Choir and the Mormon Tabernacle Choir and an Alabama chaingang, the First Amendment and the Fifth and all the others side by side, singing out the most joyous *fuck-you* ever drawn up from the well of rage and heart hurting.

The first booming verse, of course, belongs to mighty Lee Hays:

> *Well first time I seen Darling Corey*
> *She was standing by the sea*
> *Had a .45 strapped 'round her bosom*
> *She had a banjo on her knee!*
> *Maybe the words do matter.*

Like these, the beginning of the third verse, Ronnie Gilbert's alto whooshing in like cannonballs:

Oh yes, oh yes, my darling!

Lee was the reader of the group, a student of banned books and a writer of pornographic tales, so maybe he heard the Irish echo of James Joyce's Molly Bloom. "Yes I said yes I will Yes," the last words of *Ulysses*. Joyce thought Molly Bloom's "Yes" signaled the end of resistance; acquiescence. Lee heard the "Yes" of "Darling Corey" differently, louder, even, than Molly Bloom's transcendent submission, heard it to the end of his days, when he was legless in a little cottage up along the Hudson, not far from Peekskill, where he came to know and even befriend some of the men and women who'd had blood in their throats and rocks in their fists back in 1949. He heard that opening number in Carnegie Hall in the winter of 1955—sang it—like a hymn on a cold night in Arkansas. For awhile, it was possible not to be scared, even.

LARRY BLUMENFELD

BAND ON THE RUN
IN NEW ORLEANS

On the evening of Oct. 1, some two dozen of New Orleans' top brass-band players and roughly a hundred followers began a series of nightly processions for Kerwin James, a tuba player with the New Birth Brass Band who had passed away on Sept. 26. They were "bringing him down," as it's called, until his Saturday burial. But the bittersweet tradition that Monday night ended more bitterly than anything else—with snare drummer Derrick Tabb and his brother, trombonist Glen David Andrews, led away in handcuffs after some 20 police cars had arrived near the corner of North Robertson and St. Philip streets in New Orleans' historic Tremé neighborhood. In the end, it looked more like the scene of a murder than misdemeanors.

"The police told us, 'If we hear one more note, we'll arrest the whole band,'" said Tabb a few days later, at a fundraiser to help defray the costs of James' burial. "Well, we did stop playing," said Andrews. "We were singing, lifting our voices to God. You gonna tell me that's wrong too?" Drummer Ellis Joseph of the Free Agents Brass band, who was also in the procession, said, "They came in a swarm, like we had AK-47s. But we only had instruments."

The musicians were no longer playing but instead singing "I'll Fly Away" when the cops converged and the cuffs came out. A New Orleans police spokesman claimed the department was simply acting on a neighborhood resident's phoned-in complaint. And the department maintains that such processions require permits.

But when they busted up the memorial procession for a beloved tuba player, arresting the two musicians for parading without a permit and disturbing the peace, they didn't just cut short a familiar hymn—they stomped on something sacred and turned up the volume in the fight over the city's culture, which continues amid the long struggle to rebuild New Orleans.

In that fight, Tremé is ground zero. Funeral processions are an essential element of New Orleans culture, and the impromptu variety in particular—honoring the passing of someone of distinction, especially a musician—are a time-honored tradition in neighborhoods like Tremé, which some consider the oldest black neighborhood in America. For black New Orleans residents who have returned to the city, these and other street-culture traditions—second-line parades and Mardi Gras Indian assemblies—offer perhaps the only semblance of normalcy, continuity and community organization left. In a changing Tremé, within a city still in troubled limbo and racked by violent crime, long-held tensions regarding the iconic street culture have intensified. The neighborhood, the breeding ground for much of this culture, has a history of embattlement. And now more of that history is being written.

"I've been parading in the Tremé for more than 25 years, and I've never had to deal with anything like this," said tuba player Phil Frazier, who leads the popular Rebirth Brass Band. He's brother to James, who died of complications of a stroke at 34. "I told the cops it was my brother we were playing for, and they just didn't seem to care. He's a musician and he contributed a lot to this city in his short life."

Katy Reckdahl, a reporter for the *New Orleans Times-Picayune*, had rushed to catch up with the Monday-evening procession when her 2-year-old son Hector heard tubas in the distance. What she didn't expect was a sudden flood of patrol cars, sirens blaring. Her front-page, full-banner-headline report two days later described police running into the crowd, grabbing at horn players' mouthpieces, and trying to seize drumsticks out of hands. "The confrontations spurred cries in the neighborhood about over-reaction and disproportionate enforcement by the police, who had often turned a blind eye to the traditional memorial ceremonies," she wrote. "Still others say the incident is a sign of a greater attack on the cultural history of the old city neighborhood by well-heeled newcomers attracted to Tremé by the very history they seem to threaten."

It's unclear who called the police that night. But it's easy to sense the difference, longtime residents say, between North Robertson Street before and after the storm. With its proximity to the French Quarter and historic architecture, Tremé, which was not flooded, is newly attractive to home buyers within the city's shrunken post–Hurrican Katrina housing stock. Meanwhile, as in most of New Orleans, rents have sharply increased. Derrick Jettridge, who was born and raised in the Tremé, now lives in the Mid City section. "I'd never find something in Tremé for the $500 I was paying before," he says. On her New Orleans Renovation blog, Laureen Lentz wrote recently, "Since Katrina, the Historic Faubourg Tremé Association has gathered a lot of steam. Our neighborhood is changing as people have begun to realize that this area is prime, non-flooded real estate. . . . So much is happening in Tremé, it's hard to convince people that aren't here. You have to see it to believe it."

Home prices in Tremé rose nearly 20 percent immediately following the flood, settling at approximately 12 percent above pre-Katrina rates, according to Al Palumbo, branch manager for the historic districts office of Latter & Blum Realty. "Tremé, especially the area around North Robertson and St. Peter, would certainly be among my first choices for return on investment in New Orleans," he says.

But what might such development in the neighborhood ultimately cost? The intensity of the police response during the Kerwin James procession prompted a second-line of print voices, so to speak, in the *Times-Picayune*'s pages.

"If somebody is blowing a horn in Tremé and somebody else is calling the police," wrote columnist Jarvis DeBerry, "only one of those people is disturbing the peace, and it isn't the one playing the music."

Nick Spitzer, creator of the public-radio program "American Routes," wrote in an Op-Ed piece, "in a city where serious crime often goes unprosecuted and unpunished, jazz funerals make the streets momentarily sacred and safer."

"New Orleans Police Department declared a resumption of its war against our city's culture," declared columnist Lolis Eric Elie.

The day following the skirmish, discussions between community leaders and 1st District police Capt. Louis Colin yielded a temporary agreement. The evening after the arrests, Andrews, Tabb and other musicians were back on those same streets, leading another procession, this time protected by a permit, which some residents viewed as a disappointing compromise. "We don't need anyone's approval to live our lives," one resident told me.

Efforts to curtail these neighborhood processions as well as the more formal Sunday afternoon second lines hosted by social aid and pleasure clubs, who apply for official permits, continue to threaten traditions already weakened by the loss of residents in Katrina's aftermath. Participants view this as deeply hypocritical, given that so much promotion of tourism for New Orleans includes images of brass-band musicians and second-line dancers.

In April, a federal lawsuit on behalf of a consortium of social aid and pleasure clubs, aided by the American Civil Liberties Union, protested the city's hiking of police security fees—triple or more from pre-Katrina rates—for second-line parades held September through May. The suit invoked the First Amendment right to freedom of speech and expression, claiming that parade permit schemes "effectively tax" such expression. "Should the law not be enjoined," the complaint stated, "there is very little doubt that plaintiff's cultural tradition will cease to exist."

At a street-corner press conference a few days after the musicians' arrests, Jerome Smith, who runs the Treme Community Center just a block from that scene, recounted the history of an embattled neighborhood. He invoked the memory of heavy-handed police intimidation at the 2005 St. Joseph's night gathering of Mardi Gras Indians, after which Allison "Tootie" Montana, the "chief of chiefs," famously collapsed and fell dead of a heart attack while testifying at a city council meeting. He referenced the "open scar" of nearby Louis Armstrong

Park, for which the city demolished 13 square blocks of the Tremé. He spoke of how, in 1969, the creation of Interstate 10 replaced the stately oak trees of Claiborne Avenue, the neighborhood's main thoroughfare, with concrete pillars.

On the Sunday following the arrests, Councilman James Carter held a meeting with residents at Smith's center. One neighborhood activist, Al Harris, brought an enlarged copy of a photo, mounted on posterboard, of a Tremé second line in 1925. "We've been doing this a very long time," he said. Carter said that "under no circumstances is it acceptable for police to violate our cultural traditions." He announced plans for a task force organized through his Criminal Justice Committee to propose new city ordinances protecting the cultural practices under fire, and to initiate education and sensitivity training for officers and new residents of Tremé.

Such education could have easily been found in some documentaries screened last week during the city's 18th annual film festival. "Faubourg Tremé: The Untold Story of Black New Orleans," created by filmmaker Dawn Logsdon and Elie, the *Times-Picayune* columnist, offered a powerful reflection of Tremé as a place of creative ferment and political resistance for some 300 years, which included Paul Trevigne's Civil War–era founding of the country's first black newspaper, and the unsuccessful 1896 Supreme Court challenge, in Plessy v. Ferguson, to racial segregation. At one point Elie wondered in the film's narration, "How can our past help us survive this time?" Glen David Andrews, one of the men arrested Oct. 1, was featured playing his horn and as an interview subject.

Andrews also figured in "Shake the Devil Off," filmmaker Peter Entell's chronicle of a particularly cruel twist in modern Tremé history: Six months after Katrina, the Archdiocese of New Orleans decided to close the neighborhood's St. Augustine church and to remove its pastor. The historic church was founded in 1841 by slaves and free people of color. After a 19-day rectory sit-in, the parish was restored, provisionally, though its long-term fate remains in question. Near the film's climax, after footage of Jerome Harris and Jesse Jackson speaking to a crowd, the camera moved in on Andrews, who launched into "I'll Fly Away," offered as call-to-arms rather than memorial.

A question-and-answer session following a screening of "Tootie's Last Suit"—filmmaker Lisa Katzman's gloriously insightful look at the world of Mardi Gras Indians through the story of Tootie Montana's final days—drew some discussion of the recent Tremé arrests.

"We won't bow down," said Sabrina Montana, daughter-in-law of the film's main character, quoting a familiar Indian-song lyric. "This has nothing to do with our disrespect for authority and everything to do with our self-respect. Until what we do is on the city charter, second-line and Mardi Gras Indian assemblies will continue to be threatened by the whims of those who are in authority."

Following the public outcry, Sgt. Ronald Dassel of the New Orleans Police Department was quoted in the *Times-Picayune* saying, "We don't change laws for neighborhoods." But in fact the city does and always has. Special legislation protects the tourist-rich French Quarter, for example. The mostly white Mardi Gras carnival parades command a long list of specific ordinances (including much lower permit fees than for second lines). And a recent judge's order, which some critics consider unconstitutional, delineated police arrest and release protocols for municipal offenses specifically by neighborhood—with the Tremé among the neighborhoods subject to the sternest treatment.

Recently, I was walking along the bayou with Andrews when he ran into a friend. "Did you hear what they're calling you two?" his friend asked, referring to Andrews and Tabb. "The Tremé 2! We're making T-shirts."

Andrews winced. "I'm not looking to be somebody's martyr," he said.

Sure enough, a couple of T-shirts emblazoned with "Free the Tremé 2" could be seen at Vaughn's bar during a Saturday fundraiser for attorney Carol Kolinchak, to support her pro bono work for Mychal Bell, one of the defendants in the Jena 6 case. Kolinchak is also representing Andrews and Tabb, who are due to appear in court in early December.

"Of course, I wouldn't compare the situation they are facing to Mychal Bell's," said Kolinchak. "However, the discretionary decisions by law enforcement and prosecutors—on how and when to enforce the law—require attention in both situations. And those issues lie at the heart of the problems surrounding culture in New Orleans."

Tabb, the drummer who plays in the Rebirth Brass Band and is raising money to create a nonprofit music school, recoils at the thought of children watching musicians hauled off by police for making music. And he says he thinks Andrews may have been singled out by authorities; in addition to leading his Lazy Six band, Andrews is a ubiquitous presence not only at second lines, but also at civic rallies.

New Orleans after Katrina may never fully return without its iconic street culture. And its renewal—financial as well as spiritual—may be more closely tied to those traditions than city officials grasp. But those who practice the traditions know it. On Friday, Oct. 5, the nightly memorial procession for Kerwin James wove through the neighborhood, culminating on the very spot of the arrests prior that week. Andrews put down his trombone and sang "I'll Fly Away," as Tabb snapped out beats on his snare. A tight circle surrounded the musicians, as a middle-aged black woman turned to the man next to her. "They say they want to stop this?" she asked softly. "They will never stop this."

At their October 4 arraignment, Glen David Andrews and Derrick Tabb pleaded innocent to charges of parading and playing music without permits and "disturbing the peace by tumultuous manner." After first requesting a trial postponement in December, the city attorney dismissed the charges by February 20, 2008, offering no further comment.

DAVID KAMP

SLY STONE'S HIGHER POWER

Will Sly show up?

I sure hope so. I have an appointment with him. I've flown across the country and quadruple-checked to make sure that we're still on.

To cynics and music-industry veterans, this very premise is laughable: an appointment with Sly Stone. Yeah, right. For 20-odd years, Stone has been one of music's great recluses, likened in the press to J. D. Salinger and Howard Hughes. And in the years before he slipped away, he was notorious for not showing up even when he said he would. Missed concerts, rioting crowds, irritated promoters, drug problems, band tensions, burned bridges.

But in his prime, Stone was a fantastic musician, performer, bandleader, producer, and songwriter. Even today, his life-affirming hits from the late '60s and early '70s—among them "Stand!," "Everyday People," and "Family Affair"—continue to thrive on the radio, magically adaptable to any number of programming formats: pop, rock, soul, funk, lite. He was a black man and emphatically so, with the most luxuriant Afro and riveted leather jumpsuits known to Christendom, but he was also a pan-culturalist who moved easily among all races and knew no genre boundaries. There was probably no more Woodstockian moment at Woodstock than when he and the Family Stone, his multi-racial, four-man, two-woman band, took control of the festival in the wee hours of August 17, 1969, getting upwards of 400,000 people pulsing in unison to an extended version of "I Want to Take You Higher." For one early morning, at least, the idea of "getting higher" wasn't an empty pop-culture construct or a stoner joke, but a matter of transcendence. This man had power.

He also had a compelling penchant for folly. In the jivey, combustible early 1970s, when it was almost fashionable for public figures to unleash their ids and abandon all shame—whether it was Norman Mailer's baiting a roomful of feminists at New York's Town Hall or Burt Reynolds's posing nude on a bearskin for *Cosmopolitan*—Sly was out on the front lines, contributing some first-rate unhinged behavior of his own. Like marrying his 19-year-old girlfriend onstage in 1974 at Madison Square Garden before a ticket-buying audience of 21,000, with *Soul Train* host Don Cornelius presiding as M.C. Or appearing on Dick Cavett's late-night ABC talk show while conspicuously, if charmingly, high. "You're great," Stone told his flummoxed host in 1971, in the second of two notorious visits to Cavett's soundstage. "You are *great*. You are *great*. You know what I mean? [Pounds fist on heart.] *Booom!* Right on! Sure thing. No, for real. For *real,* Dick. Hey, Dick. Dick. Dick. You're great."

Cavett, grasping for some sense of conversational traction, smirked and replied, "Well, you're not so bad yourself."

"Well," said Sly, eyes rolling up in contemplation, "I am *kinda* bad. . . ."

Sly Stone is my favorite of the rock-era recluses, and, really, the only big one left. Syd Barrett, the architect of Pink Floyd's entrancingly loopy early sound, passed away last summer at the age of 60, having resisted all entreaties to explain himself or sing again. Brian Wilson, the fragile visionary behind the Beach Boys, has been gently coaxed out of his shell by his friends and acolytes, and now performs and schmoozes regularly. He doesn't count as a recluse anymore.

But Sly has remained elusive—still with us, yet seemingly content to do without us. I have been pursuing him for a dozen years, on and off, wondering if there would ever come a time when he'd release new material, or at the very least sit down and talk about his old songs. I've loved his music for as long as I've been a sentient human being—he started making records with the Family Stone when I was a toddler. And over time, as the silence has lengthened, his disappearance from public life has become a fascinating subject in and of itself. How could it have happened? How could a man with such an extensive and impressive body of work just shut down and cut out?

"I often tell people that I have more dead rock stars on tape than anyone, and they'll say, 'You mean Janis, Hendrix, and Sly?'" says Cavett today. "A lot of people think he's *gone*." Even if you're aware that Sly lives, you have to wonder what kind of shape he's in, projecting that beautiful but reckless man of 1971 into 2007, the year he turned 64. What of the dark rumors that he's done so much coke that his brain is zapped, and that he now exists in a pathetic, vegetative state? What of the more hopeful rumors that he's still writing and noodling with his keyboards, biding his time until he feels ready to attempt a comeback?

I had long dreamed of the latter scenario. Syd Barrett excepted, they *do* all come back. Brian Wilson did. The Stooges did. The New York Dolls did. Even Roky Erickson, the psychedelic pioneer from the 13th Floor Elevators, long presumed to be fried beyond rehabilitation by electroshock treatments he received in the early 1970s, has staged a robust return to the live circuit.

My hopes for a Sly comeback were highest in 2003. That year, in the back room of a music store in Vallejo, California, where Sly grew up, I sat in on a rehearsal of a re-united Family Stone led by Freddie Stone, Sly's guitarist brother. Freddie was intent on recording an album of entirely new material that he had written with his sister Rose, who played organ and shared lead vocals in the old group. "Sylvester's doing very well, by the way," Freddie told me, using his brother's given name. Gregg Errico, the band's drummer, who was also in on the reunion, explained that, while they weren't counting on Sly to join them, they had set a place for him just in case, like Seder participants awaiting Elijah. "We profess that the keyboard is on the stage, the [Hammond] B3's running, and the seat is warm for him," Errico said.

But that reunion quickly fizzled out. After that, my Sly search lay dormant; I pretty much gave up. He hadn't shown his face in public since 1993, when he and the Family Stone were inducted into the Rock and Roll Hall of Fame. Characteristically, Sly slipped in and out of the ceremony without saying much, barely acknowledging his siblings and bandmates. So why would he ever want to perform again, much less meet up with a stranger?

Then, out of nowhere, there began a series of brief, intriguing resurfacings. In August of 2005, he was sighted in L.A. on a chopper motorcycle, giving his sister Vaetta, who goes by the nickname Vet, a ride to Hollywood's Knitting Factory club, where she was performing a set with her band, the Phunk Phamily Affair. The following February came Stone's enigmatic appearance at the 2006 Grammy Awards, in which he loped onto the stage in a gold lamé trench coat and plumy blond Mohawk, performed a snippet of "I Want to Take You Higher" with some guest musicians paying him tribute, and loped off again before the song was over. And in January of this year, Stone put in a surprise cameo at Vet's band's show at the House of Blues in Anaheim, California, adding vocals and keyboards to their performances of "Higher" and "Thank You (Falettinme Be Mice Elf Agin)."

What to make of this? Was Sly's newfound·quasi-visibility a sign that, at last, his return was nigh? Early this year, I managed to get in touch with Vet Stone, who confirmed that her brother was indeed planning a return: a show in San Jose on July 7 with her band (which, with Sly's blessing, has been renamed the Family Stone), and then some summer dates at festivals in Europe. After several telephone conversations in early spring and one meeting with me in person, Vet called one day with the news: Sly would speak. We would meet up on May 9 in Vallejo, his hometown, 25 miles north of Oakland.

ARE YOU READY?

On the designated day, Vet and I arrive early at the designated meeting place: Chopper Guys Biker Products Inc., a Vallejo business that manufactures parts and frames for custom motorcycles. Sly, who lived in L.A. on and off for 36 years but recently relocated to Napa Valley, gets his bikes serviced here. As Vet and I kill time chatting, we eventually notice that it's about 10 minutes past the appointed start time of our meeting. Nothing worrying, but a long enough period to have faint thoughts of *Hmm, maybe this won't work out.* Vet tells me how many doubters she's had to deal with in booking those summer European dates, "people who wouldn't take my call, people who hung up on me, people who think I'm a delusional woman." She has been the catalyst of Sly's tentative re-emergence, the one who pulled him out of L.A. and found him a home up north, who persuaded him to play with her band and get back out on the road again. It's exhausted her, and she's openly daunted by the logistics of planning for her brother, never the smoothest of travelers, to fly to Europe and then zip from Umbria to Montreux to Ghent.

But she's gotten this far, which fuels her faith. "All I can say," she says, and it's something she says a lot, "is that I'm his little sister, and he's never lied to me." Nevertheless, even Vet is starting to get a little nervous about the interview, checking her cell phone, stepping outside the front door of Chopper Guys with me to see if anyone's coming.

And then, like John Wayne emerging from 'cross the prairie in *The Searchers* . . . a strange form advances through the wavy air in the distance: some sort of vehicle, low to the ground, rumbling mightily as it turns off the highway and into the parking lot. As it comes closer, the shapes become clearer: a flamboyantly customized banana-yellow chopper trike, the front tire jutting four feet out in front of the driver. He sits on a platform no higher than 18 inches off the ground, legs extended in front of him, his body clad in a loose, tan shirt-and-pants ensemble somewhere between Carhartt work clothes and pajamas. His feet are shod in black leather sneakers with green-yellow-red African tricolor trim. Behind him, on an elevated, throne-like seat built between the two fat back tires, sits an attractive, 30-ish woman in full biker leathers. He always was good at entrances.

Sly Stone and his lady companion, who I learn is named Shay, disembark from the chopper and walk toward the shop. He applies pink baby lotion to his hands, which I notice are huge, with elongated, tapering fingers.

He's still very slim—there was never a Fat Sly period—and he does not appear frail, as several recent reports have described him. In fact, he moves rather well, especially for a 64-year-old man who's just spent time scrunched into a custom-chopper cockpit. But he has the same hunched posture he had at the '06 Grammys—a bit like Silvio Dante's in *The Sopranos*—and he wears a neck brace.

We shake hands and say hello. I've heard he owns an old Studebaker, so I tell him I, too, own an old Studebaker. "Really, what year?" he says, looking up at me with a smile. He pulls two chairs together for our chat, a metal stool and an old barber's chair. As all these mundane things are transpiring, I realize I'm recording them in my mind like a doctor observing a patient recovering from brain trauma. *He is aware of his surroundings. He is capable of participating in linear conversational exchanges. He is able to move chairs.*

The only strange part: he is still wearing his helmet and shades when we sit down to talk. *Good lord,* I'm thinking, *is he going to wear the helmet the whole time?* Fortunately, without my prompting, Vet says, "Why don't you take your helmet off?," and Sly obliges, revealing a backward San Francisco Giants cap.

"Still sporting the blond Mohawk under there?" I ask.

"Naw, not now, it's very short," he says. Then, deadpan: "Most of it growing *under* the skin."

I start the interview in earnest with the most obvious question: "Why have you chosen to come back now?"

At this, he grins. "'Cause it's kind of boring at home sometimes."

"But it's bigger than just being bored at home, isn't it?"

"Yeah, I got a lot of songs I want to record and put out, so I'm gonna try 'em out on the road," he says. "That's the way it's always worked the best: Let's try it out and see how the people feel."

Stone tells me he has a huge backlog of new material, "a *library,* like, a hundred and some songs, or maybe 200." This subject, I come to understand, animates him like no other. With the old songs, he seems uninterested in analysis. When I ask him if he was consciously trying to do something different with his December 1969 single "Thank You (Falettinme Be Mice Elf Agin)," which, with its chanted unison vocals and slap bass, effectively invented 1970s funk—without it, no Parliament-Funkadelic, no Ohio Players, no Earth, Wind & Fire—he replies simply, "Well, the title was spelled phonetically. That was one thing different."

Likewise, on more personal matters, such as what else he was up to in his AWOL years, he's evasive: "Just traveling—going around, jumping in and out, and up and down." He doesn't flinch when I broach the subject of his hunched posture and neck brace, but it's clear he doesn't want to break out the M.R.I.'s, either. "I fell off a cliff," he says. "I was walking in my yard in Beverly Hills, missed my footing, and started doing flips. But you know what? I had a plate of food in my hand. And when I landed, I *still* had a plate of food in my hand. That's the God-lovin' truth. I did not drop a *bean*."

But when I ask Stone to describe the new songs, he straightens up, rocks forward in his seat, and starts rhyming in an insistent cadence somewhere between a preacher's and a rapper's, the rasp suddenly gone from his otherwise low, throaty speaking voice. "There's one that says, 'Ever get a chance to put your *thanks* on? / Somebody you know you can *bank* on? / Even sometimes you might embarrass them by pulling *rank* on? / Now, whatcha gonna do when you run out of them? . . . Another holiday, you're drunk and *curbing* it / You can't face a noun, so you're straight ad*verb*ing it / You had an argument at home, and you had to have the last *word* in it / Now whatcha gonna do when you run out of them?'

"There's one that's called 'We're Sick Like That,'" he continues. "It says, 'Give a boy a flag and teach him to salute / Give the same boy a gun and teach him how to shoot / And then one night, the boy in the bushes, he starts to cry / 'Cause nobody ever really taught him how to die.'"

The obvious allusion to the current war jars me, and I soon realize why: Stone has been absent from the scene for such a duration that it's hard to imagine that he was with us all along, experiencing all the things we experienced over the years—the fall of the Berlin Wall, the collapse of the Soviet Union, Nelson Mandela's release from prison, the rise of the World Wide Web, the attacks on 9/11, the invasion of Iraq.

It's almost as if he went into a decades-long deep freeze, like Austin Powers or the astronauts in *Planet of the Apes*. Except he didn't. "Did you do normal-person things?" I ask about the missing years. "Did you watch *Cheers* in the 80s and *Seinfeld* in the 90s? Do you watch *American Idol* now? Do you have a normal life or more of a Sly Stone life?"

"I've done all that," he says. "I do regular things a lot. But it's probably more of a Sly Stone life. It's probably . . . it's probably not very normal."

The Sly Stone life started getting abnormal shortly after his band's euphoric Woodstock performance. Joel Selvin, the veteran music critic of the *San Francisco Chronicle*, published a thoroughgoing, book-length oral history of the group in 1998 (simply called *Sly and the Family Stone: An Oral History*) that is as disturbing and chilling a version as you'll ever find of the "dashed 60s dream" narrative: idealism giving way to disillusionment, soft drugs giving way to hard, ferment to rot.

It's agreed upon by everyone Selvin interviewed—which is pretty much everyone in Stone's family, band, and circle of hangers-on, apart from Sly himself—that the bad craziness began when he forsook the Bay Area for Southern California, in 1970. Exit the music of hope and the gorgeous mosaic; enter firearms, coke, PCP, goons, paranoia, isolation, and a mean-spirited pet pit bull named Gun.

"There is a cloud flying over Sly from the time he moved down to Los Angeles," the Family Stone's original saxophonist, Jerry Martini, told Selvin. "Things really changed when he moved down there. . . . It was havoc. It was very gangsterish, dangerous. The vibes were very dark at that point."

Before that, though, there was the Bay Area Sly of the 1960s, a different character altogether: a personable, outgoing, uncommonly talented young man who cut quite a swath through the region's music scene. He was born Sylvester Stewart into a loving, tight-knit family presided over by a father, K.C., and a mother, Alpha, whose marriage would last 69 years. K.C. ran a janitorial business in Vallejo and was a deacon in the local Pentecostal church. From an early age, Sylvester was performing with his siblings in a gospel group called the Stewart Four. Loretta, the eldest of the five Stewart children, provided piano accompaniment, while the four Stewarts of the billing—in birth order, Sylvester, Rose, Freddie, and Vet—harmonized on vocals. "We traveled around from church to church, all over California, performing concerts," says Vet. "We thought we were just like any other family. We had no idea."

The greatest prodigy of all the young Stewarts, Sylvester was also the most driven. He was barely into his 20s when he insinuated himself into the inner circle of San Francisco's biggest music *macher*, the disc jockey and impresario Tom "Big Daddy" Donahue. In 1964, Sylvester collaborated with Donahue on the song "C'mon and Swim," a Top 10 hit for the local soul star Bobby Freeman. Shortly thereafter, he became the house producer at Donahue's label, Autumn Records, working with, among others, the Great Society and the Warlocks, the precursor bands to, respectively, Jefferson Airplane and the Grateful Dead. In the same period, under his new stage name, Sly Stone, Sylvester became a regional radio celebrity, hosting a soul show on the station KSOL from seven p.m. to midnight.

YOU CAN MAKE IT IF YOU TRY

It was all in place, the eclectic mishmash of sensibilities and influences that would inform Sly and the Family Stone: soul, gospel, pop, Haight hippiedom, sparkly showmanship. (In his D.J. days, Stone drove a Jaguar XKE he'd had custom-painted bright purple.) So when Sly decided to start up a band of his own, he knew exactly what he wanted. "It was very deliberate: men and women, different races, dressing different," says Larry Graham, the group's bassist. Martini, the saxophonist and one of the band's two white members (along with Errico, the drummer), recalls Stone playing an almost curatorial role in shaping the band's presentation. Pointing to an old publicity photo that shows him ridiculously attired in a piebald poncho, Martini says, "That was a *rug!* Sly saw a cow skin on the floor, got a rug cutter, cut a hole in it, and said 'Here, Jerry, this is gonna be your outfit.'"

Everyone had a signature look. Errico wore a leopard-print vest-and-trousers getup almost as absurd as Martini's bovine fantasia. Graham wore robes and capes. Freddy Stewart, re-christened Freddie

Stone, wore appliquéd overalls. Rose Stewart/Stone wore a variety of Ikette wigs and go-go dresses. Cynthia Robinson, the trumpet player, favored psychedelic-patterned smocks and let her straightened hair grow out into a Black Power Afro. Sly himself cultivated a neon pimp look, with flashy vests (often worn without a shirt), goggle shades, heavy jewelry, tight trousers, and muttonchop sideburns.

"I remember having lunch with Sly in my dining room, right at the beginning," says Clive Davis, who was in his first year as president of CBS Records in 1967, when its Epic subsidiary signed the group. "I told him, 'I'm concerned that the serious radio stations that might be willing to play you'—by which I meant the underground FM radio stations—'will be put off by the costuming, the hairstyles.' It was almost Las Vegas–like in its presentation. Sly said, 'Look, that's part of what I'm doing. I know people could take it the wrong way, but that's who I am.' And he was right. I learned an important lesson from him: When you're dealing with a pathfinder, you allow that genius to unfold."

Musically, too, Stone orchestrated a theoretically unwieldy but ultimately ingenious fusion of styles. "It's one of the things I really admire about Sly—we were all allowed to use our creativity, to have freedom of expression in how we played," says Graham, whose percussive "thumpin' and pluckin'" bass style became practically a new musical genre unto itself. The band's first and most conventionally soul-like album, *A Whole New Thing*, was a flop, but the exhortative title song of album two, "Dance to the Music," became their first Top 10 hit, in 1968, and remains a party standard to this day.

The album *Stand!* (1969) represented the apotheosis of both the band's signature "psychedelic soul" sound and their status as positivity-preaching messengers from the Utopian, multicultural future. Five of the album's eight songs—"Stand!," "I Want to Take You Higher," "Sing a Simple Song," "Everyday People," and "You Can Make It if You Try"—ended up on the *Greatest Hits* album that came out the following year.

Stand!, tellingly, was the album that the band was touring behind at the time of Woodstock. Graham recalls the festival as a moment when the group's members "tapped into a new zone," achieving a musical power they hadn't realized they were capable of. "It's like when an ath-lete like Michael Jordan realizes the extent of his gifts and goes, 'Oh, I can do *that*,'" he says.

But rather than return to the studio to capitalize on this momentum, Stone bunched himself up into a shag-carpeted cocoon. The year 1970 came and went with no new album and, worse, a new penchant for missing shows—26 out of 80, to be precise. Stone's decision to move to Los Angeles didn't do much for band harmony, either. In 1971, Errico quit, fed up with being summoned to L.A. from his Bay Area home for sessions on the next Family Stone album, only to be kept waiting indef-initely for Stone to use him.

That same year, Stone started renting the Bel Air mansion owned by the debauched hippie king John Phillips, of the Mamas and the Papas, which had been previously owned by Jeanette MacDonald, squeaky-clean star of corny 1930s MGM operettas. The L.A. music mogul Lou Adler, Phillips's best friend, recalls that the house across the street (which was used for exterior shots in *The Beverly Hillbillies*) was owned by a wealthy hotelier named Arnold Kirkeby. "The Kirkebys were a very conservative family," Adler says, "and they hated the flowing robes that John and his wife, Michelle, wore, the caftans and Nehru collars. They were very pleased that a 'Mr. Sylvester Stewart' was moving in. They liked the sound of that."

Needless to say, Stone and his new entourage left even John Phillips appalled. "There were lots of guns, rifles, machine guns, and big dogs" on his property, he later lamented.

"At some point, I started getting concerned about stories I heard about Sly's personal habits," says Clive Davis, who was also worried that his star artist might never deliver a new album. "But every time I met with him, he was on top of his game. I was somewhat innocent of the lifestyle going on around me, whether it was him or Janis Joplin."

SPACED COWBOY

Even though he had the Bel Air house and real studios at his disposal, Stone spent much of his time working on the new album, *There's a Riot Goin' On,* in a Winnebago motor home rigged up with recording equipment. ("There *was* a riot in that motor home," Stone says with a smile, not elaborating further.) The remaining Family Stone members played on the album, but no longer did so as a band, instead overdubbing their parts individually. They also had company, in the form of guest musicians Stone had brought aboard, among them the keyboardist Billy Preston and the guitarist Bobby Womack.

"We used to ride around in his motor home, getting high and writing songs and making music," Womack told the British rock journalist Barney Hoskyns. But what started as a lark for the soul and R&B singer-guitarist became a nightmare. "I became paranoid at everything," Womack said. "I was always thinking I was gonna get killed and that the feds were gonna bust in on Sly. Everybody had pistols. It got to the point where I said, 'I gotta get away from here.' Sly be talkin' to you, but he ain't *there*."

Somehow, the album that emerged from this chaos, which was finally released in November 1971, turned out brilliantly, if darkly. *There's a Riot Goin' On* is great "this is your brain on drugs" music. It sounds nothing like the chirpy albums that preceded it. Because Stone kept rerecording and overdubbing on the same master tape, wearing it out in the process, the overall sound is muffled and washed out—a bit of technical malfeasance that serendipitously suited the album's spacey, midtempo songs.

On many tracks, the air of dislocation is enhanced by the cold, metronomic gallop of the primitive drum machine that substituted for the departed Errico. And Stone's vocals are plain spooky—like a supine junkie's before he lapses into a coma. This is true even on the album's catchy, chart-topping single, "Family Affair." Listen to his ghoulish, meandering delivery of the line "Newly wehhhhdd a year ago / But you're still checkin' each other out / Yeahhh." It's like hearing a heat-warped 45 played at 33 r.p.m.

There's a Riot Goin' On has been as picked over and decrypted by rock critics as anything in Bob Dylan's catalogue. The opening line of the opening song, "Luv N' Haight"—"Feels so good inside myself / Don't wanna move"—is often interpreted as Stone's statement of retreat into solipsism, a repudiation of his flower-power "Everyday People" ethos of the 1960s. The late Timothy White, the *Billboard* editor and former *Rolling Stone* writer, called the album "a brooding, militant, savage indictment of all the decayed determinism of the '60s."

But Stone himself seems oblivious to the very fact of all this tea-leaf reading. "People say *Riot* is about Sly Stone's disillusionment with the 60s dream," I tell him.

"Oh, really?" he says, genuinely surprised.

"Yes, what do you make of that?"

"That may be true," he says.

"*May* be?" I say. "It's you! Is it true or isn't it?"

"I mean, I've never thought about it like that," he says. "I don't really feel like I'm disillusioned. Maybe I am. I don't think so, though."

I ask if his writing was impacted by any of the period's ugliness—the Kent State killings, the Attica prison riots, the M.L.K. and R.F.K. assassinations.

"Um, I paid attention to it," he says, "but I didn't *count* on it. I wasn't going on any other program or agenda or philosophy. It was just what I observed, where I was at."

Still, Stone doesn't totally dismiss those who ascribe loftier meanings to the album. When I ask him if he regards *There's a Riot Goin' On* in any way as a political statement, he says, "Well, yeah, probably. But I didn't mean it to be."

RUNNIN' AWAY

The success of *There's a Riot Goin' On,* which debuted at No. 1 on the *Billboard* album chart, obscured the fact that the band was further disintegrating and that Stone's unreliability was increasingly a problem to concert promoters. The no-show subject remains a sore one with Stone, who says he wasn't as bad as he was made out to be. "I got tired of going to concerts where I'd have to pay a bond, pay money in case I didn't show up," he says. Stone claims that some of his missed dates weren't his fault but acts of collusion between promoters and transportation people, who cynically exploited his reputation for flaking out. "I later found out that they had a deal going between the promoter and the guy that was taking me to the gig," he says. "So I would put up the $25,000 or the $50,000. The guy with me would help me be late, and I didn't realize that was what was going on until later. Then they'd split the money. That kind of stuff can play on your attitude a little bit. I wasn't so focused after a while."

Larry Graham bolted from the band in the tumultuous period after *Riot*'s release, having grown estranged from Stone. If the witnesses in Selvin's oral history are to be believed, each man had developed an entourage of gun-wielding flunkies, and Graham feared for his life. Graham, now a devout and unrelentingly upbeat Jehovah's Witness, is reluctant to get into the details, except to say, "Maybe things were exaggerated in the past. During those periods of time, there were a number of elements I couldn't control. I wasn't the leader. Whereas Sly was the leader: he chose to have certain people around him. Sly and I were, and still are, a family. At some point, a member of a family needs to leave home."

With a new bassist, Rusty Allen, Stone managed to put out one more great album, *Fresh* (1973), and one more pretty good one, *Small Talk* (1974). But the fragmentation of the "classic" lineup was the beginning of the end, and a prelude to Stone's reclusive, unproductive years. From the mid- to late 1970s, his output was low in inspiration and didn't sell well, notwithstanding the desperate hopefulness of the titles he gave his albums: *High on You* (not on drugs; on *You!*); *Heard Ya Missed Me, Well I'm Back;* and *Back on the Right Track.*

By the 80s, the situation was just dire—too sad to qualify as gonzo Keith Richards druggy bravado or *This Is Spinal Tap* muso-comedy. Stone was arrested several times for cocaine possession. He missed several court dates. In 1984 he shortsightedly sold his publishing rights to Michael Jackson's publishing company, Mijac Music. And creatively he'd dried up. The last new music he recorded for commercial release came out in 1986: a duet with Jesse Johnson, of the Minneapolis group the Time, on Johnson's solo single "Crazay"—an acceptable but undistinguished slice of period shoulder-pad funk. "I don't even know what that song was about, to this day," Stone says. "I just happened to go in the studio."

His drug use is another one of those subjects that Stone won't delve into too deeply. But he reckons that he got serious about getting sober around 15 years ago. "I'm pretty cool," he says. "I drink now and then, a little bit—beer. And I smoke butts sometimes." When I probe about how he managed to "clean up," he responds with a shrewd bit of verbal cryptology that sounds like one of his lyrics: "I just looked around one day, and it *was* cleaned up. Just hardly was nothing there. Just . . . certain people were not around."

I get the sense that Sly relishes this sort of opaqueness—letting people in just enough to intrigue and confound them. Some weeks later, Vet calls to tell me that Sly wants to send me a statement "about the war," by fax. It turns out to be a free-associative *pensée* that touches on our populace's divisions of opinion, the 9/11 attacks, and my own long pursuit of an interview with him. "Our demonstrative ways representing our opinions do us more harm than we are ready to admit," the fax reads in part. "I'd hate to start a fight, but I could get into fighting back. I know what you mean about being tired of callin' me. I was looking at this report having to do with reporters deserving free travel. In utter words, you are deserving of great patience and persistence and you got it. Although both of us know you must be patient before you are one. . . . Just say the truth and hope he doesn't get pissed off at you. You don't need that. I'm invincible . . . no Sly, you're washable and rinseable."

FAMILY AFFAIR

The Chopper Guys get-together was the first time I actually met Stone, but it was the second time this year I'd seen him in the flesh. On March 31, he played his first-ever scheduled concert with Vet's version of the Family Stone—which features only Robinson, the trumpeter, among the original members—at the Flamingo Hotel, in Las Vegas. By "scheduled concert," I mean that Stone was promised to the promoter and the ticket buyers as part of the show; he wasn't merely making an unbilled cameo, as he'd done in Anaheim in January.

It was a curious booking: a concert attached to the stand-up act of George Wallace, a veteran black comedian who routinely works Saturday nights in the Flamingo Showroom, a smallish theater with lounge-style banquettes and tables. The unconventional, low-wattage setup was an indicator of the industry's persistent wariness of Stone. Whereas

Brian Wilson's comeback concerts at the turn of the decade were elabo-
rately stage-managed affairs in posh venues, with an orchestra behind
him and adoring fans in front of him, Stone finds himself in the position of having to earn back the public's trust. "Somebody had to take a
chance," Wallace told EURweb.com, a black-entertainment news service, "so it's me."

As word leaked out about the Flamingo engagement, the skeptics
raised their voices. "There are some doubters who bet Sly will be a no-
show for his show," said an item in the *New York Post*'s "Page Six" column, the day before the concert. "Our bookmaker says the odds are
about even."

When I got to Vegas, I realized how jerry-rigged the Sly comeback
machinery was. There were posters up in McCarran Airport and
throughout the city advertising SLY & THE FAMILY SOTNE at the
Flamingo, but the photo displayed was a poor-quality screen grab of
Stone, with his Mohawk, from the Grammy telecast—evidently the
best the promoters could do in terms of getting a current publicity shot.

The morning of the show, I sat down with Vet Stone, Cynthia
Robinson, and some other members of their traveling troupe. With the
exception of myself and Skyler Jett, a young musician who sings Sly's
leads in the prodigal leader's absence, everyone in the room was a
woman. Among them were Lisa Stone, the pretty daughter of Rose,
who sings her mother's old parts, and Novena, Sly's daughter, a petite,
poised young woman of 25, who, when I asked, said, "My last name's
not important." (Sly also has a daughter in her 30s, Phunn, with Robinson, and a son, Sylvester junior, also in his 30s, with Kathy Silva, the
woman he married onstage at Madison Square Garden in '74 and divorced five months later.)

The matriarchal new configuration of the Family Stone makes sense—
a bosomy, embracing, welcoming change of pace from the phallic
tough-guy posturing of the old days. It's a forgiving group, too. It
couldn't have been easy for Robinson in the 1970s, carrying and raising
Sly's child while he was becoming an epic rock casualty, but here she
was, telling me that Sly's tardiness to concerts was often the result of

noble behavior. "Many times Sly was late because he came back and got the ones who were *really* late," she said. "You know, the first trip we ever made to New York, I missed the flight—and had never been on a plane before. And Sly stayed back, so I'd have somebody to ride with. I didn't ask him to, but he knew I'd never flown."

Vet Stone was never an official member of the original Family Stone, but she contributed backing vocals to their albums from the beginning and had some brief chart success in the early 70s with her own, Sly-produced group, aptly called Little Sister. As down to earth as her brother is interplanetary, she is the one who will go down in the annals as the hero in this happy coda to Sly's life, provided everything stays on track. "I was persistent. I prayed a lot," she told me of her effort to cajole her brother out of retirement.

Her campaign to reclaim Sly started in earnest with their parents' deaths, which occurred within 18 months of each other—K.C.'s in 2001, Alpha's in 2003. "They both died in my arms," Vet said, "and they both told me, 'Go get your brother.' Independent of each other—not knowing. That kind of stuck with me. And it was more than just physically 'go get him.' It was '*Support* him.' So I started going to Los Angeles, maybe sometimes twice a week, to see him. I went and told him what our parents said. He said, 'Find me a house.' And I did."

Sly's new compound, which I get to see a couple of months later, is in a bucolic, isolated spot in Napa Valley. The setting is more Francis Coppola than *MTV Cribs*, with grape arbors and topiary, but it's been Slyed up. In the driveways and garage sits an eccentric array of vehicles: the yellow chopper; a second, still bigger chopper with lightning-bolt detailing; the Studebaker, a burnt-orange Gran Turismo; a London taxi in disrepair; a Hummer that's been haphazardly spray-painted silver; and an old Buick convertible that's been spray-painted black, its front grille replaced with a rectangular length of chicken wire.

BACK ON THE RIGHT TRACK

The night of the Vegas show, after George Wallace had concluded his routine, which included some choice jokes in the "Yo mama" genre (e.g., "Yo mama's so fat, she got a *real* horse on her Ralph Lauren shirt!"), I watched the Family Stone take the stage, minus Sly. They played a proficient revue-style set, effectively a long medley of Sly and the Family Stone's greatest hits. But the audience was growing palpably restless; the fellow next to me was rather belligerently shouting, "Where's SLYYYYY! We want SLYYYYY!"

Then, sometime around midnight—the stroke of April Fools' Day— a man who looked like an extra from a blaxploitation version of *Buck Rogers* sauntered onto the stage. He was wearing a black knit cap, wrap-around white sunglasses, outrageous black platform boots with sneaker-style laces, spangly black trousers cut like newsboy knickers, a matching spangly black jacket, and a red spangly shirt. He sat down at the Korg synthesizer parked center stage and pumped his fist.

"I don't think it's him," said a woman near me, the companion of the impatient shouter. And she had a point. The figure before us was so swaddled, layered, shaded, hatted, be-scarved, and neck-braced, it really *could* have been anyone. But then he went into "If You Want Me to Stay," one of his later hits, from 1973, and everyone recognized that, *Omigod, Sly made the gig.* The place erupted in appreciative cheers, and Stone, tentative and seemingly nervous at first, grew more confident. On "I Want to Take You Higher," he got up from behind his keyboard and boogied down the center-stage catwalk, slapping hands with members of the audience.

It was not a tightly scripted show. Stone wandered the stage between songs, seemingly taking it all in, as if re-acclimating to performing life. He brought out his daughters for their own brief turns in the spotlight. Phunn performed a rap. Novena sat at a piano and played, incongruously but with great skill, "Doctor Gradus ad Parnassum," a fast, heavily arpeggiated piece by Claude Debussy. Their father loitered behind them as they did their bits, shifting from platform boot to platform boot, beaming like a dad at a school assembly.

Stone's own segment lasted a little more than half an hour. Over the course of it, he proved that he is still a limber vocalist, ad-libbing some euphoric, gospelized melismas over "Thank You (Falettinme Be Mice Elf Agin)" and re-creating the scary croak of "Family Affair." But there was one mesmerizing moment that seemed lost on the liquored-up, good-timey Vegas crowd. "Stand!" began not with the rousing drumroll you hear on the record but with Stone singing a cappella in a soft, deliberately fragile voice. ("I just felt like doing it like that—so everybody could really hear it properly," he later told me.) Some of the crowd chattered through it, but to hear him almost whisper these words—

> *Stand*
> *In the end you'll still be you*
> *One that's done all the things you set out to do*
> *Stand*
> *There's a cross for you to bear*
> *Things to go through if you're going anywhere*

—and to know the things he went through, the things he set out to do, the things he achieved, and the things he threw away; and then, to see him there, hunched and older but still standing, onstage, surrounded by family . . . well, it got to me. I misted up.

Stone is intent on getting to work on the new album in the fall, when the European tour is over. He says it will be a Sly and the Family Stone album, not the solo album. Vet's version of the Family Stone will play on it, as will his siblings Rose, who lives in Los Angeles, and Freddie, who is now the pastor of the Evangelist Temple Fellowship Center, in Vallejo.

Which is all well and good, but still: it is a tenet of rock snobbery that the founding lineup of a group must be held sacrosanct. Jerry Martini, the Family Stone's original saxophonist, joked to me a few years ago about the sadness of "reunions" that lack crucial band members. "Think of Creedence Clearwater . . . *Revisited*," he said, relishing the ellipsis. "Where are they playing? Anywhere you see a Ferris wheel!" (That said, Martini has done time in outfits called the Family Stone Experience and the Original Family Stone.)

So I put it to the main man: Is there any chance that the whole lineup from the old days will gather to play on the new album?

"I'm sure that's gonna happen, yeah," Sly says.

It almost happened last year, at the Grammys. For the first time since 1993, the year of the Hall of Fame induction, the seven original members were in the same place, and, what's more, they were poised to play together for the first time since 1971. This time, though, while Sly and his Mohawk made it to the stage, Graham fell ill and dropped out at the last minute. (His successor, Rusty Allen, filled in.)

As it turned out, Graham fared the best of anyone that night. In a bizarre miscalculation, and an affront to anyone with an appreciation of soul and rock history, the awards show's producers barely acknowledged the original group's presence. As the musicians plowed through a medley of the old hits, the cameras stayed fixed on a series of guest vocalists, who ranged from the mildly credible (John Legend, Joss Stone [no relation], Steven Tyler of Aerosmith) to the verily D-list (Fantasia, Devin Lima).

"We just kept playing, because there was really no order," says Cynthia Robinson. "There was a stage band standing in front of us, so hardly anybody knew we were there." To make matters worse, Stone had flipped his motorcycle a few days before the broadcast, damaging tendons in his right hand and making him even more uneasy with the situation than he would have been on his best day. When I ask him why the whole performance seemed so discombobulated, he says, "That wasn't my gig. Really, that wasn't my gig. I was trying to, like, cooperate with someone else that . . ." He pauses to find the right words: " . . . had their turn."

The "someone else" he's most likely alluding to, though he won't comment on him any further, is a mysterious man named Jerry Goldstein. In the deep-freeze years when no one saw Sly Stone in public—roughly from the Hall of Fame ceremony until last year—Goldstein was the man you needed to go through to get to Sly Stone: a nebulously defined manager-gatekeeper-protector. He is listed as a co–executive producer of *Different Strokes by Different Folks,* the obvious promotional tie-in to the Grammy appearance: a turgid remix CD of old Sly Stone tracks that features such artists as Legend, Tyler, Lima, Joss Stone, and Maroon 5. It was initially sold exclusively at Starbucks.

In Goldstein's defense, he is also listed as a co–executive producer of Sony Legacy's long-overdue series of Sly and the Family Stone album reissues, spanning the 1967–74 period from *A Whole New Thing* to *Small Talk*. These are terrific, with thoughtful liner notes, crisply remastered sound, and great bonus songs. The only problem is, Stone claims the reissues were prepared and released without his knowledge.

For all I know, Goldstein, who runs a Los Angeles–based company called Even St. Productions, was a positive influence on Stone and helped him get on the path to where he is now. But the thing is, Goldstein is even more elusive a figure than Stone. I know. On several occasions over the course of my Sly search, dating back to the 1990s, I tried to reach him, to see if Stone might be available for an interview. He never responded to any of my calls or e-mail messages.

I tried every tactic I could imagine to persuade him to talk to me, including contacting his old 1960s songwriting partners, Bob Feldman and Richard Gotteher. The three of them scored big in 1963 with "My Boyfriend's Back," a No. 1 for the girl group the Angels. Two years later, they had a hit of their own with the original version of "I Want Candy," which they performed under the alias the Strangeloves.

But neither Feldman nor Gotteher was able to help. (Goldstein, after the trio's split, went into management and production, with the funk band War his most famous client.) Finally, four years ago, I made a bit of headway when Lou Adler, who far out-ranks Goldstein in the L.A. music-biz hierarchy, agreed to call Goldstein on my behalf. Goldstein took Adler's call, but even Adler came up empty, telling me, "Jerry says there's nothing he can say, and there's no way Sly will talk."

Goldstein didn't return a phone message this time around, either. And, evidently, his mysterious services are no longer required. Stone has a new booking agent, Steve Green, and plans on releasing the new album on his own label, Phatta Datta. Green is the only person who will betray the slightest indication of the role Goldstein played in Stone's life. "Goldstein called me and told me him and Sly are connected at the hip," he says. "Jerry said, 'Sly's not capable of playing.'"

When I ask Vet Stone what the deal is with Goldstein, she says, "As far as I'm concerned, there is no deal with him." Greg Yates, Stone's attorney, gave me this carefully dictated statement when I called him on the matter: "I've been retained by Sly Stone to represent him regarding issues surrounding contracts with other third parties for his publishing rights. There are some significant questions about certain matters that we are investigating. We want to make certain that these things are in order, so that Sly is prepared for his return. We are concerned about certain matters that he was kept in the dark about."

So much has transpired over the last 40 years that there's bound to be some untidiness and skepticism—especially in the music business, and especially in the Sly Stone business. But then, there's also delighted disbelief that Stone has come even this far. "For me," says Green, who also represents the volatile Jerry Lee Lewis, "it's a gamble that seems less and less like a gamble."

"Certainly, I have great regrets that it's taken Sly all these years to return," says Clive Davis, "but the fact that there might be a happy ending to all this is a great feeling."

At the end of my face-to-face chat with Stone, I can't help but address something that's been nagging at me the whole time. At the Grammy Awards, he wore shades. In Vegas, he wore shades. Now, here in the front room of Chopper Guys, he's wearing shades. I'm feeling a twinge of doubt, like what that woman in Vegas felt.

"Can I see your eyes, Sly?"

"Yeah," he says, pulling down his sunglasses, revealing healthily white whites and a remarkably unlined face—the same face from Woodstock, *Cavett,* and the cover of *Fresh.* It really is Sly Stone.

BEAST FROM THE EAST

MANDRILL'S MUSICAL BREW IS EQUAL PARTS BROOKLYN AND MOTHERLAND

"When the great Roy Ayers lived next door to me up at 150th and Broadway, he'd say, 'Yo, Lou, you got too much stuff in one song! Could I just borrow the second movement?'"

—LOU WILSON

Once upon a halcyon time, when bands branded by single-word names and controlled by uncontrolled substances besotted the pop music charts, there lurked a uniquely sonic beast. Distinguished by its uncanny shape-shifting abilities, the creature was a musical omnivore, dieting on the diverse crops planted by its West Indian, Central American, and African forbearers, all the while growing stronger, tussling with its New World peers. Stamped with unmistakable colors and rippled with muscle, it was never afraid, leaving, instead, fear and wonder in its musical wake. And, though other animals that it had once bigbrothered along its creative journey would eventually surpass it in fortune and fame, no one could ever forget this remarkable beast from the East. Or could they?

"We knew there was nobody tighter. We were killers. It wasn't arrogance—just something that comes from being prepared."

—Claude "Coffee" Cave

Mandrill was nothing if not bold. Formed by a trio of Panamanian-born, Brooklyn-bred transplants, the Brothers Wilson—Lou, Ric, Carlos[1]—and their classically trained prodigy neighbor, Claude "Coffee" Cave, Mandrill was quintessential *jam* long before the term "jam band" became pejorative slander in certain circles and thick commercial booty in others. They were physically imposing and had, similar to their Parliamentary peers, honed their eclectic, powerful chops in a beauty salon. Their original grooves (the band never recorded a cover) were no flavor of the month, and, instead, feasted on anything tasty. Rock, jazz, doo-wop, psychedelia, calypso, marching band, blues, Latin, classical, and funk wouldn't just be heard at a Mandrill concert but often within each *song*. This meant you could put them on a bill with Deep Purple or Mott the Hoople, Miles Davis or Buddy Miles, Osibisa or Sha Na Na, Duke Ellington or James Brown. No matter the setting—sweaty clubs like Fillmores East and West, concert halls like Philharmonic and Carnegie, or stadium crowds six digits strong—they'd, by all accounts, turn the mutha out.

"There was a time when Earth, Wind and Fire played before us; they'd come on and *rock* the audience, and we'd have to follow that. Or War would *rock* the audience, and we'd have to follow, and we'd come with our thing. We were very fortunate to share the stage with Latin greats like Barretto, Puente, the Fania All-Stars, and *rock* the audience, then go to the Caribbean, South America, *rock* the audience. Go to Morocco with Randy Weston, Dexter Gordon, Max Roach, Odetta, and *rock* the audience."

—Dr. Ric Wilson

---

[1] Carlos Wilson was not available for interview.

Before Polydor acquired the King Records catalog and one God-father of Soul, Mandrill was the newborn label's first "Black acquisition," though the band's hippie aesthetic and Carnival approach were more Bill Graham than JB. Masters of at least twenty-two instruments, they could break beats for days, their "sound" buttressed with ubiquitous percussion and fortified with a slew of horns, guitar, organ, clavinet, vibes, and strings; all this iced with political, feel-good lyrics. In a sense, they were the embodiment of world music before "world music" came to be; they were fusion minus the noodling and mullets, sampling and mashing up genres the way hip-hop heads would do years later. The band's first two albums, *Mandrill* and *Mandrill Is*, were embraced by the experimental format of the nascent, White FM radio bandwidth and didn't truly plaster the Black music charts until they had found a White, Jewish bassist named Fudgie and an eighteen-year-old, pint-sized rhythmic powerhouse named Neftali Santiago. By their third and fourth releases—1973's *Composite Truth* and *Just Outside of Town*—the band reached a creative and commercial peak. The funk congealed on future classics such as "Fencewalk," "Mango Meat," and "Hang Loose," and got nuclear on the Nefti-penned "Two Sisters of Mystery," a song destined to provide, nearly two decades later, the heaviest sample in the history of hip-hop—P.E.'s "By the Time I Get to Arizona."

> "I remember playing drums, and it used to make me uncomfortable [with] George Clinton and Maurice White sitting right in back of me, taking notes! Then all of a sudden, Earth, Wind and Fire gets a horn section, and Funkadelic starts adding percussion, horns, and now they become Parliament, and it's like, *hmmm*, that's interesting."
>
> —Neftali Santiago

By 1974, their Polydor run came to an end, and the band's most successful lineup was done. The Wilsons and Coffee moved Mandrill to Los Angeles, signed with United Artists, then, later, Arista.

Clearly wanting more disco-lypso than polyrhythmia, neither label, nor Los Angeles, it seemed, knew what to do with them. Mandrill (now joined by the fourth Wilson brother, Wilfredo aka "Wolf") watched their success slowly wane as groups like EWF and Parliament blasted off. And though they got involved with movies (Ali's *The Greatest* and *The Warriors)*, Mandrill, still charting until 1980, finally burned out. They'd survived the '70s, churned out ten charting albums, made some nice coin, and had done, by anyone's standards, all right for themselves.

CANAL TO CROOKLYN—LOCKS AND KEYS

"The combination of the percussive instruments and the funk was a Mandrill trademark," says Lou Wilson, emphatically. "That's where we coming from, the *Caribbean*, the *Brooklyn*, the *funk*; that's what makes Mandrill *Mandrill* and separates us from whomever else is out there."

The Wilson brothers—each separated from the preceding by two years—reside on the West Coast, a decent clip from both the Bed-Stuy and Colón neighborhoods that gave birth to their "trademark." So does Claude Cave, who—unrelated by blood but eventually a key ingredient to the Mandrill family—also grew up in the same Brooklyn neighborhood around the same time, unbeknownst to the brothers. "Coffee"—a nickname he'd be given by the Wilsons years later—also had Caribbean roots and discovered he was, like his mother, blessed with "the Big Ear."

Ric: We were born in Colón [Panama], on the Caribbean side. Very Rasta, but Spanish speaking. Our grandparents moved from the West Indies to Panama with the building of the Canal, as many folks did then. Panama is such a melting pot—people from all over the Caribbean, Central and South America. Our grandparents were British West Indians, and our parents spoke English and Spanish in the home.

Lou: We lived in the Canal Zone—the American side. Dad worked as a longshoreman, mom had a beauty parlor and sold comic books while frying hair: it was called Darcy's Beauty Salon. Colón was a rough place; we'd have to rumble often. I remember the first punch I got in my eye—*bam!*—I ran to my momma's beauty parlor: "If you don't beat him, I'm gonna beat you!"

Ric: Our parents believed in self-defense. We learned to box. It came in quite handy later on when we moved to Bedford-Stuyvesant, 'cause at the time we were going to school [in Brooklyn], gangs were rampant: the Chapmans, the Stonekillers, the Rebops. We were fortunate we were four brothers, 'cause we got into fights. I'd see a crowd of people, and there's my brother in the middle, dukin' it out. He never lost a fight, nor did I.

Lou: Well, I had to set the pace; I'm the older brother. That was back in the days of honor. No guns, maybe a blade or two. No drive-by type thing. *Mano a mano.*

Ric: Eventually, word got around: "Don't mess with the Wilson brothers."

Coffee: My earliest memories are of my mother playing the piano and singing, and I'm in her lap. My father was a doctor, played the violin, and took care of a number of musicians. One of his patients was Otis Blackwell, who wrote a lot of Elvis Presley hits.

Ric: My dad had eleven sisters. He was high school educated, brilliant, but his parents died when he was fourteen, so he had to help support a big family. Dad played guitar, sang in a local group; mom sang in choir, but as we got older, the Canal took up dad's life.

Lou: Lot of their friends played calypso, pre-reggae—Sparrow, Kitchener. My dad [also] played the tres and had a picture of Duke Ellington on his mirror on the bus he drove. He played jazz records, which we soaked up, subconsciously, in the crib. The Ink Spots, Fats Waller, the Mills Brothers—a lot of jazz, man.

Ric: In Panama, there weren't many outlets in terms of college education; he didn't want us to hit the same dead end. Well, that's what they told us, anyway. They probably wanted to come to New York and party. [*laughs*] When we got off the boat. . . .

Lou: October '53, ya heard? On the SS *Honkon*. Ric and myself came first. I was eleven, Ric nine. Then they brought the others. That cold was a shock!

Ric: We're leaving paradise, and the streets here are funky and cold. We're wondering, "What the hell are we doing here?" My uncle paved the way with his family, had a brownstone on Willoughby between Nostrand and Marcy Avenue. Beautiful area: rows of houses, mixture of working-class folks, Black, Latino, Jewish, Irish. White flight hadn't taken place yet, completely.

Coffee: Initially, we were the only Black family on the block. I was one of three kids of color in grades one through eight, but, gradually, Bed-Stuy became primarily Black. There were all kinds of people—from the West Indies, India, China, Jewish grandmothers who'd escaped from Germany who'd put beach chairs out on the street. So, culturally, you got exposed. If windows were open, you'd hear calypso, Latin, classical, jazz, big band, this cacophony of sound; you'd feed on it. I'd actually ring someone's bell and ask, "What was that?"

Lou: Music was always in the air; some guys'd be playing stickball, some shooting dice, and some trying to get the latest song to harmony with their friends. *Ahhh*, the harmony groups. Funk and soul was just starting to be built off the backs of those folk.

Ric: Mom expanded what she had in Panama. As kids, we used to sing together as the Wilson Brothers, and with mom being the beautician, she was in different clubs with women, and [when they'd] have programs, we'd be featured. We'd do a lot of pop gospel stuff like "Amazing Grace," and it would go over nicely.

Coffee: I displayed an affinity for the piano and started writing my own music at six. They took me to the conservatory where there were two pianos in the room. The instructor would play a melody, then I'd play it back; and he said, "He's ready." Now, for my parents, this was a cultural thing—I wasn't gonna become a musician! I learned theory and harmony when I was nine, spent all my weekends and two nights a week at conservatory—loved it, but I wasn't learning how to read. My big ear was a gift and a nemesis.

Ric: We'd go see Frankie Lymon and the Teenagers and others at the Brooklyn Paramount Theater. A good friend of ours, Richard Harris, had a group called the Jive Five, so we were [also] doo-woppin' on the street corner. Back in the day, schools had orchestras and provided instruments for the students, so when I started in P.S. 54, I wanted to play sax. Lots of calypso would always have a sax solo, but they didn't have sax, so I started on clarinet. Lou played trumpet from the beginning, Carlos was able to play trombone, and later Wolf played clarinet. We could bring our instruments home, practice. [Later,] Carlos and Lou were part of the all-city band.

Lou: I used to mind the band room—mess with the tuba, the oboe, but the influence of Louis Armstrong was strong and the trumpet mouthpiece fit real nice.

Coffee: When I got in my teens, I started to hear things in my head involving more than just piano, like orchestras, big bands. I got transcription books of guys like Oscar Peterson who were playing beyond the speed of light. You'd look at the transcriptions, and it looked like someone'd taken a black brush and squished it across the page. This was improvisation that was transcribed. Then I started getting the records and realized sometimes the transcriptions were not accurate, 'cause I could hear what was going on and could see what was written, and some of it was not on the money. Then all of a sudden, I made a connection and realized, "They're breaking the rules." Then I got into listening to blues players, especially keyboard players, during that time when organ music was coming to the fore, when Bill Doggett, Wild Bill Davis, were grooving on the radio. After a while, I saw that the blues was in the jazz. [Eventually,] I had an opportunity to play an organ. What really interested me was you could instantly create the type of sound you wanted. It was the first synthesizer—Robert Moog was probably still up at Columbia inventing the Moog. With the use of the Hammond drawbars, you instantly could create sounds that were or that aren't. And the Leslie speaker just allured me.

Ric: Sports were also big: Lou ran track, played basketball, I was captain of the football team, Carlos ran track. Wolf played football. Boys High School offered a full meal. After high school, we all went separate ways. I went to Harvard, Lou stayed in Brooklyn, Carl was in the Navy, and Wilfredo was at Morgan Stare. Everyone was doin' their own thing,

Coffee: So I started forming bands, but, at that time, music was segmented. A jazz player didn't play Latin, a Latin player didn't play R&B, and an R&B cat didn't play straight-ahead blues. Eventually, I realized it would be fun finding the players to mix and match those elements. The other thing, because of the Caribbean influence, I got exposed to a lot of percussion—Latin bands, salsa bands, steel drums—so I also wanted to play drums. Ron Carter, who was a friend of the family, helped me get in touch with Charlie Persip, and he gave me a deeper understanding of the rhythmic thing. I taught my brother Curtis the drums, and, eventually, we started jamming together. Our house became sort of a music mecca: we had a grand piano, Hammond B–3, and a set of drums in the living room, and all these musicians would come by—like Billy Cobham, Jerry Jemmott—and jam. All kinds of young kids—we were *literally* kids.

HEART OF THE BEAST

Ric Wilson—class president, captain of the Boys High football team, and honor student—followed a full scholarship to Harvard. Wanting to become a cardiologist, he majored in biology and worked under the cutting-edge organ transplant specialist Francis Moore. Involving himself in school politics and playing football for two years further reduced music to an afterthought. "I kept my sax under my bed," Ric recalls. "Once in a while, I'd pull out some Coltrane and mess around, blow." Carlos had gone off to the nightmare unfolding in Vietnam, patrolling up and down the Mekong Delta. Lou stayed in Brooklyn. The brothers were reunited, however, when medical school brought Ric back to Brooklyn in '66. "We were fortunate to be together in Brooklyn again," Ric says. "Lou had been writing songs, Carl had taught himself how to play the guitar really well while in Vietnam—had Wes Montgomery down pat—had taught himself how to play flute, and then went to Mannes College of Music to get some classical training. So we'd mess around in clubs in the Village, and at home, [and] discovered that, creatively, we had a lot of things that felt good. We'd go to the Fillmore East at night, check out bands like the Who, Jethro Tull, and knew the instrumentation we wanted. We put together an initial group called Remedy, influenced by the fact I was in medical school, and played gigs around Brooklyn doing cover stuff. After that, we graduated to another level, called ourselves Will Power, had some serious musicians, and were booked by Norby Walters up and down the East Coast. The problem was I couldn't get away all the time, and our drummer and bass player ended up leaving. Subsequently, my brothers and I put an ad in the *Village Voice*. This was around 1968, '69."

Coffee: For many years, I was trying to get guys to incorporate R&B and Latin. I loved Santana. Greg Rollie made that Hammond sing. Phenomenal band, but they were missing the horns. I had an eighteen-piece band. Weldon Irvine, a good friend of mine, was another guy doing that. We'd go to Slugs, had these charts, and get this big band to play. Then I'd go out and play piano and vibes with Latin bands, be checking out the Fania guys, Pacheco, Harlow—phenomenal musicians! I was also working at this after-hours club in Bed-Stuy, the Golden Arrow Social Club—a legal, illegal joint, meaning things were "taken care of." At that time, clubs had to close at 4:00 A.M., so the game was you bought a membership card at the door. Bar, food, tables, big shaded green lights, cage for the stripper, bandstand, pool tables for shooting craps, and card playing. After-hours places were always jumpin' and usually paid more than a regular gig. I was the bandleader. There'd be a full show: stripper, comedian, music. The people that came through were a whole other breed. So one night, these two guys come in. . . .

Lou: Carlos and I had been roaming around. I used to carry bongos on my shoulder in a case; Carl would have his flute. So we hear this music, walk down these stairs into this funky, funky club! There's a guitar player, bass, sax, and a guy playing Hammond B–3. He looked bored—old folks grindin' out a shuttle. He was fallin' asleep and shit.

Coffee: I was playing with some guys who'd played with the Ink Spots—old-school guys. Smooth.

Lou: So when that song finished, Carl whispered to Coffee, "You know Herbie Mann's 'Comin' Home, Baby'?" Coffee sparked up. Carlos started. Coffee jumped in, I took out my bongos, and people were like, "Oh shit! We told him we had put an ad in the *Village Voice*—had cars coming from all over.

Coffee: So, then, Carlos started calling me, but my plate was full. One night, I'm waiting for James Brown to come on TV—which didn't happen often—and the phone rings. "It's this guy Carlos Wilson, and he wants to talk to you about coming down to their rehearsal!" And I'm thinking, "What's wrong with this guy? Doesn't he know JB is about to come on television?!" [*laughs*]

Lou: We would have people call and say, "Where you located? Bed-Stuy? Never mind!"

Ric: People would see the address and never get out of the car. But it was cool; it brought the folks who were real, that had no fear.

Coffee: Finally, I say okay. Went down with my brother to the beauty shop. Everything is set up between the dryers, in the stalls: amplifiers, drum kit—lots goin' on. They run through some stuff, some Latin, calypso, rock, jazz, and I'm thinking, "Hey, this is it!" They were auditioning drummers that night, and it so happened the drummer that was selected was there, Charles Padro. So I joined the group.

Ric: Charlie Padro, Puerto Rican brother, looked Caucasian, but he was down. Our first guitarist, Omar Mesa from Cuba, was down. Our first bassist, Bundie Cenac, was from the Virgin Islands, and then Coffee. That was the group for our first album.

Coffee: Omar was awesome—into rock, jazz, Latin. Had that heavy, molten rock guitar sound. [His] job was computers, coming over from Hoboken in the day. Padro was in the Bronx, Bundie was local, so we jammed and jammed. Rehearsed really hard. I came down with my rented B–3, put it in one of the stalls, then brought down vibes, a Rhodes, eventually the clavinet, which I approached like a rhythm guitar to bolster the drive. Small shop; we barely fit. When we rehearsed, there'd be a mob outside. In the summer, it was brutally hot—seven bodies crankin'. The heat had just dissipated from the hair dryers all day, and now we're crankin' up the amps, and Marshalls generate heat! [*laughs*] The Wilsons brought a strong sense of solidarity, more so than other bands. We realized we had something special, and everyone was able to make a really powerful commitment. We determined we would rehearse at least five nights a week, six hours a night. We seriously woodshedded. Finally, we played some little gigs, some picnics, then we played a club in Brooklyn on Fulton Street called the Blue Coronet, famous in the jazz world, on the same circuit as Birdland.

Ric: We built a tremendous following there, sold it out, lines around the block. Beautiful thing about the Blue Coronet, people didn't come to dance; they came to listen, because it was a jazz club. Had us in a concert setting at a very early stage.

Coffee: We created such a buzz, managers were finding the beauty shop in Bed-Stuy. In the meantime, we didn't have a name.

Lou: One day, Charlie comes from the Bronx Zoo, says he saw this animal called a mandrill. As soon as he said "man-drill," oh man, it felt right. We did some research, and we went to the zoo to see the mandrill.

Ric: Whose name happened to be Ringo. His face was mature mandrill, striking, very colorful.

Lou: With alpha males, the nose becomes very red during the season for the assault. They mourn the dead, very tight family structure, won't be intimidated. It was just so befitting and incredible how much we looked like mandrill, and it looked like us.

Ric: The name just stuck.

RECORD DEAL

The band's first major gig would be performing with the late, great Oscar Brown Jr. at the elegant Brooklyn Academy of Music, exposing them not only to thousands of new listeners but also one Beau Ray Fleming, a music biz veteran who would get the band some play in front of record execs. "He said, 'I can get you a demo showcase,'" explains Coffee. "So we went to Columbia's studio in Manhattan—it had been a church—where Miles had made *Kind of Blue*. It was like going to Mecca. We were ready to hit it. It was intense. We'd been knocking people out all over New York and were on a mission. So we do five songs, no overdubs. It was our live set with the kinks worked out, which essentially became our first album, *Mandrill*. We'd go from a Latin feel to a gospel feel to a rock feel in the same song. I used a wah-wah pedal rigged up through the organ and reverb; the system engineers went crazy. They cut an acetate, and, for some reason, Columbia slept on it. So Beau went up to Chess Records, goes into the bathroom, and a guy name Esmond Edwards comes in, asks him about the acetate he's got under his arm, says to wait, don't waste it on Chess, that he's leaving Chess to be A&R over at a new label, Polydor, [and] to bring it over there. Now, Polydor was owned by Deutsche Grammophon, who were known for their fidelity, for virtually no hiss on their classical music records. Jerry Schoenbaum, Polydor's president, hears the acetate, takes it to Fire Island with his lady for the weekend, Monday calls up Beau: 'I want to sign them now!' In the meantime, Beau sets up a showcase for us at Small's Paradise packed with industry people, and we blow everyone away," Coffee says. "Now it's on! Ahmet Ertegun wants to get us; Epic, CBS, Buddah."

Ric: We sign a deal with Polydor, then hit Electric Ladyland Studios, which is where we record our first three albums. Electric Ladyland was a trip in itself, in the Village. You went downstairs into the bowels of the earth, and a whole new world opened up. The walls were electric—reminded me of the cover *Bitches Brew*; you totally got lost. And to boot, we'd be coming in when Stevie Wonder or Jimi Hendrix was leaving and vice versa. We even talked to Jimi about collaborating, but he went to Europe on tour and never returned.

Coffee: Clive Davis, who worked for CBS, wrote in *Billboard* that two of the great things in the future were Bruce Springsteen and Mandrill; this, even though we'd signed to Polydor! First song that broke was "Mandrill." First song out the box you gotta come out hard, so Charlie said, "Man, I'm getting a gong." Bands didn't have gongs! *Mandrill* set a regional record for sales: fifty thousand albums in a month. Took FM radio by storm. Played on stations that played King Crimson, Led Zep, Paul Butterfield—White acts. See, radio was still segregated. On AM, R&B, gospel, and Latin was on the right side of the dial. Sinatra to the left. Frankie Crocker, *the man* in New York, loved our record and started to play it, and it became like the national anthem.

Ric: Mandrill blew up faster than most groups blow up. We didn't pay the kind of dues like a lot of guys working the chitlin circuit for ten years. *Mandrill* was a breakout album in New York, to the point where Sony had Mandrill do the first quadraphonic radio broadcast out of the Village Gate. And we were more international than we realized, 'cause Deutsche Grammophon was the largest label in the world. Our records were getting to all parts of the globe; [when] traveling to different places, our reputation preceded us.

But see, we were signed before I finished med school in 1970. And it was during my internship in '71, we did the Fillmore West with Miles. I couldn't get time off from the hospital, had to commute to San

Francisco every day for one week. A limo would meet me after I made rounds, go to the airport, a limo would pick me up in San Francisco, head to the Fillmore, play the gig, get back in limo, sleep on the plane, make rounds. [*laughs*] That's when I said, if I continue like this, I'm gonna be dead. "Lemme take some time off and do it right, earn millions of dollars, come back, set up my clinic, and keep on rollin'." [*Is that what happened?*] No! [*laughs*]

Coffee: Bundie left to sell Porsches. He thought, as a band, we'd copped out. Charlie left to pursue film. So Fudgie joined on bass for *Mandrill Is,* then Nefti joined for *Composite Truth.* That became *the* Mandrill lineup. It was crazy; between us, we could play twenty-two instruments. Carlos and I would write strings, horn, and vocal harmonies, and conduct. His approach to playing, his concept of rhythm, are not of this planet. Nobody had as keen a rhythmic ability, and this band was *based* around rhythm. Carlos was a powerhouse. Flute was his favorite instrument, but he was also playing formidable rhythm guitar, some guitar solos, great on trombone—one of those guys; just give him an instrument, and he can play it. One of the most gifted people I've ever met.

Ric: Bundie was a young kid, full of himself, big Afro, very cool player technically, lot of energy, speed and all that, but Fudgie *laid it down.* Fudgie, aka Fred Solomon, a White Jewish guy from the Bronx. [*laughs*] Nothing flustered him. Had experience on upright and electric, went places that your standard R&B bass player couldn't. A little behind but *funky.* Listen to his breakdown on "Ape Is High."

Coffee: Charlie said, "I got the guy: Fudgie Kae from the Bronx!" Bronx was a hotbed for bass players at the time. So he jammed with us—righteous right off the bat! He could handle anything. We showed him how to play salsa; he played like he was born with it. Sensitive, lyrical, easygoing. When you played with him, you were inspired. He played a Fender Sunburst and used acoustic bass cabinets. Bundie was more of a speed merchant. But it's not how *fast* you play, but *what* you play, and as you mature, it's not what you play, but what you *don't* play. Now, I'm not sure how Fudgie got his nickname, but he was monstrous. Ron Carter heard him and was impressed. George Clinton and Bootsy used to stand and watch us, as did Maurice White; I could see the camera goin' off in his mind. [*laughs*]

Nefti: Fudgie's so underrated. He played a very physical bass. His hands were extremely strong, but he made it sound like butter. It was scary playing with Fudgie.

COMPOSITE COMPLETE

"And then Neftali," says Coffee, "plays with his entire body. Some guys, it's all wrist and arms, but Nefti plays with body and soul. The pocket is unbelievable with him." True, before Neftali Santiago, Mandrill knew all about the pocket. With him, the pocket just got real *stanky*. Born in Spanish Harlem, raised outside of Philadelphia, Santiago brought youth, a mean 'fro, a poppin' snare, and some serious grease, which would not only help propel *Composite Truth* up the charts but also provide a stylistic blueprint for a future Philly drummer's quest for non-sampled love some years later.

Nefti: My dad's Puerto Rican; my mom's Black, American Indian, and Scottish. My mom was a 45 freak: Beatles, Sinatra, Otis, Aretha—turntable going all the time in our house. My brother played guitar in a band; they'd leave equipment at the house, and I just started playing. When I was sixteen, I went on *Ted Mack*—was like a *Star Search*. Then in '70, I started backing people on the chitlin circuit—folks like the Manhattans, Barbara Mason, the Delfonics. That's when I really learned dynamics. Those hits on all their steps—if you're not right there with them, they would yell at you! We'd play five nights a week. Buddy Miles was my favorite drummer. I was sixteen, had a mustache, big 'fro, so I could get into clubs. I was such a bad student, tired all the time, was in the tenth grade for three years. But I had the lime green pants with the green socks, platform shoes, all the killer clothes, 'cause I was making money!

Mandrill weren't only my favorite band, they were everyone's favorite around Jersey, New York. When Mandrill hit, it was like a fire went off. Yeah, you could see the Santana relationship, you could hear the Chambers Brothers and Chicago, but Mandrill were playing it all in *one set*. So they came to Philly toward the end of '72 to play the Spectrum with War opening. I got backstage and said to Carlos, "I'm gonna be your next drummer; you guys need me." Now, they didn't tell me Charlie just quit the band. This was a Friday night. Tuesday, I kid you not, the phone rang, "Kid, you've got an audition." I go to New York City, line up with thirty guys; it came down to me and Dennis Davis, who went on to David Bowie. They told me "You're the drummer but you're really young."

Ric: Neftali was a tremendous drummer. Charlie played on out ahead of the tempo, more rock and jazz, whereas Neftali stayed in the pocket, like Fudgie, a little behind but on it. Their combination was awesome. And he produced stuff like the rhythm behind "Fencewalk." Even though Carlos told Neftali what to play, he was able to manifest it—it's one of the funkiest drumbeats in R&B music—which was no easy feat.

Nefti: We go into Electric Ladyland, whoa, I've never been in a studio before! I didn't know about overdubs, so I figured out how to play all these rhythms. Then I had to travel for thirty dates before they even let me play, just to get used to being on the road. I wasn't used to flying, getting sick a lot. Padro was still drumming. He was great about it. My first gig was in Hershey, Pennsylvania, with Deep Purple and Elf. Ten thousand people. I wanted to play my drums, which were from Sears—had orange contact paper on them, looked like a Dreamsicle. [I] had them tuned just like Buddy's. But I had to play Charlie's, and my first drum solo, the bass drum *slid* off the stage. We played a lot of Southern towns for all-White audiences with bands like Savoy Brown, Status Quo. You could smell the prejudice, but we were received really well. Then Black people started catching on when *Composite Truth* hit the radio, and we played Black colleges and the big festivals.

Coffee: Finally, we got promoted on the Black side, and our music exploded.

Lou: They used that word "crossover," you know. Whatever!

Ric: It started to change, 'cause of radio play and the promotional direction of the record company. Polydor had just acquired James Brown's catalog and was able to get Mandrill promoted on Black stations throughout the country. Only problem was they forgot to keep promoting us on the White rock stations! [*laughs*] We were selling out a lot of colleges, arenas, and the [Funkadelics] were touring with us on a bus. Must've done a hundred shows with them. Lots of jamming and craziness! Lou always traveled with a bunch of paint—used to paint his face Mandrill colors. The Funkadelics didn't necessarily have a heavy wardrobe back in the day; a lot of the time, they'd just take Holiday Inn sheets and towels, and that would be their attire. George would take the sheet, put a hole in it, put Lou's paint all over and come out onstage.

Coffee: With nothing on underneath, he'd go to the foot of the stage and drop the sheet over people's heads. The *Funks*—the Parliament-Funkadelics. Loved them. They had an *entourage*, a cast of thousands coming in from all over the country. They would just *converge* on the gig.

Lou: There was a time when we were smoking, '72, '73, [and] word was headliners didn't want to go out with us. We just did what we had in the box. The variety was natural; this is what we know! never did covers, just originals. Coming from Mama Africa right out of the box created a Carnival atmosphere.

Nefti: Mandrill had no problem opening for no one. Even James Brown at Madison Square Garden. But we didn't need to; we'd already been there four times on our own, sold it out—you're talking Mandrill town, New York City. You should have brought JB in by himself! So we're jamming, and James was getting really mad. Next thing we know, we're playing off of monitors. Our road manager picks up the cord and shows us it's cut, and then James's road manager gets a gun and cuts the monitors, so we're playing just instruments. But we kept getting standing ovations.

Ric: Another highlight was when we played Philharmonic Hall in '73 with the Symphony of the New World with an eighty-piece orchestra and 200-voice chorus. Was recorded by the BBC and broadcast behind the Iron Curtain via the Voice of America.

Coffee: So many fantastic dates. One hundred fifty thousand people in Fairmont Park in Philly—people as far as the eye could see. Mandrill was huge in DC. We were advertised as headliners at RFK stadium: 80,000 people. Two babies were born during the concert!

Ric: The Funks; War; Earth, Wind and Fire—it was beautiful to share a stage with all these guys and hear one group after another.

Tremendous to be out in a sea of faces, peaceful, fun-loving. Occasionally, there'd be a riot.

Nefti: Something about getting a bunch of Black people together in the hot summertime: stuff happens. And stuff *did* happen. One concert we did with Sly at the Spectrum, I watched all these people dropping in a circle, and then I saw a guy with a butcher knife stabbing people. And then, sometimes, promoters tried to cut corners. Like at Randall's Island, summer of '73. Forty thousand people, one way in, one way out. Mandrill was headlining. We show up and find out there's this itty-bitty sound system, and nobody can hear anything. Didn't have the security for it either. Funkadelic went on for a half hour, the crowd rushed the stage, stole their equipment, beat up the vendors. Next up was Rare Earth. The stadium is oval shaped, with the backstage in the middle, so you have to drive to the stage. Rare Earth had a VW bus, didn't even make it to the stage; people just overturned it. They ran back to the dressing rooms. Chaka Khan says, "I'm not going out." Buddy Miles says, "I'm not going out either." By that time, the chief of police says to us, "Look, if you guys don't go on, I don't have enough police to cover this riot."

Coffee: These people were goin' nuts! If we go on, and the sound's not right, there's gonna be a riot, but if we don't go on, there's gonna be a riot! So we got up to the stage, lights come up, and I realize immediately there's a mob of people behind me, around the Leslie, the equipment. Just standing. I go to start to play and can't step forward—look around and this chick has her hand down my pants on my ass! So I gently pull her hand out, start to play, and the whole system, sound, lights, everything, just dies. Could only hear a cowbell.

Nefti: Then somebody threw a bottle at my face. I had a boom [mic] right in front of me—bottle just splattered. I played barefoot, so I went to pick up my platform shoes, and they'd already started taking stuff. I look up, and there goes the band. They'd forgot me. And now I'm in the hands of the fans.

Coffee: All of a sudden, I see this mass of humanity pouring out of stands, coming towards us. Now it's an all-out run, a dead heat. I didn't know where anybody was, so I dove underneath this trailer, looking at feet go by, then realize someone's next to me. It's this guy who'd grown up across the street from me and now was a policeman. He'd just come to see the show. I'm like, "Richard? Is that *you*?" So we stayed there and caught up; it was just surreal.

Nefti: Two girls tried to take my scarf around my neck and were choking me. Others were pulling out chunks of my hair. I'm all ripped up like the Hulk, just humiliated. Cops are doin' their tear gas thing. I get to the dressing room, had no clothes. That night we fly to California to do *Soul Train* the next day. So that's why I'm wearing Carlos's clothes and shoes for that.

Coffee: The promoter tried to short us on the deal, so I impounded the tickets, put these huge bags of ticket stubs in my mother's living room.

Nefti: Mandrill headlined most of those funk festivals, but War [and] Earth, Wind and Fire—these bands had hits. Yet, when it came to the box office, Mandrill was the big-ticket draw, and promoters knew that. And it was a problem. War, they'd pull a "Hey, our record's number one; we're headlining." But we'd say, "Well, the contract *says* Mandrill's the headliner." The people would suffer, 'cause an hour would go by, and no one's onstage. Finally, [we] took the stage, and War never did that again, 'cause with their energy, people would walk out on them. They slowed their songs *down*, 'cause they didn't want to compete with that Mandrill energy, and you can quote me on that!

Lou: Let me say this: every group we played with was significantly influenced by us. I'm not trying to blow any horns here, but go back to when we first started, to the groups that were happening around 1970. Santana: had percussion, guitar, Hammond, but no horns; Sly: had horns, didn't have percussion; Chicago: had horns, no percussion; Earth, Wind and Fire: didn't have horns and had a paucity of percussion—I mean, Maurice always had that timbale but no wall of percussion like Mandrill from the get-go. And the Funkadelics: maybe one conga and a bell, no horns. After a number of these groups left playing alongside Mandrill, the horns and percussion became significant parts of their presentation. Even Motown, as big as Motown was, [if] you listen to Motown, you didn't hear a lot of percussion. R&B and percussion didn't go together! Today, it's commonplace.

DISCO'S TAMING OF THE BEAST

By 1974, Mandrill was again a different band. Mesa, a disciple of guru Sri Chinmoy, apparently disagreed with the abundance of women and drugs in the band's circle and left. Betty Davis/Santana/Voices of East Harlem vet Doug Rodrigues took his chair for the double LP, *Mandrilland*, an eclectic release recorded in the swamps of Louisiana. Soon, Nefti Santiago, tired of the road, drugs, and the Wilson's tightening grip on the band, also left, but would come and go over the years. "Mandrill was a democracy in the beginning," Nefti says. "We all had a song on each record. But the brothers kind of did us wrong on *Mandrilland*. Went back in the studio, didn't tell us. But, you see, I love the music enough to overlook that kind of stuff, 'cause I'd rather still be a part of the culture and a part of the whole legacy. And then there was the road life, going from city to city to city—wake up sometimes and not even know where I was. Now, you could do a couple of different things to deal with the ups and downs of the whole thing. Fudgie's drug of choice was heroin; he chose to deal that way, and, eventually, [it] took him out.[2] Others' was cocaine; mine was weed. All these excuses were made for Sly, for Mandrill, for why you didn't show up. Last time we played the Spectrum, we headlined over Sly—a big deal—Bobby Womack was opening. Well, Carlos and Lou missed the plane, couldn't get to the show on time, and we never played the Spectrum again. That was around '75. That's when things started kind of folding."

Coffee: War left United Artists for LAX Records, so UA needed someone to fill their spot. We moved to L.A., did *Beast from the East* and *Solid*. Decent albums, but UA was slowly imploding. We couldn't get out of there fast enough. So we were looking for another label. A bidding war ensued with mega-offers—I was *shocked* at the numbers—including Philly International, Capitol, CBS, who said, "We'll let you produce Sly Stone" (they couldn't get him in the studio), and I said, "Uh, I'll Pasadena, thanks." We signed as artists and producers with Clive Davis and Arista, who had told me, "When I didn't sign you

---

[2] Fudgie is believed to have overdosed in the late '70s.

before, I went after Earth, Wind and Fire and signed them. I think I did all right!" [*laughs*] So we put out a couple of albums with them, but I just got burnt out. Focused on scoring commercials, movies, which I still do.

Nefti: Mandrill got caught up in: "Do we stay Mandrill, or do we start writing disco songs?" The band started writing disco songs, moved to the West Coast. Wait, Beast from the East moves West? The whole rhythm section changed—Fudgie didn't go—changed the sound of the band. Now you see what the Wilson brothers sound like on their own.

Ric: We could see the changes coming. Listening to radio, you could hear the changes. We were resisting that. When we played live, our folks loved what we did, so we didn't feel we needed to get caught up in that, but the challenge, as the challenge is today, was to get the music that you recorded heard on the radio. It's never the people; once you expose them to the shit, they will appreciate it. That's the crux of the matter, and today that's what we're dealing with. We've come full circle in a way, like we're living in a disco era where the good shit isn't being played. Have a consultant from Scarsdale coming to Harlem to tell the DJ what he should play? C'mon. Thank God the Internet has opened up the situation for new artists and old that aren't necessarily kowtowing, and that's how it needs to be.

Lou: It allows the people to enjoy variety, as in the '70s. Every group that came out rose above the din, had something to say, man.

AFTERWORD

The Wilson Brothers still push the Mandrill mantle today, while most folks their age push buttons on a remote control and look for AARP discounts. Believe me when I say they still look capable of landing a few left hooks. Not all of their albums have been reissued, but thankfully shows like *Soul Train* and *Don Kirchner's Rock Concert* preserve Mandrill's prize-fighting attack, as does a recent DVD performance at the Montreux Jazz Festival. A new album is in the works, and, of course, they live vicariously via hip-hop. "It's a humbling experience to have a younger generation lean on our music as a carriage for their messages," Ric says. "We're looking to collaborate."

Oliver Wang

BOOGALOO NIGHTS

Since the 1960s, Latin music legend Joe Bataan has played venues from East Harlem to East Berlin, but sometimes even he can be surprised by a new audience. Last June he headlined a show in a trendy Brooklyn club near the Manhattan Bridge, where he was backed by Bronx River Parkway, a multiracial band made up of Latin aficionados, most of them four decades his junior. Bataan described the mostly white and Asian-American crowd as "a lot of hippies" until he was gently corrected: "Oh, I meant hipsters."

Bataan might as well get used to it. Though he still draws crowds of middle-aged fans who grew up on his unique blend of sweet soul singing and Afro-Cuban rhythms, a younger generation is rediscovering the Latin boogaloo sound that Bataan found fame with. Born somewhere between Chicago and New York, between black and brown, the music's initial era burned bright but briefly—yet forty years later, the boogaloo is back.

The very term "boogaloo" invokes a sensation of something both familiar and exotic, slick with lubricious grooves and a punch of funk. It began as a dance but with no set steps or patterns. Dancing the boogaloo was about letting loose in whatever way possible—tossed heads, flailing limbs, kicking feet and all. Little wonder that musicians would find ways of translating that kinetic energy into rhythm. According to lore, in 1965 the Detroit R&B duo of Robert "Tom" Tharpe and Jerry "Jerrio" Murray attended a hop sponsored by Herb "Kool Gent" Kent, a DJ from Chicago's WVON. There, they saw black teenagers performing a frenzied, energetic dance. When they asked its name, the teens replied it was from Spanish Harlem and called the boogaloo.

Tom and Jerrio recorded a seven-inch titled "Boo-Ga-Loo," a thunderous, proto-funk jam filled with rumbling drums, swinging hand claps, and vaguely salacious grunts and yells. The song was an instant hit, rocketing to more than a million sales, and immediately inspired a series of boogaloo-themed songs in R&B and jazz, ranging from A. C. Reed's scorching funk single "Boogaloo Tramp" to the freewheeling grooves of the Jazz Crusaders' "Ooga-Boo-Ga-Loo."

Like the dance that inspired it, boogaloo in the R&B and jazz worlds were freestyles, with no set formula. Notably though, for a music fad inspired by a dance purportedly from Spanish Harlem, these boogaloos bore no discernible Latin influences. It wasn't until the boogaloo returned home to New York in 1966 that it acquired a Latin *sabor*, one intermeshed in both African-American and Latin-American rhythmic traditions.

There's little agreement over who transformed the R&B boogaloo into the Latin *bugalú*, but the first to market its name was probably Brooklyn band leader Ricardo "Richie" Ray. On his 1966 album *Se Soltó*, Ray prominently announced the debut of the "bugaloo," a Latin rhythm that he described as a "Phunky cha cha." For Ray, the bugaloo meant more than just a new style; his liner notes also proclaim that it was "the first real bridge" to bring Latin- and African-American dance and music styles together. Ray's was a bold claim but not particularly accurate. Jazz had already served as a crossroads of exchange for black and Latin music, beginning as early as Dizzy Gillespie and Machito's Afro-Cuban suites of the 1940s. By the early '60s, there were any number of big R&B/Latin crossover hits, especially the slinky 1963 remake of Herbie Hancock's "Watermelon Man" by Cuban master percussionist Mongo Santamaria.

What made *bugalú* different was as much generational as it was musical. The players who led the movement were an emergent cadre of

"Nuyoricans," New York–born and –raised Puerto Ricans. They came of age in and around working-class black and Latino neighborhoods, in a musical polyglot where the honeyed doo-wop sounds of Frankie Lymon and the Teenagers were as resonant as Tito Puente's spirited mambos. When mambo's crown venue, the Palladium Ballroom, closed in 1966, *bugalú* was already rising to provide the next big thing.

The clarion call came with the 1966 single "Bang Bang," by the Joe Cuba Sextet. Headed by veteran *conguero* Cuba and his "velvet"-voiced singer Jimmy Sabater, the Sextet built "Bang Bang" around a hammering piano riff that leads into a series of loud hand claps and a chorus of beeps and sighs, and climaxes with a nonsensical hook of "Bang! Bang!" Outside a few random Latin culinary references (*lechon!*), the song had no real songwriting, but its propulsive energy and memorable chants transcended culture and language. "Bang Bang" was a massive success, charting more than a million copies and all but kick-starting the *bugalú* craze. Within months, *bugalú* bands had all but taken over New York's Latin dance halls and radio playlists.

The sound's colorful flair and spirit of self-invention were matched in the new personalities who rode its initial wave. Self-proclaimed as *el rey* (king) of *bugalú*, Pete Rodriguez, depicting himself as a swinging '60s bachelor on his record covers, scored two immense hits, "I Like It Like That" and "Oh, That's Nice!" Contrasting with Rodriguez's dapper playboy image was the brooding, gangster-obsessed Willie Colón. The future megastar of salsa was only 17 when he cut *bugalús* like "Willie Baby" for his provocatively titled *El Malo* (The Bad One) album.

The real gangster, though, was Bataan. Born to a Filipino father and a black mother, Bataan passed for Puerto Rican in East Harlem—so much so that he led the Nuyorican street gang the Dragons in the early '60s. Bataan was a respected street fighter whose short jail stints persuaded him to seek a more productive form of expression.

This complex cross-cultural heritage seeped into his music; his first major hit came in 1967 with a *bugalú* cover of the Impressions' "Gypsy Woman," a song originally influenced by Curtis Mayfield's interest in Latin rhythms. Bataan borrowed more than just Mayfield's song—unlike other *bugalú* vocalists with their showy, belting voices, Bataan preferred the sweet, soulful touch of Mayfield and the Impressions, Lymon and the

Teenagers, and other sensitive soul men. Bataan was a gifted arranger and bandleader, but his greatest mark came in how he drizzled his richly emotive voice over his band's chattering Afro-Cuban rhythms.

The *bugalú* formula itself was consistent. Simplicity was central. The catchiest *bugalús* kept the core rhythm uncluttered—a simple bass line or piano riff would suffice—with some blaring brass on top and rollicking percussion beneath. Unlike their older Latin forebears, who sang in Spanish, Nuyorican songwriters penned their catchy hooks in English. These choices endeared *bugalús* to a large cross-cultural audience and made them exportable. By 1967 and '68, bands from Puerto Rico to Panama, Colombia to Peru, expanded *bugalú*'s popularity across the Latin Caribbean and South America. "Black" and "brown" musical styles had been in conversation for years, from the Cuban clave rhythm powering the famed "Bo Diddley beat" to Perez Prado's mambo-fying of Hank Ballard's "The Twist." But the *bugalú* existed at the busiest of these crossings, the cross-pollination of disparate strands of African musical traditions in the New World that the slave trade had previously thrown asunder. Few American-born Latin music styles had ever had such an impact abroad.

Yet even as *bugalú* created new fans, it was attracting enemies as well. New York's Latin music machine was run through the loose collusion of record labels, club promoters, and radio programmers. Traditionally, they had been able to use their muscle to force bands into deals that maximized profits for the owners but stiffed the players. When *bugalú* bands treatened to unite against the oligarchy, they found themselves blacklisted from radio play and ballroom bookings.

Meanwhile, *bugalú* had left former mambo giants like Tito Puente and Charlie Palmieri on the sidelines, overshadowed by the popularity of their younger peers. The *bugalú* blacklist emboldened these elders to reclaim the dance halls and record charts with the blessing of a Lagin music industry happy to have more familiar faces to work with. The strength of the backlash was great enough that, by 1969, the once flourishing music was floundering. In the words of Bataan, "They assassinated the *bugalú*."

The main power identified with the blacklist was Fania Records. When attorney Jerry Masucci and band leader Johnny Pacheco founded Fania in 1964, they were in the shadow of older Latin labels such as

Tico, Alegre, and Cotique. But *bugalú* acts such as Bataan, Bobby Valentin, and Monguito Santamaria helped Fania catch their rivals. By the end of the '60s, Fania was well on its way to eclipsing all other American Latin labels.

Eager as Fania had been to capitalize on the *bugalú* craze, it was also quick to join the blacklist once its artists started asking for more money and control. The suppression was complete once salsa became the next major Latin movement out of New York in the early '70s. Salsa, with the styles based around more traditional Latin rhythms than *bugalú*'s corss-cultural fusion, proved to be even more successful, and labels like Fania found it easy to abandon the *bugalú*.

Even though *bugalú* vanished from mainstream view and its records went out of print by the early '70s, the music maintained a cult following for decades. Bootlegs and compilations have kept many songs in rotation. More recently, Fania has led an unprecedented revival. When the Emusica Entertainment Group bought Fania's catalog in 2005 (for a reputed $10 million), it astutely perceived a continuing market for the music. It has since re-released many of Fania's *bugalú*-era albums—most for the first time on DC. Emusica has also commissioned tastemaker DJs like London's Gilles Peterson and New York newcomer DJ Rumor to assemble album-length Latin soul mixes in an attempt to introduce the music to a new generation.

Bugalú was always a great bridge between communities; in its heyday, ballrooms would draw black, white, and Latino fans from across New York's boroughs to boogaloo the night away. With an equally diverse fan base in this emergent generation, *bugalú* continues to live up to the cross-cultural ideal it was born out of. That sentiment of unity is brought home on one of the new Fania anthologies, *Latin Soul Man*, dedicated to the late, great percussionist Ray Barretto. A Nuyorican from an older generation, he was an undisputed forefather of the *bugalú*. However, unlike his scornful peers, Barretto embraced the style; he even titled his 1967 album *Latino Con Soul*. The title track of another LP, *Together* (1969), appears on *Latin Soul Man*. On it, Barretto expresses the social idealism of the *bugalú* era, singing, "I know a beautiful truth and it's helped me be free / I know I'm black and I'm white and I'm red / The blood of mankind flows in me."

Sam Kashner

FEVER PITCH

WHEN TRAVOLTA DID DISCO;
THE MAKING OF *SATURDAY NIGHT FEVER*

In 1976, producer Robert Stigwood placed a million-dollar bet on a young TV star, signing John Travolta to a three-movie deal. First up, a low-budget production based on a *New York* magazine article about disco-crazy Italian-American kids in Bay Ridge, Brooklyn: *Saturday Night Fever*. From Travolta's famous "Stayin' Alive" strut to the mid-filming death of his girlfriend, to three harrowing nights on the Verrazano-Narrows Bridge, Sam Kashner has the story of a culture-bending hit, whose music—by a revitalized 60s band called the Bee Gees—became the best-selling soundtrack of its time.

Robert Stigwood, the 42-year-old Australian impresario known as "the Darryl Zanuck of pop," was out of his mind. That was the talk in Hollywood, Bill Oakes remembers, on September 25, 1976, when his boss held a lavish press conference at the Beverly Hills Hotel to announce that the Robert Stigwood Organisation—RSO—had just signed John Travolta to a million-dollar contract to star in three films. Oakes, then in his mid-20s, had worked for the Beatles and had once been Paul McCartney's assistant. By this time he was running RSO Records, which boasted Eric Clapton and the Bee Gees among its roster of pop stars. "Everyone thought it was madness," says Oakes, "because nobody had ever made the transition from television to movie stardom. So, a lot of us thought to pay a million dollars for Vinnie Barbarino [Travolta's character on the TV sitcom *Welcome Back, Kotter*] is going to make us a laughingstock."

Stigwood wanted Travolta to star in the movie version of *Grease*, the long-running Broadway musical (in which Travolta had already appeared as Doody, one of the T-Bird gang members, in a road company). Five years earlier, Stigwood had auditioned the actor—then just 17—for *Jesus Christ Superstar*, and though Ted Neeley got the job, Stigwood had penciled himself a note on a yellow pad: "This kid will be a very big star."

But Stigwood's option for *Grease* stipulated that production could not begin before the spring of 1978, because the musical was still going strong. While they waited, Stigwood and his lieutenants began to look around for a new property.

A few months before, an English rock critic by the name of Nik Cohn had published a magazine article entitled "Tribal Rites of the New Saturday Night." Appearing in the June 7, 1976, issue of *New York*, the article followed the Saturday-night rituals of a group of working-class Italian-Americans in Bay Ridge, Brooklyn, who held dead-end jobs but lived for their nights of dancing at a local disco called 2001 Odyssey. Cohn's hero, named Vincent, was a tough, violent guy but a great dancer who yearned for a chance to shine, and to escape the mean streets of Brooklyn.

On an icy winter night in 1975, Cohn had made his first trip to Bay Ridge with a disco dancer called Tu Sweet, who would serve as his Virgil. "According to Tu Sweet," Cohn later wrote, "the [disco] craze had started in black gay clubs, then progressed to straight blacks and gay whites and from there to mass consumption—Latinos in the Bronx, West Indians on Staten Island, and, yes, Italians in Brooklyn." In 1975, black dancers like Tu Sweet were not welcome in those Italian clubs; nonetheless, he liked the dancers there—their passion and their moves. "Some of those guys, they have no lives," he told Cohn. "Dancing's all they got."

A brawl was in progress when they arrived at 2001 Odyssey. One of the brawlers lurched over to Cohn's cab and threw up on his trouser leg. With that welcome, the two men hightailed it back to Manhattan, but not before Cohn caught a glimpse of a figure, dressed in "flared, crimson pants and a black body shirt," coolly watching the action from the club doorway. "There was a certain style about him—an inner force, a hunger, and a sense of his own specialness. He looked, in short, like a star," recalled Cohn. He'd found his Vincent, the protagonist of his New Journalism–style piece.

Later, Cohn went back to the disco with the artist James McMullan, whose illustrations for the article helped persuade Cohn's underwhelmed editor in chief, Clay Felker, to run it. The title was changed from "Another Saturday Night" to "Tribal Rites of the New Saturday Night," and a note was added insisting that "everything described in this article is factual."

In the 1970s it was almost unheard of to buy a magazine article for a movie, but "Tribal Rites" attracted enough attention that producer Ray Stark (*Funny Girl*) and a few others bid on it. Cohn had known Stigwood back in London and liked him. Stigwood came from humble stock: farm people in Adelaide, Australia. He'd made his way to London in the early 1960s and ended up managing the Beatles organization for Brian Epstein. Ousted in the power struggle that followed Epstein's death, Stigwood went on to create RSO Records, and in 1968 he branched out into theater, putting together the West End productions of *Jesus Christ Superstar*, *Hair*, and *Grease*. His movie-producing career began five years later, with the film version of *Jesus Christ Superstar*, followed by *Tommy*, the rock musical written by the Who and directed by the flamboyant Ken Russell, which became one of the biggest movies of 1975.

So the deal was made, and Cohn was paid $90,000 for the rights.

Now they had to find a director.

In Los Angeles, Stigwood's assistant, Kevin McCormick, a brilliant, lean 23-year-old from New Jersey, went from office to office looking for one. "Kid, my directors do movies," one agent promptly told him. "They don't do magazine articles." But while McCormick was packing to return to New York, the phone rang, and it was the agent saying, "Kid, you're in luck. My client came in and looked at this, and he's interested. But you should see his movie first."

"So we saw *Rocky* on Monday, and we made a deal," recalls McCormick, now executive vice president of production at Warner Bros. The client was director John Avildsen, and he brought in screenwriter Norman Wexler, who had earned his first Academy Award nomination for the screenplay for *Joe*, the popular 1970 film about a bigoted hard hat, played by Peter Boyle. (Incidentally, the film gave Susan Sarandon her first screen role.) Wexler had also co-adapted Peter Maas's *Serpico* for the screen (which brought him a second Oscar nomination). That seemed fitting, as Al Pacino was something of the patron saint of Cohn's article, as well as of the film—in the story, Vincent is flattered when someone mistakes him for Pacino, and in the movie, the poster from *Serpico* dominates Tony Manero's Bay Ridge bedroom, going face-to-face with Farrah Fawcett's famous cheesecake poster.

Wexler, a tall man, often wrapped in a trench coat, puffed on Tarrytons so continuously he was usually wreathed in cigarette smoke. McCormick thought of him as "a sort of tragic figure, but enormously sympathetic." A manic-depressive, Wexler was on and off his meds; when he stopped, all hell broke loose. Karen Lynn Gorney, who played Stephanie Mangano, Tony's love interest in the movie, remembers, "He would come into his agent's office, or try to pitch a script to somebody, and start giving nylons and chocolates to the secretaries." He could turn violent, and was known to sometimes carry a .32-caliber pistol. In the grip of a manic episode, he once bit a stewardess on the arm; on another flight he announced that he had a plan to assassinate President Nixon. "You've heard of street theater?" he yelled, holding up a magazine picture of the president. "Well, this is airplane theater!" He was arrested and escorted off the plane.

But McCormick was pleased when the script came in. At 149 pages, "it was way, way, way, way too long, but quite wonderful. I think what Norman did so well was to create a family situation that had real truth, an accurate look at how men related to women in that moment, in ways that you would never get away with now." Wexler transformed Vincent into Tony Manero and gave him a young sister and a favored older brother who breaks his mother's heart by leaving the priesthood.

During one row at the dinner table, Tony explodes at his mother when she refuses to accept that her eldest has turned in his collar: "You got nuthin' but three shit children!" he yells. Tony's mother—played by acclaimed stage actress and Off Broadway playwright Julie Bovasso—bursts into tears, and Tony is overcome with remorse.

Before John Travolta became a teen idol, he was a dancer. "I think my first turn-on to dance was James Cagney in *Yankee Doodle Dandy*, when I was five or six," recalls Travolta on a break from filming the musical version of John Waters's *Hairspray* in Toronto. "I used to try to imitate him in front of the television set. I liked black dancing better than white dancing. I used to watch *Soul Train*, and what I wanted to create was a *Soul Train* feel in *Saturday Night Fever*." That famous strut to the Bee Gees' "Stayin' Alive" in the opening scene? "It was the walk of coolness. I went to a school that was 50 percent black, and that's how the black kids walked through the hall."

"Nobody pushed me into show business," Travolta says. "I was aching for it." Born in 1954 in Englewood, New Jersey, he was one of six kids, five of whom pursued careers in show business. His mother, Helen, was an actress who taught in a high-school theater-arts program and who set a record for swimming the Hudson River. His father, Salvatore (known as "Sam"), once played semi-pro football and was a co-owner of Travolta Tyre Exchange. John's parents agreed to let him drop out of Dwight Morrow High School, in Englewood, at 16, for one year, to pursue a theatrical career. He never went back. Soon after, in 1970, Travolta caught the attention of agent Bob LeMond when he appeared as Hugo Peabody in a production of *Bye Bye Birdie* at Club Benet in Morgan, New York. LeMond quickly got him work in dozens of TV commercials, including one for Mutual of New York, in which Travolta played a teenager crying over the death of his father.

Travolta moved to Los Angeles in 1974 and auditioned for *The Last Detail*, but lost the role to Randy Quaid. He landed a small role as Nancy Allen's creepy, sadistic boyfriend in Brian De Palma's *Carrie*, just before auditioning for *Welcome Back, Kotter*, the ABC sitcom about a group of unteachable Brooklyn high-school students called the "Sweathogs" and their local-boy teacher, played by the show's creator, Gabe Kaplan.

After signing to play the dumb but sexy Italian kid, Vinnie Barbarino (who thrilled the girls with his goofy grin, curly forelock, and swiveling snake hips), Travolta landed the lead role in Terrence Malick's *Days of Heaven*. But ABC wouldn't let him out of the *Welcome Back, Kotter* production schedule, and Richard Gere took his place. "I thought, What's happening here? Will I ever get my big break?" Travolta recalls.

What Travolta didn't know was that he had already gotten his big break. The network was receiving 10,000 fan letters a week—just for him. Soon there were beefcake Vinnie Barbarino posters everywhere—that cleft chin, those cerulean eyes. His public appearances were mobbed. When his 1976 debut album was released, thousands of female fans packed E. J. Korvette's record department in Hicksville, Long Island, and an estimated 30,000 fans showed up at what was then the world's largest indoor mall, in Schaumburg, Illinois. When *Carrie* was released, Travolta's name appeared above the title on some movie marquees.

ABC asked him to star in his own show, based on the Barbarino character, but Travolta turned it down, worried about ever getting a major film role. Then Robert Stigwood called.

While still appearing on *Welcome Back, Kotter*, Travolta had played the lead in an ABC-TV movie called *The Boy in the Plastic Bubble*, the true story of a teenage boy who had been born without an immune system. It aired November 12, 1976, and his co-star was Diana Hyland, who played his mother. Hyland—often described as "a Grace Kelly type"—had appeared on Broadway with Paul Newman in *Sweet Bird of Youth*, but was best known as Susan, an alcoholic wife on the TV series *Peyton Place*. A romance flowered between 22-year-old Travolta and 40-year-old Hyland, which baffled many who knew the young actor, and was toned down so as not to raise too many eyebrows in the press or alienate his teen fan base.

It was Diana who persuaded Travolta to take the role of Tony Manero. "I got the script, I read it that night," Travolta recalls. "I wondered if I could give it enough dimension. Diana took it into the other room, and in about an hour she burst back in. 'Baby, you are going to be great in this—great! This Tony, he's got all the colors! First he's angry about something. He hates the trap that Brooklyn and his dumb job are. There's a whole glamorous world out there waiting for him, which he feels only when he dances. And he grows, he gets out of Brooklyn.'" Travolta remembers answering, "'He's also king of the disco. I'm not that good a dancer.' 'Baby,' she said, 'you're going to learn!'"

Stigwood "just had blithe confidence that the movie's going to be up and ready to go," according to McCormick. "And he had no financier. He was financing it himself with his new partners, for two and a half million dollars. I knew that the budget was at least $2.8 [million] already. I had a stomachache every day. We were making this low-budget movie out of 135 Central Park West—we literally put together the soundtrack in Stigwood's living room."

And they had to hurry: Travolta and Stigwood were slated to film *Grease* soon after. This was just a little movie to get out of the way.

After six months of prepping, a huge problem reared its head: the director turned out to be all wrong. McCormick noticed that Avildsen was becoming increasingly difficult. "First he couldn't figure out who the choreographer should be. We met endlessly with [New York City Ballet principal dancer] Jacques D'Amboise. [Alvin Ailey star] Judith Jamison we talked to for a while. So, it just got to a point where Avildsen wanted to be put out of his misery. He was acting provocatively: 'Travolta's too fat. He can't dance, he can't do this, he can't do that.'"

Avildsen brought in a trainer, ex-boxer Jimmy Gambina, who had worked with Sylvester Stallone on *Rocky*, to get Travolta into shape, "which was really good," McCormick says, "because Travolta is prone to be soft and not that energetic, and Gambina ran him like he was a fighter." But Avildsen still wasn't satisfied, and wondered if maybe Travolta's character "shouldn't be a dancer—maybe he should be a painter. It was just weird. It became Clifford Odets," recalls McCormick. Travolta, ultimately, wasn't happy with Avildsen, either; he felt the director wanted to smooth Tony's rough edges, make him the kind of nice guy who carries groceries for old ladies in the neighborhood—another Rocky Balboa.

Just weeks before filming was set to begin, Stigwood summoned Avildsen to an emergency meeting. That morning, Stigwood had learned, Avildsen had been nominated for an Oscar for Rocky. McCormick says, "Robert walked in and said, 'John, there's good news and bad news. The good news is you've just been nominated for an

Academy Award. Congratulations. The bad news is you're fired.'"
(Avildsen won the Oscar.)

"Now what do we do?" McCormick asked Stigwood.

"We get another director."

So, John Badham came on the scene, three weeks before principal
photography was to begin. Badham was born in England, raised in Alabama, and educated at the Yale School of Drama. Like Travolta, he
came from a theatrical family. His mother was an actress and his sister,
Mary, had played Scout, Atticus Finch's daughter, in *To Kill a Mocking-
bird*. It was her connection to Gregory Peck that had gotten her
brother's foot in the door in the industry: in the mailroom at Warner
Bros. At 34, Badham still had few credits to his name—some television
and a baseball movie starring Billy Dee Williams, Richard Pryor, and
James Earl Jones (*The Bingo Long Traveling All-Stars & Motor Kings*).
He had just jumped from—or been pushed out of—directing *The Wiz*,
because he objected to 33-year-old Diana Ross being cast as Dorothy.
McCormick sent him the *Saturday Night Fever* script and promptly
flew him to New York.

When Travolta met Badham, he was surprised that his new director
knew so little about New York. The actor took it upon himself to show
Badham Manhattan and Brooklyn. "I said, 'Let me be your guide. Let
me take you by the hand and show you New York and its environs—the
real New York. I know this town.'" He was a quick study, says Mc-
Cormick. "Badham, the most unmusical guy in the world, brought in
the choreographer, who was fantastic"—Lester Wilson. Travolta had already been working with Deney Terio, a disco dancer who would later
host a TV disco competition called *Dance Fever*, but it was Wilson,
many in the crew believe, who breathed life into the movie.

Wilson was a black choreographer who had worked with Sammy
Davis Jr. as a featured dancer in *Golden Boy* on Broadway and in London. A legend in gay dance clubs, he'd won an Emmy for choreograph-
ing Lola Falana's television specials. Paul Pape, who played Double J,
the most aggressive member of Tony Manero's entourage, says, "Deney
Terio did show John the moves, and I give him credit for that. But I
don't think Lester Wilson got nearly the credit that he deserved. The
movie was Lester."

Travolta describes Wilson as "such an interesting guy. He taught me what he called his 'hang time.' He would smoke a cigarette to greet the day, and he infused my dancing with African-American rhythm. I'm the kind of dancer who needs thought and construction—an idea—before I dance. I need an internal story. Lester would put on some music and he would say, 'Move with me, mother-fucker—move with me!'"

Before they could start filming, they had to get the setting just right. Lloyd Kaufman, co-founder of Troma Entertainment and the film's executive in charge of locations, says, "We looked at every disco in Manhattan, Brooklyn, and Queens, and even considered converting a loft to our own specifications, before deciding to go with 2001 Odyssey, in Bay Ridge. That was always our first choice, since that's where the story really happens." The movie, except for two days' filming on the West Side of Manhattan and the Verrazano-Narrows Bridge scenes, was shot entirely in Bay Ridge.

Filming in Brooklyn brought a whole new set of challenges. It was a rough place, and the production started to have some neighborhood problems. A firebomb was thrown at the discotheque, but it didn't cause any serious damage. McCormick asked John Nicolella, the production manager on the shoot and a tough Italian character, "'What the fuck is this about?' And he said, 'Well, you know, it's a neighborhood thing. They want us to hire some of the kids.' Then these two guys appeared on the set, pulled me off to the side. 'You know, you're being disruptive to the neighborhood. You might need some security. And if you want to put lights on the bowling alley across the street, Black Stan really wants seven grand.'" They paid him.

Tom Priestley, then a camera operator on his first feature film, says, "We all grew up on locations in New York because Hollywood had all the studios. We had one or two stages that were decent. But most of the time, all our work was in the streets. We didn't have all the bells and whistles that Hollywood had. And that's what made us, I think, tough and adaptable. You figure if you can work in New York you can work anywhere."

To research his character, Travolta began sneaking into 2001 Odyssey with Wexler. So great was his popularity as Vinnie Barbarino he had to disguise himself in dark glasses and a hat. Before he was spotted, he watched the Faces—the cool, aggressive dancers Cohn had based his article on—concentrating on every detail of their behavior. When he was recognized—"Hey, man! Hey, it's fuckin' Travolta!"—the actor noticed how the disco's alpha males kept their girls in line. "Their girlfriends would come up, and they'd say, 'Hey, stay away from him, don't bug Travolta,' and they'd actually push the girls away. Tony Manero's whole male-chauvinist thing I got from watching those guys in the discos," says Travolta.

Priestley remembers, "I would've thought the real guys [in Brooklyn] would have resented a film like this, like we've come to make fun of them or something, but they loved it. There was one brother-and-sister team that was very good. Remember, all those people in the show are extras. You see them dancing next to Travolta and Donna Pescow [who played Annette]. They were really good dancers."

There were no special effects in *Saturday Night Fever*, except for the smoke rising from the dance floor. Bill Ward, the film's sole gaffer, explains that it wasn't from dry ice or a smoke machine—it was "a toxic mix of burning tar and automobile tires, pinched from a Bay Ridge alley." It created such heat and smoke that at one point they had to wheel in oxygen for Travolta. The filmmakers also went to great trouble and expense—$15,000—to put lights in the dance floor, designed to pulsate to the music. The walls were covered with aluminum foil and Christmas lights. When the club's owner saw the dailies for the first time, he said, "Holy shit, you guys made my place look great!"

Filming began on March 14, 1977. "The first day's location was outside the dance studio," recalls McCormick. "I got a phone call from the production manager, and he said, 'This is chaos!' I came out and there were 10,000 kids on the streets, and we only have four security guys. So we had to shut down for a couple of hours while we just regrouped and tried to figure out a way to make it work. It was the first time that we actually had a sense of who John was." By the end of the first day, they had to shut down and go home because "there was no place you could point the camera without seeing 15,000 people. We'd have to put out fake call sheets and get out there at 5:30 in the morning" to avoid the crush of fans.

Brooklyn-born actress Donna Pescow, who breaks your heart as Annette, the foolish local girl whose adoration of Tony nearly destroys her, was in the makeup trailer with Travolta when fans surrounded them and started rocking the trailer back and forth. "That was terrifying," she remembers. "So, they got the right people in the neighborhood, who said, 'Don't do that anymore.' They were practically paying protection—I mean, it was really tough." Karen Lynn Gorney, however, felt that the sheer energy released by thousands of Travolta's female fans yelling "Barbarino!" added to the set. "It helped the film," she says. "A lot of female hormones raging around—that might have been a good thing. Women aren't supposed to express their sexuality, but that's what you get, all that screaming and crying, because they're sitting on their gonads."

A personal tragedy was unfolding for Travolta, however: Diana Hyland's struggle with breast cancer. By the time he began preparing to play Tony Manero, she was dying. Travolta made many trips from New York to Los Angeles to be with her through her illness, so he was in a state of constant jet lag and distress. Two weeks after shooting began, he flew to the West Coast to be with Diana one last time. "He did not know Diana was sick when he fell in love," Travolta's mother, Helen, later told *McCall's* magazine, "but he stuck with her when he did know." On March 27, 1977, Hyland died in his arms.

Andy Warhol was on Travolta's return flight to New York. He later wrote in his diary, "John Travolta kept going to the bathroom, coming out with his eyes bright red, drinking orange juice and liquor in a paper cup, and he put his head in a pillow and started crying. I saw him reading a script, too, so I thought he was acting, really cute and sensitive-looking, very tall. . . . You can see the magic in him. I asked the stewardess why he was crying and she said, 'death in the family,' so I thought it was a mother or father, until I picked up the paper at home and found out that it was Diana Hyland, who'd died of cancer at forty-one, soap-opera queen, his steady date."

Karen Lynn Gorney later said that she could feel Diana's spirit on the set, "protecting him, because he was going through deep grief and he had to get through it. If he fell into the grief, he wouldn't be able to pull himself out of it. But he was very professional and he was right there on the money. I remember the scene at the Verrazano Bridge when I lean over and kiss him. The poor thing was suffering so, and that kiss was totally spontaneous. That wasn't Tony and Stephanie—that was because I really saw he was hurting."

There's another lovely scene between Travolta and Gorney, when Stephanie agrees to accompany Tony to a Brooklyn restaurant. "We wanted to see how much of it we could do in one shot," Badham says about that scene, which was filmed through the restaurant's window, so you see them through a glorious, dreamlike reflection of a city skyline—"magic and distant." They try to impress each other with their savvy and their cool, but they are hilariously unpolished. (Stephanie informs Tony that worldly New Yorkers drink tea with lemon.) "These kids are trying to pretend like they're a lot more sophisticated than they are," Badham says, "though obviously anybody that says 'Bonwit Taylor' hasn't quite got it all together." As the scene unfolds, the light subtly changes, late afternoon moving into dusk.

Badham and Travolta clashed on a number of occasions. When Travolta first saw the rushes of the opening scene, in which a stand-in—shot from the knees down—takes that famous walk along Brooklyn's 86th Street to the beat of "Stayin' Alive," he insisted that his character wouldn't walk like that. He made Badham reshoot the scene, this time with Travolta strutting down the avenue. Later, when Travolta got his first look at how his big dance solo had been edited, he had a meltdown. "I was crying and very angry because of the way the dance highlight was shot. I knew how it should appear on-screen, and it wasn't shot that way. You couldn't even see my feet!" The sequence had been edited for close-ups, so that all his hard work—the knee drops, the splits, the solo he had labored over for nine months—had been cut off at the knees. He knew that for the scene to work, he had to be seen head to toe, so no one would think someone else had done the dancing for him. One of the most famous dance numbers in the history of film almost didn't make it to the screen.

"I called Stigwood," Travolta says, "crying and furious, and said, 'Robert, I'm off the movie. I don't want to be a part of it anymore.'"

Stigwood gave Travolta license to re-edit the scene, over Badham's objections. At 23, Travolta knew what he wanted and what he could do, and he was protecting his character and his dazzling moves.

"The Bee Gees weren't even involved in the movie in the beginning," says Travolta. "I was dancing to Stevie Wonder and Boz Scaggs." Once they came in, however, everything changed.

Afterward, Stigwood thought of the Bee Gees as co-creators of the movie. "Those first five songs," says Bill Oakes, "which I put on the first side of the soundtrack double album—'Stayin' Alive,' 'How Deep Is Your Love,' 'Night Fever,' 'More than a Woman,' and 'If I Can't Have You' [written by the brothers Gibb but sung by Oakes's wife at the time, Yvonne Elliman]—that's the side you couldn't stop playing." But in 1976, before Stigwood bought the rights to Cohn's article, "the Bee Gees were broken," remembers McCormick. "They were touring Malaysia and Venezuela, the two places where they were still popular. They were a mess. Everybody [in the group] had their own little soap opera." But Stigwood "still had this innate ability to spot where a trend was going, like he had this pop gyroscope implanted in him," he adds.

The Bee Gees are three brothers—Barry, Robin, and Maurice Gibb—who were born on the Isle of Man and grew up in Australia, and whose first big hit, "New York Mining Disaster 1941," had some people believing that it was secretly recorded by the Beatles under a pseudonym. It was followed by two more hits: "To Love Somebody" and "How Can You Mend a Broken Heart." Quick fame and riches put tremendous strains on the group—they broke up, tried solo acts, regrouped, and by the time of *Saturday Night Fever* were considered a dated 60s band, awash in drugs and alcohol and legal problems. Nonetheless, Stigwood signed them to his record label and released "Jive Talkin'" to radio stations anonymously, because no one wanted to hear from the Bee Gees. Oakes recalls that in the early 1970s "it was hard just getting the Bee Gees back on the radio, because they were virtually blacklisted." But when "Jive Talkin'" hit, people were surprised to learn that "these falsetto-singing disco chaps were in fact your old Bee Gees—that again was Stigwood's genius." The song and the album it came from, *Main Course*, were huge hits. Even though they weren't a disco band—they didn't go to clubs, they didn't even dance!—Stigwood felt they had "the beat of the dance floor in their blood," Oakes says.

When Stigwood told the band about Cohn's article and asked them to write songs for the movie, they were back living on the Isle of Man, for tax reasons. Barry Gibb suggested a few titles, including "Stayin' Alive" and "Night Fever," but it wasn't until they convened at the Chateau D'Heuroville studio, in France, to mix a live album called *Here at Last Live*, did they flesh out those songs—and they wrote them virtually in a single weekend.

Stigwood and Oakes turned up in Heuroville, and the Bee Gees played their demos: "How Deep Is Your Love," "Stayin' Alive," "Night Fever," "More than a Woman." "They flipped out and said these will be great. We still had no concept of the movie, except some kind of rough script that they'd brought with them," according to Barry Gibb. "You've got to remember, we were fairly dead in the water at that point, 1975, somewhere in that zone—the Bee Gees' sound was basically tired. We needed something new. We hadn't had a hit record in about three years. So we felt, Oh jeez, that's it. That's our life span, like most groups in the late 60s. So, we had to find something. We didn't know what was going to happen."

Oakes mixed the soundtrack on the Paramount lot. Senior executives would call across the commissary to ask, "'How's your little disco movie, Billy?' They thought it was rather silly; disco had run its course. These days, *Fever* is credited with kicking off the whole disco thing—it really didn't. Truth is, it breathed new life into a genre that was actually dying."

The music had a profound effect on cast and crew. Priestley remembers, "We all thought we'd fallen into a bucket of shit, and then we heard that music. It changed everything. We didn't hear the soundtrack until we were about three weeks into the movie. But once you heard it, you said, 'Whoa!' An aura came over it. I mean, I'm not a disco fan, but that music transcends disco." For the first time, everyone dared to think this movie could be big. Gorney, whose father was Jay Gorney, the songwriter who wrote such hits as "Brother, Can You Spare a Dime" and "You're My Thrill," had the same reaction: "The first time I heard the music I said, 'Those are monster hits.'"

"How long was the *Fever* shoot?" asks Karen Lynn Gorney rhetorically. "Three months and 30 years, and it's not over yet. I seemed to be always working on the film, because of the dancing. Physically, I was weak when I started. I was terrified, because the first time I danced with

John he'd been working for half a year on this stuff. I felt like I was try-ing to dance with a wild stallion—he was that strong."

An actress and dancer who was well known at the time as Tara Mar-tin Tyler Brent Jefferson on ABC's endlessly running soap opera *All My Children*, Gorney landed the part after sharing a cab with Stigwood's nephew. When he described the movie to her, she asked, "Am I in it?" She then auditioned for Stigwood in his apartment in the San Remo, on Central Park West. "I remember this giant silk Chinese screen along the wall—the whole history of China. I did the best acting of my life in front of him." She landed the part of Stephanie, a Brooklyn climber who has already made the big move to "the city" and is hell-bent on self-improvement—taking college courses and drinking tea with lemon. Tony reminds her of the neighborhood she's trying to escape. It's a touching and comic role—at one point, while showing off her erudition in her Brooklyn accent, she insists that *Romeo and Juliet* was written by Zefferelli. "I was trying to convince myself to stay away from Tony," she says about her role, "because he wasn't going to get me anywhere. I wanted you to see the voices in her head saying, 'Oh, he's too young. He doesn't have any class.'"

There was some early grumbling about Gorney when filming began. Certain crew members felt she was too old for the part, and that her dancing wasn't up to par. (She had sustained serious injuries in a motor-cycle accident a few years earlier.) But Pauline Kael, in her review of the film, found the performance affecting: "Gorney wins you over by her small, harried, tight face and her line readings, which are sometimes miraculously edgy and ardent. The determined, troubled Stephanie is an updated version of those working girls that Ginger Rogers used to play." Her toughness, her ambition—even her comic cluelessness—con-tribute to the authenticity of the film. As does an accent so thick it needs subtitles.

The other important female character is Annette, played by Donna Pescow. She auditioned for the role six times—three for Avildsen, three for Badham. When she got the part, at 22, she said it was the first Christmas in years she wouldn't have to work at Bloomingdale's selling ornaments. She had spent two years at the American Academy of Dra-matic Arts, in New York, trying to get rid of her Brooklyn accent, but when she finally landed the role, she had to reclaim it. Legendary casting director Shirley Rich told her, "Donna. Move back home, hang out with your parents. You sound like you don't come from anywhere."

"I grew up never calling it 'Manhattan.' It was always 'the city'— 'We're going to the city,'" Pescow recalls. "I was living with my folks because it was close to the set, and I didn't drive. And so the Teamsters used to pick me up. My first night of shooting, my grandfather Jack Goldress drove me to the set in Bay Ridge. He was a former lighting man in vaudeville and then a movie projectionist at the RKO Albee, so movies were not a big thing for him. He was more interested in finding parking."

Badham rehearsed Pescow and the Faces for a couple of weeks, "just to get us to be kind of a gang. We went to the clubs together. Travolta couldn't go because he was too recognizable, but the other guys went. I'd never been in a discotheque, ever."

One of the first scenes shot with Donna was the gang-rape scene, still a harrowing thing to watch. An acting coach at the American Academy once told her, "If you play a victim, you're lost," and she seems to have followed that advice. Though we cringe at the way her character is abused, we see her strength and her resilience. In her effort to become the kind of woman who can attract Tony, she allows herself to be abused by the boys she probably grew up with, went to school with, danced with. Yet her character has the most insight into how women's roles were changing: Tony contemptuously asks her, "What are you anyway, a nice girl or you a cunt?" To which she replies, "I don't know—both?"

"John Badham and I had a running disagreement" about that scene, Pescow remembers. "I said, 'She's a virgin.' He said, 'No, she's not.' That's why I never played it as if she were really raped—she wasn't— she was off in her own little world," offering up her virginity, by proxy, to Tony Manero.

Pape admits how difficult it was to film that scene. "What Donna did was an incredible piece of acting. We were really worried it was going to affect our friendship. We talked about it a lot before we did it. We had to go into this choreographed situation where you're violating your friend with no concern for her feelings whatsoever. We had to go to a place where we weren't protecting her at all. She was willing to give it up to the wrong guy. And what did she really want? She just wanted to be loved."

Everyone on the set seemed to respond to Pescow's vulnerability. Says Priestley, "The crew just loved her. She was so great. But we all felt sorry for her. There's that great scene where she walks up to Tony and says, 'You're gonna ask me to sit down?' And he says, 'No,' but she said, 'You'd ask me to lie down.' She was perfect—it was so Brooklyn. I mean, the little outfit with the white fur jacket? It makes you feel bad for every girl you screwed over."

Tony Manero's Faces—his entourage of homeboys who watch his back, admire his dancing, keep the girls from bothering him, and rumble with the Puerto Ricans—were played with pathos and humor by Pape (Double J), Barry Miller (Bobby C.), and Joseph Cali (Joey). When he first moved to New York from Rochester, Pape says, "Pacino was the actor to be—he was the hottest thing. He was the presiding spirit of the movie. When Tony comes out of his room in his underwear and his Italian grandmother crosses herself, he says, 'Attica! Attica!'—that's from *Dog Day Afternoon.*" Pape managed to land this, his first film role, on his first audition—almost unheard of—and his character was a kind of "lieutenant figure who could easily have been the leader. But he had one flaw: he had a bad temper. That's why he was in second position."

Like his cohorts, Cali, a stage-trained actor, would end up being typecast by the role of Joey. "People thought I was that street guy. I had to be Joey," he later said. Miller, as the hapless Bobby C., has the most shocking moment in the film when he falls—or jumps—to his death from the Verrazano Bridge. He's depressed because his girlfriend is pregnant and he knows he has to marry her, ending his carefree days as one of Tony's entourage.

The actors rehearsed for a few weeks in Manhattan, around Eighth Street and Broadway. "We just played basketball together and did that scene where we're making fun of the gay guys," Pape says. "We were all brand new—it's what we'd been dreaming about, having a chance to prove ourselves. We all improvised well together." (Travolta, in fact, was an inspired improviser. Manero's overbearing father slaps him on the head during an argument at the dinner table. Travolta improvised,

"Would you just watch the hair? You know, I work on my hair a long time, and you hit it! He hits my hair!")

In prepping for their roles, the Faces went to Times Square with the costume designer, Patrizia von Brandenstein (who would later win an Oscar for her art direction on *Amadeus*). The wardrobe was bought off the rack, adding to the film's authenticity. "We were buying all these polyester things, picking out all this costume jewelry. She had a great feel for it," Pape says. Von Brandenstein found Travolta's famous white suit at a boutique in Bay Ridge just under the El. "It was 1977," says Priestley. "You had to have bling—all the gold around your neck, the pointy shoes. You had to have the suit. It was called 'the Hollywood Rise.'"

Pape took inspiration from the crush of local Barbarino fans hanging around the shoot. "It wasn't just that they were there to see Travolta," he says. "If they could get within five feet of you, they wanted to be sure you were doing them right. They didn't want Hollywood bullshit. These were the guys who went to the clubs on the weekends, who worked in the paint stores, who had the dead-end jobs. This was important to them. It wasn't just about hanging around movie people. It was like, Yeah, you're welcome to be here. But regardless of what you think, respect it. This is our life, this is our world. One of the guys said, 'You can touch it, but don't spit on it.'"

The Verrazano-Narrows Bridge looms over *Saturday Night Fever* as a nearly mythical structure. Named after the 16th-century Italian explorer Giovanni da Verrazano, the bridge is a source of ethnic pride for Italian-Americans. When it opened, on November 21, 1964, it was the longest suspension bridge in the world, connecting Brooklyn and Staten Island. An American achievement with an Italian name, it symbolizes the realization of unreachable dreams. Tony knows that bridge, and in one scene he lovingly describes its history, its dimensions, its grandeur. It's where Tony's entourage—full of alcohol and sheer animal energy—hang from the girders and dare one another to climb higher. The crew spent three harrowing nights filming on the Verrazano, and it was a nightmare, as the March weather veered from freezing on one occasion to nearly 90 degrees on another. The high winds posed additional threats to the camera crew and stuntmen. Doubling as Travolta's stand-in and wearing Tony Manero's shoes and pants, Priestley, the camera operator for the scene, took a handheld camera out on the bridge's main beam and filmed himself with just a key grip holding his waist. "I was young. You couldn't sense danger then. But you're 600 feet off the water. I had my camera in my hand and we just did it. We wanted to show Hollywood we could make great films."

"They were talking about putting a guy wire on us," Pape reminisces, "and I said, 'No.' I just jumped up on the cable to show them I could swing around. There was no safety net. I was [hundreds] of feet above the water. All that was improvised—it wasn't planned. I just jumped up there and said, 'Let's do it, let's get it done.'"

The cast and crew thought that Paramount didn't care about *Saturday Night Fever*. "They gave us an office on the lot the size of a broom closet," Oakes says. "They didn't believe in it. Only Stigwood knew it was going to be something big. It was just the studio's 'little disco movie'—that was the phrase that haunted me."

In fact, word was getting back to Michael Eisner, newly ensconced as Paramount's head of production, that the movie was too vulgar. At previews in Cincinnati and Columbus, half the audience walked out because of the language and sex scenes. McCormick remembers being paged in Kennedy Airport: "I pick up the phone and it's Eisner, who starts screaming at me because we'd only taken two 'fuck's out. It became one of those ridiculous arguing sessions, where they said, 'Take out two "fuck"s and I'll let you have one "spic."'" Stigwood finally agreed to take two 'fuck's out of the movie, and that was it—he wouldn't change." They did leave in the term "blow job," however, which, some believe, is the first time the phrase was uttered in a feature film. (Attempts to reach Eisner were unsuccessful.)

It wasn't just the language. Some of the suits at Paramount were made uncomfortable by the way Travolta was so lovingly photographed in one scene—preening in front of the mirror in his bikini briefs, his gold chain nestled in his chest hair—by the cinematographer Ralf D. Bode. "We got all kinds of hassle," remembers Badham. "We were letting some man walk around in his underwear, showing his body off." The image of lean, sexually vibrant Travolta was so homoerotic that the production designer, Charles Bailey, put up that Farrah Fawcett poster just to cool things off.

There was another little problem that Paramount had to deal with before the film could ever be released. *Hairspray* would not be the first time John Travolta dressed in drag. Letting off steam at the end of the shoot, Travolta and members of the crew filmed a mock wedding at the disco—for laughs—with John dressed as the bride and one of the grips appearing as the groom. "They wanted to blow Paramount's mind," Bill Ward explains. But when the studio executives arrived, according to Tom Priestley, "they didn't see the humor in it. They sent someone to take control of the film, and I'm sure they burned it."

Stigwood released the music before the film—his strategy not only worked, it changed the game. "He basically pioneered an entirely new way of doing business in the distribution of films, records, stage, and television," Oakes believes. "I think his being from Australia had a lot to do with it—that sort of buccaneering adventurism, that entrepreneurship. I don't think he would have been as successful if he'd been English."

Eisner was skiing in Vail two weeks before the movie opened, on December 7, 1977. "I heard 'Stayin' Alive' at the lift, at the bottom, and then we went up to the top, to the restaurant, and they were playing 'Stayin' Alive' there, too, so I called up Barry Diller, head of Paramount, and I said, 'Do we have a hit here?' And then it opened," Eisner recounted, and Travolta "was the biggest thing that ever happened." When the film debuted, at Grauman's Chinese Theatre, it was a phenomenon. In its first 11 days, it grossed more than $11 million—it would go on to gross $285 million, and the soundtrack became the best-selling movie soundtrack album of all time (until Whitney Houston's *The Bodyguard*, in 1992).

Travolta, who thought they were just "doing a little art film in Brooklyn," was stunned. Not only did it breathe new life into disco, it changed the way American youth looked: "Thousands of shaggy-haired, blue-jean-clad youngsters are suddenly putting on suits and vests, combing their hair and learning to dance with partners," wrote *Newsweek*. The Abraham & Straus department store in Brooklyn even opened a "Night Fever" men's-wear boutique. John Travolta look-alike contests were drawing lines two blocks long. Fans no less prominent than Jane Fonda and *Chicago Tribune* movie critic Gene Siskel—who saw *Saturday Night Fever* 20 times—bid on Travolta's suit when it was auctioned at a charity benefit in 1979. Siskel outbid her at $2,000. (It's now valued at $100,000 and has ended up in the Smithsonian Institution.)

Pape and Pescow went to see the film in a theater in Brooklyn. "It was my first time seeing it with the people that we made it about," recalls Pape. "It was amazing. They were talking back to the screen, they were screaming and yelling, and as we came out of the theater, we were caught. But the crush was not mean—the crush was, 'You nailed it! What part of Brooklyn are you from?' It was a crush of affirmation."

The film was, finally, so authentic, Karen Lynn Gorney believes, that it was more of a documentary. "We improvised for two weeks, so that by the time it came to filming, Badham just shot what was happening. It wasn't acting."

For the Bee Gees, once the music hit, life became insane. "*Fever* was No. 1 every week," remembers Barry Gibb. "It wasn't just like a hit album. It was No. 1 every single week for 25 weeks. It was just an amazing, crazy, extraordinary time. I remember not being able to answer the phone, and I remember people climbing over my walls. I was quite grateful when it stopped. It was too unreal. In the long run, your life is better if it's not like that on a constant basis. Nice though it was."

When the reviews came out, Travolta noticed his manager, Bob LeMond, quietly weeping in the Palm Court of the Plaza Hotel. He was reading Pauline Kael's review in the December 26, 1977, *New Yorker*. To this day, Travolta treasures Kael's words: "[He] *acts* like someone who loves to dance. And, more than that, he acts like someone who loves to act. He expresses shades of emotion that aren't set down in scripts, and he knows how to show us the decency and intelligence under Tony's uncouthness. . . . he isn't just a good actor, he's a generous-hearted actor."

The Academy of Motion Picture Arts and Sciences nominated Travolta for a best-actor Oscar, along with Richard Dreyfuss, Woody Allen, Richard Burton, and Marcello Mastroianni (Dreyfuss won, for *The Goodbye Girl*). But the Bee Gees were snubbed. Stigwood threatened legal action, and McCormick threw an "anti–Academy Awards party" at his house, in Los Angeles, in protest. The guest list included Marisa Berenson, Tony and Berry Perkins, Lily Tomlin, and the writer Christopher Isherwood—even Ava Gardner showed up. "It was the last blush of *Saturday Night Fever*," for McCormick. "It was over after that, for me."

The movie changed John Travolta's life. What Brando and James Dean had been to the 1950s, Travolta was to the 1970s. *Saturday Night Fever*, believes Travolta, gave the decade its cultural identity. Pape felt that it was just Travolta's fate: "Sometimes it's time for you to have the brass ring. It's like, in John's life, it was meant to happen, and everybody just has to get out of the way." When movie stardom hit for Travolta, there was no one else in his stratosphere. "I had the field to myself," he recalls. "A few years later, Cruise would come along, and Tom Hanks, and Mel Gibson, but for a long time there was no one else out there. It was like Valentino-style popularity, an unimaginable pinnacle of fame. It's not that I wanted competition. I just wanted company."

For Pape, the movie "was like getting strapped onto a rocket ship. I became almost a victim of my own success. All the stage training I'd had, all the stuff that I'd done, it was starting to work against me, because the only work I was being offered were similar kinds of things. The very thing that made us trapped us." Pescow, who won the New York Film Critics Circle Award for best supporting actress for the film, later got rave reviews playing a waitress on television in the short-lived *Angie*. After that, she "spent years waiting for a film part to come through. And when it didn't I realized I was turning my entire life into a waiting room. I wasn't going to do that anymore." Today, Pape is in demand doing voice-overs for television and film, and he's C.E.O. of his own production company, Red Wall Productions. And Pescow's return to acting was not an insignificant one. As if to forge a link between Tony Manero and Tony Soprano (could there possibly be a white suit hanging among the other skeletons in Soprano's closet?), Pescow appeared in the controversial final episode of *The Sopranos*.

By the end of the 90s, Joseph Cali had occasionally turned up on television, in shows such as *Baywatch* and *Melrose Place*, but he now primarily sells high-end home-theater equipment for Cello Music & Film Systems, a company he founded six years ago. Gorney has appeared in dozens of independent films since *Saturday Night Fever*. She might well have ushered in the era of the tough heroine with the thick Brooklyn accent, embodied by actresses such as Marisa Tomei, Debi Mazar, and Lorraine Bracco.

McCormick now says that working on *Fever* "was the most exciting time of my life. I couldn't get up early enough, and I couldn't wait to see the dailies every night. It went from a dark winter of John losing Diana to a glorious summer. And we didn't know at the end how it was going to work out. All I prayed for was that it would be enough of a success that I'd get to work on another movie." His prayers were answered. At Warner Bros., McCormick has overseen such films as *Syriana*, *Charlie and the Chocolate Factory*, *The Perfect Storm*, *Divine Secrets of the Ya-Ya Sisterhood*, *Fight Club*, and *Blood Diamond*.

Stigwood's comet also continued to burn—for a while. *Fever* was followed by *Grease*, which did even better at the box office. But inevitably, perhaps, Stigwood and the Bee Gees fell out. The band filed a $120 million lawsuit against him, which would later be settled out of court. RSO folded in 1981. "I know I'd worked for a magician—an alchemist," McCormick says, but after *Saturday Night Fever* "you could never get him interested in anything again. He really had no serious desire. He wanted to be safe. And all that money went offshore to Bermuda," where Stigwood maintained a baronial estate for a number of years. Oakes says, "He removed himself from everyday life, almost like Howard Hughes. He was literally on his yacht, or in a suite somewhere. To get him to go out was a major achievement."

Travolta believes that "the big difference between me and Stigwood was, when something is that big, people feel in a way that they'd rather get out if they can't replicate that incredible success. He pulled up his ladder, moved to Bermuda, decided to get out of the game." For Travolta it was different. "It was never just about money. I'd wanted to be a film actor my entire life. For Stigwood, if it wasn't the pinnacle every time, he wasn't going to stay."

Travolta found himself in the wilderness, too, after the success of *Grease*. His third film for RSO, *Moment by Moment*, with Lily Tomlin, was a disappointment for everyone. (Critics nicknamed it *Hour by Hour*.) In 1983, Stigwood co-produced a sequel to *Saturday Night Fever* called *Staying Alive*, with its writer-director Sylvester Stallone. Although Norman Wexler co-wrote the screenplay, the movie was a disaster. "I called it *Staying Awake*—it was ego gone mad," recalls Oakes. "It was shorter, five times more expensive, and not any good." Oakes withdrew from Hollywood soon after. "That's when I said, 'I'm putting down my tools.'" After writing a film for Arnold Schwarzenegger (*Raw Deal*, in 1986), Wexler started turning down work. "I was fired by my agent," he told friends gleefully, before returning to playwriting. His last play, in 1996, was a comedy, *Forgive Me, Forgive Me Not*. He died three years later.

Travolta's career had a brief boost with two comedies, *Look Who's Talking* and *Look Who's Talking Too*, in 1989 and 1990, but by 1994, when he came to the attention of an intense young filmmaker new in Hollywood, his asking price had plummeted to $150,000. Quentin Tarantino was a huge fan of Travolta's, and he cast him in the role of Vincent Vega, a hit man who can dance, in *Pulp Fiction*. After *Welcome Back, Kotter* and *Saturday Night Fever*, it was the third time a character named Vincent would transform Travolta's career.

As for Nik Cohn, he admits that "in America I have always, and will always be, the guy that did *Saturday Night Fever*." Twenty years after its release, he published an article in *New York* magazine explaining how he had come to create the character of Vincent, cobbling him together from all the Faces he'd seen while trawling through pop-culture venues in the U.K. and America. There was in fact no Tony Manero, except for the one made flesh by Wexler's screenplay and Travolta's performance. For Cohn, "the whole phenomenon was just Travolta, because his particular gift is sympathy. There's something about those puppy-dog eyes and the wetness around the mouth. And the other ingredients—my character, the Bee Gees' music, Wexler's script—they all had their function. But it would not have been a touchstone, it wouldn't have worked with anybody else—nobody else could have done it."

In the early 80s the disco craze ended with a thud, followed by a backlash, from which the Bee Gees have never quite recovered. Those embarrassing white suits and platform shoes went to the back of the closet, or have been sold on eBay, and the disco sound evolved into the four-on-four beat of club divas such as Madonna and hip-hop artists such as Wyclef Jean (who remade "Stayin' Alive" as "We Trying to Stay Alive"). In 2005, a memorabilia company called Profiles in History put the 2001 Odyssey dance floor up for auction, but the attempt just ended up in a lawsuit. The nightclub continued to exist, for a while anyway, at 802 64th Street in Brooklyn, with a new name—Spectrum—ending its life as a gay, black dance club, where the disco craze first began.

But the characters of *Saturday Night Fever* live on in the collective imagination. I remember a moment nearly 10 years after the film when the poet Allen Ginsberg asked the Clash's Joe Strummer if he believed in reincarnation, and Strummer jumped the gun and said he'd like to come back as "Tony Manero, the guy from *Saturday Night Fever*—he had great fucking hair." Bay Ridge calling! Bay Ridge calling!

SEAN NELSON

DEAD MAN TALKING: "KURT COBAIN: ABOUT A SON"

A NEW EXPERIMENTAL DOCUMENTARY LETS
KURT COBAIN DELIVER HIS OWN EULOGY

The chief criticism of the new experimental documentary *Kurt Cobain: About a Son*, advanced by Manohla Dargis in the *New York Times* and furthered by clever bloggers everywhere, is that were he alive, Kurt Cobain would hate it. This projection isn't relevant—since he's *not* alive—nor particularly damning, because, frankly, who cares?

Why should the subject like the documentary? Did those greedy Bible hucksters like *Salesman*? Did Robert Crumb like *Crumb*? Could anything matter less? More importantly: The whole point (I hesitate to use the word "tragedy," though it certainly felt like one) about Cobain, consecrated by his mirthless image on posters down the ages and reinforced dramatically in the film, is that he didn't like anything about himself for very long. Cobain's plain voice, edited from tapes of 25 hours of interviews with journalist/biographer Michael Azerrad (with lo-fi sound shrewdly intact), "narrates" the film, a visual poem of the Pacific Northwest that corresponds to its subject's life. Aerial views of the cities where Cobain was a kid (Aberdeen), where he got serious about music (Olympia), and where he wound up (Seattle) set the tone from the outset: *About a Son* is about place—the place that spawned him and formed the unconscious foundation of his perspective on the world, on morality, on love, on ambition, on sex, on drugs, on rock 'n' roll, and so forth.

At times the visuals are literal. Kurt talks about his insensitive dad bringing him to work—cut to a lumberyard in Aberdeen. He talks about sitting in his dad's office—cut to the desk and the file cabinet. He talks about listening to Queen's *News of the World* while waiting for his dad to finish work—cue Freddie Mercury singing "It's Late" and a shot of a pile of logs. We get it. At other times, the images are poetic, journalistic, or just random, like a dead bird fanned out on a forest floor. Before long, these literal and abstract correspondences take on their own life as both illustration of and commentary on the narration. The most powerful image, however, is the one that doesn't appear until the last minute of the film: Cobain's face. We spend the whole film not seeing it, but imagining it superimposed over footage of the places he grew up seeing, hating, struggling to escape.

The fact that this footage is reward not archival adds a layer of meaning that might not register so much outside the Northwest— which is fine; if it's about place, let it be about place. Seeing the familiar sights of present-day Seattle—there's Neumo's (instead of old Moes's), there's the library, there's an embarrassment of new condos—under Cobain's soliloquies is a powerful reminder that he's a building block of both the psychic and physical architecture of the Northwest. And absurd though it may sound, it also suggests that he's in danger of being forgotten—not as a face or a voice, obviously, but as an exponent of a certain regional character that's hard to detect under all this prosperity. When Cobain was alive, the desire to escape your small town, make a name for yourself, make some music, and make some money presented a genuine dilemma for people schooled in what Cobain (sounding a bit like Courtney Love) disdainfully called "the bohemian theory of musical revolution."

By the time the film's interviews took place, Nirvana was a global phenomenon and its frontman had had to reconcile himself to being thought of as a hypocrite by the devotees of this theory, whose spiritual center, not for nothing, was Olympia, the very town whose "taste of culture" made him get real about his music. Though he sounds convinced that the bohemian theory was full of holes, there can be no question that the man with a K Records tattoo on his arm was tortured by it while he lived. Surely, Nirvana was the first band for whom the appropriate way to demonstrate true appreciation was to *not* wear the T-shirt. The then-prevailing bohemian revolutionary rock ideal that being punk meant being real, and being real meant rejecting fame, money, and attention—that barely exists anymore, except as a marginal objection or a quiet personal choice. Even the notion that there's such a thing as selling out is largely obsolete today, partly because of Nirvana's success. In 1992, that notion was central to music culture in the Northwest (and plenty of other places), even as bands vied to swim in Nirvana's wake. If Cobain is a martyr to anything, it's not rock 'n' roll, it's that brutal ideology, which, like all ideologies, was utopian, and therefore built to fail. The film never says any of this, but the thwarted anger in Cobain's voice, and the scenes of a changed Seattle (including Sub Pop's well-appointed new offices) make it impossible not to consider.

Well, impossible for *me* not to consider, because that's my Cobain mythos. There are many others: a tragic story of an undiagnosed depressive (though a self-diagnosed schizophrenic); an inspiring bildungsroman about a backwoods hick who made it big but couldn't take the pressure; an infuriating session of "brooding and bellyaching" by (to borrow Cobain's own words) "a product of a spoiled America." It's all of these things, too. The depth of the film's investigation of Cobain's identity resides in its refusal to be definitive. *About a Son* isn't an argument about Cobain, or even a plea to remember him. It's a eulogy, spoken by the deceased, who, despite receiving as much exposure in the last three years of his life as a human can possibly get, died feeling like he hadn't been heard.

Though cinema has concerned itself with musicians since it learned to speak—the first talkie wasn't called *The Jazz Singer* by accident—it wasn't until the rock 'n' roll era that the medium started to expand to contain the complexity of the interaction between a person and a persona. The two landmarks of this expansion were, fittingly, about the Beatles and Bob Dylan. *A Hard Day's Night* and *Don't Look Back*, a pair of low-budget black-and-white films that established a precedent that prevails to this day: Rock movies that succeed tend to feature the heroism of self-determination. Whether biopics (from *8 Mile* to *Coal Miner's*

Daughter), documentaries (from *Some Kind of Monster* to *The Filth and the Fury*), or dramas (*Hustle & Flow* to *Tender Mercies*), good rock films—and hiphop films, which in film terms means basically the same thing—turn on the observation that making music does not make you better than human; it's just that in many cases, it's the only recourse available to humans who are practically useless at everything else.

And so it is with *About a Son*, a reminder of the other side of that equation: The self-determination was essential because rock 'n' roll really was Cobain's only choice. Most of what he talks about in the film is boilerplate rock star, with all the narcissism and paranoia that go along with the job of constructing your own narrative. Typical Northwest forced humility trades off with self-consciously enigmatic non sequiturs. But hearing him bemoan his contempt for society, journalists, and his small-town roots, then extol his love for his wife, his daughter, and heroin leaves you with the impression that had he not become what he became, it's reasonable to believe that his fate would've been no different. Cobain spent a short life trying to create a persona to deliver him from the torpor of his rural ordinariness, then battling with the perceptions of that persona. But the warring desires that defined him and his creation—to be a rock star and to demystify the rock-star myth, to be aesthetically true to the punk rock that changed his life and to reach a huge audience, to deliver "anti-drug tirades" while rhapsodizing about a $400-a-day heroin habit, etc.—all point to the more fundamental desire to not be whatever he was. And no one can do that.

The distance of 13 years since the death of *About a Son*'s subject was essential—Cobain's audience wasn't ready until now, but it's possible that the medium wasn't quite ready either. The formal conventions of rock cinema have always tended to mirror the tenor of rock itself: The '50s were all good times and cheeseburgers, exploitation pictures built to cash in on a craze; the '60s saw Beatlesesque romps give way to psychedelic experimentalism; the '70s begat the born dead concert film; with the '80s came the music video; and the '90s recycled all these styles. Now that the rock 'n' roll era is well and truly dead, the boutique of rock lives on in a proliferation of documentaries—some more or less homemade—enabled by advances in cheap digital video technology and the growth of the consumer DVD market (inversely proportionate, it seems, to the death of the CD market). *About a Son* isn't technically revolutionary (though it is beautifully made); its biggest stylistic debt is owed to Godfrey Reggio's hypnotic *Koyaanisqatsi*. But for a mainstream motion picture, even an indie, to dedicate itself to examining not just an icon, but iconography itself, by treating the biggest rock star of the last 20 years to a *Koyaanisqatsi*-esque approach is a major development.

It only works because you don't see Cobain's face. This daring choice allows director A. J. Schnack to construct a physical reality that's defined by both Cobain's absence and the suggestion of his presence. It forces you to remember your own version of the man from the videos and the magazines. It also allows you to forget that image, and affect your own personal deconstruction and reconstruction. Because you don't see him, because he never stops talking, and because the film provides relentless visual context, it pulls off the fascinating trick of being both subjective and objective—not alternately, but simultaneously. And while you're interrogating your assumptions, Schnack is asking questions, too.

If the questions were along the lines of "How vulnerable was he?" this would've been the shortest documentary of all time. The interesting question, the one *About a Son* asks, is how could such obvious vulnerability march in time with such calculation? Cobain's contradictions— guilelessness and craftiness, insecurity and ambition, self-love and self-hatred, pride and shame, punk and corporate—have fueled marathon hours of argument between devotees and haters alike. *About a Son* wisely makes no attempt to reconcile these irreconcilable conflicts of character. It simply understands that such things are human and lets Cobain do all the talking.

And while it's probably true that he wouldn't have liked the film— too indulgent, too whiny, too many shots of Aberdeen—one can at least imagine that Cobain would've appreciated the opportunity to speak for himself, without the constant interpretation that he so despairingly resisted when he was alive. This is probably the ultimate reason that *About a Son* is the only way to do a film about Kurt Cobain, who was, for all important reasons, the last rock star: There's no thesis, no exegesis, no attempts to put him in a frame he didn't choose. It's just: Here he is, his words, his version—unfiltered, unmitigated, unmagnified even by his own blinding beauty. And for those of us who really did hang on his every word when he was alive, getting frustrated along with him at the way no one seemed to like him for the right reasons, the film's mandate to humanize a musician who has been handed down to history as a glowering 2-D icon is a welcome innovation.

But that still doesn't make it easy to watch, even all these years later.

JODY ROSEN

A PIRATE LOOKS AT 60

Jimmy Buffett's Midlife Crises

Jimmy Buffett turned 60 this past Dec. 25, a day he undoubtedly spent in a lower latitude, in a meditative frame of mind, in close proximity to a tankard of Captain Morgan. At least that was the case with birthday number 50, which, as recounted in his autobiography *A Pirate Looks At Fifty* (1998), Buffett celebrated by piloting his private jet from the Cayman Islands to Costa Rica to Colombia and drinking copiously, while contemplating "spirituality" and his goals going forward: "Learn celestial navigation," "Swim with dolphins," "Start therapy." Anyone who has heard a Jimmy Buffett record will know that therapy is unnecessary. Buffett has been writing and singing confessional songs for three decades, but he's never shown the slightest sign of discontentment—shrugging away the world's sadness, and his own indulgences, with an amused "I know it's all my fault" while oozing over to the bar for another round.

And who can blame him? Buffett is one of the music business' singular success stories. He has parlayed an unlikely subject—getting shitfaced while cruising the Gulf Coast in your power boat, basically—into a multimillion-dollar industry, a perennial place on *Forbes'* list of highest-grossing entertainers, and the most passionate concert audience this side of the Deadheads. (He also has written a couple of *New York Times* best sellers, operates a chain of seaside bars, and has his own seaplane airport, Lone Palm. Take that, Jay-Z.) Buffett has done all this without altering his music one iota—indeed, without any evident effort at all. He's a bard of hedonism, the sunbaked, can't-be-bothered-to-stir-from-this-beach-chair variety. His songs are nudged along by lazy rhythms and gentle country-rock acoustic strumming, and accented by the rounded ping of steel drums—the universal sonic signifier of Caribbean languor. He takes the stage of sold-out arenas in the same T-shirt and baggy beach shorts that he wears aboard ship, and can't even bring himself to put on a pair of shoes. Does he even own shoes?

I learned about the Buffett dress code the hard way, when I turned up wearing street clothes at a Madison Square Garden concert on a chilly evening last September. I had heard tales of Buffett's rabid fans, the Parrotheads, and was prepared for an onslaught of Hawaiian shirts. But that was just the beginning of the Club Med–wear. I came up the subway stairs to find a phalanx of men in their 40s striding down Seventh Avenue in plastic leis and grass skirts. Headgear ranged from Carmen Miranda–style fruit baskets to baseball caps topped with foam shark fins. Waiting in line at the Garden turnstiles, I stood next to a fellow with a papier-mâché outboard motor belted around his waist.

Buffett sells a lot of records. (His latest album, *Take the Weather With You*, topped the country charts when it was released last October). But it's touring that has made his fortune, and to really understand Buffett, you have to spend a couple of hours in a room with 15,000 people shouting along with every lyric while batting giant inflatable sharks overhead. "Parrotheads are known, to, um . . . begin their preparations early," Buffett said to cheers shortly after taking the stage, and sure enough, much of the audience was unmistakably blotto well before the first steel drum sounded. Buffett sang a stately new song, "Here We Are," which marvels at the enduring, well-soused fellowship of Parrotheads: "Who would have thought this game, this flame would still be burning?/ Who would have guessed that all these blenders would still be churning? . . . Here we are, with our fins up and our feathers flashing/ Here we are, with our coconut shell brassieres, chanting." Video screens flanking the stage played footage of the Parrotheads' famous parking lot antics. It looked like a giant frat party—a *Girls Gone Wild* video, with the part of the 19-year-old co-eds played by paunchy middle-aged men—but for Buffett, Parrotheads are heroic nonconformists, and their bacchanals have spiritual overtones. In "Here We Are" he sings: "Here we are, all the black sheep family outcast and a freak or two. . . . We're the offbeat Uncle Freds who spill their wine on you. . . . We're the dreamy Deadheads who just like us and Dave Matthews."

He's right, Parrotheads are as devoted as Deadheads and Dave Matthews fans—doubtless many in attendance at the Garden had followed Buffett up the coast in their minivans. But musically, Buffett has nothing in common with jam bands. He fronts a slick 12-piece group, the Coral Reefers, and they breeze through the same songs, in the same way, note for note, night upon night, year after year. Buffett has a knack for ingratiating singalong melodies and sharply detailed lyrics, and he's ruthlessly single-minded. Few pop stars have carved out so distinct a theme and stuck to it unwaveringly for so long, with such fearless zeal for bad puns: "Last Mango in Paris," "Changes in Latitudes, Changes in Attitudes," "Off to See the Lizard," "Floridays," "The Weather Is Here, Wish You Were Beautiful," "Jamaica Mistaica," "License to Chill."

Buffett is not the first American pop singer to sell tropical fantasies. The tradition stretches from Tin Pan Alley's Hawaiian ballads of the 1910s, to Bing Crosby's and Elvis Presley's revivals of the theme, to '50s and '60s exotica and Don Ho, on down through Buffett to country beach bum Kenny Chesney. But where the other performers have mystified the islands, Buffett is unsentimental and journalistic. In admirable detail, his songs depict tourist traps, where the locals exist only to pour your drinks and cheeseburgers in paradise are on the menu. Buffett is unambivalent about this ugly Americanism—he's all for it. He's tacky, but you have to give him credit for capturing a milieu and a mindset. He'll never get the respect given to his generation's more celebrated troubadours, but he may prove more valuable to future social historians as a chronicler of late–twentieth-century American folkways. Go to Bob Dylan and Paul Simon for poetry and pretty tunes, but if you want to know how baby boomers ate, drank, and screwed on vacation, reach for *Boats, Beaches, Bars, and Ballads*.

By all accounts, Buffett lives the life he sings about. For his fans, most of whom aren't multimillionaires with large pleasure craft, the experience is vicarious: The closest many will come to a Caribbean lagoon is a kiddie pool in the parking lot of a Jimmy Buffett concert. Yet Buffett's songs are not so much about an escape to a place as a flight from time. His theme is the Me Generation midlife crisis. Buffett's tunes are sunny and easygoing, but they have a desperate undercurrent: the hopeless hope that the party need never end, that you can, as one song put it, "grow older but not up," remaining reckless and responsibility-free deep into adulthood.

Two decades ago, in "Pirate Looks at Forty," Buffett cast his plight in mock-historical terms: "Yes I am a pirate, two hundred years too late/ The cannons don't thunder, there's nothing to plunder/ I'm an over-40 victim of fate." More recently, in the Parrothead anthem "Here We Are," Buffett put it in starker terms. "It's the child in us we really value," Buffett sings. That message has proven very good for business, and there's no reason to doubt Buffett's sincerity. Somewhere right now—a warm, palmy place—the pirate is looking at 60 in the same way that he will look at 70, and, if his liver holds up, 80. Through a boozy haze, with the blue ocean gleaming on the horizon just over the rim of a shot glass, it looks an awful lot like 18.

ALAN LIGHT
ADDITIONAL REPORTING BY
PAUL FARBER AND JAIME LOWE

THE WONDER YEARS

THE NOTORIOUS B.I.G.

He was a straight-A student and a drug dealer, a romantic and a player, an "ugly sex symbol," a jokester who was often depressed. He counseled kids to stay in school, then dropped out himself. He listened to country music and tore apart stages with his freestyles.

When Christopher Wallace became the Notorious B.I.G., he channeled all of his contradictions into rhymes of unparalleled depth and emotion. But before his debut CD *Ready to Die* catapulted him to fame in 1994, his experiences on the streets of Brooklyn forged him into a complicated young man.

The only child of a single immigrant mother, Biggie came of age in hip-hop's golden era. But as Biggie grew up, though, there were two things Voletta Wallace didn't know about her son. First, he had fallen for the lure of the streets and was selling crack. And second, he had aspirations for his music beyond just being a hobby.

"People don't know that he spent four or five years working on musical ideas to get to the level that he was on," says his former neighbor and mentor, jazz trumpeter Donald Harrison. *Blender* spoke to dozens of Biggie's friends, lovers and collaborators, who told the story of his early years—and the dreams and disappointments, the joy and pain, that helped create the greatest MC of them all.

Christopher Wallace grew up in the Bedford-Stuyvesant section of Brooklyn, a borderline neighborhood—striving and working-class on one side, urban wasteland on the other. His father, George Latore Wallace, abandoned the family when Chris was 2 years old, leaving him to be raised by his Jamaican-born mom, Voletta. School came easy to him, so from a young age he put his efforts into something that interested and challenged him: hip-hop.

Voletta Wallace (mother): Christopher was a sweet, loving, friendly little boy. He started to write at 2, 2 1/2. I walked into his classroom once and the teacher said, "This little boy is going to be something great." I wasn't the only one who thought that anything he touched would turn to gold.

Sam Hubert (childhood friend): Me and Chris linked up in kindergarten. We both had single, West Indian mothers, so they kind of clicked. Our mothers were very protective. I think that's why the streets were so attractive to us, because we were so sheltered.

Chico Delvec (childhood friend; member of Junior M.A.F.I.A.): Chris's mom was really strict with him. She bought him a bike for Christmas, and she told him not to ride around the corner—that was where I used to live, and it just looked hood-ified. So he rode around the block, and a friend of mine took the bike from him, and the guy let me get a ride. I guess Chris seen me on his bike, so when I came back around his momma came with him and, you know, she screamed on me.

Wallace: I did what any loving mother would do. I wanted my son to be safe, to be a decent human, to be morally sound, and I wanted to shelter him from the filth of the world. I don't call that overprotective. I call it being a mother.

Hubert: Chris was really smart. He was always on the honor roll. Every week or so, they would post everyone's grades to help motivate us, and it got to the point where he didn't even have to look, he knew his name was in the top percentage. It came effortlessly to him, so he wouldn't brag. He'd just knock out his schoolwork and have the rest of the day to be Chris.

Sean "Diddy" Combs (recording artist, producer; CEO, Bad Boy Entertainment): In his rhymes, he always sounded like a straight-A student, like someone who read a lot. Funny thing was that he hadn't actually read that much, but he used words that I had to look up in the dictionary.

Donald Harrison (jazz musician, neighbor): Christopher was always on his front stoop because his mom wouldn't let him leave the block. I was around, so he would strike up conversations with me. He was precocious, very intelligent. He said he wanted to get into music. I initially thought he would be a jazz musician. One of the things I do is to have young people who want to play music learn a song and sing it. I had him learn a Cannonball Adderley song. And he did. He could sing it—on pitch!

Hubert: We were writing stuff together since he was little, 10 years old, already doing routines in the house. If you could hear those tapes, he really had a lot already.

Abraham Widdi (friend; former coworker, Met Foods supermarket): I met Chris when we were working in the store together. He was about 10 or 11, and I was 17. He used to rhyme while he was packing bags, just rhyming to himself. Nobody took him seriously.

Delvec: I used to come to his house and eat dinner and play his games—he had ColecoVision and Atari. He would charge us money to come in his house to play his games, a dollar to play 10 games.

Michael Bynum (childhood friend): Most of the time me and Chris would be indoors, just mixing on the turntables, rapping, trying to make up songs. When we were about 13, we formed the Technique Crew. Big was the leader, and I used to do the music. The Techniques was me, Big Chris, Hubert, a guy named Sal, a guy named Tyrone, and another guy named Jase. We made two songs. One was "We Don't Care," based on this beef between KRS-One and Queensbridge, going back and forth about where hip-hop started. So we made up a song: "We don't care where hip-hop started."

Harrison: I recorded those guys on my little eight-track deck. I have the tapes somewhere. I have some old things Chris wrote; one rhyme started, "Savor the flavor/'Cause I'm your brand-new neighbor." I actually took his tapes up to Def Jam, and they couldn't hear it at the time.

They said he was young to be speaking on those topics—what life was like on the rough edge of our neighborhood.

Hubert: Chris would listen to the white radio stations and know all types of songs. One time he came to my house and he was like, Yo, I'm having trouble sleeping, put on some country music mad low. It was something he probably did at his house. He was . . . eclectic.

As Christopher reached his teens, his interests broadened beyond music and school. He entered his first serious relationship, and—seeing other neighborhood kids starting to reap the riches of crack slinging—took to the streets himself.

Jan Jackson (former girlfriend; mother of Biggie's daughter, T'Yanna Wallace): I met Chris when I was coming home from work. I didn't know him, but we had common friends. I was on a bank of pay phones and he brought his big ass in the booth with me and started making jokes and asking me why I was serious all the time. He was a wonderful artist—he drew me a picture of a ghetto Bart Simpson holding a gun in kind of a street pose, and he put my name underneath it in graffiti.

Robert Izzo (teacher, Westinghouse High School): Chris was naturally outgoing. I ran a Big Brother and Sister program. Biggie was one of our original Big Brothers. He may not have graduated, but a lot of kids stayed in school because of him. He could sit down and talk to kids. He would just tell them to stay in school and struggle through—he gave advice that he hadn't even followed.

Bynum: Westinghouse was a vocational school. We had a Bunsen burner, we would burn pennies and throw 'em at people. We would smoke weed in class. We acted stupid, so they kicked us out.

Delvec: When I was 13, I got into my little hustling thing on the block. I used to tell Chris, "Why don't you come and hang with me?" And he was like, "Naw, naw, you know my moms, she be wilding if she found out I be outside with you on the block." After a while, he was like "Yo, fuck that, I'ma come hang with you on the block and see what's up." And with the pimps hustling, the ho's and all that—he was kind of nervous because he had never been in that environment before. But he started seeing me with different sneakers every day, different coats, bikes, all of that. He was like, "Damn, son, I wanna get weed; I wanna do what you do." So after a while, we hooked him up. And he started getting his own money.

Widdi: He just dealt drugs for entertainment; he never was really a drug dealer.

Hubert: I went to high school in East New York. I'd come back down here and see that raw hustler that he turned into. I was like, Whoa, what the fuck is he doing? I knew Chris, and he could've done anything he wanted, but this is what he chose.

Wallace: I never knew. As far as I knew he was packing at the supermarket. Whatever he was doing, he hid it well. And whenever I asked, he denied it. After he died, I read in a magazine that I once took a dish out of his room and it was full of crack—that it was, excuse my words, what he called "his shit." But I never knew—to this day I don't know what crack looks like.

Despite his extracurricular activities, Christopher hadn't lost sight of the music. A chance connection to Big Daddy Kane's DJ led him to a young hip-hop executive with a funny nickname—it turned out to be the break that would jump-start his career.

Delvec: I hooked Chris up with a friend of mine called D-Roc. That's when he really started getting on the mic and rocking. A guy named 50 Grand was one of the old timers we used to hang out with down there. Big used to come to his house, and Grand always had turntables. Biggie used to get on the mic at parties, baby showers, shit like that.

Easy Mo Bee (producer): He was trying to make the transition from selling drugs to music. He wasn't happy selling drugs. He used to say, "Mo, I gotta get out of this shit."

Mister Cee (producer): At the time, I was DJ-ing for Big Daddy Kane. And DJ 50 Grand said, I got this kid from around the way and he's nice. I was getting ready to go on tour with Kane, so I said I'd listen to him when I got back. And the night I came back, I didn't even unpack—50 Grand brought me the cassette and I played it and it was incredible. So Big and 50 Grand came by the house, and I got the idea to redo the demo. They had only a few tracks and one was [built on the

Emotions song] "Blind Alley." I thought we should re-record it with the beat from Kane's "Ain't No Half Stepping" and send it to *The Source* for their Unsigned Hype contest.

Matty C (former journalist; A&R executive): I received Big's demo from DJ Mister Cee. I was blown away—to me, this was the second coming of Big Daddy Kane. Especially because he was rhyming over the original break from "Ain't No Half Stepping." There were a few other songs on the demo that were freestyles over instrumentals. They were tight, but you didn't need to go past the first one to be like, This dude needs a deal. And that's all I needed to play for Puff.

Combs: I was putting feelers out because I had some budget to sign a couple of acts. I called up *The Source*. L.L. Cool J was big then, that sex-symbol R&B rap—so I was looking for a sex symbol, somebody that would drive the girls crazy. Matty C told me about Biggie, so I said send me a picture. He said, No, no, let me just send you the demo.

Matty C: After hearing the first bars of that first song, Puff wanted to know more about him—what does he look like? That was the comical part of the conversation—me trying to tell him that Big's not exactly an image-driven artist, that he was heavy. And Puff's trying to figure how heavy: "Is he Heavy D heavy? Or is he Fat Boys heavy?"

Mister Cee: Puffy paged me and said he wanted to set up a meeting. I played Puffy some other demos we had and he said to Big, who didn't do much talking, "I want you to rhyme for me, right here." As soon as Biggie kicked a rhyme, Puffy said, "I can have a record out by the summer, how would you like that?"

Combs: When he first walked in, he was so big, so dark—like Liberian, Ethiopian, African dark. I didn't care, though—his energy overrode that. He was so charismatic. This big guy who looked like a security guard, you wanted to know what was behind these lyrics he was writing.

Faith Evans (recording artist; former wife): Puff said to me, "I'm gonna make him the first ugly sex symbol."

Hubert: Everything was going wrong for Chris until that Bad Boy business card popped up. He carried that card around—not like it was an idol or anything, but it was just that something could come out of this and change everything.

Jackson: Right around when I was pregnant, he met Puffy. He thought he was a dedicated businessman, that he had his head on straight.

Wallace: I resented Puffy because I'm very education-minded and I wanted Puffy to encourage my son to go to school, not to make this noise and dream of being a millionaire.

As Biggie found out, it's a long road from getting a deal to getting an album out. His frustration with the delays, though, was tempered by the addition of a new family member.

Ed Lover (radio personality): I left the soundtrack to my movie *Who's the Man?* in the hands of Andre Harrell and Uptown Records, and Puff, who was doing A&R for Uptown, made sure he got his own artists on the soundtrack. Biggie's "Party and Bullshit" really represented Brooklyn—nobody had that street cred that Biggie had.

Easy Mo Bee: We got to the part in "Party and Bullshit" where Biggie says, ". . . and a fucking fight broke out," and he said, "Yo, Mo, this is what I want. We're all gonna pile into the booth, and we're gonna take some chairs, some tables, and just kinda throw shit around, make it sound like a fight in a club." If you listen really hard in the background you can hear me say, "Yo, what happened to the music?!'"

Dream Hampton (journalist, filmmaker): There were a lot of stops and starts to Biggie's career. There was a complete album he gave to Andre, and Andre waffled on the project. Uptown was an R&B label, and this wasn't like anything Andre had put out before. He wanted Puff to recut the original version. Shortly thereafter, Andre fired Puff anyway. Puff said, I'm taking Big with me, and Andre said, Whatever. Biggie was discouraged, though. He was broke, and he really believed his record was never going to come out. And he had a baby on the way.

Jackson: When we had the baby, he said, I'm not doing the diaper thing. He maybe changed T'Yanna's diapers three times. The first time he was alone with her, she started crying. He called his mother, and she came home from work. When I got home, T'Yanna was sitting there with a bag of Cheese Doodles. He said that's the only way she wouldn't cry.

Wallace: Chris became a different person when T'Yanna was born. He said he had a princess now. He loved being a father. I never saw him so happy.

Hampton: People told him he was ugly his entire life, and he knew it was true, so when he showed me his baby, he said, "She cute, right?" He used to sleep with the bassinet right next to his bed—not in the bed, 'cause he thought he was gonna roll over.

Jackson: We broke up when T'Yanna was 6 months old. He came to me one day and said, "This relationship is not where I want to be right now." I was hurt, but I respected that he didn't lead me on.

Evans: The first time we met was at a photo shoot of the new Bad Boy artists—myself, Big, and Craig Mack were the only ones who showed up. At lunch break, we started conversating. He asked me to take him and his boys home, and I said OK, because I had room in my truck. About two weeks later, Puff had a Father's Day party at this club on the Upper East Side. Big and I talked, and he performed that night—and then he went home with me. And from then on we were a couple. It was two months from the time we met until we got married.

Wallace: As a mother, I had questions about that. Who meets someone—and a few weeks later they get married? That must be the love of the century! But I never said I told you so, never said he wasn't ready. And I liked Faith, and later, I adored my grandson.

Now that Biggie had a daughter to support, Puffy needed to keep him busy with one-offs and guest spots, so he didn't lose him to the hustle. But from those one-verse gems and a growing reputation as a live performer, the Notorious B.I.G. soon found himself with one of the most-anticipated debut albums ever.

Eddie F (recording artist, producer): My production company had done about half of Mary J. Blige's *What's the 411?* album. Around that time, Puff was staying with me, and Big started coming around the office. Puff was doing remixes on the songs, and if he had a hot rapper or someone who he thought was promising, he'd put them on the remix.

Mary J. Blige (recording artist): Big performed on the "Real Love" remix, but I hadn't met him or even seen him yet. I became a fan the

first time I heard his voice. The things he said, just in his pocket—
"Look up in the sky, it's a bird, it's a plane!/Nope, it's Mary J/Ain't a
damn thing changed." . . . I lost my mind like the rest of the world.
When we did the "What's the 411" remix, he was just leaning on the
wall, listening to the music, writing the rhyme in his head, I guess, since
I never saw him write anything down. He went into the booth and
killed it. It was like watching something supernatural.

Da Brat (recording artist): Jermaine Dupri told me Big wanted do a
song ["Da B Side"] with me. JD did the beat, and we went to his little
basement studio. Big didn't use pen and paper. He said he was almost
done, and I had my paper, like, halfway done with my lyrics. I'm like,
OK, how is this dude almost done? And he just went in the booth and
did it. No paper, no anything. Mind you, this dude smoked like Bob
Marley. I was just impressed that his memory was so great.

Nas (recording artist): I saw him perform before I knew him. He
came into this club, and guys were like, Who does this guy think he is?
They kinda chuckled. 'Cause any new guy had to be brave to step onstage with established artists. And all of a sudden, he takes the stage
and he rocks some fucking freestyle and just grabbed people's attention,
and then left without a smile and walked out of the club.

Combs: Biggie was such an incredible performer, which is especially
hard if you don't dance. It was like his eyes rolled to the back of his
head—not a lot of movement but captivating and intense, like watching
Miles Davis or Billie Holiday. If he moved a little bit, just moved his
head, people would go crazy.

Hubert: I saw Big write "Juicy" [from *Ready to Die*] up in his mom's
crib. There was, like, 50 people in that little room. He'd be on the bed,
weed smoke all around. And just thinking, thinking, thinking.

Mister Cee: People heard a lot of *Ready to Die* before the CD officially came out. There was a huge frenzy around it. DJ Clue put five or
six songs from it on a mix tape, and Biggie and Puffy were ready to beat
his ass. Everybody was buying that tape. It was a gift and a curse—
nothing like that had ever happened to a debut artist.

Craig Mack (former Bad Boy recording artist): When Arista
Records sent us on the Bad Boy promotional tour, Big and them didn't

have any luggage. We were leaving for, like, seven days, and Big showed up at the airport with a hundred little Pathmark plastic bags tied up as their luggage.

Matty C: The richness of *Ready to Die* came from Big's willingness to trust himself musically and creatively. Puff did a lot, but a lot was Big's visions—tracks he picked and said, I'ma rhyme to this. It just showed his confidence, his intelligence to really see his vision through.

Nas: When *Ready to Die* came out, you could feel it—a big change was about to happen.

ALEX ROSS

APPARITION IN THE WOODS
RESCUING SIBELIUS FROM SILENCE

Composing music may be the loneliest of artistic pursuits. It is a laborious traversal of an imaginary landscape. Emerging from the process is an art work in code, which other musicians must be persuaded to unravel. Nameless terrors creep into the limbo between composition and performance, during which a score sits mutely on the desk. Hans Pfitzner dramatized that moment of panic and doubt in "Palestrina," his 1917 "musical legend" about the life of the Italian Renaissance master. The character of Palestrina speaks for colleagues across the centuries when he stops his work to cry, "What is the point of all this? *Ach*, what is it for?"

The Finnish composer Jean Sibelius may have asked that question once too often. The crisis point of his career arrived in the late nineteen-twenties and the early thirties, when he was being lionized as a new Beethoven in England and America, and dismissed as a purveyor of kitsch in the tastemaking European music centers, where atonality and other modern languages dominated the scene. The contrasts in the reception of his music, with its extremes of splendor and strangeness, matched the manic-depressive extremes of his personality—an alcoholic oscillation between grandiosity and self-loathing. Sometimes he believed that he was in direct communication with the Almighty ("For an instant God opens his door and *His* orchestra plays the Fifth Symphony," he wrote in a letter) and sometimes he felt worthless. In 1927, when he was sixty-one, he wrote in his diary, "Isolation and loneliness are driving me to despair. . . . In order to survive, I have to have alcohol. . . . Am abused, alone, and all my real friends are dead. My prestige here at present is rock-bottom. Impossible to work. If only there were a way out."

Sibelius, who was born in 1865 and died fifty years ago this September, spent the better part of his life at Ainola, a rustic house outside Helsinki. On his desk for many years lay the Eighth Symphony, which promised to be his summary masterpiece. He had been working on it since 1924 and had indicated several times that it was almost ready for performance. In 1933, a copyist transcribed twenty-three pages of the score, and at a later date Sibelius's publisher may have bound the manuscript in a set of seven volumes. There were reportedly parts for chorus, as in Beethoven's Ninth. But the Eighth never appeared. The composer finally gave in to the seduction of despair. "I suppose one henceforth takes me as—yes!—a *fait accompli*," he wrote in 1943. "Life is soon over. Others will come and surpass me in the eyes of the world. We are fated to die forgotten. I must start economizing. It can't go on like this."

Aino Sibelius, the composer's wife, for whom the house was named, recalled what happened next. "In the nineteen-forties there was a great *auto da fé* at Ainola," she said. "My husband collected a number of manuscripts in a laundry basket and burned them on the open fire in the dining room. Parts of the 'Karelia Suite' were destroyed—I later saw remains of the pages which had been torn out—and many other things. I did not have the strength to be present and left the room. I therefore do not know what he threw onto the fire. But after this my husband became calmer and gradually lighter in mood."

Ainola stands much as the composer left it. The atmosphere of the house is heavy and musty, as if Sibelius's spirit were still pent up inside. But you get a different feeling when you walk into the forest that abuts one side of the house. The treetops meet in an endless curving canopy. The ground is uncluttered: many paths fork among the trunks. Venturing a little farther into the wood, you lose sight of all human habitation.

A profound stillness descends. The light begins to fail, the mists roll in. After a while, you may begin to wonder if you will ever find your way back. Many times in Sibelius's music, the exaltation of natural sublimity gives way to inchoate fear, which has less to do with the outer landscape than with the inner one: the forest of the mind.

Milan Kundera, in his 1993 essay collection "Testaments Betrayed," anatomizes the more peripheral European cultures, using his native Czechoslovakia as a specimen. "The small nations form 'another Europe,' " he writes. "An observer can be fascinated by the often astonishing intensity of their cultural life. This is the advantage of smallness: the wealth in cultural events is on a 'human scale.' " Kundera warns, however, that the familial feeling can turn tense and constricting: "Within that warm intimacy, each envies each, everyone watches everyone." If an artist ignores the rules, the rejection can be cruel. Even those who rise to fame may experience isolation at the summit—the burden of being a national hero.

In the nineteenth and twentieth centuries, each of the "small nations" had a celebrity composer. Edvard Grieg in Norway, Antonín Dvořák in Czechoslovakia, and Carl Nielsen in Denmark, among others, served as ambassadors for their local cultures. In Russia and Britain, too, composers took on outsized roles, embodying ideas of national greatness, whether or not they desired the assignment. A little later in the twentieth century, certain composers who had come of age around 1900 became symbols, in a wider sense, of a rapidly fading pre–First World War world. They tended to be conservative in style, and they were haunted by feelings of obsolescence, to the point where they found it difficult to keep writing. The iconic British composer Edward Elgar, who died in 1934, failed to finish another large-scale work after his supremely elegiac Cello Concerto of 1918–19. Sergei Rachmaninoff produced only five major works from 1917 until his death, in 1943.

"I feel like a ghost wandering in a world grown alien," Rachmaninoff wrote in 1939. "I cannot cast out the old way of writing, and I cannot acquire the new. I have made intense effort to feel the musical manner of today, but it will not come to me. . . . I cannot cast out my musical gods in a moment and bend the knee to new ones." Sibelius felt the same pang of loss. "Not everyone can be an innovating genius," he wrote in his diary. "As a personality and as an apparition from the woods you will have your small, modest place."

And yet the so-called "regional" composers left an imposing body of work, which is integral to the century as a whole. Their music may lack the vanguard credentials of Schoenberg's or Stravinsky's, at least on the sonic surface, but Nielsen, in his 1925 book "Living Music," makes a good counter-argument: "The simplest is the hardest, the universal the most lasting, the straightest the strongest, like the pillars that support the dome." And, precisely because these composers communicated general feelings of mourning for a pre-technological past, or, more simply, a yearning for vanished youth, they remained acutely relevant for a broad public.

Mainstream audiences often lag behind the intellectual classes in appreciating the more adventurous composers, but sometimes they are quicker to perceive the value of music that the politicians of style fail to comprehend. In 1952, Nicolas Slonimsky put together a delightful book, *Lexicon of Musical Invective*, an anthology of wrongheaded music criticism in which now canonical masterpieces are compared with feline caterwauling, barnyard noises, and so on. Slonimsky should also have written a "Lexicon of Musical Condescension," gathering high-minded essays in which now canonical masterpieces were dismissed as middlebrow, with a long section reserved for Sibelius.

Sibelius was not merely the most famous composer Finland ever produced but the country's chief celebrity in any field. He played a symbolic but active role in the drive toward Finnish independence, which was finally achieved in 1917. When Finns are asked to characterize their culture, they invariably mention, along with such national treasures as the lakeside sauna, Fiskars scissors, and Nokia cell phones, "our Sibelius." Mostly because of him, classical music has retained a central role in Finnish culture. The country's government invests enormous sums in orchestras, opera houses, new-music programs, and music schools. The annual Finnish expenditure on the arts is roughly two hundred times per capita what the United States government spends through the National Endowment for the Arts.

Finns are strangers to the European family. Descendants of an errant Mongolian tribe, they speak a language unrelated to the Indo-European linguistic group. For centuries, they were governed by the Swedes; then, in 1809, they became a semi-autonomous grand duchy of tsarist Russia. In the late nineteenth century, the Swedish influence remained strong, with a minority of Swedish-speakers forming the élite. Sibelius belonged to this group; he learned Finnish as a second language. Yet, like many of his generation, he avidly joined in the independence campaign, which became more urgent after Tsar Nicholas II introduced measures designed to suppress Finland's autonomy.

The national legends of Finland are contained in the "Kalevala," a poetic epic compiled in 1835 by a country doctor named Elias Lönnrot. Cantos 31 through 36 tell of the bloodthirsty young fighter Kullervo, who has his way with a young woman who turns out to be his sister. She commits suicide; he goes off to war. One day, finding himself again in the forest where the rape occurred, he asks his sword what kind of blood it wishes to taste. The sword demands the blood of a guilty man, whereupon Kullervo rams his body on the blade. In 1891 and 1892, Sibelius, who had just completed two final years of study in Berlin and Vienna, used this dismal tale as the basis for his first major work, "Kullervo," an eighty-minute symphonic drama for men's chorus, soloists, and orchestra.

The Finnish epic has a metre all its own: each line contains four main trochaic beats, but vowels are often stretched for dramatic effect. Instead of smoothing out the poetry into a foursquare rhythm, Sibelius bent his musical language in sympathetic response: in the third movement, for example, the orchestra maintains a pattern of five beats in a bar, while the chorus elongates its lines to phrases of fifteen, ten, eight, and twelve beats, respectively.

In 1892, "Kullervo" had a decisively successful première in Helsinki. For the remainder of the decade, Sibelius worked mainly in the tone-poem genre, consolidating his fame with such works as "En Saga," "The Swan of Tuonela," the "Karelia Suite," and the tuneful "Finlandia." Sibelius's mastery of the orchestra, already obvious in "Kullervo," became prodigious. "The Swan of Tuonela," which was conceived as the overture to an unfinished "Kalevala" opera, begins with the mirage-like sound of A-minor string chords blended one into the next over a span of four octaves.

Sibelius finished his first two symphonies in 1899 and 1902. On the surface, these were typical orchestral dramas of the heroic soul, although Sibelius's habit of breaking down themes into murmuring textures sounded strange to many early listeners. Finns quickly appropriated the Second as an emblem of national liberation; the conductor Robert Kajanus heard in it "the most broken-hearted protest against all the injustice that threatens at the present time," together with "confident prospects for the future." In other words, the symphony was understood as a gesture of defiance in the face of the Tsar. Although Sibelius rejected this interpretation, images of the Finnish struggle may have played a role in his thinking. In the finale of the Second, a crawling, rising-and-falling figure in the violas and cellos evokes a recurring pattern in the second scene of Mussorgsky's "Boris Godunov"—the scene in which Pimen the monk records the villainies of Tsar Boris.

Sibelius's other "hit" scores of the period, the brilliantly moody Violin Concerto and the affectingly maudlin "Valse Triste," cemented his international reputation and therefore increased his stature at home. Around this time, though, alcohol became an issue. Sibelius, who often conducted his own works, would fortify himself with liquor before engagements, then disappear for days. A widely discussed painting by the Finnish artist Akseli Gallen-Kallela, "The Problem," depicted Sibelius drinking with friends, his eyes rolled back in his head. Although he was supported by a state pension, he ran up large debts. He was also beset by illnesses, some real and some imagined. Fissures were appearing in the façade that "Finland's hero" presented to the world.

In 1904, Sibelius tried to escape the embarrassments of his Helsinki life style by moving with his wife and three daughters to Ainola. There he set to work on his Third Symphony, which was itself a kind of musical escape. In contrast to the muscular rhetoric of "Kullervo" and the first two symphonies, the Third speaks in a self-consciously clear, pure language. At the same time, it is a sustained deconstruction of symphonic form. The last movement begins as a quicksilver Scherzo, but it gradually, almost imperceptibly, evolves into a marchlike Finale: the listener may have the feeling of the ground shifting underfoot.

Shortly after finishing this terse, elusive work, Sibelius got into a debate with Gustav Mahler on the nature of symphonic form. Mahler went to Helsinki in 1907 to conduct some concerts, and Sibelius presented his latest ideas about "severity of form" and the "profound logic" that should connect symphonic themes. "No!" Mahler replied. "The symphony must be like the world. It must be all-embracing."

Sibelius kept a close eye on the latest developments in European music. On visits to Germany, he became acquainted with Strauss's "Salome" and "Elektra" and Schoenberg's earliest atonal scores. He was variously fascinated, alarmed, and bored by these Austro-German experiments; more to his taste was the sensuous radicalism of Debussy, whose "Prelude to 'The Afternoon of a Faun,'" "Nocturnes," and "La Mer" revealed new possibilities in modal harmony and diaphanous orchestral color.

Sibelius, in his Fourth Symphony, completed in 1911, presented his listeners with music as tensely forbidding as anything from the European continent at the time. (Perhaps the most searching rendition of this symphony on disk is Osmo Vänskä's, with the Lahti Symphony, on the Bis label. Herbert von Karajan's recordings of the last four symphonies, on D.G., remain satisfying, and Leif Segerstam recently conducted a superb complete cycle for Ondine.) Sibelius wrote the Fourth in the wake of several risky operations on his throat, where a tumor was growing. His doctors instructed him to give up drinking, which he agreed to do, although he resumed in 1915. The temporary loss of alcohol—"my most faithful companion," he later called it—may have contributed to the claustrophobic grimness of the music, which, at the same time, bespoke a liberated intellect. The first few bars of the symphony extrapolate a new dimension in musical time. The opening notes, scored darkly for cellos, basses, and bassoons, are C, D, F-sharp, E—an ambiguous whole-tone collection. It feels like the beginning of a major thematic statement, but it gets stuck on F-sharp and E, which oscillate and fade away. Meanwhile, the durations of the notes lengthen by degrees, from quarter notes to dotted quarters and then to half notes.

It's as if a foreign body were exerting gravitational force on the music, slowing it down.

The narrative of the Fourth is circular rather than linear; it keeps revisiting the same insoluble conflicts. An effort at establishing F major as the key of the initially sunnier-sounding second movement founders on an immovable obstacle in the form of the note B-natural, after which there is a palpable shrug of defeat. The third movement dramatizes an attempt to build, note by note, a solemn six-bar theme of funerary character; the first attempt falters after three bars, the second after five, the third after four, the fourth after three. The fifth attempt proceeds with vigor but seems to go on too long, sprawling through seven bars without coming to a logical conclusion. Finally, with an audible grinding of the teeth, the full orchestra plays the theme in a richly harmonized guise. Then uncertainty steals back in.

The finale thins out as it goes along, as if random pages of the orchestral parts had blown off the music stands. This is music facing extinction, a premonition of the silence that would envelop the composer two decades later. Erik Tawaststjerna, Sibelius's biographer, reveals that the middle section of the movement is based on sketches that Sibelius made for a vocal setting of Poe's "The Raven," in a German translation. It is easy to see why a man of Sibelius's psychological makeup would have been drawn to its melancholia. The German translation follows the rhythm of the original, so Sibelius's music can be matched up with lines in Poe's poem. Softly crying flute and oboe lines in the epilogue fit the famous words "Quoth the Raven 'Nevermore.' " The symphony closes with blank-faced chords that are given the dynamic marking mezzoforte—half-loud. The instruction is surprising. Most of the great Romantic symphonies end with fortissimo affirmations. Wagner operas and Strauss tone poems often close pianissimo, whether in blissful or tragic mood. Sibelius's Fourth ends not with a bang or a whimper but with a leaden thud.

"A symphony is not just a composition in the ordinary sense of the word," Sibelius wrote in 1910. "It is more a confession of faith at different stages of one's life." If the Fourth is a confession, its composer might have been on the verge of suicide. Yet, like so many Romantics before him, Sibelius took a perverse pleasure in surrendering to melancholy, and finding joy in darkness. "Joyful and sorrowful," he wrote in his diary. In his next symphony, he set himself the goal of bringing to the surface the joy inherent in creation.

Joy is not the same thing as simplicity. The Fifth begins and ends in crystalline major-key tonality, but it is a staggeringly unconventional work. The schemata of sonata form dissolve before the listener's ears; in place of a methodical development of well-defined themes, there is a gradual, incremental evolution of material through trancelike repetitions. The musicologist James Hepokoski, in a monograph on the symphony, calls it "rotational form"; the principal ideas of the work come around again and again, though each time they are transformed in ways both small and large. The themes really assume their true shape only at the end of the rotation—what Hepokoski calls the "telos," the epiphanic goal. Music becomes a search for meaning within an open-ended structure—an analogue to the spiritual life.

At the beginning of the Fifth, the horns present a softly glowing theme, the first notes of which spell out a symmetrical set of intervals: fourth, major second, fourth again. Fifty years later, John Coltrane used the same configuration in his jazz masterpiece "A Love Supreme." Sibelius's key is E-flat major, but the melody turns out to be a flighty thing, never quite touching the ground. A rhythmic trick adds to the sense of weightlessness. At first, it sounds like a standard 4/4 metre, but, after a syncopated sidestep, it turns out to be 12/8. A rotation process begins: the melodic material is broken into fragments and repeatedly reshaped. In the fourth iteration, an electrifying change occurs: the tempo accelerates by increments, until the music is suddenly hurtling forward. Sibelius achieved this effect by way of an exceptional feat of self-editing. After the première of the first version of the symphony, in 1915, he decided to rework it completely, and one thing he did was cut off the ending of the first movement, cut off the beginning of the second, and splice them together. The accelerating passage becomes a cinematic "dissolve" from one movement to another.

The second movement of the Fifth provides a spell of calm, although beneath the surface a significant new idea is coming to life—a swaying

motif of rising-and-falling intervals, which the horns pick up in the finale and transform into the grandest of all Sibelian themes. The composer called it his "swan hymn"; he recorded it in his diary next to a
description of sixteen swans flying in formation over Ainola. "One of
my greatest experiences!" he wrote. "Lord God, that beauty! They circled over me for a long time. Disappeared into the solar haze like a
gleaming, silver ribbon. . . . That this should have happened to me, who
have so long been the outsider." The swans reappeared three days later:
"The swans are always in my thoughts and give splendor to [my] life.
[It's] strange to learn that nothing in the whole world affects me—
nothing in art, literature, or music—in the same way as do these swans
and cranes and wild geese. Their voices and being."

The swan hymn transcends the depiction of nature: it is like a spiritual force in animal form. When the horns introduce the theme, during
a flurry of action in the strings, it's as if they had always been playing it,
and the listener had only begun to hear it. A moment later, a reduced
version of the theme is heard in the bass register of the orchestra at one-
third the tempo, creating another hypnotic Sibelian effect of layered
time. Then the winds launch into their own melody: a wistfully circling
figure that bears an odd resemblance to Erik Satie's "Gymnopédies."

This is not "masculine" heroism on the order of Beethoven's
"Eroica," which is also in the key of E-flat major. As Hepokoski suggests, Sibelius's later music implies a maternal rather than paternal
logic—God-given themes gestating in symphonic form. Only by way of
wrenching dissonances does the music break loose from its endlessly
rocking motion and push toward a final cadence. The swan hymn, now
carried by the trumpets, undergoes convulsive transformations, and is
reborn as a fearsome new being. Its intervals split wide open, shatter,
and re-form. The symphony ends with six far-flung chords, through
which the main theme shoots like a pulse of energy. The swan becomes
the sun.

Sibelius was at the height of his powers, yet he had precious little music left in him: the Sixth and Seventh Symphonies, the tone poem
"Tapiola," incidental music for a production of Shakespeare's *The*

Tempest, a smattering of minor pieces, and the phantom Eighth. His pursuit of a final symphonic synthesis made the process of composition almost impossibly arduous. Suddenly dissatisfied with the fluid form that had evolved in the Fifth, he began to dream of a continuous blur of sound without any formal divisions—symphonies without movements, operas without words. Instead of writing the music of his imagination, he wanted to transcribe the very noise of nature. He thought that he could hear chords in the murmurs of the forests and the lapping of the lakes; he once baffled a group of Finnish students by giving a lecture on the overtone series of a meadow. Whatever he succeeded in putting on paper seemed paltry and inadequate. As the revisions of the Fifth show, he looked at his own creations with a merciless eye, slashing away at them as if they were the scribblings of an inept student.

Harbingers of silence proliferate in Sibelius's last works. As Hepokoski writes, his sonic narratives end not in a blaze of victory, as in the Fifth, but in "dissolution," "decay," "liquidation." The Sixth Symphony echoes the sober spirit of the Third, with antique modes underpinning the harmony; it's as if the composer were trying to flee into a mythic past. Yet brutal choirs of brass keep slicing into the gossamer string textures and through the neat ranks of dancing winds. The Seventh Symphony is anchored on a grand theme for solo trombone, which sounds three times against a mercurially changing background. In its final appearance, it generates such a heat of elation that it teeters on the edge of chaos. The "dissolution" takes the form of a metallic smear of dominant-seventh chords in chromatic sequence followed by a high, exposed line in the violins. And "Tapiola," a twenty-minute tone poem conjuring the Finnish forest, turned out to be Sibelius's most severe and concentrated musical statement. In a central section depicting a physical or mental storm, whole-tone harmony crumbles into near-total chromaticism—upward- and downward-slithering patterns of notes. Like a wanderer lost in the woods, the listener struggles to find a path through the thicket of sound. When the home chord of B minor is finally reasserted in the brass, it has a hollow ring, its middle note pushed deep into the bass. We are apparently back where we started, with no exit in sight.

Finally came the music for "The Tempest," commissioned by the Danish Royal Theatre, in 1925. Perhaps Sibelius felt some conscious or unconscious identification with the figure of Prospero, who, at the end of the play, decides to set aside his magic powers and resume a semblance of normal life:

> *But this rough magic*
> *I here abjure. And when I have required*
> *Some heavenly music—which even now*
> *I do—*
> *To work mine end upon their senses that*
> *This airy charm is for, I'll break my staff,*
> *Bury it certain fathoms in the earth,*
> *And deeper than did ever plummet sound*
> *I'll drown my book.*

Sibelius wrote no music for this tremendous speech, but its rhetoric infuses the cue for "solemn music" that follows, with dissonances sounding at earsplitting volume. Then the chaos melts away into a clean open fifth, which sounds alien in context. All this evokes Prospero dimming the sun, setting sea and sky at war, waking the dead. A quiet hymn for strings follows, in which the chromaticism of the tempest is woven back into classical harmony. It is "heavenly music," but also sweet, ordinary music, dispelling the rage and pain that fuel Prospero's art.

Did Sibelius, like Prospero, think about abjuring his magic and drowning his book? If so, he gave no sign of it in the late nineteen-twenties and the early thirties. The Eighth Symphony was under way, and the composer seemed happy with it. He is known to have worked on the piece in the spring of 1931, while staying alone in Berlin. Writing home to Aino, he said that the symphony was "making great strides," although he was puzzled by the form it was taking. "It's strange, this work's conception," he told his wife. That is all we know about it.

Fame can confuse any artist, and it had an especially disorienting effect on Sibelius. Why his symphonies struck such a chord with Jazz Age audiences is difficult to explain. Perhaps they achieved mass popularity precisely because they were foreign to the neon light and traffic noise of contemporary urban life. In any case, no composer of the time caused such mass excitement, especially in America. Celebrity conductors vied for signs of favor from Ainola. New York Philharmonic listeners voted Sibelius their favorite living symphonist. His name even cropped up as a plot point in Hollywood movies. In Otto Preminger's chic 1944 thriller "Laura," a detective, played by Dana Andrews, interrogates a shady Southern gentleman, portrayed by Vincent Price:

> **Dana Andrews:** You know a lot about music?
> **Vincent Price:** I don't know a lot about anything, but I know a little about practically everything.
> **Dana Andrews:** Yeah? Then why did you say they played Brahms's First and Beethoven's Ninth at the concert Friday night? They changed the program at the last minute and played nothing but Sibelius.

"Nothing but Sibelius" comes close to summing up American orchestral programming of the period. Serge Koussevitzky, the conductor of the Boston Symphony, presented a cycle of Sibelius symphonies in the 1932–33 season, and hoped to cap the series with the world première of the Eighth.

Olin Downes, who from 1924 to 1955 served as music critic of the *Times*, was crucial to Sibelius's American reputation. The son of Louise Corson Downes, a crusading feminist and Prohibitionist, Downes believed that classical music should appeal not just to élites but to common people, and in the *Times* he condemned the obscurantism of modern music—in particular, the artificiality, capriciousness, and snobbery that he perceived in the music of Stravinsky. Sibelius was different; he was "the last of the heroes," "a new prophet."

Downes travelled to Finland in 1927 to meet Sibelius. The composer had fallen into one of his periodic bouts of depression. Meeting Downes temporarily lifted his spirits, although, in the long term, Downes's devotion may have had a deleterious effect. Glenda Dawn Goss, in a book-length study of this singular composer-critic relationship, suggests that Sibelius was in some way crushed by the attention that Downes heaped on him.

In the early thirties, just as Koussevitzky was expecting to conduct the première of the Eighth Symphony in Boston, Downes pestered Sibelius for the completed score. In 1937, Downes wrote a follow-up letter in which he passed along the sentiments of none other than Louise Corson Downes: "My mother and I often speak of you and she asked me again about the Eighth Symphony. . . . 'Tell Mr. Sibelius that I am not concerned or anxious so much about his Eighth Symphony, which I know he will complete in his own good time, as about his *Ninth.* He must crown his series of works in this form with a ninth symphony which will represent the summit and the synthesis of his whole achievement and leave us a work which will be worthy of one of the elected few who are the true artistic descendants and inheritors of Beethoven.' "

As if pressure from music critics' mothers were not enough, Sibelius was also brooding over his music's reception in Europe. Paris had no time for him. Berlin, before Hitler came to power, viewed him with condescension bordering on contempt. In those cities, expansive symphonies and evocative tone poems had little intellectual market value. The critic Heinrich Strobel referred to Sibelius's Violin Concerto as "boring Nordic dreariness."

In America, Downes's pugilistic praise of Sibelius aroused resentment among Stravinsky's many followers and admirers. In 1940, Virgil Thomson became the music critic of the New York *Herald Tribune,* and in his début review he tore lustily into Sibelius, calling the Second Symphony "vulgar, self-indulgent, and provincial beyond all description." Equally venomous attacks emanated from the Schoenberg camp. The émigré theorist Theodor W. Adorno prepared a dire analysis of the Sibelius phenomenon for a sociological think tank called the Princeton Radio Research Project: "The work of Sibelius is not only incredibly overrated, but it fundamentally lacks any good qualities. . . . If Sibelius's music is good music, then all the categories by which musical standards can be measured—standards which reach from a master like Bach to most advanced composers like Schoenberg—must be completely abolished." Adorno sent his essay to Thomson, who, while agreeing with its sentiments, sagely advised that "the tone is more apt to create antago-nism toward yourself than toward Sibelius."

Sibelius's confidence was by that time already gone. You can see it slipping away in his correspondence with Koussevitzky, which is pre-served at the Library of Congress. The conductor sends letters and telegrams almost every month, pleading for the Eighth. Sibelius replies in an elegant, slanting hand on parchment-like paper, tantalizingly mentioning a symphony that is almost, but not quite, finished.

In January, 1930, Sibelius reports, "My new work is not nearly ready and I cannot say when it will be ready." In August, 1930, he is more sure: "It looks as though I can send you a new work this season." But he is worried about American copyrights, which do not protect his music. Koussevitzky reassures him that the symphony will be safe from piracy. In the end, it does not appear. Then, in August, 1931, in the wake of his productive stay in Berlin, Sibelius writes, "If you wish to perform my new Symphonia in the spring, it will, I believe, be ready." In December, the information is leaked to the Boston *Evening Tran-script:* "Symphony Hall has received an important letter from Sibelius, the composer, about his new Symphony, the Eighth. It is completed, and the score will soon be on the way to Boston." Another apologetic telegram from Finland arrives two weeks later. Sibelius probably heard of the *Transcript* article and panicked.

The following June, the Eighth is back on its feet: "It would be good if you could conduct my new symphony at the end of October." Then comes a fresh panic. "Unfortunately I have named October for my new symphony," he writes just a week later. "This is not certain, I am very disturbed about it. Please do not announce the performance." Eventu-ally, it is promised for December, 1932. Koussevitzky sends a "restless" telegram on New Year's Eve, as if he had been checking the mailbox every day. Two weeks later, he receives yet another terse telegram, yet another postponement. There are a few more tentative mentions of the Eighth in subsequent correspondence, then nothing.

In the late thirties, Sibelius again hoped to set the Eighth free from its forest prison. By that time, he knew better than to say anything to the garrulous Koussevitzky. Then, in 1939, Hitler invaded Poland, and Finland became part of a chess game between Nazi Germany and the

Soviet Union. Early in the war, Finland was applauded in the West for its hardy stand against the Soviets, and Sibelius was more popular than ever. In 1941, though, Finland aligned itself with the Germans, partly because Fascist elements had infiltrated the government and the Army, and partly because the Nazis would have taken over the country anyway. Sibelius went from being a symbol of freedom to serving as an apparent Nazi stooge. As a Nordic, "Aryan" composer, he had enjoyed glowing notices in Nazi Germany. Now he became almost an official German artist, receiving as many performances as Richard Strauss. He allegedly said, in a message to Nazi troops, "I wish with all my heart that you may enjoy a speedy victory."

Sibelius was privately tormented by the promulgation of Nazi-style race laws in Finland. In 1943, he wrote in his diary, "How can you, Jean Sibelius, possibly take these 'Aryan paragraphs' seriously? . . . You are a cultural aristocrat and *can* make a stand against stupid prejudice." But he made no stand. As the culture god of the Finnish state, he had long since ceased to see a difference between music and history, and now with the world in flames his music seemed destined for ruin. At the same time, obscure private agonies consumed him. The diary again: "*The tragedy begins. My burdensome thoughts paralyze me. The cause? Alone, alone. I never allow the great distress to pass my lips. Aino must be spared.*" The final page of the diary, in 1944, contains a shopping list for champagne, cognac, and gin.

Sibelius lived to the age of ninety-one, making wry jokes about his inability to die. "All the doctors who wanted to forbid me to smoke and to drink are dead," he once said. In a more serious mood, he observed, "It is very painful to be eighty. The public love artists who fall by the wayside in this life. A true artist must be down and out or die of hunger. In youth he should at least die of consumption." One September morning in 1957, he went for his usual walk in the fields and forest around Ainola, scanning the skies for cranes flying south for the winter. They were part of his ritual of autumn; when he was writing the Fifth Symphony, he had noted in his diary, "Every day I have seen the cranes. Flying south in full cry with their music. Have been yet again their most assiduous pupil. Their cries echo throughout my being." When, on the third-to-last day of his life, the cranes duly appeared, he told his wife, "Here they come, the birds of my youth!" One of them broke from the flock, circled the house, cried out, and flew away.

There is a curiously moving photograph of Igor Stravinsky kneeling at Sibelius's grave, a horizontal metal slab on the grounds at Ainola. The visit took place four years after Sibelius's death. The master of modern music had practical reasons for making the pilgrimage: the Finnish government had promised him the Wihuri Sibelius Prize, worth twenty-five thousand dollars. But the gesture had a certain gallantry. In the past, Stravinsky had belittled Sibelius: on the occasion of the old man's death, he had slammed down the phone when a reporter called for a comment. In his last years, though, Stravinsky warmed to a few Sibelius scores, and made an arrangement for octet of the Canzonetta for strings.

The notion that there might be something "modern" about Sibelius was risible to self-styled progressives of the immediate postwar era. The Schoenbergian pedagogue René Leibowitz summed up the feelings of many new-music connoisseurs when, in 1955, he published a pamphlet titled "Sibelius: The Worst Composer in the World." Surveys of twentieth-century music labelled the composer a marginal figure in the central drama of the march toward atonality and other intellectual landmarks. Yet performances of Sibelius's music continued unabated; conductors and audiences had it right all along.

In the last decades of the century, the politics of style changed in Sibelius's favor. He began to be understood in terms of what Milan Kundera called, in another meditation on the culture of small nations, "antimodern modernism"—a personal style that stands outside the status quo of perpetual progress. Suddenly, composers and scholars were paying heed to Sibelius's effects of thematic deliquescence, his ever-evolving forms, his unearthly timbres. New-music luminaries, from the hyper-complex Brian Ferneyhough to the neo-Romantic John Adams, cited him as a model. Among them was a group of Finns—Magnus Lindberg, Kaija Saariaho, and Esa-Pekka Salonen—who found new respect for the national hero after having rejected him in their punkish youth. Lindberg made his name with a gripping piece called "Kraft" (1983–85), whose orchestra is augmented by scrap-metal percussion and a conductor blowing a whistle. At any given point, it sounds nothing like Sibelius—Lindberg cites the influence of German noise-rock bands—but the accumulation of roiling sonic masses from microscopic material feels like a computer-age reprise of "Tapiola."

In 1984, the great American avant-garde composer Morton Feldman gave a lecture at the relentlessly up-to-date Summer Courses for New Music, in Darmstadt, Germany. "The people who you think are radicals might really be conservatives," Feldman said on that occasion. "The people who you think are conservative might really be radical." And he began to hum the Sibelius Fifth.

GARY GIDDINS

BACK TO BOSSA

ROSA PASSOS AND FIFTY YEARS OF BOSSA NOVA

Rosa Passos is often described as the heir to, or female equivalent of, João Gilberto, which is a way of saying that she is a distinguished interpreter of bossa nova at a time when gifted young Brazilian singers, like Marisa Monte, have adopted more fashionable pop styles. This won't necessarily sound appealing to those who recall bossa nova as an easy-listening diversion of the Kennedy years, epitomized by Astrud Gilberto's girlishly vacant invocation of "The Girl from Ipanema." But there has always been a difference between the musical phenomenon that began in Brazil in the late fifties and the watered-down version that flourished in the United States. Though the latter inspired brilliant collaborations—Stan Getz and João Gilberto; Frank Sinatra and Antonio Carlos Jobim—bossa nova quickly became a lounge-music punch line. "Blame It on the Bossa Nova," Eydie Gormé wailed, as Sergio Mendes and Brasil '66 made a sedative of "The Look of Love." In Brazil, the perspective is entirely different. While João Gilberto reigns as a god, Astrud is hardly known on the beaches of Ipanema. And many key bossa-nova figures, including the incomparable Elis Regina, never found a North American audience. The divide between the domestic bossa and its export-market derivative is sure to be much brooded over next year, when Brazil celebrates bossa nova's fiftieth anniversary.

Bossa nova grew out of long-standing samba traditions, but its emergence is usually traced to a 1958 album, "Canção do Amor Demais," by the hugely popular singer Elizete Cardoso. The album had a strange evolution. A few years earlier, Vinicius de Moraes, a playwright, poet, and diplomat, hired Jobim to write music for his play "Orfeu da Conceição." The play, a retelling of the Orpheus and Eurydice myth, was a success and generated interest in a film—the 1959 hit "Black Orpheus." But the French production company wanted a new score, leaving Vinicius scrambling for a way to introduce the songs he had written with Jobim. He chose Cardoso for her popularity and musicality, and, though initially reluctant, she agreed to make the record. (Imagine Lennon and McCartney, unable to get a record deal, having to persuade Vera Lynn to introduce their songs.) But the interpretative twist that gave the music a genuinely new feeling came from the participation of an obstreperous guitarist from Bahia, João Gilberto.

Jobim and Gilberto belonged to a generation that had grown up with bebop. While the tunes written by bebop innovators like Charlie Parker, Dizzy Gillespie, and Bud Powell were often too volatile and complicated for contemporary listeners, Jobim found a way of using bebop harmonies—especially the tritone, or flattened fifth—as the basis for irresistibly lyrical melodies. One of his most famous songs, "Desafinado"—the title means "slightly out of tune," or "off key"—is built almost entirely on discords. Gilberto, meanwhile, refined rhythms, banished vibrato, and subdued emotion, forging a style that was neither Brazilian samba nor American jazz. The music historian and producer Zuza Homem de Mello says that the first use of the phrase "bossa nova" was in a liner note that Jobim wrote for Gilberto, describing his "new way" of doing things; the phrase also appears in the lyric of "Desafinado."

In 1958, Rosa Passos was six years old and had been playing piano for three years. She grew up in Salvador, the capital of Bahia, her imagination fired by the early recordings of Gilberto and by the success of

"Black Orpheus" (with its Luiz Bonfá score). By the age of fifteen, she was performing on local television. Yet her career was slow in taking off. She made an album in 1979, "Recriação," introducing songs written with her longtime collaborator, Fernando de Oliveira, and then retired to Brasilia, where she married and raised a family. She rarely performed during the next decade and did not record again until 1991. In 1996, her album "Pano Pra Manga" brought her renewed attention, including an appearance at the Hollywood Bowl. Jazz musicians began to discover her: she performed in Japan, Cuba, Germany, Denmark, Switzerland, and Russia, and returned to the United States for a New Orleans concert in 2001. She made several more albums, with ensembles ranging from small jazz groups to orchestras, among them "Entre Amigos," "Festa," "Eu E Meu Coraçâo," "Azul," and "Amorosa." Yet, as good as the recordings are, Passos belongs to that dwindling tribe of performers who do their best work before an audience.

Recently, she gave her début performance at the Blue Note. She began with two songs by Dorival Caymmi, whose sambas helped define the development of Brazilian popular music during the nineteen-thirties, the period of Carmen Miranda's pre-Hollywood stardom. On "Vatapá," with its clipped, fizzy rhythm, her right hip bumped upward on the offbeats as her hands elaborated the melody, and, for a moment, you could imagine her in a fruit-bowl hat. The ballad "Marina" was a more emblematic Passos vehicle: tender, stylish, knowing. She laid out her phrases with the deliberation of an instrumentalist, behind or on the beat, conveying, even to listeners, like me, whose Portuguese is limited to "*Uma caipirinha, por favor*" and "*obrigado*," a conversational spontaneity that seemed to illuminate the emotional core of the piece.

Yo-Yo Ma, who has toured and recorded with Passos, has described her voice as "the most beautiful in the world." That's an overstatement, but only in degree. Her voice has the clarity of water, and her phrasing, all but free of vibrato and ornamentation, is colored only by the nasality that is embedded in the Portuguese language. If it isn't the most beautiful voice, it is surely one of unusual splendor, especially bewitching in the upper register, where it suggests fragility but never breaks. Whether she whispers or shouts, her intonation is reliably solid—a crucial asset in music that values dissonance and verbose lyrics.

And she is more than a singer. Passos is a prolific songwriter and a superb rhythm guitarist in the manner of her idol, João Gilberto. When she accompanies herself, the intimacy of her style and her harmonic sophistication are underscored; her fretting hand is in constant motion, adding transitional chords to already copious harmonies, and her grasp of the fretboard is so sure that she produces far less "surface noise"—those scratching sounds made when sliding from one chord to another—than many full-time guitarists. Her most recent album, "Rosa," released last year on Telarc, is the long-awaited testimony to her self-sufficiency: she arranged the entire album for voice and guitar (except for an introductory a cappella number) and composed nearly half of it. The confident delicacy of her attack masks fascinating details—her varied articulation of different words in the same phrase, as on the intricate "Molambo," arranged with a bolero beat, and, in her own haunting "Sutilezas," an exquisitely plaintive series of rising four-bar phrases that resolve and then rise again.

At the Blue Note, she fronted a quartet with the saxophonist Rodrigo Ursaia, the pianist Helio Alves, the bassist Paolo Paulelli, and the drummer Celso de Almeida. Passos absorbs the enthusiasm of the audience; at intervals, she plucked a flower from a vase onstage and presented it to someone sitting ringside. Short and stocky, she has a strong face with prominent cheeks and a generous mouth. She speaks little English—her stage announcements were translated by the saxophonist—but she commands attention by her emotional resolve. In this respect, she is not Gilberto's heir; she is his better. On Jobim's ingenious "Fotografia," backed by the band, she telegraphed its flirtatious romance with lilting high-note inflections and an occasional wink; in the same composer's heartbreaking "Dindi," she sighed the words; and on Ary Barroso's jubilant "É Luxo Só," accompanied only by her own acoustic guitar, she opened up her lungs and transformed a crowded downtown night club into Carnival. Then she handed out another flower.

DAVID MARGOLICK

THE DAY LOUIS ARMSTRONG MADE NOISE

Fifty years ago this week, all eyes were on Little Rock, Ark., where nine black students were trying, for the first time, to desegregate a major Southern high school. With fewer than 150 blacks, the town of Grand Forks, North Dakota, hardly figured to be a key front in that battle—until, that is, Larry Lubenow talked to Louis Armstrong.

On the night of Sept. 17, 1957, two weeks after the Little Rock Nine were first barred from Central High School, the jazz trumpeter happened to be on tour with his All Stars band in Grand Forks. Larry Lubenow, meanwhile, was a 21-year-old journalism student and jazz fan at the University of North Dakota, moonlighting for $1.75 an hour at The Grand Forks Herald.

Shortly before Mr. Armstrong's concert, Mr. Lubenow's editor sent him to the Dakota Hotel, where Mr. Armstrong was staying, to see if he could land an interview. Perhaps sensing trouble—Mr. Lubenow was, he now says, a "rabble-rouser and liberal"—his boss laid out the ground rules: "No politics," he ordered. That hardly seemed necessary, for Mr. Armstrong rarely ventured into such things anyway. "I don't get involved in politics," he once said. "I just blow my horn."

But Mr. Lubenow was thinking about other things, race relations among them. The bell captain, with whom he was friendly, had told him that Mr. Armstrong was quietly making history in Grand Forks, as he had done innumerable times and ways before, by becoming the first black man ever to stay at what was then the best hotel in town. Mr. Lubenow knew, too, that Grand Forks had its own link to Little Rock: it was the hometown of Judge Ronald Davies, who'd just ordered that the desegregation plan in Little Rock proceed after Gov. Orval Faubus of Arkansas and a band of local segregationists tried to block it.

As Mr. Armstrong prepared to play that night—oddly enough, at Grand Forks's own Central High School—members of the Arkansas National Guard ringed the school in Little Rock, ordered to keep the black students out. President Dwight D. Eisenhower's meeting with Governor Faubus three days earlier in Newport, R.I., had ended inconclusively. Central High School was open, but the black children stayed home.

Mr. Lubenow was first told he couldn't talk to Mr. Armstrong until after the concert. That wouldn't do. With the connivance of the bell captain, he snuck into Mr. Armstrong's suite with a room service lobster dinner. And Mr. Armstrong, wearing a Hawaiian shirt and shorts, agreed to talk. Mr. Lubenow stuck initially to his editor's script, asking Mr. Armstrong to name his favorite musician. (Bing Crosby, it turned out.) But soon he brought up Little Rock, and he could not believe what he heard. "It's getting almost so bad a colored man hasn't got any country," a furious Mr. Armstrong told him. President Eisenhower, he charged, was "two faced," and had "no guts." For Governor Faubus, he used a double-barreled hyphenated expletive, utterly unfit for print. The two settled on something safer: "uneducated plow boy." The euphemism, Mr. Lubenow says, was far more his than Mr. Armstrong's.

Mr. Armstrong bitterly recounted some of his experiences touring in the Jim Crow South. He then sang the opening bar of "The Star-Spangled Banner," inserting obscenities into the lyrics and prompting Velma Middleton, the vocalist who toured with Mr. Armstrong and who had joined them in the room, to hush him up.

Mr. Armstrong had been contemplating a good-will tour to the Soviet Union for the State Department. "They ain't so cold but what we couldn't bruise them with happy music," he had said. Now, though, he confessed to having second thoughts. "The way they are treating my people in the South, the government can go to hell," he said, offering further choice words about the secretary of state, John Foster Dulles. "The people over there ask me what's wrong with my country. What am I supposed to say?"

Mr. Lubenow, who came from a small North Dakota farming community, was shocked by what he heard, but he also knew he had a story; he skipped the concert and went back to the paper to write it up. It was too late to get it in his own paper; nor would the Associated Press editor in Minneapolis, dubious that Mr. Armstrong could have said such things, put it on the national wire, at least until Mr. Lubenow could prove he hadn't made it all up. So the next morning Mr. Lubenow returned to the Dakota Hotel and, as Mr. Armstrong shaved, had the Herald photographer take their picture together. Then Mr. Lubenow showed Mr. Armstrong what he'd written. "Don't take nothing out of that story," Mr. Armstrong declared. "That's just what I said, and still say." He then wrote "solid" on the bottom of the yellow copy paper, and signed his name.

The article ran all over the country. Douglas Edwards and John Cameron Swayze broadcast it on the evening news. The Russians, an anonymous government spokesman warned, would relish everything Mr. Armstrong had said. A radio station in Hattiesburg, Miss., threw out all of Mr. Armstrong's records. Sammy Davis Jr. criticized Mr. Armstrong for not speaking out earlier. But Jackie Robinson, Sugar Ray Robinson, Lena Horne, Eartha Kitt and Marian Anderson quickly backed him up.

Mostly, there was surprise, especially among blacks. Secretary Dulles might just as well have stood up at the United Nations and led a chorus of the Russian national anthem, declared Jet magazine, which once called Mr. Armstrong an "Uncle Tom." Mr. Armstrong had long tried to convince people throughout the world that "the Negro's lot in America is a happy one," it observed, but in one bold stroke he'd pulled nearly 15 million American blacks to his bosom. Any white confused by the Rev. Dr. Martin Luther King Jr.'s polite talk need only listen to Mr. Armstrong, *The Amsterdam News* declared. Mr. Armstrong's words had the "explosive effect of an H-bomb," said *The Chicago Defender*. "He may not have been grammatical, but he was eloquent."

His road manager quickly put out that Mr. Armstrong had been tricked, and regretted his statements, but Mr. Armstrong would have none of that. "I said what somebody should have said a long time ago," he said the following day in Montevideo, Minn., where he gave his next concert. He closed that show with "The Star-Spangled Banner"—this time, minus the obscenities.

Mr. Armstrong was to pay a price for his outspokenness. There were calls for boycotts of his concerts. The Ford Motor Company threatened to pull out of a Bing Crosby special on which Mr. Armstrong was to appear. Van Cliburn's manager refused to let him perform a duet with Mr. Armstrong on Steve Allen's talk show.

But it didn't really matter. On Sept. 24, President Eisenhower sent 1,200 paratroopers from the 101st Airborne into Little Rock, and the next day soldiers escorted the nine students into Central High School. Mr. Armstrong exulted. "If you decide to walk into the schools with the little colored kids, take me along, Daddy," he wired the president. "God bless you." As for Mr. Lubenow, who now works in public relations in Cedar Park, Tex., he got $3.50 for writing the story and, perhaps, for changing history. But his editor was miffed—he'd gotten into politics, after all. Within a week, he left the paper.

ON LYNYRD SKYNYRD AND THE WHITE TRASH THING

In a pub on Achill Island, in West Ireland, I'm hanging out with Anarchists. The Anarchists are having a gathering along a lake down the hill from the pub where we've been drinking. The pub is full of Irish Nationalists; they're cool with the Anarchists, because both are against the English rule. I'm along for the ride.

A band of Irish guys are playing country and western music with fake Southern accents or simply American accents to them. It's as goofy as it sounds, but everybody's tossing back pints and having good times. I've got my arm around a blue-eyed black Irish girl named Karen, between a lot of beery snogging, I'm telling her all about where I come from, but only because she's asking.

The band breaks into their last song, the Irish National Anthem. The Nationalists stand up. The Anarchists stay seated. Except for one guy, a new recruit; Kieran, I think he's called; who recently jumped from Sinn Fein for something more radical. He, resolutely and yet with a goofy grin, stands up and sings with the rest of the pub. After the anthem is over Karen whispers in my ear that we need to leave, as the rest of the bar stares us all down. She grabs my hand and we head for the door with the rest of the group.

Torn between autonomy and the place he calls home, Kieran is still singing the National Anthem and doing a jig before he breaks into a round of "Joe Hill" with the rest of the group as we drunkenly stagger back to our camp.

My buddies Mark and Ray and me are barreling down the backroads in Mark's beat up old black '85 Ford Ranger. It's a sunny Southern Indiana day. Both of them are fubared. I take up the backseat with sober resignation the guitarist's long-ass guitar solo rips its way through Lynyrd Skynyrd's, "Sweet Home Alabama." The sun hits the rebel flag hanging in the back where the window should be and it silhouettes me. Mark takes hard turns and the big truck fishtails on the loose gravel. Ray grabs the vise grips that are hanging from the door where the window handle should be and rolls it all the way down. He sets his full beer in the cup holder attached to the crack in the window, and grabs an empty beer bottle from the floorboard. He shoves his broad shoulders out the window and chucks it at a road sign that shows a crooked arrow. The bottle misses and hits the grass without a sound. "Faggot," Mark shouts at him as he jerks the wheel to the left. "Suck my dick," Ray yells back.

We're thirty miles north of the Kentucky border in a county called Crawford. This is where we tell people we're from because the town we live in is too small for anyone to have heard of it. We're sticking to the backroads because two thirds of us are shitfaced. We're also sticking to the backroads because we can tear it up out here and we really don't have anywhere else to go. It's summer vacation, but that only matters to Mark, because he's the one third that's still enrolled.

They want me to drink because they're eighteen and nineteen and think I look up to them. I'm the one that's not drinking. I don't drink because that's fucking redneck shit. I don't look up to them because I'm a city boy "transplant," and I think I'm better than them. Mark hits fast forward on the dubbed Lynyrd Skynyrd tape.

"I'm up," I say to Ray.

"Ya gotta drink one of these, if ya wanna throw it, fag."

"Just give 'im a fucking bottle," Mark shouts at Ray. Ray tosses an empty Budweiser bottle back to me.

"Ya wanna get up here fer that," he asks.

"Nah, I got it," I say and head to the back of the truck. I push the flag aside and post up on the back hatch.

"Oh, shit," Ray says.

"Dude, be careful back there," Mark hollers, stopping the cassette at "Free-bird." The song gets me pumped.

"Just fuckin' punch it," I yell back.

"Grab somethin'," he says and hits the gas. I wing the bottle at a brown sign that says "entering Crawford County." It shatters against it loudly.

"Fuck yeah, little man," Mark shouts.

"Motherfucker," Ray turns and says to me, smiling and shaking his head.

"Ya gotta be able to see straight, bitch," I say.

Down the road a bit, somewhere in the middle of "Freebird," right around the instrumental part, the tape makes a shrill noise.

"Motherfucker," shouts Mark as he pulls out the cassette. Its black tape is stretched out and snapped. He chucks it on the floorboard and puts in that rap song about liking big butts.

I liked to consider myself a city boy. The last place we lived was a rough, violent, white working-class suburb of Gary, Indiana. Except I shortened it to just, "used to live in Gary." It left 'em a stronger image. A stronger image of what I *wanted* them to picture anyway.

They called us "transplant hicks" as they call city folk who get stuck down there. A tag I vigilantly denied. Then, maybe they just called them "transplants" and I tacked on the "hick." Can't remember for sure.

In small town Indiana, the Confederate flag drapes windows of trailers, just like the Marlboro jackets are worn and Taz cartoons are tattooed on shoulders draped by those t-shirts with pictures of Indians surrounded by wolves and lightning that you can find at any truck stop. To put it bluntly, the Indiana redneck has no culture, they cling to these symbols of badassness, because they have nothing to hold them together. They have no stories so they're falling for anything. And they're falling apart.

I eventually move to Louisville, Kentucky. A town that was my former respite when I got my first car in Crawford County. Back then I would take off by myself and shop in record stores or hang out in coffee shops taking it all in. It was the place that I'd go to see my first punk rock shows. The big city. It's an old story, but yeah, I took off for the city.

I'm actually from Kentucky in the most literal sense of the word. I was born in Ashland. A small coal mining town. At least that's what I hear. I only lived there until I was one or two, before my dad moved our family all around the country; leading me, my mom and my brother down a downward spiral until we ended up in Crawford County, Indiana.

If you live in Louisville for just a few years, people start taking you in as one of their own:

"How long have you been in Louisville?"

"A few years."

"Oh, well you're a local now."

I guess it's that Southern Hospitality thing. But I went with it, attempted to turn my back completely on my white trash roots. I started saying that I was from Louisville or else that I was from Kentucky. Both could be true, the latter probably more so depending on how you look at it. But Louisville was a wonderful place and Kentucky people are still the best I've ever met. I really wanted to be a part of it and leave everything else behind. The more they knew about me, the more they accepted me as one of them.

Maybe where you're from can be that fluid, but it's the past that holds weight. And there were things that I couldn't let go. I began walking between worlds. Louisville might have accepted me as their own, but inside I knew better. My redneck roots lay in small town Indiana; I'd come up around all of the stereotypes the rest of the country holds the South to, yet I did so on the other side of the Mason-Dixon. Everybody I associated with came up in the city going to magnet schools and hanging out on Bardstown Road, the kind of arty

Bohemian Street that every city has. Just like I felt like an outsider in Crawford County, I often felt alienated in Louisville. My friends didn't understand the anger and self-hatred and sadness that poured out of me. They just didn't get me sometimes. The way that I was always on a high horse. The way I could laugh at incest, rape and fetal alcohol syndrome. They had grown up in the South, but came up in the normalcy and safety of the city.

I guess trash is trash no matter how you cut it.

Me and some of my college buddies are heading down to the river to watch Lynyrd Skynyrd play a free show. That is, if you could call them Lynyrd Skynyrd, considering that most of the band had died in a plane crash, including the main songwriter. This doesn't matter to us though, because we're really going down there to check out the spectacle of thousands of wasted hicks rocking out and to laugh our asses off. When we get there the football field–sized lawn is packed with a buttload of drunk rednecks. Most of them are probably from small Southern Indiana towns in or not far from Crawford County. The rest are probably from the South End of Louisville.

We sip whiskey out of a flask and laugh at all the girls on shoulders flashing titties and shirtless, long-haired, toothless hicks falling all over each other.

After the concert is over, I kick my way through all the beer cans and garbage that drapes the field. I'm shouting, "Freebird" and "the South's gonna do it again," at the dispersing crowd, they shout back "hell yeah" and "fuck yeah" as they head back to their cars and trucks. My friends put up with it for a little, then they get impatient. They drop me off at my apartment in Old Louisville before they go to their condos in the East End and I decide that I don't like them anymore.

Funny thing about Lynyrd Skynyrd is that they're from Florida. Not funny because they're not from Alabama like the song says. Funny because Florida ain't the South. At least that's what you'll hear from Southerners from the other parts. Hell, folks have even said the same thing about Kentucky, but we won't get into that.

I'm taking Adam, a Louisville friend of mine, to visit Billy, an old friend of mine in Crawford County.

Billy is the only bridge that I haven't burned in my old town. We've stayed good friends over the years. He was a few years younger than I was. I took him to his first punk show in New Albany, a town right across the river from Louisville. That was a long-ass tone ago.

Billy is having a party when we arrive at his doublewide trailer. When I walk in I see Misty, an old friend of mine. She sees me and breaks into tears.

"Oh my God, I can't believe it. How've you been? I can't believe it's you," she says between sobs, "it's been so long." It's been years since I've seen her. When I last saw her she was fourteen years old, now she's nineteen. I feel glad to see her, yet I'm uncomfortable about all the blubbering. Me and Adam have a seat at the kitchen table across from her. She brings me up to date on everything that's happened in her life. Her big sister Cassie married one of my old buddies. They had a couple of kids and are breaking the cycle, as in they've actually been happy. It all goes downhill from there. Misty has moved the topic of conversation on to her late father, Jake. I've heard a bit about this from Billy before. He was murdered in a bad meth deal. Dragged behind a truck for miles. His body was never found, but bloody shreds of his clothes were. She tells me that she was asked to identify these rags. She starts crying again. I reach my hand across the table and wrap it over hers.

I never liked her father. Not since he tried to fuck my ex-girlfriend, Jenny. Jake was married to Jenny's aunt, Misty's mother. I didn't give a fuck about Jenny anymore, but I could never hang with that kind of shit, nor could I get used to it. And for the last five or so years I've no longer had to.

Misty's friend, a young, kind of pretty, but disturbingly thin girl comes over and wraps her arms around her.

"Don't worry. Let's get out of here. Let's just go to Denver, mah cousin lives there," she says.

"But what about alla them niggers there," Misty asks.

Adam gets up and walks into the other room. I hold onto Misty's hand as she cries. Then I get up and give her a big hug.

Across the room, Billy's roommate turns on 100.5 The Fox; the opening lines of "Freebird" fill the room.

"Fuck yeah," he yells and starts riffing on his air guitar.

"Get that fuckin' shit off my stereo," Billy says and throws on a Dead Kennedys CD.

An hour later, I go into the living room. Adam is watching cable TV.

"What's up, with all that racist shit," he asks me.

I look down at the ground. "You really don't know where you are, do you?" I ask flatly. It's all I can think to say.

It was Lynyrd Skynyrd's label that posed them in front of the Confederate flag. They thought it would solidify their tough image.

Maybe it took an outsider to see just how fucked up Crawford County was. To tell its story. I know that sounds pretentious. But I'm humble enough to also know the reason that I got out of there, without a prison sentence, a tour of duty in Iraq, a hearse or strung out on meth, was because I knew there was something better than that place. I'm not always cool with the fact that I had the privilege of that knowledge, sometimes I'm struck with a kind of weird guilt.

Maybe I should have let it all go back then and just lived it up in the city. Maybe I should have just been happy to get the hell out of the sticks. But I couldn't just let it all go. It almost seemed that I took it all in for a reason.

I still can't let it go.

I'm in Amsterdam, smoking weed in a park with a few dudes. Two of them are young English guys on vacation. The other two are living in Amsterdam. One of the latter group is a black man with a European accent. He asks me where I'm from. I tell him that I'm from Kentucky.

"That's the South, right. Are you some kind of redneck?"

"Sure, yeah, I'm a fuckin' redneck, whatever." I reply.

"You like stringin' black people from trees."

"Man, I think you got the wrong idea. I'm not a racist."

"Well, you said you were a redneck. You must be in the Ku Klux Klan."

"I've organized against the Klan. Have you ever been to the South?"

"No."

"Have you ever even been to the states?"

"What's this got to do with you bein' redneck?"

"Have you?"

"No?"

"So you've never even been to the states. Let alone the parts I come from. You have no idea what you're talking about. Your stereotyping me based on some bullshit European hearsay and I'm the bigot? You're a fucking idiot."

He smiles and starts singing Billie Holiday's "Bitter Fruit." I let it go and walk away.

"Sweet Home Alabama," is a controversial song. Vastly misunderstood and carrying with it a truckload of mythology. It's pretty much common knowledge that it's a song calling out Neil Young for his one-sided take on the racism in the South in his song "Southern Man." All that aside, if you can get behind the idea that it's not a racist song (which is vigilantly argued by rock fans on both sides of the fence), "Sweet Home Alabama" in it's dismissal of George Wallace is very accurate to the sentiment of poor white folks. *"In Birmingham they loved the governor/well we all did what we could do."* I can almost hear the character of the song shrugging as he says it. It's a simple dismissal of some accusatory city boy or Yankee or whoever. A dismissal of someone who wants to hold them personally responsible for all the racism in the country. Meanwhile, unlike their ac-cusers they actually know black folks, work alongside them at the con-struction site. They're also barely getting by and have little time for some uppity fuck who won't get off his horsey long enough to listen to them anyway. Same goes for Watergate. They had nothing to do with it and they rest easy at night. That's always what I got out of the song.

As far as what the people in the town where I come from got that out of the song, well I've always assumed they just liked it because it was badass. But a part of me hates where I come from. Maybe they need to write a song dismissing me.

I was wasted in a pub in Achill Island once, snogging on a Black Irish girl named Karen who'd been pulling for me all night. She's an Anarchist, actually they're all Anarchists, everybody I've been hanging out with anyway. Everybody else in the pub is an Irish Nationalist, but they're cool with the Anarchists because neither of them like the English rule.

She asks me where I'm from in the states. I tell her that I'm from the south. I tell her that I'm from a small redneck town. Then the band rips into "Freebird." I get up and shout every verse and pump my fist, acting the fool as white trash does. I tell her it has something to do with where I come from.

AROUND THE BEND

My friend Josh will warn people not to talk shit about Creedance around me. This is because of the time I got drunk and punched him in the balls as a result of his doing just that. He also tells them that it's best not to step on Creedance around me, because that band is responsible for me kicking the Christ out of my life.

There's a bunch of misunderstanding going on here, all of it coming from a drunken *volley* of misunderstandings that we had one evening.

First of all, he wasn't quite talking shit about Creedance at all. He was in the process of trying to remember the name of that shitty fake band Creed and in the process rattled off "Creedance." I, being so offended by hearing the two bands in the same sentence, swung at his shoulder or some similarly benign part of his body, and drunkenly connected directly with his balls. Thus leaving him crumpled and convinced that to me Creedance was not to be mocked. After I apologized to him, I could only explain my actions as being because Creedance got me out of the Christ.

The last misunderstanding was the most important, because it's the one he takes most literally. It's true, sure. But in a much more indirect way than I was able to articulate all wasted like I was. You see, Creedance was the first rock and roll band I got into. And it was rock and roll that put me on the path to dropping everything that bound me or repressed me, not the least of those being Christianity. It was the gateway that led me out of the narrow, repressive and buttclenched world that I was raised in. If it wasn't them it would've been something else, but it couldn't have been any other *band* but Creedance Clearwater Revival.

I was raised in a Pentecostal Christian family. Pentecostalism was a religion based on bonds and fear. I lived in a binary world where everything was either black or white. Anything and everything that was not directly related to God fell under the umbrella of witchcraft or secular humanism. Conspiracies abounded which tied anything cultural that spoke not of religion to the Devil himself.

The "flesh" was a word that my parents, my father especially, threw around a lot. The flesh was something else that I was told to look out for. The flesh was what I wanted that was not of God, sinful desires, or desire, period. We were to seek God and to avoid the trappings of the Devil and the flesh.

At church my parents, my brother, the congregation and myself, would get the Holy Spirit and speak in tongues, cast out demons and dance and fall flat on our backs "slain in the Spirit." In an evil world I found my outlet in an angry and overbearing God. When I was in the Spirit I felt the presence of God, joy could be had with no fear of the Flesh. The rest of the time that fear was all there was.

Of course, worldly music was an abomination of God and it worked in cahoots with the Devil and me flesh to lead people into sin and darkness and finally Hell. Not unlike *anything* ultimately liberating or even simply fun. I was warned that if I listened to rock music I was inviting evil spirits in, to possess me. That it would lead me astray from the ways of the Lord and into Hell for an eternity. The thing was, I'd heard the Devil's Music before, and it seemed to draw me in, like I was being tempted. It had a beat to it that was appealing, yet with it came the grievance of the Holy Spirit that I felt in my guts. Under my breath I rebuked it in the Lord's name. But to use the church's lexicon, seeds were being planted.

My parents kept my brother and me from a lot of things when we were kids. We never got to do Halloween and instead spent that time in church dressed as bible characters. When fantasy movies were played in elementary school, we had to sit in the hall so evil spirits wouldn't possess us. This is all pretty boring, garden variety, Christian paranoia and child rearing, but you'll need it for background. But yeah, that was the way I was raised and it sucked.

I read a *Peanuts* comic strip when I was a little kid. It sticks with me to this very day. Linus is sitting and playing with a bunch of toys. His big sister Lucy comes by scoops them all up and takes all of them away. Then she tosses him a rubber band and says, "here, you can have this." Linus picks up the rubber band and stretches it between his hands. Then stretches it a little more. And then he's pulling it and stretching it all over the place and having a fucking blast. Lucy comes into the next panel and snatches it from him. "You weren't supposed to have that much fun with it," she says.

When my brother and me were not quite teenagers, my parents suffered the oldie station to be played in our rooms. I guess they thought it was innocent compared to how sinful the world has become. Or maybe they thought by conceding some songs about flying purple people eaters and Alley Oop, King of the Jungle would sate our curiosity enough to keep us from delving further into the Devil's music.

They fucked up.

> *There's a place up ahead and I'm goin', just as fast as my feet can fly.*
> *Come away, come away if you're goin' leave your sinkin' ship behind.*
> —CREEDENCE CLEARWATER REVIVAL
> FROM "UP AROUND THE BEND"

It was the song "Up Around the Bend" that first got me. In this song there was joy, motion, and riffs that gave me butterflies. These guys were onto something. They weren't messing around. I didn't know what was around that bend nor was I even fully aware that I was on a sinking ship. I really didn't pay too much attention to what was being sung anyway, but more just the whole essence of the song itself. It was a goddamn bursting kernel of pure uncut, feverish lust for life. It did so without apology. It did so without glorifying or projecting it onto some dickhead god. It had zeal without being tied to fear, guilt, and regret, it asked for no forgiveness. If it were Hell itself around that bend they would follow through without complaint.

My father broke away from his own father's business, into more chains, more rules, more Gods. More masters more authoritarian bullshit. He burned his bridges to end up locked inside an iron door. He found Jesus. Was filled with the Holy Spirit. Spoke in tongues and cast out spirits. And for all the exorcism and spiritual abandon, he only boxed himself in. My father's rebellion was another set of laws.

For myself, coming into my own was much simpler. It was not through some contradiction-spouting atheist, or through the pursuit of knowledge, or some shattered faith, or Jimmy Swaggart blubbering on television that made me throw off my father's God and to live for myself. To pursue life. Just a voice full of promise and a goddamn happy, rock guitar lick beckoning me to come away with them, because there were better things around the bend.

TEN YEARS

When I was pretty young one of my first shows was Rancid at the Emerson Theater in Indianapolis. I was pretty young, but probably not as young as some of you were when you saw your first shows, because I had just got out of a tiny town where there weren't any. So enough with the beating around the bush about how old I was, trying to be vague about it is my intention.

So anyway, I was at this Rancid show and let me tell you, I was so completely into it. Keeping in context, it was one of my first shows and all, well, fuck context, it was a great show. Rancid was out there in all their full punk glory. Charged and studded. And there was much love in the pit. I shouted all the lyrics and piled on with all the punks. Some skinhead got onstage and sang along with Lars (or whoever the

lead singer is). I walked away from the show with a Rancid T-shirt
and a set list, smiling from ear to ear. Even my brother, who was
smoking a lot of weed and into "heavy shit" at the time, begrudgingly
admitted that they were pretty good.

Most of these specifics I am only just now having a foggy recollec-
tion of as I write. For some reason, though, my strongest memory was
Lars pointing to some punk kid near the stage and saying, "fuck you,
where are you gonna be in ten years?"

The whole crowd then flipped off and pointed and laughed at the
guy. I'm not sure what the kid did, but Lars sure was pissed. I wondered
what Lars meant when he said that.

The next day, oddly enough, I recall with more clarity. I went into
the good record store in town, decked out in my new Rancid T-
shirt. The older punk guy behind the counter asked me how the
show was, then sat back and patiently listened, while I raved about
how great it was and how some skinhead got on stage and skanked
with Lars and there was stage-diving and blah, blah, blah. I'm sure I
sounded like a fucking idiot. Not wanting to burst my bubble, he
just sat and smiled and listened like old punks should do. I'm sure all
the while thinking, "he'll learn." Having heard me, another employee, also young, but older than me, walked up and said that he
didn't like Rancid. He said that they were dicks to the sound guy
and that the only good band was the opening band (a band which,
by the way, I can't recall for anything and in retrospect, probably
were better). The older punk didn't stop him either, but still held
that same knowing smile, as if to say, "yep, he'll learn, too."

I walked out of there with a few more punk CDs and thought about
it. Yeah, they *were* kind of dicks to the sound guy.

It's been several years and Rancid have gone on to buy a mansion and
spray paint it with words like "chaos" and "oi." They tattooed "punx"
across their knuckles and got punched out at ABC No Rio for being
"sellouts."

I went on to see plenty more punk shows, for better or worse. Shaved my hair into a mohawk and went from that to a devil's lock, then grew it into a normal hair cut and put on a studded jacket with band names all over it. Then I ditched the jacket and shaved my hair into a mohawk again and changed it, but only for a driver's license picture, then I shaved it off.

I probably didn't need to go into that whole montage. But whatever, time passed. People change. So on so forth. Every now and then, when someone brings up Rancid, I think about Lars yelling, "fuck you! where will you be in ten years?" I still don't know what he meant by that. And I've had over ten years to figure it out.

Tom Ewing

THE HISTORY BOOK ON THE SHELF

In ABBA's "On and On and On" the singer's at a party and gets into a conversation with someone who's worried about the world. He turns out to be a Swedish government minister and shouldn't really be saying that stuff (so they sing a stomping Beach Boys pastiche instead). Like a lot of ABBA's more rocking songs, it doesn't quite work but fails in an endearing way—but beyond that it struck me as an odd thing to be singing about.

I'm sure that in 1980 the band were something like royalty in Sweden and almost certainly were really going to dinner parties and meeting ministers. It's the matter-of-fact way they mention it that surprised me. I can only think of one other song about meeting a politician at a party—Pulp's "Cocaine Socialism." The Pulp song takes the meeting as a springboard for a savage attack on Tony Blair's Labour Party, as well as Cool Britannia and cocaine and corruption. "Cocaine Socialism" is a fine record, but it never struck me as odd—biting outsider opposition was the tone I expected a record about politicians at parties to take. As opposed to ABBA's convivial reasonableness.

Of course I go to dinner parties sometimes myself, and though there aren't any politicians involved, convivial reasonableness seems a fine aim. Maybe that's a reason I find myself enjoying ABBA more the older I get. Actually I can't remember not enjoying them: They were my favorite band at seven; they're one of my favorite bands at 34. What I want to explore in this column, though, is how ABBA often seem a very adult band, writing songs squarely set in the adult (as opposed to adolescent or teenage or college-age) world, coping with adult emotions, and particularly adult compromises and disappointments.

I'll admit I'm talking here mostly about the later ABBA, roughly from 1976's *Arrival* onwards. The earlier, goofier ABBA is also terrific—and was the version that launched Europop as we knew it (try Holland's Luv' for a marvelous band that uses the ABBA of "King Kong Song" and "Ring Ring" as a springboard). I don't find myself feeling the songs as much as their later records, though, possibly because I think Bjorn Ulvaeus and Benny Andersson are excellent lyricists, and on the earlier albums their confidence in their English wasn't up to showing that.

Critical wisdom has it that ABBA material darkened in the late 1970s because the two couples who formed the band both split up. There's surely a lot of truth in this—their later albums are studded with fantastic, rueful break-up songs—but I don't necessarily want to confuse "adult" and "dark" here. ABBA songs aren't "dark" just because of the intra-band divorces, they're more universal than that: the sorrow in them is often a sense that the best of times, the most lived parts of life, have already, irretrievably happened. "Having the time of your life"—the chorus of "Dancing Queen" is literally and painfully felt: this is as good as it gets. In so many ABBA songs the important stuff has all happened in the past—when Chiquita was sure of herself, when Fernando crossed the Rio Grande, when the narrators of "One of Us" or "Thank You For The Music" made the decisions they're looking back on in the songs.

And what happens afterward? "Now you're working in a bank, a family man, a football fan, and your name is Harry"—this from "Our Last Summer," a relatively jolly song about lost first love that still fits in "a fear of getting old, a fear of slowly dying." Fears come true: dreams don't. But one of the things that makes ABBA adult rather than adolescent is that they're usually sympathetic to their fading everymen protagonists. Harry may just be a bank clerk, but his life isn't horrible or wrong or a betrayal, it's just a bit more boring than it once was. "Should I Laugh Or Cry," a portrait by his tired, frustrated wife of an absurd domestic Napoleon, is probably the saddest record ABBA ever made, but even this pathetic individual, shouting in too-short trousers, is no monster.

Compare, if you like, the ridiculous paroxysms of agony and disgust a band like Radiohead go through contemplating the simplest of socializations on "Fitter, Happier" or "Paranoid Android." ABBA understand and will not condemn compromise, and contentment, and dull satisfaction, and the flipside to the songs where they lament past excitement are the songs in which something immense does disrupt the adult world and its settlements. "Lay All Your Love On Me"—not by accident the most irresistibly physical of any ABBA track—spells it out: "a grown up woman should never fall so easily." On "The Visitors," set in a Soviet-occupied country, the European bourgeois world the band generally documents becomes a terrified but precious pretense, one that can be shattered by a stranger's hand rattling the doorknob.

Strangest and maybe best of all is "The Day Before You Came," a simple portrait of an ordinary adult life on the day before it is changed forever: By what, we never learn. As the UK journalist Taylor Parkes notes in his fantastic 1995 essay on ABBA, the spectral choirs of backing vocals suggest a murderer as much as a lover. Here is the central ABBA theme: life is trivial and nothing happens, but the somethings that might happen are worse.

"The Day Before You Came" is full of awkward conversational lyrics: "I must have gone to lunch, at half past 12 or so, the usual place, the usual bunch." Their slight stiltedness is what makes ABBA great lyricists—as non-native speakers they rarely risked too many metaphors or much poetic imagery, preferring a matter-of-fact reportage of feeling. Combined with Agnetha and Frida's occasionally halting pronunciation this could make them sound devastatingly direct and vulnerable.

Sometimes ABBA could be high-falutin', though: "Happy New Year" has a death's head lyric, which pins down the essential, horrid sameness of January 1st and concludes that "man is a fool and he thinks he'll be OK, dragging on feet of clay, never knowing he's astray." Of course "Happy New Year" also has a chorus that goes "Happy New Year! Happy New Year!" and ABBA were a band that didn't know how not to write a catchy song, so it has a use-value that fights against its bleakness—thank goodness, or it would just be a moan. Because of the sheer sticking power of ABBA's melodies, their lyrics can often be safely ignored—in a pub quiz once I asked teams to identify a verse from "Knowing Me, Knowing You"—"In these old familiar rooms, children once played. Now there's only emptiness, nothing to say." The song is one of the band's most famous in Britain, but nobody got it right.

In other words, ABBA's adultness, or darkness, is mostly strictly optional. In the same way as their characters lead well-ordered lives while suffering the occasional regret and pang of anxiety, ABBA never let their existential worries get in the way of their day job: writing immediately fabulous pop music. "The Visitors" may be about political paranoia but it's also got a blazing synthpop chorus. "The Day Before You Came" makes the rare move of putting its music where its mentality is and was one of the band's first flops.

Sometimes ABBA's musical instincts seem to sabotage the band's emotional impulses. "Our Last Summer" sticks to your head as doggedly as any of the band's hits until its bittersweet mood is jarred by a really downright vulgar guitar solo. Even this fits the mood, though. Then we were Summer heroes, it seems to be saying, now we're grown-up and awkward and the kind of basically not very cool people who think this song could use a bit of ill-placed axe work. Which is fine—when the band did try and be fashionable (their recording jaunt to Miami at the mainstream height of disco, for instance) the results were even more inelegant than usual.

As a fan, I indulge ABBA's sometime musical inelegance as much as I enjoy their terrific songcraft, but what I keep coming back for is the sadness and richness in their songs. I've concentrated here on the lyrics because I think they're undervalued, but in the end the hooks are always going to be what sells ABBA, and this is probably as it should be. If you're fond of their hits at all though, keep their records around, sniff about their back catalog a little more, and don't dismiss them: You may find that your life ends up more like an ABBA song than you imagine.

OTHER NOTABLE MUSIC WRITING OF 2007

MISS AMP, "Grinderman: Nick Cave's League of Extraordinary Gentlemen," February 2007, *Plan B.*

Anthony Bartkewicz, "Justin Broadrick," March 2007, *Decibel.*

Gavin Bertram, "Room That Echoes," May 2007, *Real Groove.*

Mark Binelli, "Punk Rock Fight Club," August 23, 2007, *Rolling Stone.*

Garrett Caples, "Hyphy and Its Discontents," July 11, 2007, *San Francisco Bay Guardian.*

Jon Caramanica, "The Education of Kanye West," August 26, 2007, *New York Times.*

Arielle Castillo, "Undercover Boy Wonder," June 12, 2007, *Miami New Times.*

Jeff Chang, "Movin On Up," January 22, 2007, *The Nation.*

Susan Choi, "Three Mix Tapes," March 2007, *Moistworks.*

Jace Clayton, "Muslin Gaze," Summer 2007, *Bidoun.*

Kandia Crazy Horse, "Digital Venuses," May 9, 2007, *San Francisco Bay Guardian.*

Jane Dark, "The Five Paragraph Essay: 'It's Britney Bitch'," November 15, 2007, *Jane Dark's Sugarhigh.*

Justin Davidson, "The Strange Case of Joyce Hatto," 2007, eMusic.

Elizabeth Donnelly, "For Harry Potter Fans About to Rock, We Salute You," July 14, 2007, *Salon.*

Warren Ellis, "John Allyn Smith Sails," August 9, 2007, *Warren Ellis's blog.*

Matt Fink, "Modest Mouse: On Their Own Terms," Winter 2007, *Under The Radar.*

Bill Friskics-Warren, "Adding Notes to a Folklorist's Tunes," December 2, 2007, *New York Times.*

Greg Garry, "Black Magic Woman," October 2007, *Radar Magazine.*

Thomas Golianopoulos, "I'm Real What Are You," July 2007, *XXL.*

Michael Gonzales, "Down With the King: Black Folks & Elvis," August 16, 2007, *Blackalicious Pop.*

Kory Grow, "Grinderman 'No Pussy Blues,'" December 17, 2007, *Paper Thin Walls.*

David Hadju, "Songbook Jam," March 19, 2007, *The New Republic.*

Ernest Hardy, "Kiss The Boys," July 18, 2007, *LA Weekly.*

Rob Harvilla, "Hot Hot Heat," March 6, 2007, *Village Voice.*

Katie Hasty, "Independents' Day," June 30, 2007, *Billboard.*

Geoffrey Himes, "Epitaph," July 2007, *Downbeat.*

Dustin Horwitt, "Rockin' in the Free World," September 19, 2007, *Washington City Paper.*

Hua Hsu, "Young Jeezy: The Inspiration," February 2007, *Vibe.*

Stevie Kaye, "Cansei De Ser Sexy," February 2007, *Real Groove.*

Dana Kletter, "Eminence grise," March 27, 2007, *The Boston Pheonix.*

Luciana Lopez, "Quiet Portland Life of a Top Tanguero," November 5, 2007, *The Oregonian.*

Michael Martin, "Springtime for 'Xanadu,'" May 28, 2007, *New York Magazine.*

Michaelangelo Matos, "Bringing the Family Along," July 7, 2007, *Idolator.*

Kelly Mellott, "Life Takes a Visa," Spring 2007, *Venus Magazine.*

Nakesa Moody, "Rap Backlash," February 28, 2007, *Associated Press.*

Paul Morley, "Northern Lights," September 16, 2007, *The Guardian.*

Jenny Offill, "Candy Says," March 2007, *Moistworks.*

Mark Owens, "Graphics Incognito," February 2007 (Issue 12), *Dot Dot Dot.*

Randall Roberts, "Are You Not Devo? You Are Mutato," December 5, 2007, *LA Weekly.*

Chris Ryan, "Kingdom Come," February 2007, *Vibe.*

Sukhdev Sandhu, "Mingering Mike Superstar," Winter 2008, *Bidoun.*

Kelefa Sanneh, "How Don Imus's Problem Became a Referendum on Rap," April 25, 2007, *New York Times.*

Makkada Selah, "The Motormouth of the South," June 12, 2007, *Village Voice.*

Peter S. Scholtes, "This Atlas Rocks," December 19, 2007, *City Pages.*

Rob Sheffield, "Still Hairmetal After All These Years," December 27, 2007–January 10, 2008, *Rolling Stone.*

Patti Smith, "Ain't It Strange?," March 12, 2007, *New York Times.*

Ian Svenonius, "Rock 'n' Roll as Real Estate," February 2007, *Dot Dot Dot.*

Dave Tompkins, "The Night-Time Master Blaster," Spring 2007, *Stop Smiling.*

Tom Turrell, "On the Corner," liner notes, 2007, *Miles Davis's "On The Corner"* box set.

Michael C. Vazquez, "Disorientalism," Spring 2007, *Bidoun.*

Gene Weingarten, "Pearls Before Breakfast," April 8, 2007, *Washington Post.*

Daniel Wolff, "Patti Scialfa's Passionate Gamble," October 20–21, 2007, *Counterpunch.*

Annie Zeleski, "Radiohead's *OK Computer* Turns Ten," July 12, 2007, *Riverfront Times.*

LIST OF CONTRIBUTORS

While he's busy missing deadlines for such publications as *Decibel, Revolver, Rock Sound* (UK), and *Alternative Press*, **J. Bennett** enjoys pork products, WWII–era side arms, and long walks on the beach. He is currently working on an authorized biography of monkey gladiator Jacco Macacco and lives in an abandoned missile silo on the outskirts of Los Angeles.

Noah Berlatsky writes ill-tempered criticism for *The Chicago Reader* and *The Comics Journal*. He is a failed poet, an artist who can't draw, and, inevitably, a blogger (http://hoodedutilitarian.blogspot.com/). He recently edited an online forum on the *Gay Utopia*, which includes contributions from Ursula K. Le Guin, Dame Darcy, and a Giant Squid, as well as penis collages, lascivious transgender assassin fan fic, the insect-sex zombie apolcalypse, and vile chutney recipes. You can find it here: http://gayutopia.blogspot.com/.

Marke B., aka Marke Bieschke, is Senior Culture and Web Editor of the *San Francisco Bay Guardian* and writes a biweekly clubs column called *Super Ego*. A Detroit native, he's been covering Bay Area nightlife for 12 years, despite encroaching crow's feet. His "Fag Fridays: 10 Years of Faggotty Goodness" was a *Best Music Writing 2007* notable essay.

Larry Blumenfeld's writing about music and culture has appeared in *The Wall Street Journal, The Village Voice, The New York Times*, and *Salon*, among other publications. He was a 2006–2007 Katrina Media Fellow for the Open Society Institute, researching cultural recovery in New Orleans, and a 2001–2002 Fellow in the National Arts Journalism Program at Columbia University. His essay, "Exploding Myths in Morocco and Senegal," appeared in *Music in the*

Post–9/11 World (Routledge). He is editor-at-large of *Jazziz* magazine. He lives, writes, and plays basketball in Brooklyn, New York.

Jonathan Cunningham is a literary rose that grew up through concrete streets of Detroit. As a Bahamian-American writer/editor/columnist, he enjoys covering the global urban beat from São Paolo to Soweto. He can't get a freelance assignment to save his life these days and the rejection/motivation is a better indoctrination into this craft than any journalism degree could ever offer. He's currently the music editor of the *New Times Broward–Palm Beach*, where he enjoys stirring up trouble. His works have appeared in *Fader, Elemental, Metro Times*, and the annals of his own hard drive.

Niki D'Andrea joined the staff of *Phoenix New Times* in 2004 and has been music editor since 2006. Since coming to *New Times*, she has been honored with awards from the National Association of Black Journalists and the Arizona Press Club. D'Andrea has been writing about music since the 1990s, when, as a teen, her first pieces were published in 'zines including *Tailspins* and *Flipside*. Over the course of one year—all in the name of covering the Phoenix music scene—D'Andrea danced with Arizona Governor Janet Napolitano and drank with singer Johnette Napolitano (no relation).

Tom Ewing has had an unrequited crush on pop music since 1980. To express it, he founded the online community ILX and the pop culture zine freakytrigger.co.uk, where he writes regularly about music and anything else.

David Kamp is a longtime contributing editor for *Vanity Fair* and the author of the food-world history "The United States of Arugula," as well as the humor books *The Rock Snob's Dictionary, The Film Snob's Dictionary, The Food Snob's Dictionary*, and *The Wine Snob's Dictionary*. He likes quixotic pursuits of reclusive subjects such as Sly Stone, and considers it his greatest regret that George Harrison had agreed to an interview with him but died before the meeting could occur.

Sam Kashner is the author of three nonfiction books and one novel, *Sinatraland,* and is a frequent contributor to *Vanity Fair, Esquire,* and *GQ.* He lives in New York City with his wife, Nancy Schoenberger.

Alan Light is the former editor-in-chief of *Vibe* and *Spin* magazines, and a former senior writer at *Rolling Stone*. A frequent contributor to the *New York Times*, he is the author of *The Skills to Pay the Bills: The Story of the Beastie Boys*, and is a two-time winner of the ASCAP–Deems Taylor Award for excellence in music writing.

David Margolick is a longtime contributing editor at *Vanity Fair*, where he writes about culture, the media, and politics. He served as national legal affairs editor at *The New York Times*, where he wrote the weekly *At the Bar* column for seven years. He is the author, most recently, of *Strange Fruit: The Biography of a Song*. He lives in New York City.

Sean Nelson is a writer and musician in Seattle. His most recent recording is *Nelson Sings Nilsson*, an LP of Harry Nilsson songs. He will also appear on the next album by Robyn Hitchcock & the Venus 3 (he is the fourth). Nelson writes most frequently for *The Stranger*, where he is associate editor emeritus, a title he invented. He also wrote the 33 & 1/3 installment about Joni Mitchell's *Court and Spark*. He updates www.seannelson.net every so often.

Eric Pape was a 2007–2008 John S. Knight Fellow at Stanford University, where he investigated the ways that creativity can grow from war, post-war, and other extreme hardships. While there, Eric helped to produce the graphic novel, *Shake Girl*, based on a poor Cambodian girl who gets caught up in events beyond her imagining. (It is available at http://www.stanford.edu/group/cwstudents/shakegirl/index.html.) Previously, Eric spent five years based in Paris as a special correspondent and regular contributor to *Newsweek* magazine, covering politics, urban strife, immigration, war, and wine. Prior to that, he wrote long-format features for the *Los Angeles Times* Sunday magazine, *Spin*, *Vibe*, and dozens of other publications, while reporting around the world.

Brandon Perkins is the senior editor for *URB Magazine*, sure, but he'll never have a shot at an Olympic medal. Perhaps that degree from Emerson College and gigs writing for the *Los Angeles Times*, *SOHH.com* and others look damn good on a dating résumé, but he can't read hieroglyphics. The next great American novel may indeed be living inside his fingertips but not enough of it has leaked onto a page for anyone to actually get a proper plot synopsis from him. But what does any of it mean when, as he stands to meet his maker, he'll have to say he spent his entire life scared of birds? Even if this is his second straight inclusion in Da Capo's *Best Music Writing* series.

Nadia Pflaum has been a staff writer at *The Pitch* in Kansas City since 2004. She is a graduate of Loyola University in Chicago, a former Village Voice Media fellow, and a 2007 ASCAP award winner for music writing, and has also contributed to *Salon.com*.

Ann Powers is chief pop critic at the *Los Angeles Times*.

Craven Rock has lived all over America and has inside knowledge of Middle American small town life. He works seasonally as a cab driver, having commuted there for seven years to fleece rich folks at the Kentucky Derby. Time not working he strives to write seven hours a day. He has done a 'zine called *Eaves of Ass* for the past seven years. He has also done freelance work for Razorcake, Avow, and a few others. He can be contacted at eavesofass@yahoo.com.

Matt Rogers is a Harlem-based writer and documentary filmmaker. As a contributing editor at *Wax Poetics*, he really enjoys talking to "old" musicians. One of his favorite foods when he's hangin' loose is fresh mango meat.

Jody Rosen is the music critic for *Slate* magazine. He is author of *White Christmas: The Story of an American Song* (Scribner, 2002), and the producer of the CD *Jewface* (Reboot Stereophonic, 2006), an anthology of vaudeville-era Jewish novelty records. He lives in Brooklyn.

Alex Ross has been the music critic of the *New Yorker* since 1996. *The Rest Is Noise: Listening to the Twentieth Century*, his first book, won the National Book Critics Circle Award for Criticism and was a finalist for the Pulitzer Prize.

Solvej Schou has a Danish name people have always had difficulty pronouncing. She graduated from Barnard College in New York and the University of Southern California Annenberg Graduate School of Journalism. She works for The Associated Press and has contributed to the *L.A. Weekly, People, Fashion Wire Daily, CMJ New Music Report*, and *Mean* magazine, among other publications. Solvej also plays music and lives in Los Angeles.

Jeff Sharlet is the author of *The Family: The Secret Fundamentalism at the Heart of American Power*, coauthor of *Killing the Buddha: A Heretic's Bible*, and author of a short history of American protest music, *The Hammer Song*, forthcoming from Basic Books. He's a contributing editor for *Rolling Stone* and *Harper's* and has also written for *Mother Jones, The Nation, New York*, and *Pakn Treger*, the world's only Yiddish magazine in English.

Ben Sisario is a reporter at the *New York Times* and the author of *Doolittle* in the acclaimed 33 & 1/3 series. He teaches at the Tisch School of the Arts at New York University and contributes to *Blender* magazine and WFUV public radio.

Danyel Smith is the editor-in-chief of *Vibe* magazine and the vice president and editorial director of VIBE Media Group. Smith is a former editor-at-larger for Time Inc. as well as former editor-in-chief of *Vibe* (1997–1999). She has written for *Elle, Time, Cosmopolitan, Essence*, the *Village Voice*, the *New Yorker, Entertainment Weekly, Rolling Stone, Spin*, the *San Francisco Bay Guardian, Condé Nast Media Group*, and the *New York Times*. Smith is the author of *San Francisco Chronicle* best-selling novel *More Like Wrestling* (Crown 2004) and wrote the introduction for the *New York Times* best-seller *Tupac Shakur*. Her second novel, *Bliss* (Crown), was published in July 2005. A regular guest host at WNYC, Danyel is quoted often in major publications, and she comments on pop culture for VH1, BET, A&E, and CNN. Born and raised in California, she lives in Brooklyn, New York.

Phil Sutcliffe is a freelance journalist born and based in London (contact greyhair@nildram.co.uk). He served a proper indentured apprenticeship on the *Newcastle Evening Chronicle* 1969–1971, then gradually got lost in music. Or possibly found. He has written quite a lot for *Mojo, Q, Blender, Smash Hits, The Face, LA Times, eMusic*, also done some radio and TV. He is a member of honour and national executive council member of the National Union Of Journalists of UK and Ireland.

Andy Tennille is a convicted vinylphile who likes grooving to some vintage slabs of soul in the shitty apartment he shares with his wife and dog, Jolene, in the Tenderloin Heights neighborhood of San Francisco. An associate editor at *BLURT*, Tennille has contributed to such fine publications as *Harp, Paste,*

SF Weekly, and the *San Francisco Chronicle*, as well as a legion of nefarious Web sites too numerous to list. Visit his online self at LinerNoteJunkie.com.

Clive Thompson is a contributing writer on science and technology for the *New York Times Magazine* and *Wired Magazine*. He also runs the science culture blog *Collision Detection*, at www.collisiondetection.net.

Oliver Wang is an assistant professor of sociology at CSU–Long Beach. He regularly contributes to *NPR, The Los Angeles Times, LA Weekly, Vibe*, and *Wax Poetics*. He also hosts the audioblog soul-sides.com.

Bill Wasik is a senior editor of *Harper's Magazine* and editor of the anthology *Submersion Journalism: Reporting in the Radical First Person from* Harper's Magazine (The New Press). His book on new-media culture will be published by Viking in 2009.

Jeff Weiss is a Los Angeles–based writer whose work has appeared in *The Los Angeles Times, The LA Weekly, The Arizona Republic, Idolator*, and *Stylus Magazine*. He also maintains the music blog *The Passion of the Weiss* (http://passion oftheweiss.com). While he has never "cranked that" nor "suppermanned a ho," he takes great pride in his ability to do the Electric Boogaloo, the Electric Slide, and the Electric Company (a little-known dance fad that briefly swept Menlo Park, New Jersey, in the late 1880s.)

Carl Wilson runs the popular music blog Zoilus.com and is a writer and editor at the *Globe and Mail*, Canada's national newspaper, based in Toronto. His work has also appeared in *Pitchfork, Slate, The New York Times, Blender*, and many other publications.

CREDITS

"Gayest. Music. Ever.," by Marke B. First published in the *San Francisco Bay Guardian*, September 26, 2007. Copyright © 2007 *San Francisco Bay Guardian*. Reprinted with permission.

"Dimm Borgir," by J. Bennett. First Published in *Decibel Magazine*, June 2007. Copyright © 2007 *Decibel Magazine*. Reprinted with permission.

"Underrated Overground," by Noah Berlatsky. First published as "Ridiculed and Belittled" in *The Chicago Reader*, January 19, 2007. Copyright © 2007 Noah Berlatsky.

"Band on the Run in New Orleans," by Larry Blumenfeld. Originally published at www.salon.com on October 29, 2007. Reprinted with permission.

"Freaks Come Out at Night," by Jonathan Cunningham first published in *New Times Broward–Palm Beach*, May 17, 2007. Reprinted with permission of Village Voice Media.

"Bad Habits," by Niki D'Andrea first published in *Phoenix New Times*, April 5, 2007. Reprinted with permission of Village Voice Media.

"The History Book on the Shelf," by Tom Ewing first published by *Pitchfork Media*, June 19, 2007. Copyright © 2007 Pitchfork Media, Inc.

"Back to Bossa," by Gary Giddins. First published in *The New Yorker* on November 26, 2007. Copyright © 2007 Gary Giddins.

"Sly Stone's Higher Power," by David Kamp. First published in *Vanity Fair*, August 2007. Copyright © 2007 David Kamp.

"Fever Pitch," by Sam Kashner. First published in *Movies Rock*, Fall 2007. Copyright © Sam Kashner.

"The Wonder Years," by Alan Light. First published in *Blender*, April 2007. Copyright © Alan Light.

"The Day Louis Armstrong Made Noise," by David Margolick. Published in the *New York Times*, September 23, 2007. Reprinted by permission.